CAMBRIDGE STUDIES IN AMERICAN LITERATURE AND CULTURE

The Color of the Sky

Other books in the series

Robert Zaller: *The Cliffs of Solitude*
Peter Conn: *The Divided Mind*
Patricia Caldwell: *The Puritan Conversion Narrative*
Stephen Fredman: *Poet's Prose*
Charles Altieri: *Self and Sensibility in Contemporary American Poetry*
John McWilliams, Jr.: *Hawthorne, Melville, and the American Character*
Mitchell Breitwieser: *Cotton Mather and Benjamin Franklin*
Barton St. Armand: *Emily Dickinson and Her Culture*
Elizabeth McKinsey: *Niagara Falls*
Albert J. Von Frank: *The Sacred Game*
Marjorie Perloff: *The Dance of the Intellect*
Albert Gelpi: *Wallace Stevens*
Ann Kibbey: *The Interpretation of Material Shapes in Puritanism*
Sacvan Bercovitch and Myra Jehlen: *Ideology and Classic American Literature*
Karen Rowe: *Saint and Singer*
Lawrence Buell: *New England Literary Culture*
David Wyatt: *The Fall into Eden*
Paul Giles: *Hart Crane*
Richard Grey: *Writing the South*
Steven Axlerod and Helen Deese: *Robert Lowell*
Jerome Loving: *Emily Dickinson*
Brenda Murphy: *American Realism and American Drama, 1880–1940*
George Dekker: *The American Historical Romance*
Lynn Keller: *Remaking It New*
Warren Motley: *The American Abraham*
Brook Thomas: *Cross Examinations of Law and Literature*
Margaret Holley: *The Poetry of Marianne Moore*
Lother Hönninghausen: *William Faulkner*
Tony Tanner: *Scenes of Nature, Signs of Man*
Eric Sigg: *The American T. S. Eliot*

The Color of the Sky

A Study of Stephen Crane

DAVID HALLIBURTON

Stanford University

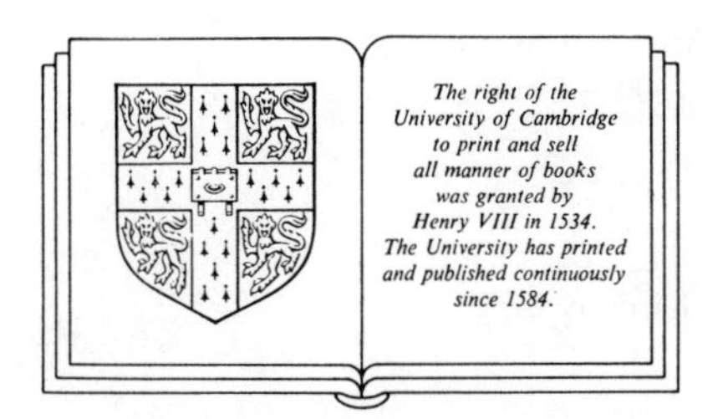

CAMBRIDGE UNIVERSITY PRESS

CAMBRIDGE

NEW YORK NEW ROCHELLE MELBOURNE SYDNEY

Published by the Press Syndicate of the University of Cambridge
The Pitt Building, Trumpington Street, Cambridge CB2 1RP
32 East 57th Street, New York, NY 10022, USA
10 Stamford Road, Oakleigh, Melbourne 3166, Australia

First published 1989

Printed in the United States of America

Library of Congress Cataloging-in-Publication Data

Halliburton, David.

The color of the sky: a study of Stephen Crane / David Halliburton.

p. cm. – (Cambridge studies in American literature and culture)

ISBN 0–521–36274–1

1. Crane, Stephen, 1871–1900 – Criticism and Interpretation.
I. Crane, Stephen, 1871–1900. II. Title. III. Series.
PS1449.C85Z646 1989 88–23686
813′.4 – dc19 CIP

British Library Cataloguing in Publication Data

Halliburton, David

The color of the sky: a study of Stephen Crane. – (Cambridge studies in American literature and culture).

1. English literature, American writers.
Crane, Stephen, 1871–1900 – Critical studies
I. Title
818′.409

ISBN 0-521-36274-1 hard covers

Contents

1

Introduction

In the preface he wrote for Thomas Beer's biography of Crane, Joseph Conrad recalls a visit from his young American friend when to both men life was being, to use a phrase from "The Open Boat" that was a favorite of Conrad's, "barbarously abrupt." The crucial exchange between the two on that occasion, though familiar to Crane specialists, is worth retelling since it raises issues central to the present study.

> After a longish silence, in which we both could have felt how uncertain was the issue of life envisaged as a deadly adventure in which we were both engaged like two men trying to keep afloat in a small boat, I said suddenly across the width of the mantelpiece:
>
> "None of them knew the colour of the sky."
>
> He raised himself sharply. The words had struck him as familiar, though I believe he failed to place them at first. "Don't you know that quotation?" I asked. (These words form the opening sentence of his tale.) The startled expression passed off his face. "Oh, yes," he said quietly, and lay down again. Truth to say, it was a time when neither he nor I had the leisure to look up idly at the sky. The waves just then were too barbarously abrupt.[1]

The veteran sailor's own knowledge of dangers at sea might have been enough to make him appreciate the appropriateness of Crane's comment. But his reaction says more than that. All the while that he was needling Crane with references to "barbarously abrupt" this and "barbarously abrupt" that, Conrad was storing the longer phrase for a suitable occasion, which is to say that the statement had general power for him; it represented a veracity, a wisdom, applicable in any number of circumstances other than exposure at sea. The fact that both men were facing difficulties at the time of Crane's visit was such a circumstance, hence Conrad's utterance. The range of application was wider still, however: "It opens with a phrase that anybody could have uttered, but which, in relation to what is to follow, acquires the poignancy of a meaning almost universal."[2] Conrad's recitation of the sentence is itself unexpected, and

Crane is accordingly surprised. Crane is always being surprised, for his is a world of wonder, a state of feeling that has taken on a peculiarly American flavor:

> From the start 'wonder' was put to much more far-ranging uses in American writing than in any other literature. The American writer faced different problems and had different needs, and 'wonder' became a key strategy where in Europe it tended to remain one idea among others. . . . The second consideration is this. The stance of wonder has *remained* a preferred way of dealing with experience and confronting existence among American writers.[3] [Italics in original.]

Many passages in Crane testify to a felt wonder, which Tony Tanner associates with naïveté and youthfulness; the sketch of the Greek dancer, to be discussed below, is one such passage. Rather than pursue this theme explicitly, the present study, assuming its presence, attends to particular effects that derive from the state (and to its counterpart, a state of detachment or coolness that is equally characteristic) and to the techniques employed (ranging from scannable prose rhythms to dithyrambs of the sublime) in expressing them.

One needs to be naïve, in any case, about naïveté, at least where Crane is concerned. In years he was never anything but young, and youthful characters frequently occupy his pages. Henry Fleming is a youth, Maggie is first seen as a girl, and "babes" abound – Conrad said the only times he heard Crane laugh were when the latter was with the former's baby. But if Crane's eye retains a certain innocence, he speaks from the beginning with the tongue of experience. At an age when most writers are struggling with influences or snatching at novelties for the sake of novelties, Crane crafts an unmistakable style. Not less remarkably, while still in his twenty-first year he begins the recasting process that produces a series of styles or at least very distinctly marked stylistic patterns, all unmistakably his own, but each, in notable respects, different from the others. The breezy cleverness of the hunting and fishing sketches is the first style, which Crane, in a much-quoted letter, describes himself as having renounced in 1892. Then come other styles hard to tie to strict chronology (for the boundaries are necessarily approximate, and elements of one enter another). Besides the early "clever" style, we find in the slum novels a blaring, highly percussive sort of ragtime; in *The Red Badge of Courage* a to-and-fro rhythm that gives the novel both a balladlike air and an epic cadence; in the newspaper reports a mélange of streetwise descriptiveness, dramatic miniatures, and mood-inducing changes of pace; in the romantic novels more mélange, with a dose of the old cleverness thrown in to leaven the self-conscious, quasi-parodic narrative movement; in the major tales a masterful style-of-all-work that ranges far and wide but is always under control, moving in stately dignity without the least loss in intensity; in "The Monster" a chastened, more matter-of-fact style closer to the Howells norm – though with colorful moments – that in large part carries over into *Tales of Whilomville,* where it mixes with authorial self-awareness, a large element of lightness, and sharp-tongued irony; in the late war reports a quality that in feeling, diction, and tone more nearly satisfies criteria for the sublime than one might have thought likely (its counterpart being the plain, all-business style that usually surrounds it in these works); in *The O'Ruddy* a lively, workmanlike quality full of gallop and a gusto that even Hazlitt could applaud; while in the poetry a repertoire of techniques larger and more diverse than some readers have been prepared to recognize combines with an arsenal of philosophical and metaphysical ideas to forge a poetic style remarkable not so much for texture and finesse as for economy and power. It should be added that two other strains weave in and out of these patterns, one being parody, which is especially conspicuous early on, and dialect, which also starts early but lasts on into *The O'Ruddy*.[4]

Like Crane's styles, his famous irony, which waits in the wings when it is not on stage and which supplies much stylistic energy, also smacks of much longer seasoning than it in fact enjoyed: The kind of overview that usually comes, if it comes at all, with long time, appeared to come to Crane virtually *ab ovo*. He seemed always to be ahead of himself:

> Before his community could impose its standards upon him, before his mother, widowed when he was nine, could impose her Methodism on him, before his friends could explain the terms on which the gang played, Stephen Crane had developed a set of responses that anticipated the reality. These responses were formed in great part from the shreds and patches of the conventions being imposed upon him: His anti-Methodism assumed gods, angels, and sinful men; his rejection of the boys' world led to his studious proficiency at baseball and his rigor in captaining the corps at his military preparatory school. But these were strengthened by an inner consciousness that told him that whatever was accepted was suspect; that there was an inside story behind every public history.[5]

Many readers took *Maggie* for a rendering of New York life based on Crane's intimate knowledge of that city; but that knowledge came later, during his days as a reporter. Before experiencing war, Crane wrote such a convincing war novel that a veteran officer distinctly recalled Crane's serving with him in the Union Army. Similarly, "The Reluctant Voyagers" describes men stranded offshore by chance before being safely plucked from the sea; only later did Crane himself become stranded in like manner, thus living the experience that would become "The Open Boat." If such now-familiar facts surprise on first encounter, so does the acuity of Crane's artistic intelligence and of his no less precocious sensibility. His knack for applying that intelligence and that sensibility by anticipation suggests a capacity for extrapolating from types. Having sampled conflict in baseball and military life on the parade ground, and having discerned the patterns followed by storytelling veterans and historians, he can "predict" what a certain war in general, and one war in particular, must have been like. Sartre predicts the life of Jean Genet in much the same way, slyly showing how the prediction comes true. Kenneth Burke's version of the technique is "prophesying after the event," an interpretative strategy in which the reader first ascertains the essence or principle of the object in question, then, to test the formulation, derives the object from the principle.[6]

At least in part Crane's typological imagination, which also prompts him to use the word *type* with great frequency, is a legacy of the American Protestant tradition, and in particular Puritanism, with its disposition for figural types symbolizing the design of deity. From a more secular side of the matter Crane's formative years as a reporter could only have reinforced whatever native disposition he had for nosing out all manner of typicalities – of qualities, form, meaning, structure, character, attitude – in the pageant of American life. One sense of the noun, while not necessarily religious in nature, has more affinity than other senses with the typological tendencies of the early American imagination: "That by which something is symbolized or figured; anything having a symbolical signification . . ." (*OED* 1, 1470): "But at length emerged this fact – the Porto Rican, taking him as a symbolized figure, a type, was glad, glad that the Spaniards had gone . . ." (IX, 177); "He was become a philosopher, a type of the wise man who can eat but three meals a day . . ." (VIII, 297).

Three other senses, all emerging in Crane's century, attest to a desire for a terminology to meet changing needs, a terminology that could discriminate among proliferating forms and patterns by some sort of classification. In "It was essential that I should make my battle a type and name no names . . ." (*Letters,* 84) the sense is "a pattern or model after which something is made" (*OED* 5. *transf.,* 1843). What is paradigmatic in the pattern gets embodied, as it were, in "the old English type of chair" (VIII, 87), meaning "a typical example or instance" (*OED* 7. *transf.,* 1842). When, five years later, Emerson makes Goethe "the type of culture," he coins a new sense, "A person or thing that exemplifies the ideal qualities or characteristics of a kind or order; a perfect example or specimen of something" (*OED* 7.b *spec.*), which Crane takes up by remarking "It should be a well-known fact that . . . the engine-driver is the finest type of man that is grown" (VIII, 746).

These, then, are a few, almost randomly selected examples of why Crane has received so much attention and why continuing attention is warranted. Like other authors securely berthed in the canon, but in his own way, Crane is both benefactor and beneficiary: Benefactor not only because of particular works he has contributed to the canon, but because his writings register his own era in a unique way even as they uniquely anticipate the era that follows; beneficiary because, having gone through a slump in scholarly attention, recalling those experienced by Poe and Melville – though one that was less protracted and less pronounced – Crane has received the acknowledgment from the scholarly community and from the general public that other established writers of his time gave freely from the start. These writers include Conrad, William Dean Howells, Hamlin Garland, H. G. Wells, Edward Garnett, Harold Frederic, Henry James, and Ford Madox Ford, who testifies to having heard James say repeatedly of Crane, "He has great, great genius."[7] "Genius" testimonials, indeed, compose a kind of subgenre within the critical literature on Crane. The present study may be regarded as such a testimonial insofar as it succeeds in further elucidating Crane's accomplishments, a generalization that applies to most of its predecessors in the field. But "proving" that a writer is gifted or a work major is notoriously difficult, which is why critics who try to do so, such as Yvor Winters and F. R. Leavis, bank on the reader's readiness to accept force of assertion and apposite quotations as an adequate basis for judgment. Notwithstanding that the former critic was an important influence on its author, this book concentrates instead on textual particulars both in themselves and in the way they aggregate to form larger and more general patterns of intelligibility. "God lives in detail," says an old German saying, reminding the interpreter that large meanings are mediated by little ones, and vice versa. The type of meaning at issue here is the type Burke calls poetic, as distinguished from semantic meaning. We employ semantic meaning when we point to a chair and state that the thing being pointed at is a chair, whereas poetic meaning occurs when someone exclaims, "Ho, ho! a chair!" The exclamation is stronger in feeling than the bare statement; it indicates more than the figure points to, hence it means more. Thoreau employs the same distinction when he remarks that "The volatile truth of our words should continually betray the inadequacy of the residual statement."[8] That volatile truth differs in nature from residual statement is shown by the fact that the latter, or semantic meaning, operates on an either–or principle, according to which "New York City is in Iowa" is false because it is not true. But by the criterion of poetic meaning New York City can indeed be in Iowa:

> Has one ever stood, for instance, in some little outlying town, on the edge of the wilderness, and watched a train go by? Has one perhaps suddenly felt that the train, and its tracks, were a kind of arm of the city, reaching out across the continent, quite as though it were simply Broadway itself extended? It is in such a sense that New York City can be found all over the country – and I submit that one would miss very important meanings, meanings that have much to do with the conduct of our inhabitants, were he to proceed here by the either–or kind of test.
>
> "New York City is in Iowa" is "poetically" true. As a true metaphor, it provides valid insight. To have ruled it out, by strict semantic authority, would have been vandalism.[9]

Crane's creation of works replete with meaning, expressing a singular vision in a singular style, does more to account for his elevation to his present status than the fact that he "is frequently spoken of as the most legendary figure in American letters since Edgar Allan Poe."[10] Indeed, the legends about Crane, by concentrating on the flashier aspects of his turbulent life, many have diverted attention away from the substance of his writings. In any event, Edwin H. Cady accurately characterizes Crane's current standing when he observes that "what was twenty years ago something like a frontier, sparsely and unevenly inhabited, uncertainly developed, has been largely occupied. Crane is now an established, major American author, a specialty, a 'field' with a gigantic CEAA Edition and a secondary bibliography so large it has called forth half a dozen surveys of itself."[11]

For the largest concern to be addressed in the following pages there may be no better name than the human condition, to borrow the phrase of a writer peculiarly akin to Crane not only in temperament but in his way of regarding the changing worldly scene. Montaigne writes:

> The world is but a perennial see-saw. All things in it are incessantly on the swing, the earth, the rocks of the Caucasus, the Egyptian pyramids, both with the common movement and their own particular movement. Even fixedness is nothing but sluggish motion . . . . I do not portray the thing in itself [*être*]. I portray the passage.

And finally: "every man carries within the entire form of the human condition."[12] The first statement catches the verve of Crane's temperament, which is ever on the move, now shifting as the world shifts, or shifting independently, now trying one perspective only to swap it for another. It may be objected that this is simply a trait of modernity, which it is; but on this score Crane is "more modern" than others: His kinetic energy never stops flowing, its direction and tempo being itself subject to change, interruption, and resumption. We have it on the authority of another French writer that in this respect Crane is quintessentially American. "The whole life of an American," says De Tocqueville, "is passed like a game of chance, a revolutionary crisis, or a battle."[13]

The second statement by Montaigne relates back to the phenomenon of the type. In each individual human being Crane, like Montaigne, sees all other human beings collectively, so that anyone's experience is precisely everyone's experience. Hence the things Crane hears from a series of individual veterans forms a composite representation of an army, saying in effect what the army might say if it could speak with a single voice. It should be added that Crane, like Montaigne, understands the human condition not as something discrete but as a nexus of relations connecting it with the nonhuman realm of animals, the natural landscape, and the cosmos.

Two major themes that emerge from this background are the same two Toynbee discovers at the heart of civilization: "Social injustice has been one of the two specific diseases of civilization since the earliest date to which our surviving records go back. Its other specific disease has been war."[14] The first disease spreads its contagion through *Maggie: A Girl of the Streets, George's Mother,* "The Monster," and a number of sketches and reports, including "An Experiment in Misery," "An Experiment in Luxury," and "The Men in the Storm"; it appears as well in several poems, and takes the form in *Tales of Whilomville* of the unfairness with which children treat each other. The second disease runs its long course from *The Red Badge of Courage* through the stories in *The Little Regiment, Wounds in the Rain,* the Spitzbergen tales, and *Great Battles of the World* to several poems in *War Is Kind* as well as in *Black Riders,* the tales of the Wyoming Valley, and dispatches on the Spanish–American and Greco–Turkish war, not to mention Crane's projected novel on the American Revolution. If war is broadened to embrace any conflict as such, then there is almost nothing in Crane that would not qualify as pertinent.

If Crane's characters are individuals, they are individuals in a community, a phenomenon always of interest for Crane, but especially when it is in crisis, is just forming, or is breaking up. The relatively spontaneous and emotional nature of such formations derives from a social impulse that takes the form, in American life, of association. Building on De Tocqueville, who may be credited with first pointing out the importance of association in this country, Johann Huizinga observes:

> Just as with individuals, the social impulse displays itself in America principally in a primitive form, that is, as a spontaneous and strongly emotional combination of forces for a concrete goal, with a pronounced need for secret forms and a far-reaching readiness to place personal energies without reservation at the service of the goal of the association, in brief, in the formation of a club or the foundation of a fraternal order.

> We have an involuntary tendency to assume that the sense of social organization is directly governed by objective interests. But it is a question whether the history of civilization does not have to take another primary factor into account at least as much – the concentration of common activity for the sake of the effect of fellowship, or to express it less barbarously the enthusiasm and the energy which arise from the powerful feeling of striving together for any goal whatever.[15]

In a later section of the book I will take up the question of Crane's aesthetics of war, which derives from such spontaneous striving, an aesthetics that includes what I will call the military sublime.

Some of Crane's best moments occur when opportunities arise for a fraternity that is more than contingent association. This is conspicuously the case in "The Open Boat," where Crane states the truths of experience that "the ethics of their condition" do not allow the characters to express; while a more apocalyptic moment of fraternity occurs in "When a people reach the top of a hill" and the "Blue Battalions" poem, where the visionary impulse in Crane takes center stage.

On the whole, however, the question of community in Crane's writings is both problematic and complex. His individualist heritage may be said to put him, on the one hand, at a certain distance from the association he desires to find or form, an association that would be, ideally, a genuine fraternity. The solitary strain in Puritanism, which in *Pilgrim's Progress* sanctions Christian's abandonment of his family to save his own soul, the Methodist acceptance of individual conversion, late nineteenth-century competitiveness and social segmentation – all of these factors may have weighed against finding a viable social order representing the authentic interests both of the individual and of the community. On the other hand, the same factors point in a different direction when read from a different angle. For the Puritan heritage is collectivist as well as individualist: The New Israel of New England is by definition a covenant community;[16] Methodism was an important agency in the Great Awakening of the eighteenth century, a group phenomenon by any standard; and if the late nineteenth century had little to show in the way of exemplary solidarity, it at least had its visionaries, such as the Howells of *The Traveller from Altruria* or the Frederick Law Olmstead who crusaded for parks and recreational facilities to reduce urban isolation and distrust.[17] It was Crane's good fortune, in any case, to find community when chance and character and circumstance converged in the seminal experience leading to "The Open Boat."

Despite his admiration for Tolstoy, Crane in his tales of war does not deal with armies in Tolstoy's way. The object of Crane's desire is an ideal, a military fraternal order or society of warriors that would replace *homo oeconomicus,* along the lines suggested by Brooks Adams. Such an order is incompatible with the scale and anonymity of an army, hence Crane's emphasis on the smaller unit – the regiment, for example, or the squad, or, as in "The Upturned Face," a pair of comrades. This emphasis, combined with a continuing concern for the individual character and a willingness to shift at any time to an omniscient or even a cosmic overview, makes for a complex perspectivism, to adopt a term that characterizes a notable pattern in nineteenth-century American letters.

It was the practice of the romantic historians of nineteenth-century America to devise scenes that are at once visual shows and moral dramas. The scenes exploit contrasts; they invoke a sense of grandeur; and they appeal strongly to the eye. W. H. Prescott finds such an object in the Mexican temple, which plays a central role in his *Conquest of Mexico*; John Lothrop Motley finds such a figure – or rather, forms one – by personifying the human capacity for challenges: "Through the mists of adversity, a human figure may dilate into proportions which are colossal and deceptive."[18] Prescott's use of the temple may serve to exemplify the practice of the artist whose perspectives are in some sort inspired by things or events, while Motley's invention of a figure may serve to exemplify the practice of the artist whose perspectives depend more upon self-inspiration or the mediation of cultural tradition. The author of "The Story of a Year," published the month before Lee's surrender at Appomattox, is an artist of this type. Before leaving for military duty, the hero and his sweetheart climb to a height from which they enjoy the following perspective:

> As Ford looked at the clouds, it seemed to him that their imagery was all of war, their great uneven masses were marshalled into the semblance of a battle. There were columns charging and columns flying and standards floating, – tatters of the reflected purple; and great captains on colossal horses, and a rolling canopy of cannon-smoke and fire and blood . . . . The tumult of the clouds increased; it was hard to believe them inanimate. You might have fancied them an army of gigantic souls playing at football with the sun.[19]

Henry James had previously established, in the story, an authorial position like the one Crane might have assumed, describing Ford's appearance and explaining how it might be interpreted by a "spectator." When James's character then becomes *himself* the spectator, as in the passage just quoted, he assumes the second of the two roles – that of the character as *subject* of perspectives – which, as in Crane, is the complement of the previous representation.

The narrator of Ambrose Bierce's Civil War tale "The Mirage" is riding ahead of some advancing troops when he beholds

> . . . a truly terrifying spectacle. Immediately in front . . . was a long line of the most formidable looking monsters that the imagination ever conceived. They were taller than trees. In them the elements of nature

> seemed so fantastically and discordantly confused and blended, compounded, too, with architectural and mechanical details, that they partook of the triple character of animals, houses and machines . . . . Among them, on them, beneath, in and a part of them, were figures and fragments of figures of gigantic men. *All* were inextricably interblended and superimposed.[20] [Italics in original.]

To this classic grotesque vision the soldiers respond with emotion. But the narrator's reaction is more like the reaction one might expect from a man who, like Bierce, had done cartographic work in the Civil War, surveying, measuring, judging from afar:

> The mirage had in effect contracted the entire space between us and the train to a pistol-shot in breadth, and had made a background for its horrible picture by lifting into view Heaven knows how great an exent of country below our horizon. Does refraction account for all this? To this day I cannot without vexation remember the childish astonishment that prevented me from observing the really interesting features of the spectacle and kept my eyes fixed with a foolish distension on a lot of distorted mules, teamsters and wagons.[21]

The fiction has entered what is for Bierce a typical perspectival phase: We are now over here with the author, quietly interested, while the terror is safely back there in time. It is a moment of judgment made possible by the safety of distance.

Compare this with the version of a classic grotesque Crane offers in a newspaper sketch of 1892:

> Two Italians . . . recently descended upon the town. With them came a terrible creature, in an impossible apparel, and with a tambourine. He, or she, wore a dress which would take a geometrical phenomenon to describe. He, or she, wore orange stockings, with a bunch of muscle in the calf. The rest of his, or her, apparel was a chromatic delirium of red, black, green, pink, blue, yellow, purple, white, and other shades and colors not known . . . . Beneath were those grotesque legs: above, was a face. The grin of the successful midnight assassin and the smile of the coquette were commingled upon it. When he, or she, with his, or her, retinue of Italians, emerged upon the first hotel veranda, there was a panic. Brave men shrank . . . . Since then, he, or she, has become a well-known figure on the streets. People are beginning to get used to it, and he, or she, is not mobbed, as one might expect him, or her, to be. (VIII, 513–14)[22]

The language is freighted with feeling: *impossible, delirium, fantastic.* Yet the object remains at a remove: There is no attempt, for example, to sympathize with the creature. Nor does the locus in question desire to resolve the question of the creature's identity. *Locus* here and in the pages that follow is meant to be a more flexible term than point of view or standpoint. By convention these terms are sited in individual characters, James being the master of such siting, which is also sighting, if you will, because the individual character is the place from which everything is seen. But the place from which we see in Crane's writings is anywhere and everywhere, now a character, now a group, now a "somewhere" from which an indeterminate voice – if it is a voice – says things only the author would know, but does not seem to be the author's. A later discussion of an early tale will clarify the matter.

If not knowing the color of the sky is a matter of great earnest in an open boat, it is a matter of great jest in the Greek dancer sketch. It is not that the questions about "what it is" are genuinely ontological, or even that they are genuinely questions. Rather, the pretended inability to know licenses a certain freedom, a freedom to play, for example, with the taboo subject of hermaphroditism. That this play does not go further suggests how one always has to stop at "the point of reticence,"[23] to borrow Arthur Waugh's *Yellow Book* phrase. (The force of that reticence helps to explain why Crane never wrote his projected novel about a male prostitute.) Such constraint may result, as in the portrait of the Greek dancer, in a "surface" treatment. But the surface is often sufficient for the purposes that perspectivism has in view. Between it and its object there exists a zone in which limited knowledge – the knowledge of appearance – becomes a virtue; a zone in which attention can probe, then pull back, advancing and then retreating, even as Henry and his fellows do on the field of battle. Here is a locus fascinated by what is "other" but determined to maintain such otherness in a state of comparative mystery. As a result the writing seems pervaded by a kind of radical indeterminacy, as though the author feared that a premature commitment to anything too *particular* would prevent him from being sufficiently *general*.

The amount of energy in any artistic economy is finite. The cost of indulgence here is abstinence there. Or to paraphrase Virginia Woolf: In order to do something significant, there are a lot of things one must decide not to do. The cost of Crane's desire to see much is sometimes a willingness to know little, or to be ambiguous about what he does know. The question of knowledge, or more precisely of its relation to experience, nonetheless remains central to the artistic economy to which I have referred. In *The Red Badge of Courage* there are 350 examples of words connected with visual perception, such as *perceive, observe,* and *discover,* and more than 200 of words such as *seem, appear,* and *exhibit*.[24]

As to ambiguity, a certain degree of it may attend any perspectivism, which is not to imply that perspectives cannot also be strong and clear, Crane having provided many of the latter. It is just that the perspectivist, within the constraints of language and genre and tradition, wants to remain as free as possible as often as possible for as long as possible – thus Crane's preference for provocative open-endedness over "well-made" closures.

This pattern is connected with the "somewhere" locus noted above, which, in "The Blue Hotel," for example, pulls back from the immediate scene to so remote a distance that the entire planet appears to be a mere bulb. It is what makes Crane a literary version of that legal perspectivist, Justice Oliver Wendell Holmes, whose attention to whatever plain of battle comes before him is typically fixed from afar. If the cost in this case is that even large figures come to look small, the reward is that the overall picture can better be seen and known and judged.[25] To the figures in the battle, it may seem that Holmes and Crane are looking on with indifference, as the correspondent in the open boat thinks nature does, or that they are watching the figures have their fling before felling them, as in the last poem in *Black Riders*. But Holmes and Crane are simply insisting that it is easier to know and judge a thing when one is not too close to it: in the same way painters stand back from the canvas. Describing Cervantes's linguistic counterpart to American perspectivism, Leo Spitzer attests to the "almost cosmic independence of the artist."[26] Although the point is well taken, artistic independence is constrained, at least where Crane is concerned, by the same nexus that operates in his fictional world – by the character he has, by the opportunities or deprivations chance throws his way, and by the particular circumstances that prevail when he writes. Nor does Crane forget that the cosmos itself is independent too, and only problematically comes within the artist's sway.

To say that Stephen Crane is a perspectivist is to recognize that several desires in him lay claim to the same aesthetic territory, sometimes serially, sometimes all at once. At the close of a work it becomes theoretically possible to bring an end to the shifting – to stop the kaleidoscope of perspectives, as it were. Success would presumably enhance the cause of what Crane calls "the ethical sense," in contrast to the "anarchy," which he appears to invoke as an opposing term. The opposition, however, is a friendly one. In writing to the publisher of his first collection of poems, Crane objects to the exclusion of certain works: "It seems to me that you cut all the ethical sense out of the book. All the anarchy, perhaps. It is the anarchy which I particularly insist upon" (*Letters,* p. 40).

Ultimately, Crane, like the prophet–bard of Whitman's *Song of Myself,* would have it both ways:

> Apart from the pulling and hauling stands what I am,
> Stands amused, complacent, compassionating, idle, unitary . . . .
> Both in and out of the game and watching and wondering at it.
>
> *(ll. 75–9)*

In and out of the game at the same time, Crane would be both the soloist and the social person, both the writer and the warrior, both the catcher and the reporter who describes the victory of his baseball team over the nine from another school (VIII, 567–9).

In conclusion let us glance back at our point of departure, "None of them knew the colour of the sky," which Conrad said was a phrase that anybody could have uttered, but that took on a meaning almost universal. Conrad may well have believed that anyone could have uttered it; or the statement could be a rhetorical strategy to set up a contrast with the concluding point of the sentence. To the extent that the words in the phrase are available to anyone, Conrad's observation is valid, but the choice of just these words, when taken together with the way they relate to one another, is unmistakably Crane's. The verb and both of the nouns are among his favorites. To Crane experience is a process not only of feeling but of coming-to-know; color is a general word typifying the essence of a given phenomenon; and the sky, in which the famous wafer is pasted, is at once a part of the natural scene and a kind of transcendental background against which key objects the more visibly stand out. Even the innocent-looking pronoun carries the Crane trademark. *None* is a syncategorematic, one of those helper words that mainly serve to make connections. Everyone uses them, of course, but Crane does noteworthy things with them, and with numerous other words, as a subsequent chapter will attempt to demonstrate. In reading Crane it is as helpful to work to this level of detail as it is to work at a more general level. What Josephine Miles says about *Leaves of Grass* applies equally to the better works of Crane:

> Every particular has its place in the list, every list its place in the whole poem, and every whole poem its place in geography and universe. Smallness and greatness are equal in this cycle of meaning. Through Whitman, Emily Dickinson, Marianne Moore and others, America has fostered the sense of size not only in greatness, but in smallness also, in the most minute and loving detail.[27]

The present study proceeds in a similar vein, delving into details that combine to form a larger horizon of meaning and investigating that horizon in its own right. In the pages that follow, comparisons between Crane and other American writers or with writers in other languages are not based, for the most part, on the phenomenon of influence. One reason is that the problem of what writers and what works influenced Crane remains an open question. He seems to be about as spontaneously "original" as any writer in the canon, Emily Dickinson being in this respect the other nineteenth-century author of which the same might well be said. A second reason is more positive, namely, that wirters talk to one another through their works irrespective of whether they have met one another directly. This is the grounding assumption behind intertextual interpretation, of which this study will provide examples. It lies, too, behind T. S. Eliot's idea of a tradition that readjusts itself each time a new author is assimilated into it, and Jorge Luis Borges's suggestion that one can profitably think of Kafka, for example, as in some ways a forerunner of Hawthorne, the paradigmatic text in this case being "Wakefield." In this study I will make the best use I can not only of the many insights provided by previous students of Crane, but of ideas from intellectual and social history, philology, lexicography, stylistics, and philosophical discourse. In short, the present study attempts to follow Kenneth Burke's admonition to use all that there is to use. The subject demands no less.

2

The Little: Early Writings

No one seems to have written a history of the little, or, for that matter, of the large. Given the authority and charisma associated with great size, the latter optic might seem the more obvious of the two. Vico's version of history is a case in point. According to *The New Science* (Book 2, Chapter 3), gentile humanity was founded by people who renounced the true religion of Noah and then, because of their hard life in the forests that sprang up after the Flood, grew to be giants. The Hebrews meanwhile retained a normal human size, to which the giants returned. Largeness remains a convenient way of figuring the paradigmatic and the powerful. The little has a history in its own right, however, and one of particular interest since at least as early as the Renaissance.

A LITTLE HISTORY

In the story of scale, the invention of the compound microscope in 1590 and the telescope in 1605 are important landmarks.

> One invention increased the scope of the macrocosm; the other revealed the microcosm: between them, the naive conceptions of space that the ordinary man carried around were completely upset: one might say that these two inventions, in terms of the new perspective, extended the vanishing point toward infinity and increased almost infinitely the plane of the foreground from which those lines had their point of origin.[1]

One key consequence in the history of ideas is a growing sense of relativity. Phenomena become appearances perceived from this or that perspective; the success of the immensely influential Cartesian methodology depends on the determinacy that phenomena have in the cognition of an eye of an I. The radical perspectivism of a Swift or of a Voltaire depends in turn, at least in part, on the relativity of things as they appear to an eye whose vision has been influenced by the new science: It is impossible to imagine a Lilliput or a *Micromégas* in a world without the microscope or the telescope. The essential point, however, is not the role of technology and science in forging perspectivism, but that perspectivism itself, and in particular its focus on the little.

Often the little is what can be brought within view, comprehended, controlled, possessed. A privileged littleness, for the bourgeoisie, is the commodity that can be purchased and permanently withdrawn from the public realm. Hannah Arendt sees this privatization as an essential aspect of French life following its descent from the heights of European power:

> Since the decay of their once great and glorious public realm, the French have become masters in the art of being happy among "small things," within the space of their own four walls, between chest and bed, table and chair, dog and cat and flowerpot, extending to these things a care and tenderness which, in a world where rapid industrialization instantly kills off the things of yesterday to produce today's objects, may even appear to be the world's last, purely humane corner.[2]

To the veracity of this thesis Proust offers much testimony. One thinks of the "little phrase" of music that weaves its way through pages concerned with Swann. Even closer to the spirit of Arnedt is this typical behavior of Odette: "Odette had gone to sit on a tapestry-covered sofa near the piano, saying to Mme. Verdurin, 'I have my own little corner, haven't I?' " When Swann a moment later praises Mme. Verdurin's sofa the latter replies:

> And these little chairs, too, are perfect marvels. You can look at them in a moment. The emblems in each of the bronze mouldings correspond to the subject of the tapestry on the chair; you know, you combine amusement with instruction when you look at them; – I can promise you a delightful time, I assure you. Just look at the little border around the edges; here, look, the little vine on a red background in this one, the Bear and the Grapes. Isn't it well drawn?[3]

It is not accidental that Proust has his roots in the nineteenth century. The nineteenth century is, to a singular degree, an age of detail. The passion for small things is more than a French phenomenon, as anyone can tell from an inspection of Victorian furnishings at the Victoria and Albert Museum, and the same affection for little touches in precisely the note, as Henry James would say, of the Biedermeier period in Germany and Austria. Although Swinburne has rightly been called a master of detail, the epithet applies equally to Browning, Tennyson, and Hopkins. And what are those loose and baggy monsters called novels if not huge metonymies of little touches? Only in the nineteenth century, moreover, does that little person, the child, come into literary prominence, the author of *Little Dorrit* being the novelist who perhaps makes the most of the youthful perspective.

Someone with an eye for the little can make surprising observations. The reader of Pater's *The Renaissance* hardly expects "The School of

Giorgione" to produce an insight into paradigmatic smallness. Giorgione, Pater remarks,

> is the inventor of *genre,* of those easily movable pictures which serve neither for uses of devotion, nor of allegorical or historic teaching – little groups of real men and women, amid incongruous furniture or landscape – morsels of actual life, conversation or music or play, but refined upon or idealised, till they come to seem like glimpses of life from afar.[4]

In American letters littleness is frequently a function of age, the little person being focused on in such a way as to illuminate the larger, older world. This is the case in Hawthorne's handling of Pearl, the gentle boy, and the Robin of "My Kinson Major Molyneux"; in James, who uses Miles and Flora, in *The Turn of the Screw,* as prisms to refract evil, or the suspicion of evil; and in Harriet Beecher Stowe, whose Little Eva helps throw into relief the horror of "the peculiar institution." The little personages of *Little Lord Fauntleroy, Little Women,* and *The Adventures of Tom Sawyer* reflect a yearning to preserve if not recover the relative innocence of an American past. Though this is partly the case in *Adventures of Huckleberry Finn,* that novel tries to steer wide of the sentimental devices employed in the books just mentioned. A story more likely to have influenced Crane, Garland's "The Return of a Private,"[5] employs such devices extensively, in particular exploiting the appeal of the little. Private Smith is young and, as in Private Fleming's case, his first significant act is to retire and think over his situation. As Smith and his three companions return from the Civil War to their rural homes, they form "the little group" and "the little squad" (pp. 122–3). As "fuzzy little chickens" come from their coops on the Smith farm and a calf in a little pen answers the call of a cow, Smith's wife appears: "Seeing all this, seeing the pig in the cabbages, the tangle of grass in the garden, the broken fence which she had mended again and again – the little woman, hardly more than a girl, sat down and cried" (p. 129). With her "little ones" (p. 131) in their Sunday best, "the little wife" (p. 135) visits a neighbor who prophesies, from the configuration of "two little tea stems" (p. 135) the return of Private Smith. The family becomes "the little group" (p. 136) hurrying to spot the soldier, who looks at "the little unpainted house" that is also "a little cabin" (p. 136) and who calls his little son "My little man!" (p. 137). The story concludes with a set piece that epitomizes the domesticity of what might be called the Sentimental Little:

> Oh, that mystic hour! The pale man with big eyes standing there by the well, with his young wife by his side. The vast moon swinging above the easter peaks . . . the little turkeys crying querulously as they settled to roost in the poplar tree near the open gate. The voices at the well

> drop lower, the little ones nestle in their father's arms at last, and Teddy falls asleep there. (p. 140)

In the scene that closes "Chickamauga," a story of suffering soldiers from the locus of a small boy, Bierce twice takes advantage of littleness, though in a manner closer to Crane. Like the shepherd boy in "Death and the Child," the protagonist looks at the spectacle around him without knowing what it means; when knowledge does come to him, it strikes with terrible force: "He stood considering [the outbuildings] with wonder, when suddenly the entire plantation, with its enclosing forest, seemed to turn as if upon a pivot. His little world swung half around; the points of the compass were reversed. He recognized the blazing building as his own home!"[6] The littleness and the turkey that subsequently appear after the boy sees his mother's corpse indicate the difference that separates Bierce's vision from Garland's:

> The child moved his little hands, making wild, uncertain gestures. He uttered a series of inarticulate and indescribable cries – something between the chattering of an ape and the gobbling of a turkey – a startling, soulless, unholy sound, the language of a devil. The child was a deaf-mute.[7]

The commitment to shock effect, so different at first glance from Garland's idyll, is responsible for an excess in language hardly superior to, and in a way not even unlike, the sentimental effect. I refer not to the analogies of ape or turkey, though these are strong medicine, but to the rhetorical overkill of *startling* and *soulless* and *unholy* and *language of the devil.* This takes the perspective away from the little locus and, more importantly, it identifies this, and not the war, as the locale of evil. The little boy too suddenly and gratuitously becomes the grotesque child, a nineteenth-century literary creation some of whose traits are exemplified by, *inter alia,* Hawthorne's Pearl or, more problematically, the children in *The Turn of the Screw.* Crane himself flirts with this type in the little brat who causes chaos in "The Angel–Child," a Whilomville tale.

The little occupies a large place in the nonfictional canon, where it is always perspectivistic and where the perspective connects human beings with nature. In the "Nature" of his second series of essays Emerson holds that we lacked perspective until geology introduced us to "her large style," as a consequence of which every little entity can be seen in its relation to the universal. Like eternity in Blake's grain of sand, or like the definition written on a blade of grass in "Death and the Chid," nature's code of laws "may be written on the thumbnail, or the signet of a ring."[8] Thoreau reminds his readers that Walden scenery is on a humble scale, celebrating its beauties by humbly measuring things, such as the depth of the pond, with consummate care. At the same time he makes gentle fun of the tradition of the sublime.

While only "the insight and the far sight of the geologist" would prove to inhabitants that their "smiling valley" was once a " 'horrid chasm,' " a discerning eye – such as Thoreau's – can see the true history, and can use that history to suggest that the humble scale has a grandeur of its own.[9] Santayana goes a bit further, finding in littleness a synecdochic relation to what is vast and even sublime: In the following passage one can also hear the same stoic note, which is almost a note of resignation, that one hears not infrequently in Crane: "No doubt the spirit or energy of the world is what is acting in us, as the sea is what rises in every little wave; but it passes through us, and cry out as we may, it will move on."[10]

The time now comes to examine that crucial figure called the little man.

THE LITTLE MAN

One of the more interesting Sullivan takes, "Four Men in a Cave," begins as follows:

> The moon rested for a moment in the top of a tall pine on a hill. The little man was standing in front of the camp-fire making oration to his companions.
>
> "We can tell a great tale when we get back to the city, if we investigate this thing," said he, in conclusion. (VIII, 225)

That the experience is not sought for itself but as material makes even more crucial the role of the little man's utterance, which launches the adventure, precipitates the confrontation in the cave, and rounds out the narrative. The effect of this first utterance is, through its persuasive force, to transfer the group from its present, recognizable space into a wonderland which at the outset appears to be as otherworldly as the realm into which another curious little person once fell.

From the temporal point of view, the adventure occurs during an intercalary period in which, since the outdoors has become practically synonymous with leisure, everything one does there is "extra" or superfluous. Indeed, if the tale is to be tall, it must claim its own portion of that special type of excess validated by its own tradition. Often, the excess takes the form of the verbal swagger characteristic of Mike Fink or of Twain's Child of Calamity, in the raft passage Twain deleted from *Huckleberry Finn*.[11] Such a language would not come easily, perhaps, to a New Jersey boy transplanted to New York. For Crane, in any case, it is the attitude that counts, and it is this attitude that, on the one hand, leads him later to prick the bubble of Henry Fleming's self-centeredness and, on the other, that motivates his not infrequent and mostly sardonic asides on oratory and "eloquence." The attitude is exemplified in the text before us when the little man attempts to be bigger than he is by stretching himself forensically. For Twain, to stretch is to feign, exaggerate, invent, but without lying; as Huck says, *The Adventures of Tom Sawyer* "was mostly a true book; with some stretchers, as I said before." In Crane's treatment, on the other hand, stretching is a reaching toward something unknown and at the same time an egoistic overreaching, an extension and reinforcement of the self in its competition with others. In this sense Crane does not stand within tradition but appropriates it.

Inevitably, anything that an author thus appropriates bears the dual imprint of the convention and of his own vision. Consider the relation, in tall tales, between what might be called kinesis – headlong, wild, or otherwise extravagant activity – and a countervailing stasis or calm. In the raft passage it is the raftsman who is, in this understanding of the term, kinetic; Huck, except during his arrival and departure, remains motionless in the episode (though the entire episode is kinetic in the sense that the raft is continuously in motion). In "The Story of the Good Little Boy" Twain plays off the imperturbability of narrative tone against the motion of a boy sent hurtling through a roof with fifteen dogs trailing after him like the tail of a kite; in Jim Blain's "Story of the Old Ram" the headlong series of disconnected episodes, leading to the accident that turns Parson Hagar into a carpet, ends in the comic calm of the narrator's slumber; while in "The Celebrated Jumping Frog of Calaveras County" the contrast is between the expected movement of the frog and the immobility caused by the load of buckshot it secretly carries.

That the kinetic moments in Crane are also frequently kaleidoscopic is not, then, in itself unique. What is distinctive is their connection with the problem of appearance, which interests Crane from the beginning of his career. "A scrawny stone dam, clinging in apparent desperation to its foundation, wandered across a wild valley" (VIII, 230). In this sentence from "The Octopush" we recognize *Webster*'s third sense: "appearing (but not necessarily) real or true; seeming." A sentence in "The Last Panther" reads: "So it is apparent that travelling by night was once a dangerous practice in Sullivan County" (VIII, 208). Here two lexical senses apply: "visible; readily seen," and "readily understood; evident, obvious." Although one might argue that the second sense suffices, this would undervalue the importance of Crane's appeal to the eye. "Apparent" and its variants preserve the etymon "appear": To have "readily understood" is to have "readily seen." In "The Cry of a Huckleberry Pudding" the kaleidoscope is formed by the four men themselves as they respond to a noise: "There was instant profound agitation, a whirling chaos of coverings, legs and arms; then, heads appeared" (VII, 255); the kinesis reaches extreme proportions with the statement "There was a pause which extended through space. Comets hung and worlds waited" (VIII, 256).

Such motifs, with their built-in theatrics, can become a facile effect, as in the fall described in "Four Men in a Cave":

> They slid in a body down over the slippery, slimy floor of the passage. The stone avenue must have wibble-wobbled with the rush of this ball of tangled men and strangled cries . . . . The adventurers whirled to the unknown in darkness. The little man felt that he was pitching to death, but even in his convolutions he bit and scratched at his companions, for he was satisfied that it was their fault. The swirling mass went some twenty feet and lit upon a level dry place in a strong, yellow light of candles. It dissolved and became eyes. (VIII, 237)

While this is style for its own sake, or close to it, one can see in it "the beginnings of the later, penetrating style,"[12] and also something that the word "style" does not quite cover. I refer to the pell-mell shifting in the passage – to its structural kinesis, if you will; for each of the seven sentences has a different subject. One might argue that each subject identifies a point of view. This term usually refers, however, to a center of consciousness associated with a particular character, and that is the case in only three of the sentences (the first, fourth, and fifth). One might do better either to condense the term and speak simply of this or that view, or better still, as already proposed, of this or that locus. A locus, as distinguished from a point of view, can remain almost defiantly indeterminate, as may be seen in "The Open Boat," where it is easier to locate what the men do not know than to determine who it is that knows that they do not know.[13] At the same time, it is clear that, as the story develops, there are durations in which the locus does become that of a particular character, namely, the correspondent. The passage before us presents a series of loci, each depending upon the identical grammatical sequence (subject followed by verb) but upon a "revolution" – as Crane might call it – of subjects. The subject of the first sentence is "They," the men; of the second, "The stone avenue"; of the third, "The torches"; of the fourth, "The adventurers"; of the fifth, "The little man"; of the sixth, "The swirling mass"; and of the seventh, "It," referring to the antecedent phrase, "a strong, yellow light of candles." The passage thus bodies forth, sentence by sentence, the very swiftness, interpenetration and confusion that are its subject. The process is like a dialectic without a synthesizing term. If we miss the effect on a quick reading it is because of the speed with which each locus gives way to the locus that follows. The structure, sentence for sentence, is: Group (they); Scene (avenue); Scene (torches); Group (adventurers); Individual (little man); Scene (swirling mass); Scene (it: candlelight). The centrality of the little man is more pointed, however, than this schematization indicates, for he emerges at the end of sentence three; sentence four then characterizes the action of the other men so that sentence five can describe the little man's attitude toward them. He experiences the fall, moreover, primarily in relation to his own attitude: "for he was satisfied that it was their fault." Anticlimactically, the men learn that the vampire–ghoul–Druid–Aztec–witch doctor who has been tormenting them is merely an old man driven out of home and mind, and into the cave, by his mania for gambling.

> "Oh well," the pudgy man said, "we can tell a great tale when we get back to the city after having investigated this thing."
>
> "Go to the devil!" replied the little man. (VIII, 230)

The sketch thus ends, as it began, with the little man's outburst, the ending being doubled insofar as the outburst finishes the framing narrative. Each outburst, furthermore, is in the imperative, each expresses an attitude of rejection, and each employs a conception that sets the tall tale within a perspective enabling the reader to see the stretching *as* stretching. This is what I meant when I said that Crane appropriates, rather than stands within, the tradition. The kinesis in the narrative belongs essentially to the story-within-the-story, to the action in the cave; outside, in the framing narrative, comes *desengaño,* as the guide's illuminating calmness is contrasted with the shadowy frenzy in the cave. Although this is not the equivalent of that "area" of Jim Blaine's "Story of the Old Ram" which Twain reserves for the perspective of the storyteller, it has a similar perspectival effect. The afterview in the closing section forces the little man to see that his fear is excessive. At the same time it highlights the discrepancy between the cave experience and the matter-of-fact appearance it assumes once it has been debunked.

In "A Ghoul's Accountant" another strange scene unfolds:

> Once a campfire lay dying in a fit of temper. A few weak flames struggled cholerically among the burned-out logs. Beneath, a mass of angry, red coals glowered and hated the world. Some hemlocks sighed and sung and a wind purred in the grass. The moon was looking through the locked branches at four imperturbable bundles of blankets which lay near the agonized campfire. The fire groaned in its last throes, but the bundles made no sign. (VIII, 240)

Such a description could be related to the nineteenth-century environmental determinism which Poe and Balzac, each in his own way, make poetic and "atmospheric." Atmosphere, in any case, furnishes an appropriate horizon for interpreting the passage; the question is, what type of atmosphere? There is little sense in this passage or anywhere else in these works of the deep resonance one finds in Poe or Balzac, who understood, in accordance with then-current notions about ambiance and milieu, "that the organic being must be explained by the environment just as the environment bears the imprint of this being."[14] Crane's vision is not that holistic, or at least it is not holistic in that way. In Crane one finds the atmosphere without the guiding strength of an underlying and widely shared conception. It is as if Crane, shedding belief, had kept mood. Or, better: He backs the mood with a new belief, which sees a unity of human being and nonhuman environment only in the sense that opponents need the active presence of entities different from themselves. Hence the menace is there as "other," as something alien from what is human, whereas for Poe and Balzac it is there as essentially "the same."

In Crane, if fear is abroad it is a projected fear, a fear emanating from a human center; but it is not an absurd one because for Crane's characters the nonhuman really does oppose the human. That fear is one source, at least, of the demonic strain in Crane's writings. As for the contention that the environment is not synthesized with its human counterparts, as in the atmospheric writing of Poe or Balzac, the best proof is the most obvious: The menacing presence takes the form, ultimately, of an actual human being whose advent precipitates the crisis in the narrative. That is, Crane differentiates between the generalized menace of the natural environment and the particularized menace of a certain human being. Pursuing this line of thinking into considerations of technique, one finds that his treatment of atmosphere can be traced, at least in part, to the need for a contrast with the deflating, comic ending – a build-up of terror that comedy can tear right down. It can also be traced partly to the sheer effect of piling up conventional motifs from the tradition of the grotesque, such as the ghastly grin, the mysterious house, and the "ghoul" himself.

At the conclusion of the story it is Crane's own conventions of which the reader is most aware. There is a vocal outburst, then another that is evidently still more violent, and finally a kick – inflicted on the little man by the ghoul – that is the vocal outburst's gestural equivalent.

THE MAN AND THE BEAR

"Killing His Bear" stands out for several reasons. For one, it is more concerned than other Sullivan County writings with the hunt as, literally, a matter of life or death. Secondly, the little man appears pitted in single combat with his prey. Third, the tales and sketches do not in general transpire in the cold, snowy, and hence more dramatic weather that prevails in "Killing His Bear." Finally, the sketch reverses the pattern of deflating setbacks, and the little man comes for the first time into his own, capitalizing on the assertiveness that is the corollary of the curiosity that keeps getting him into trouble.

> In a field of snow some green pines huddled together and sang in quavers as the wind whirled among the gullies and ridges. Icicles dangled from the trees' beards, and fine dusts of snow lay upon their brows. On the ridge-top a dismal choir of hemlocks crooned over one that had fallen. The dying sun created a dim purpose and flame-colored tumult on the horizon's edge and then sank until level crimson beams struck the trees. As the red rays retreated, armies of shadows stole forward. A gray, ponderous stillness came heavily in the steps of the sun. A little man stood under the quavering pines. He was muffled to the nose in fur and wool, and a hideous cap was pulled tightly over his ears. His cold and impatient feet had stamped a small platform of hard snow beneath him. A black-barrelled rifle lay in the hollow of his arm. His eyes, watery from incessant glaring, swept over the snowfields in front of him. His body felt numb and bloodless, and soft curses came forth and froze on the icy wind. The shadows crept about his feet until he was merely a blurred blackness, with keen eyes. (VIII, 249)

If it would be excessive to speak, in connection with the other pieces, of an encounter between man and nature, it is not excessive here because of the hunter's isolation, because of the challenging environment, because of the foreshadowing Crane achieves through the "dismal choir," the one hemlock that had fallen, and "the dying sun," and because of that reference to the horizon's edge that lets the scene stretch out into its own symbolic distance.

"Off over the ridges, through the tangled sounds of night, came the yell of a hound on the trail. It pierced the ears of the little man and made his blood swim in his veins. His eyes eagerly plunged at the wall of thickets across the stone field, but he moved not a finger or foot. Save his eyes, he was frozen to a statue" (VIII, 249). There is something behavioristic, if you will, about this account. While we are in some sense "with" the little man, we are certainly not within him. We begin with the sound he hears at its point of origin *prior* to the moment it penetrates his ears, tracing the trajectory of the stimulus from that point. Yet even then the reader is not truly inside, for it is not the little man who perceives himself as a statue; neither is the reader entirely outside: The locus is at once inner and outer. The account of the hound's approach concludes: "A hound, as he nears large game, has the griefs of the world on his shoulders and his baying tells of the approach of death. He is sorry he came" (VII, 249–50). Here, too, the inner–outer polarity no longer applies. To be sure, the account is "outside" of the little man, that is, external to his consciousness. But that is no longer the point of reference. Nor, as we shall see below, is the perspective the same as the one Crane employs when he later shifts the locus from the man to the bear. The limitation of the inner–outer polarity is that it applies to the particularity of a single consciousness. The account we have just read is also particular to the extent that it states, anthropomorphically but perhaps not inaccurately, that the hound is sorry he came; but it is at the same time general in a way that places it beyond the reach of the animal, just as it is already beyond the reach of the little man. The statement is not a universal truth: It is a generalization of the feeling anyone might have on hearing a hound bay. In this sense the thought expressed "belongs" to the little man, regardless of the fact that the author describes no moment in which that thought is distinctly registered.

The nearest Crane comes to the imaginative space of his character is this:

> The trees kept up their crooning, and the light in the west faded to a dull red splash, but the little man's fancy was fixed on the panting, foam-splattered hound, cantering with his hot nose to the ground in the rear of the bear, which runs as easily and as swiftly as a rabbit through brush, timber and swale. Swift pictures of himself in a thousand attitudes under a thousand combinations of circumstances, killing a thousand bears, passed panoramically through him. (VIII, 250)

This focus – now near, now far – is developed within a larger pattern of motion and stasis. The suspence of the narrative, the buildup of pressure that vents itself in a dual outburst at the end, arises from the relation between the immobility of the little man and the rapid motion, first of the hound, and then of the bear. But something else happens, too, for the movement in space is perpetuated in consciousness; the hound canters, the bear runs easily, swift pictures pass through the little man's brain. More than before, Crane tries to peer beneath the shimmering surface of event.

The corollary of the relation between motion and stasis is a relation between magnitudes. The game the hunter seeks is "large," the bear "great"; the hunter, by comparison, is little. The bigness associated with him consists, on the one hand, in that fanciful killing of a thousand bears, and on the other hand, in his reaction to the hound's baying, which smites him as "a call to battle" (VIII, 250), echoing the image of "armies of shadows" (VIII, 249) from the opening passage. Meanwhile, the little man is acting little. Hearing the cries of the hound, "his eyes gleamed and grew small" (VIII, 250). But something subtler than a mere contrast is involved. As the moment of the kill approaches, the moment when the little man is to make his big move, he is glimpsed from a different angle: He resembles in the shadows "a fantastic bronze figure, with jewelled eyes swaying sharply in its head" (VIII, 250), a description which makes him look for a moment more than human or less but which by no means belittles him. The bear's terrific movement has its parallel, furthermore, in the sensorium of the little man, who "listened so tremendously that he could hear his blood surge in his veins" (VIII, 250).

This likeness between the two antagonists never effaces their respective identities. While the two converge, they do so as beings essentially apart and opposed. Yet the very fact of this convergence brings them together in a peculiar way:

> The thicket opened and a great bear, indistinct and vague in the shadows, bounded into the little man's view, and came terrifically across the open snowfield. The little man stood like an image. The bear did not "shamble" nor "wobble"; there was no awkwardness in his gait; he ran like a frightened kitten. It would be an endless chase for the lithe-limbed hound in the rear.
>
> On he came, directly toward the little man. The animal heard only the crying behind him. He knew nothing of the thing with death in its hands standing motionless in the shadows before him. (VII, 250–1)

Although the bear dominates the opening sentence, it is into the little man's view that the animal emerges. Sentence three, similarly, appears to belong to the bear, yet each of its three clauses is a miniature interpretation from the locus of the little man, who underlines the difference between the way the bear actually moves and the way it would be conventionally represented as moving. The shift to the locus of the bear recalls the shift to the locus of the dog; there is something significant it does not know. The same may be said of the four men in the open boat except that there Crane will stress the fact of their ignorance rather than the thing of which they are unaware. The situation of the bear is like the dark side of the little man's curiosity: He gets in trouble for wanting to know, the bear for failing to know. "It was a wee motion, made with steady nerves and a soundless swaying of the rifle barrel; but the bear heard, or saw, and knew" (VIII, 251). In this moment in which the little man finally acts something vast occurs, not merely because of what the hunter does, but because of his peculiar unity with the hunted. Tremendously, the conflict is played out. One is reminded that William Dean Howells, after reading *Maggie,* praised Crane for achieving the same quality of fatal necessity that we admire in Greek tragedy. "Killing His Bear" possesses something of that quality, a sense of watching a destiny – the shape of which is already known – unfold before our eyes. If the action seems full despite the brevity of the piece, it is because we feel both forces in the agon. We feel them both separately and together and yet in relation to an overview that has access to the agon without being confined to it. This overview – this locus that is everywhere and nowhere – enlarges and at the same time diminishes. It declares that the event is grand while implying that it involves, after all, only a little man and a bear. Here is the grand effect:

> The earth faded to nothing. Only space and the game, the aim and the hunter. Mad emotions, powerful to rock worlds, hurled through the little man, but did not shake his tiniest nerve.
>
> When the rifle cracked it shook his soul to a profound depth. Creation rocked and the bear stumbled. (VIII, 251)

This grand effect depends upon ringing words in much the same way as a comparable effect in the section of *Robinson Crusoe* called "A Dreadful Deliverance": "I shot at a great bird which I saw sitting upon a tree on the side of a great wood. I believe it was the first gun that had been fired there since the creation of the world . . . ."[15] The historical perspective, mediated by Defoe's first person, heightens the reader's sense of the land's long past and the novelty of Crusoe's intrusion upon it. Crusoe's laconic manner is an essential aspect of such perspectivism, expressing as it does both the literalist disposition of the hero and the match between that disposition and the facts. It is probably a fact that this is the first time since creation that a gun has been fired here; of this Crusoe is aware and this he reports.

The difference between the two conceptions is that Defoe, through the single locus of a first-person report, makes the past significantly, distantly visible against the present, whereas Crane, through a locus that is at once differentiated and fused, assimilates the past into the present, which is all. It is now as though nothing matters *but* the now, as though all creation *is* now; and yet we know that the greatness of the moment has entirely to do with the littleness of the man. Crane achieves this complex perspective by taking us very swiftly from the breadth and generality of earth, space, game, to the specificity of the aim and the hunter, then from emotions powerful enough to rock worlds to the rush of these through the little man, with attention to so fine a focus as his tiniest nerve. This is what I mean by differentiation. But differentiation works only with and through the identification of the present totality of the world with the immediate project of the little man: It is for him as hunter that the earth fades to nothing, for him that his emotions are powerful to rock worlds, for him that creation itself rocks. In this sense Crane presents a fused vision, letting the great appear little, that the little may take upon itself, with irony, whatever of greatness is its due.

If the little man's desire is satisfied it is because, through the concerted action of hunter and hound, the situation is so much in hand. The situation embodies, indeed, the desiderata of prediction and control that had already become, by Crane's time, bonded specifically with the notion of science and collaterally with technology. To predict and control, to shift from an "objective" attitude toward "nature" to a posture extending the range of human power, is a long-standing goal not only of the "savage mind," as Lévi-Strauss reminds us, but of all technology and profit-seeking enterprise. The figure of the hunter merges with that of the Gilded Age's man of business who, by hitting his economic target, can capture a market, even "make a killing."

Nothing would be worse than to view all this within the ideology of the pastoral. If anything, it is antipastoral. Nature solicits pastoral desire with the promise of communion (with nature itself and frequently with companions) that is simultaneously a denial of confrontation. Crane, reversing the pattern, offers confrontation, denies communion. This explains a seeming discrepancy between stories like "Four Men and a Cave," where the four men drop out of nature for a time, as it were, and "Killing His Bear," where the little man is plunged back into it. The supposed discrepancy is merely a difference depending on what, at a given moment, Crane chooses to emphasize. In "Four Men in a Cave" the movement indoors takes the men from their natural setting into an area of human conflict. In "Killing His Bear" and "The Mesmeric Mountain" Crane offers a conflict between man and nature. If "Four Men in a Cave" tends to drop the human being out of nature, "Killing His Bear" drops him out of society: The little man appears all by himself. Thus the two works present, each in its own way, denials of communion – of a human being either with nature or with other human beings – and climaxes of confrontation – of human beings either with one another or with nature itself.

The final, dual outburst in the story, consisting of the gunshot and of the little man's outcry, initiates a train of doublings that go off like pairs of firecrackers on a string:

> The little man sprang forward with a roar. He scrambled hastily in the bear's track. The splash of red, now dim, threw a faint, timid beam on a kindred shade on the snow. The little man bounded in the air.
>
> "Hit!" he yelled, and ran on. Some hundred of yards forward he came to a dead bear with his nose in the snow. Blood was oozing slowly from a wound under the shoulder, and the snow about was sprinkled with blood. A mad froth lay in the animal's open mouth and his limbs were twisted from agony.
>
> The little man yelled again and sprang forward, waving his hat as if he were leading the cheering of thousands. He ran up and kicked the ribs of the bear. Upon his face was the smile of the successful lover. (VIII, 251)

The little man's antics are like the echo of his ballistic outburst, at once kinetic (he springs, scrambles, bounds, waves his hat, runs, kicks) and vocal (he roars, yells, and yells again). On the most obvious level his actions are circumstantially structured in that he pursued his game in order to confirm the kill. The repetitiveness of his actions does not show compulsiveness so much as the eruption of emotion bottled up: The bear has heaped him, as Ahab would say. This very repetitiveness brings out the equally significant excess of pride he feels – his glory and his glee. I should also point out that these antics directly follow the lines in which the little man feels world-rocking emotions and in which creation itself rocks. In the concluding description of the little man we have, in short, a meiotic or diminishing effect that shows the man unchanged, still little, still keen to conquer, vainglorious and – as the kick in the ribs demonstrates – still full of aggressiveness and resentment.

The two effects are less sharply distinguished than these citations may indicate. The diminishing effect, in one of its aspects, begins at least as early as the analogy between the little man and the bronze figure, an analogy which makes it possible for Crane, if briefly, to dehumanize him: The head that a moment before would have been "his" head has become "its" head (VIII, 250). If Crane nudges the little man, experimentally, toward thingishness, he nudges him also toward animality, for the terms "yell," twice applied to the little man, was first applied to the dog. One could argue that if this makes the hound anthropomorphic it makes the man zoomorphic: Similarly, the limbs of the dead bear as "his" not "its" limbs. The point is that Crane, by playing with identities, explores the way in which beings from different ontic realms shade toward one another even as they hold back from each other. Crane shares Hõlderlin's sense of the dynamic intimacy by which things that are held apart in *polemos* even as they are bound, all strangely, together. Readers sympathetic to such a conception will observe how, at the end of the story, the great themes of man and nature and battle and death are joined by the theme of love.

Liebestod? Hardly. Eros? Yes, but an eros of aggression, as shown by victor's kick and victor's glee: The other exists in order to be conquered. Here, man and animal come together in a meeting less egalitarian than hierarchical. Before the hunter's outburst, the object of desire is high, the desiring subject low: great bear, little man. The consequence of fulfilled desire is a reversal wherein the subject towers above the object he has brought down from a kind of greatness. There is for the little man, *post coitum,* no sadness, but a potent *ergo sum*. Negating the other, the little man affirms himself: He *is* more now that the other is less.

Aggressive eros seeks possession: The lover would be master, the loved his slave. But when the lover masters by killing, possession can only be *post mortem*. From the little man's point of view the prey, as the title indicates, is "his." That the bear, as we have seen, also gets that possessive pronoun draws the animal away from the status of "it" and toward a status nearer the human, not only because "his" applies conventionally to human beings but because it is also applied by them to nonhuman beings to which they feel close. Thus the little man's hound is "he." Closer to the little man in this sense, the bear yet remains himself: It is his nose in the snow and his limbs that are twisted from agony. The "his" that Crane applies to the little man in the concluding passage refers to what he possesses already: his hat, his face. The man and the animal resemble each other in that each, in his own way, is self-possessed. It is a different yet similar self-possession shown earlier by the little man's patience in awaiting the kill. There it was necessary, in order to be in charge of the hunting situation, to be in control of oneself: to endure the cold, to keep alert, to aim with care. But once he has loved in his killing way, the need for such control ends. His outbursts, a way of letting go, show the little man expressing in gesture the feeling that had earlier caused swift pictures of himself, killing a thousand bears, to pass panoramically through him. The little man who waves his hat to the cheers of thousands is the same little man who challenges the cave because it would furnish a tale to tell. What the little man loves successfully is himself, though not strictly *for* himself. The little man would never savor an accomplishment in solitude, because he loves himself for the being he is to others. It is the loving gaze of others that he seeks, a gaze that recognizes him as a hunter. The little man's eros is, after all, social. The bear signifies possession, itself a signifier, whose signified is status.

The final struggle in this early collection is not between man and animal, but between man and mountain. Some preliminary skirmishing occurs when the pudgy man complains about the excessive dishwashing he has had to do. The little man, however, is preoccupied by mysterious prospects of interest to him alone. Appropriately, he is by himself when the story begins.

THE MAN AND THE MOUNTAIN

Crane's deflating, anticlimactic endings doubtless owe much to that parodic disposition described by Eric Solomon.[16] It is one of the features that makes it possible to see in Crane a pioneer of the modern tradition of the antinovel and the antihero. Crane goes against the grain of the "well-made" theory by unhorsing the reader's expectations; at the same time, as odd as it sounds to say so, there is something a little neoclassical about this tendency, suggestive as it is of the *Dämpfung,* or restraint in that literary mode. What is true of Crane's endings is often true of his beginnings as well. Crane will have nothing of the attention-getting of George Herbert, who launches "The Collar" with "I struck the board, and cried, No more. / I will abroad." Crane sneaks up on you, letting you suppose that nothing much is happening, the better to make it interesting when something does. One of the first of this type is the opening of "The Mesmeric Mountain":

> On the brow of a pineplumed hillock there sat a little man with his back against a tree. A venerable pipe hung from his mouth and smoke-wreaths curled and slowly sky-ward. He was muttering to himself with his eyes fixed on an irregular black opening in the green wall of forest at the foot of the hill. Two vague wagon ruts led into the shadows. The little man took his pipe in his hands and addressed the listening pines.
> "I wonder what the devil it leads to," said he. (VIII, 268)

The statement initiates a quest. But for what? And why does the narrative concern a mountain?[17]

To answer these questions one must consider the relation of landscape and movement in the context of the Sullivan County writings as a whole. That country is largely a place of caves or cavelike interiors. In "The Last Panther" two boys venture into a cave to face a wounded panther, and the two men in "Bear and Panther" watch a bear moving in and out of a cave. The first of the little-man stories revolves around a cave, while some of the others involve a complementary space made by man: a tent, a house, a room within a house. In "Hunting Wild Hogs" we learn that "In the holes and crevices, valleys and hills, caves and swamps of this uneven country, the big game of the southern part of this State have made their last stand" (VIII, 202–3).

A cave provides a kind of topographical perspectivism. Depending on the terrain, a cave may present itself as a space on one's own level, or it may be lower or higher, making it possible for an adventure to be not only an exploration inward but also a descent or an ascent, the former being associated with the demonic, loss of control and the like, the latter with a more directed type of quest. In "Four Men in a Cave" the principal experience is a descent; in "The Holler Tree" the little man goes up in order to go down; in "The Black Dog" the four men move laterally into the interior of the house only to ascend into an old man's room. All make explicit the function of passage that is the *raison d'être* of all the movements. Passage entails change. Through passage the situation of a character is altered topographically (one is now at a different place), existentially (one enters a different state of being), or socially (one attains a new relation to one's fellows). Passage is the process that brings one from the known to the unknown, from sameness to otherness, and may be viewed as the objective correlative of one's desire. What matters is neither the point of departure nor the direction of the movement: Neither ascent nor descent is privileged. What matters is movement as kinetic embodiment, as bodying-forth, of desire.

In "The Mesmeric Mountain" the little man first descends from his high position: "Keeping his eyes fixed he slid dangerously to the foot of the hillock and walked down the wagon-ruts" (VIII, 270). He must then go up "over pine-clothed ridges and down through water-soaked swales" (VIII, 270). On the way he climbs a tree, descends from it, and continues. Nearing the mountain, "He dived at a clump of tag-alders and emerging, confronted Jones's Mountain" (VIII, 270). If this is not an ascending movement, neither is it clearly a descending one: The little man may be diving in the sense of plunging forward or in the sense of plunging down. A similar ambiguity attends his passage through the area between hillock and camp. Crane never states that he went down to the camp or that, on returning, he again went up. As for the final section of the narrative, it is an ascent leading to a descent leading to an ascent. It is at the same time an attack leading to a retreat leading to an attack (a seesaw pattern on which *The Red Badge of Courage* will elaborate). The effect of all this scrambling is not to complicate the tracery of the little man's progress, but to etch it ever more deeply, such repetition serving, as Lévi-Strauss has shown, to make the structure of the "myth" clear.[18] The ups and downs reveal the little man's persistence, the power of the urge within. They are like the ups and downs of an entire life compressed, a way of showing that this is how the little man chooses to live. The little man takes a different direction from the others; he goes "elsewhere." Looking back, we can see that Crane was not silent on the spatial relations that obtained before he set out. Crane ignores the up-and-down possibilities between camp and hillock because it is not in that direction that the quest lies: On this score he is indifferent. But about the relation of the little man's hillock to the forest he says this: "The little man went to the edge of the pine-lumed hillock and, sitting down, began to make smoke and regard the door to the forest" (VIII, 269). This edge is at once a border, in the sense of a present limit, and a frontier, in the sense of a limit that is also a possible new beginning; it is an expression in space of the moment-before-acting. The contiguity of edge and door illustrates the manner in which Crane brings things together in this narrative, for if the little man is to pass over the border, if he is truly to experience his own frontier, he requires a point of entry. "On the most archaic levels of culture this possibility of transcendence is expressed by various *images of an opening*. . . ."[19] (Italics in original.) Through such an opening to a higher world, humans can ascend while the gods descend. The present opening is immediately given as an opening inward, but one that leads in the end to the victorious ascent of the little man to the mountain top. In this towering mass that menaces him, there is, furthermore, something of the awesome otherness that underlies the experience of the holy. Finally, the passage of the little man – as a movement from the known to the unknown, from the same to the other – has overtones of the rite of passage in which the initiate dies away from his or her present world. After the little man has slid dangerously to the foot of the hillock, he passes from the sunshine into the gloomy woods. Then: "The green portals closed, shutting out live things. The little man trudged on alone" (VIII, 270). This borrowing of "archaic" elements lends a kind of mythic resonance. Measured against Lévi-Strauss's requirements, however, the narrative does not qualify as mythic since it does not reconcile oppositions through equivalents mediated by a third term. In Crane's work one opponent merely defeats the other. But the way to victory twists in a peculiar manner, through reversals and reversals that are themselves reversals. There are other surprises as well, for example the encounter between the pudgy man and the skeptic who retorts, " 'Fool, what does it lead to, then?' " The result is a work that appropriates various generic features much as it appropriates elements from archaic cultural sources, a mixed work that never ceases to be a hunting tale and never quite attains the status of a fable, as Crane seems to have understood that term.[20] We shall see below that the mythic overtones that readers feel are justified on another basis than the one we have so far noted. For the moment we know enough to avoid the mistake of taking the little man's confrontation with the mountain in a manner too narrowly psychological. What Crane gives us is bits of psychology and bits of fable blended together.

With the approach of evening, both the atmosphere and the little man appear to grow somnolent:

> The wanderer sat down in a clear place and fixed his eyes on the summit. His mouth opened widely and his body swayed at times. The little man and the peak stared in silence.
>
> A lazy lake lay asleep near the foot of the mountain. In its bed of water-grass some frogs leered at the sky and crooned. The sun sank in red silence and the shadows of the pines grew formidable. The expectant hush of evening, as if some thing were going to sing a hymn, fell upon the peak and the little man. (VIII, 270–1)

A natural vocalizing expressive of world harmony, a convention Crane occasionally uses,[21] here sounds more religious than usual; "hymn" belongs to that higher diction in his canon, along with "portals" (VIII, 270) and "smite" (VIII, 271), which contrasts with the lower diction of the little man's oral, largely dialectal style, with the rest of the diction somewhere in between, in what may be regarded as a middle style. The higher diction does not prepare for a contrast with a small or deflating action, but affirms by anticipation that something out of the ordinary is about to happen. A contrast is there, but it is short term – a contrast between the stasis of the little man and his sudden movement, between a hypnagogic or semihypnagogic period and an abupt self-arousal.

> A leaping pickerel off on the water created a silver circle that was lost in black shadows. The little man shook himself and started to his feet,

> crying: "For the love of Mike, there's eyes in this mountain! I feel 'em! Eyes!"
> He fell on his face.
> When he looked again, he immediately sprang erect and ran.
> "It's coming!"
> The mountain was approaching. (VIII, 271)

Except in one crucial regard the relation between man and mountain, beginning from the time the little man fixes his eyes on the summit, parallels a possible relation between a mesmerist and his subject. William James had pointed out two years earlier that "The 'hypnotic,' 'mesmeric' or 'magnetic' trance *can be induced in various ways,* each operator having his preferred method."[22] (Italics in original.) The method closest to the relation Crane describes was one practiced at the time in Britain, in which the subject stares fixedly and abstractedly at some object not likely to stir interest in itself. Literary antecedents may be found in certain Poe narrators, especially the narrator of "Berenice," who uses much the same means to achieve self-induced mesmeric states.

When I say that the relation resembles that of mesmerist and subject except in one crucial regard, I refer to the fact that the little man reverses the normal pattern. His gaze should be unseeing and his mind empty, the better to be filled by the communicated will of the operator; above all, he should not interrupt the continuity of the spell. But that is exactly what he does. The episode is an account of loss and recovery of consciousness, of submission to an influence and rejection of that influence – a pattern to be repeated in his fight with the mountain, in which he gives in to its superior power, then rejects it in a final surge to victory.

It can be objected that what he sees is not there: that the mountain has no eyes, and that the little man is under no hypnotic suggestion. But if I am right in thinking that the narrative is not so much an exercise in the narrowly psychological as in the broadly marvelous, then a mountain *can* have eyes. What the work gives us is an imaginative truthfulness conveyed in a tall tale. Where then is the deflation, the putdown, which occurs in the other Sullivan County writings? It is within the tale; at issue here is not the author's resistance to the claims of a genre but his character's resistance to the claims upon him of something "wholly other." His ability to resist underlines not merely his willfulness, which is evident throughout the little-man series, but his ability to improve his status. His last attempt to assert himself proves to be his best.

Generally in these early works the other in a confrontation is defined either temporally (older or more venerable) or spatially (larger). In light of that pattern the mountain in the present work is fitting. It is not only greater temporally and spatially, it is vastly so, a fact which in itself supports the tall-tale effect. It is, possibly, the biggest thing Crane could think of; certainly it is the big thing, the great thing, in the experience of the little man. If one now considers that this great thing constitutes a mystery in a sense that one may speak of as broadly religious, the reaction of the little man has a definite coherence. For if his attitude toward the mountain resembles a trance, it also resembles traditional – or again, if you will, "archaic" – reactions to the *mysterium tremendum*. "We need an expression for the mental reaction peculiar to it," writes Rudolf Otto, "and here, too, only one word seems appropriate, though, as it is strictly applicable only to a 'natural' state of mind, it has here meaning only by analogy: it is the word 'stupor.' *Stupor* is plainly a different thing from *tremor*; it signifies blank wonder, an astonishment that strikes us dumb, amazement absolute."[23] The difference between the attitude of the little man and the attitude of someone more strictly religious does not immediately emerge. For the little man's first reaction, on shaking off his stupor, is one of profound fear, as befits an encounter with the *mysterium tremendum*. His flight expresses that fear. Only with the reversal of movement, only with the little man's decision to turn around and attack, does Crane represent him as coming into his own. This pattern deserves a closer look.

The action, as physical movement, evolves in parallels and contrasts. At first the little man moves while the mountain remains motionless: This is the period of his approach. He then becomes motionless, like the mountain, as he sits and stares, the stasis ending with his self-arousal. Now he moves again and the mountain moves for the first time. Pursued becomes the pursuer until the cycle ends with the little man standing atop the mountain, which is once gain motionless. A simple structural paradigm is established as follows:

Man moving, mountain motionless
man motionless, mountain motionless

man moving, mountain moving
man motionless, mountain motionless

The space between the first and second sets reflects the caesura between immobility and kinetic outbreak; if the pause with which the story ends aims to repeat the period in which man and mountain were both motionless, following the little man's approach, a circularity emerges. Two considerations, however, must be taken into account. The first is that each of the sets, despite the similarity of their concluding phase, expresses a perspective of its own. The perspective of the opening set is, for want of a better term, naturalistic: In everyday existence it is a fact that human beings move toward mountains while mountains remain motionless. The second perspective is not naturalistic but fabulous, as when the mountain comes to Mohammed. In the combat of man and mountain there is a kind of magic. It is a magic, moreover, which would not be possible were it not for Crane's handling of repetition, which, by bringing out a similarity of development, allows the naturalistic phase to serve in part as a model for the mythical phase, strengthening the believability of the latter.

The second consideration is the struggle and a reversal that transpires entirely within the second phase. In formal terms, the reversal is signaled by a shift separating the perspective of the naturalistic phase from that of the fabulous. This is like the shift in one of Crane's most characteristic poems, which advances by negating a premise or reversing an expectation. The reversal occurs just when the little man seems to have been defeated:

> "God!" he howled, "it's been follerin' me!" He grovelled.
>
> Casting his eyes upward made circles swirl in blood.
>
> "I'm shackled I guess," he moaned. As he felt the heel of the mountain about to crush his head, he sprang again to his feet. He grasped a handful of small stones and hurled them.
>
> "Damn you!" he shrieked, loudly. The pebbles rang against the face of the mountain.
>
> The little man then made an attack. He climbed with hands and feet, wildly. Brambles forced him back and stones slid from beneath his feet. The peak swayed and tottered and was ever about to smite with a granite arm. The summit was a blaze of red wrath.
>
> But the little man at least reached the top. Immediately he swaggered with valor to the edge of the cliff. His hands were scornfully in his pockets.
>
> He gazed at the western horizon edged sharply against a yellow sky. "Ho!" he said. "There's Boyd's house and the Lumberland Pike."
>
> The mountain under his feet was motionless. (VIII, 271)

The turning point is the outburst, at once oral and gestural, in which the little man acts out his defiance of the menacing, older, bigger "other."

The ensuing battle may be related, for its part, to a combat myth in which the champion nearly loses the battle with the enemy, finally destroys and disposes of him, and celebrates his victory. The first of these three stages casts light upon the fact that the little man suffers what seems to be a defeat before recovering and resuming the fight. "Obviously a story about someone who simply goes out and wins is much less effective (hence less perfect) than a story about someone who nearly loses, then wins at the last moment as the result of a new development." The combat myth, it may be said, is somewhat misnamed: "It is really a 'victory myth.' It isn't just the story of a fight; it is the story of a radical triumph. . . ."[24] Such a story may be a more satisfactory parallel for Crane's narrative than the "purer" mythic models of Lévi-Strauss.

Whereas the latter provide solutions to contradictions by generating new oppositions with mediating terms, Crane's model is distinctly one-sided. There is an opposition between man and mountain, and man wins. There is nothing, in Lévi-Strauss's terms, that fits between the two, as the carrion-eating animal fits between the carnivore and the herbivore, or as mist between water and air. The two sides are not less opposed; it is just that one of them has been subdued. Crane's is an individual creation conditioned by collective factors (the English language at a particular stage, received modes of representation, norms of characterization and action, social assumptions, the publishing market, and the like). It is, furthermore, specifically literary. One finds in it neither a mediation derived from the terms of opposition, as in the Hegelian model, nor a mediation that splits the difference between the term, as in the Lévi-Strauss model. The "other" term offered by Crane is not, strictly, a third at all, though it may be regarded as serving in lieu of such. But it is most definitely other: other than the basic opposition (man versus mountain) and other than the solution (man triumphs over mountain). It is the complex of attitudes and effects that situates the represented action. Both the opposition and the solution of the opposition hang suspended within a framework consisting of the fact that the path does go just where the pudgy man had said it would, thus diminishing the little man's triumph; and of the fact that the little man goes from one extreme to another, starting out little when he suffers excessive fear, growing figuratively bigger during his display of courage, then submitting in the end, in a way that again diminishes him, to a pride as excessive in its own way as his original fear.

Having apparently decided in favor of the antagonist, the mountain, Crane withdraws his support, as if to say, "Winner loses." In this way a two-part opposition is decided, only to be itself opposed. The result is nothing more definite than a sense that opposition is in the nature of things, a sense that, depending on changing perspectives or changing circumstances or mere chance, victory is not very different from defeat. The ethical burden imposed by such an attitude is picked up characterologically, as it were: To compensate for lack of resolution through plot Crane attaches particular value to the resoluteness of his character. One understands that while the little man's opponents change he remains the same, as admirable in his assertions as in his pretensions he is absurd.

3

Conflict as Condition: *Maggie: A Girl of the Streets*

The opening of Crane's first novel, which appeared in 1893 as *Maggie: A Girl of the Streets (A Story of New York),* recalls the close of "The Mesmeric Mountain": "A very little boy stood upon a heap of gravel for the honor of Rum Alley. He was throwing stones at howling urchins from Devil's Row who were circling madly about the heap and pelting at him" (p. 3). The protagonist of each narrative is little, isolated, elevated, and menaced, and each reacts defiantly, the one throwing pebbles, the other stones.[1] As the occupant of the heap, the little boy is a version of the little man as the heap of gravel is a version of a mountain; but there is a difference. While the man's position, having been freely assumed, lends a splendor of isolation, the boy's does not. Social reality has become so much a matter of mere oppugnancy that conflict goes on by itself, interminably: Conflict, to use a word that becomes prominent in the New York City sketches, is a "condition."

CONFLICT AS CONDITION

A current of energy that must always flow somewhere, conflict can be interrupted, stalled, or diverted, but it cannot be shut off. In this strange economy of strife the advent of Pete, who breaks up the fight, illustrates the significance in Crane of the outsider, who appears as the novice or the innocent one (*The Red Badge of Courage,* "Death and the Child"); the monster, in the story of the same name; the newcomer ("The Bride Comes to Yellow Sky"); the foreigner ("One Dash – Horses," "A Man and Some Others"), or the newcomer who is also a foreigner ("The Blue Hotel"). In *Maggie* the ultimate outsider, in the end, is Maggie herself.

Being an outsider is a matter of degree. Pete is an outsider in that he does not belong to the nuclear family. Through his friendship with Jimmie – one of those fraternal relations that are a leading medium of social sympathy in Crane's Bowery world – Pete enters the family system in a way that causes Maggie – dramatically and ironically – to depart from it; he leaves, rejecting it, and having left, rejects Maggie as well. For her part Maggie, having departed, returns to be rejected again.

Maggie's fate is in part determined by the pairing of Jimmie and Pete. As we have seen, it is through this relation that the first conflict in the story is interrupted. Subsequently the relation is neatly – almost too neatly – reversed: Jimmie enters into conflict with Pete as if by the throwing of a switch, though "It occurred to him to vaguely wonder, for an instant, if some of the women of his acquaintance had brothers" (p. 85). Jimmie maintains his "moral" equilibrium by concentrating on the wrong done to his own honor: "He suddenly broke out again. 'I'll go t'ump hell outa deh mug what did her deh harm. I'll kill 'im! He t'inks he kin scrap, but when he gits me a-chasin' 'im he'll fin' out where he's wrong, deh damned duffer. I'll wipe up deh street wid 'im' " (p. 88).

The series of fights in the first pair of chapters demonstrates the sheer inertia of the violence unleashed (in Crane's view) *within* the Bowery *by* the Bowery. But the repetitions do something else Crane has not before attempted. First Jimmie fights the urchins of Devil's Row, then he fights one of his own allies, Blue Billie, to demonstrate the prowess that he thinks Pete will doubt later and that he thinks Blue Billie doubts even now. The third outbreak pits son against father. When Maggie cries on seeing that Jimmie has been brawling again, he hits her as well. She, meanwhile, has been jerking baby Tommie along against his will. The trail thus leads from extrafamilial intergroup conflict (between Devil's Row and Rum Alley) to extrafamilial intragroup conflict (between Jimmie and a Rum Alley friend) to a series of conflicts within the nuclear family (between father and son, brother and sister, mother and children, husband and wife). The picture of the family Crane goes on to present adds something qualitatively by showing the manner – verbal, emotional, and physical – of the conflict, and quantitatively by showing that in the Johnson flat there is simply more of it. The parental pair are creatures of excess, the mother playing a role closest to that of the giant mother in a Sullivan County tale entitled "An Explosion of Seven Babies": "The mother's massive shoulders heaved with anger. Grasping the urchin by the neck and shoulder she shook him until he rattled. . . . Jimmie screamed in pain and tried to twist his shoulders out of the clasp of the huge arms" (pp. 15–16).

SUBMISSION

If the family's conflicts are largely due to the father's submission to the bottle, they are also due to his submission to the mother, which derives in turn, circularly, from her submission to the bottle. Appropriately, her power lies in that very submission, which, in its excessiveness, makes her too much to handle. For there exists in her none of that moderation and self-control, that sense of measure, that Crane admires in the discipline of the military life, with its interlocking levels of compliance and command. In the army authority reigns; in the Johnson family it riots. That the mother frequently breaks into tears is a part of the pattern, for where measure is wanting there can only be swings between extremes.

The woman is a synecdoche of an environment that is a virtual exercise in expressionist violence:

> Eventually they entered into a dark region where, from a careening building, a dozen gruesome doorways gave up loads of babies to the street and the gutter. A wind of early autumn raised yellow dust from the cobbles and swirled it against an hundred windows. Long streams of garments fluttered from fire-escapes. In all unhandy places there were buckets, brooms, rags and bottles. In the street infants played or fought with other infants or sat stupidly in the way of vehicles. Formidable women, with uncombed hair and disordered dress, gossiped while leaning on railings, or screamed in frantic quarrels. Withered persons, in curious postures of submission to something, sat smoking pipes in obscure corners. A thousand odors of cooking food came forth to the street. The building quivered and creaked from the weight of humanity stamping about in its bowels. (pp. 12–13)

A basis for Crane's emphasis on female presence is the absence of men, who are away at work. More specifically, the children of this "mother-environment" are disgorged in parodic parturition; the garments shown are things washed by the mothers; the cleaning articles are things wielded by mothers. A hint at rejection is afforded by a juxtaposition of statements, which brings these infants who are threatened in the street into contiguity with the "formidable women." The giving-up of babies is reinforced by the odors, which are the excess of food – the part of food that goes off in the cooking process. The concluding sentences widen the context, for to say that the environment is dominated by child-bearing females is not to say that it is identical with them. The environment is made general by number (a thousand odors) and by introducing the most general statement in the description, not through women or infants, but through the less specific figure of the "person": "Withered persons, in curious postures of submission to something . . . ." Such descriptions point back to the taste for urban exoticism that the brothers Goncourts developed and refined as well as to contemporary interest in the depiction of American lowlife.[2]

In an age less genteel Crane might have shown more graphically some postures of submission available to a girl of the streets. In any case, the scene that opens Chapter 12 portrays her in a posture that dramatizes her submission to Pete: "From her eyes had been plucked all look of self-reliance. She leaned with a dependent air toward her companion" (I, 51). The picture of Maggie that emerges thereafter is done in tones similar to the ones that Crane applies to her environment:

> In a hall of irregular shape sat Pete and Maggie drinking beer. A submissive orchestra dictated to by a spectacled man with frowsy hair and a dress suit, industriously followed the bobs of his head and the waves of his baton. A ballad singer, in a dress of flaming scarlet, sang in the inevitable voice of brass . . . . She returned attired in less gown, and sang again. She received another enthusiastic encore. She reappeared in still less gown and danced. (p. 105)

The parallel between the orchestra's and Maggie's submissiveness is sufficiently obvious, as are the sexual implications of the scarlet gown and the disrobing. Less obvious is the link between the word "shape," denoting the room, and Pete's remark to Maggie: " 'Say, Mag, I'm stuck on yer shape. It's outa sight' . . ." (p. 49). That comes six chapters earlier, and is placed in the same relative position (that is, at the opening of the scene) as in the passage before us. The resulting resonance helps the word "irregular" cast a little moral shadow of its own, with prophetic implications for Maggie, whose name, appropriately, is the first word to appear at the end of that description.

Her brother's submission is also made explicit: "Jimmie came when he was obliged to by circumstances over which he had no control. His well-trained legs brought him staggering home and put him to bed some nights when he would rather have gone elsewhere" (pp. 67–8). The specificity of the second statement covers for the vagueness of the first in a typical way. About the importance of the Bowery's dependence on drink Crane is as clear as any reformer; about some other factors he seems less sure. To what does everyone submit? To "something." Why does Jimmie keep coming home? Because of "circumstances over which he had no control." If his account of Pete's power over Maggie is more satisfactory it is not merely because Crane gives it more space, but because Maggie's vulnerability provides a ready-made structure, as visible as the orchestra's relation to the conductor: "Maggie was dazed. She could dimly perceive that something stupendous had happened. She wondered why Pete saw fit to remonstrate with the woman, pleading for forgiveness with his eyes. She thought she noted an air of submission about her leonine Pete. She was astounded" (p. 124).

PERCEPTION: THE SURPRISING ELEMENT

Crane shares Peirce's fascination with what the latter calls the surprising element in experience, "the sense of something opposing one's Effort, something preventing one from opening a door slightly ajar;

which is known in its individuality by the actual shock, the Surprising element, in any Experience which makes it *sui generis*."[3]

That Crane differentiates among types of surprise, wonder, and astonishment is suggested in "A Grey Sleeve," where, regarding the young girl, we are told: "The flying open of the door had obviously been an utter astonishment to her and she remained transfixed there in the middle of the floor . . ." (VI, 71). The same differentiation obtains in "Three Miraculous Soldiers": surprise on the part of the soldiers and overwhelming wonder on the part of the child, who seems to witness the bodily disappearance of the soldiers she has hidden: "The result was a stupefaction of her mind. She was astonished out of her senses at this spectacle of three large men metamorphosed into a handful of feed" (VI, 37). This susceptibility to surprise, to which the female and the young are supposed to be especially prone, makes them likely to be overwhelmed, though in the stories just cited the danger is minimized by characters – not female and young but male and, relatively speaking, old – who function somewhat in the manner of wards. This presence, in any event, is missing in *Maggie*. The girl blossoms alone, famously, in a mud-puddle, her purity appearing in the context of impurities to which she is directly exposed. Now this notion of the child as a figure of contrast may owe something to the Wordsworthian strain in English Romanticism wherein the child functions by negative association, invoking that from which it differs, the better to show *that* it differs. The author of *Maggie* reminds us perhaps less of Wordsworth, however, than of Dickens, who explains in the preface to *The Old Curiosity Shop* "that, in writing the book, I had it always in my fancy to surround the lonely figure of the child with grotesque and wild, but not impossible companions, and to gather about her innocent face and pure intentions, associates as strange and uncongenial as the grim objects that are about her bed when her history is first foreshadowed."[4] The principle of contrast operates powerfully, in any case, in both the English and the American works, and is a key source of surprise as well as a key factor in perception. For while Maggie's innocence is not in itself enough to see her through, it stands in vivid opposition to her environment.

In *Maggie* characters live in a state of wonder not far removed from shock. To Jimmie "Foot-passengers were mere pestering flies with an insane disregard for their legs and his convenience. He could not conceive their desire to cross the streets. Their madness smote him with eternal amazement" (p. 37). The "mere boy" (p. 118) whom Nell abandons for Pete declares to Maggie "how amazing it was that anybody should treat him" (p. 125) in such a way. When Maggie later tells him she is going home instead of accompanying him, he is "struck with amazement" and "stupefied" (p. 129). Even Pete is capable of being shocked; refused a kiss, he walks off with "something of an astonished expression upon his features" (p. 64). Maggie's wonder is everywhere in evidence: "It was apparent to her that [Pete's] condescension was a marvel . . . . With Maggie gazing at him wonderingly, he took pride in commanding waiters who were, however, indifferent or deaf" (p. 105). We saw, above, Maggie's reaction when Pete submitted to Nell. An astonishment more akin to fear, of a type that Darwin discusses in his *Origin of the Emotions,* is registered visibly when Pete turns the girl away from his bar: "Astonishment swept over the girl's features. 'Why, Pete! yehs tol' me – ' " (p. 139).

Maggie goes where her perception leads her, though in saying this it is well to remember the degree to which the meaning of the word "perception" has changed. In Crane's day it still designated a true apprehending; to perceive was to see, to behold accurately. More recently the word has come to suggest the reverse: When one states that one has a perception, one is saying simply that one has a point of view; perception becomes a claimed apprehending. Maggie's perception verges upon being perception of this kind: "Maggie perceived that here was the beau ideal of a man. Her dim thoughts were often searching for far away lands where, as God says, the little hills sing together in the morning. Under the trees of her dream-gardens there had always walked a lover" (pp. 47–8). These words put a wide distance between perceiver and perceived or, more precisely, they define percepts in terms of opinion. A few pages later, "Maggie perceived that Pete brought forth all his elegance and all his knowledge of high-class customs for her benefit. Her heart warmed as she reflected upon his condescension" (pp. 58–9). Here we are still more aware of Maggie's attitude toward Pete's behavior than of the behavior itself; we are aware, too, that Pete's manners are anything but elegant. Yet Maggie's attitude has relative validity; may one then say that Maggie perceives as much as the horizon of her past and her present situation allow? Such a view risks placing too narrow a limit on the range of perceptual possibilities – risks suggesting that Maggie is fated to remain to the end as ignorant as she was in the beginning. This is not, I think, the case. The more Maggie enters into the life of the saloon and the dancehall the more she perceives: "As they went out Maggie perceived two women seated at a table with some men. They were painted and their cheeks had lost their roundness" (p. 108). Appearance emerges as an issue for Maggie at the same time as we become conscious of the nature of her perception. "Perceived" first occurs in connection with Maggie herself in the concluding paragraph of Chapter 5 (the sentence concerning Pete as the ideal man). Early in the next chapter we read: "As he became aware that she was listening closely, he grew still more eloquent in his descriptions of various happenings in his career. It appeared that he was invincible in fights" (p. 49). Wonder has its negative moment, in the sense that head and heart, drawn toward the future in a new way, must in some sort revolt against the present. As Robert Musil's man without qualities comes to understand, to be surprised at the way things are is to infer that they might be otherwise. Through the mediation of Pete, Maggie's perspective is altered:

> The almost vanished flowers in the carpet-pattern, she conceived to be newly hideous. Some faint attempts which she had made with blue ribbon, to freshen the appearance of a dingy curtain, she now saw to be piteous.
>
> She wondered what Pete dined on.
>
> She reflected upon the collar and cuff factory. It began to appear to her mind as a dreary place of endless grinding. (pp. 51–2)

We might say that Maggie here *con*ceives, rather than *per*ceives, in that the object does not stand forth, under its own power, in a full, self-given appearance. The flowers are the same as always, but she has come to interpret them differently. Indeed, it is here that we see Maggie forcefully, almost creatively, extending herself toward an entity which remains fixed, inert. If, on the other hand, Maggie is more passive with Pete, it is because Pete's appearance is full, an uprearing "thereness," which overwhelms her: "Swaggering Pete loomed like a golden sun to Maggie. He took her to a dime museum where rows of meek freaks astonished her . . . . Pete did not appear to be particularly interested in what he saw" (p. 68).

Here Maggie seems to be at the center of the perception: Pete appears *to her* to be uninterested. As the book goes on, however, this centrality fades, as I have already suggested. Near the end of Chapter 12 we can still read: "The men made Maggie fear, but she blushed at Pete's words as it became apparent to her that she was the apple of his eye" (p. 107). A few pages later Maggie perceives the woman who is "painted with no apparent paint," and in the same scene she dimly perceives that something has gone wrong in her relationship with Pete. But in general there is a shift away from Maggie's perceptions, as the way is being prepared by the parallelism between Jimmie's relation to Hattie, "the forlorn woman," and Pete's relation to Maggie. After turning Hattie away, Jimmie watches her: "on the brilliantly lighted avenue he perceived the forlorn woman dodging about like a scout" (I, 63). In the following chapter Pete gives the same treatment to Maggie, the sequence being inverted so that the rejection follows Pete's sighting of her: "he went hastily over to the side door. Opening it and looking out, he perceived Maggie standing as if undecided, at the corner" (I, 66). Maggie is no longer the one who looks but the one who is looked at. Appropriately, in the homecoming scene between these two episodes, she becomes the focus of an overtly visual attention:

> His mother, tottering about the room, pointed a quivering forefinger.
> "Lookut her, Jimmie, lookut her. Dere's yer sister, boy. Dere's yer sister, Lookut her! Lookut her!" (pp. 130–1)

As this takes place, there is an increasing use of the word "apparently": "As the woman walked down between the rows of tables, Pete was at her shoulder talking earnestly, apparently in explanation" (p. 124; *cf.* pp. 125, 140). If Crane's use of "appear" and related words throughout the text already distances the object of perception, "apparently" tends to increase the distance. The word does not express a state of ignorance so much as a desire to remain general by avoiding particularity, or at least, overparticularity. This is at least part of the reason for abstaining – after the chapter in which Maggie perceives the two other women – from further more or less direct representation of Maggie's consciousness. After that passage we have Crane's description of her astonishment at Pete's submission to Nell, a description relatively "close" to Maggie's mind, but briefer than the description of her reaction to her home after she gets to know Pete. It is the last account of its kind. Later "Maggie was paying no attention, being intent upon the doors" (p. 126), and "The girl was still staring at the doors" (p. 126). While both statements account for her present state, they do so from the outside, being visual notations of attitude, both in the sense of an affective and cognitive orientation, and in the sense of a posture.

SIGHT AND SPEECH

Maggie's corollary status as the one-who-is-looked-at, established in the subsequent rejection scene with the family, is reinforced in the rejection scene with Pete. Although she does find speech again, her words are ineffectual: "Finally she asked in a low voice: 'But where kin I go?' " (p. 140). Her final reduction to silence epitomizes her descent to the status of an object: "She wandered aimlessly for several blocks. She stopped once and asked aloud a question of herself: 'Who?' " (p. 140). Speech for Maggie is no longer interpersonal; it is the communication of a sensibility with itself, confirming isolation, registering despair. This bad girl of the streets is henceforth a visible body moving silently in space, the kinetic center of the book, so far as Maggie is concerned, being Chapter 18, where Crane records the utterances of the men who pass her in silence. Their words are random and typical: The one name by which the girl is addressed (Mary) is generic, and complementary to the name Pete employs (Mike) in his encounter with Nell in Chapter 14.

Among the parts of the body, the face may be the most conspicuously social. The face turns to others a reflecting surface on which feeling and intentions visibly appear. But whereas another writer might present modeled, three-dimensional features, Crane is inclined to offer none at all. No need to be bothered with noses and chins when the face is at once a physiognomic signature of a particular mode of being and a type of general sign. In Hofmannsthal's words, "a human face is a hieroglyph, a sacred, definite sign."[5] This does not mean that one has only to look at a countenance in order to know what an individual "is" once and for all, for the essential, in Crane, has a way of getting mixed up with the contingent. In learning what someone is, we are to a degree learning what that person is *now*; in learning what that person is now, we are to a degree learning what that person *is*. In Chapter 1 we see Jimmie fighting in Rum Alley: "His infantile countenance was livid with fury" (p. 3). Now that is the contingent Jimmie – the boy who happens to be involved, at the moment in a battle. But it is also the essential Jimmie, because this experience establishes a pattern of combative behavior that will persist throughout his life.

The face belongs to a gestural world of sight and space. Sight facilitates vividness; it helps the reader to feel a sense of direct experience; yet it also creates a sense of separation in space, for sight – as compared, for example, with taste, touch, or smell – can also establish a feeling of distance. Sight shares these characteristic with space which, as Whitehead explains, is both "separative" and "prehensive": It keeps things apart and at the same time, precisely because it relates them to one another spatially, keeps them together.[6]

The scene in which Maggie appeals to her seducer for support is ostensibly a dialogue; but consider what happens when we remove the spoken words and attend only to the miming:

> He went hastily over to the side door. Opening it and looking out, he perceived Maggie standing, as if undecided, on the corner . . . .
>
> As she turned her face toward him Pete beckoned to her hurriedly . . . .
>
> Maggie came to him, the anxious look disappearing from her face and a smile wreathing her lips . . . .
>
> The bartender made a violent gesture of impatience . . . .
>
> Astonishment swept over the girl's features . . . .
>
> [Pete's] countenance reddened with the anger of a man whose respectability is being threatened . . . .
>
> The girl's eyes stared into his face . . . .
>
> The girl . . . was apparently bewildered and could not find speech. . . . He slammed the door furiously and returned, with an air of relief, to his respectability. (pp. 138–40)

The scene suffers little if at all when stripped of speech. Normally, speech is interpersonal, it being understood that the words I hear come from "inside" the one who speaks to me, just as my words to the other come from "inside" me; but speech in *Maggie* is peculiarly externalized. Pete's words belong as much to the social field as to himself. When Pete speaks he aligns himself with a type of action in that field and borrows its word-set. This may be the word-set of the seducer, who says sweet things, or the tough, who says hard ones; they are in every case the lines that go with the part: Thus Maggie's mother, when she speaks, portrays the Parent of the Ungrateful Child.[7] This is not to suggest a discrepancy between expression and feeling, nor is it to suggest a discontinuity between the speaker's sense of identity and her social role. On the contrary, the former is assimilated to the latter, the social role drawing the character away from individuation toward the type. It is as if to say: The outside of a person may be all the inside a person has. One is reminded of the fact that, as Jan Mukařovský reminds us, the writer must borrow language from standard, public speech:[8] The writer's choice of style is always in some sort an appropriation. In *Maggie* Crane suggests that the voice of the public, as Valéry calls it, is itself an appropriation. Through the words I say I move away from myself as individual toward the crowd, which is the composite of all the faces that gaze at me, expecting certain things of me and leading me in certain directions. I live in the gaze of these faces, I depend upon it for sustenance, I draw it into myself just as I breathe the air by which I am enveloped. I am what these others make of me and thus I speak the words they exact from me even as I, as part of that crowd of others, exact words from them, drawing them out of that individuation from which, by the social force that pulls us all, I am equally drawn. Speech in *Maggie,* then, is precisely a form of alienation.

Maggie, too, as we have seen, has her speech stolen from her. Even if she were "allowed" to continue speaking, her words would no longer express the individual Maggie, but a role player, "a girl of the painted cohorts" (p. 144). A girl of the streets communicates through her glances, her smiles, her walk, presenting an appearance which is in fact her reality. Maggie thus lives, in Chapter 17, the deprivation of speech that, as I have tried to show, was already implicit in the chapter that precedes it. In the eyes of Pete, Maggie is already the type which she does not literally become until the following chapter. Maggie's claim to a self-respecting, independent existence is undermined, of course, long before this. Maggie's view of things, and the words that express this view, belong to the book as much as they belong to Maggie herself: "The theatre made her think. She wondered if the culture and refinement she had seen imitated, perhaps grotesquely, by the heroine on the stage, could be acquired by a girl who lived in a tenement house and worked in a shirt factory" (pp. 72–3). Take away that parenthetic phrase "perhaps grotesquely" and you have a fair representation of Maggie's view. But the full statement, incorporating that phrase, presents a shift in perspective, the main statement expressing Maggie's vision, the "aside" expressing a judgment that is not hers. The same may be said of the opening passage of the book, with its stamping humanity, gruesome doorways, and curious postures of submission.[9]

THE GROTESQUE

Crane likes to draw on conventional grotesque motifs, such as the ghoulish grin and the humorless laugh, the demonic physical object, the monster and the freak, and the word "grotesque" itself. When Pete and Jimmie fight, "The faces of the men began to fade to the pallor of warriors. Their lips curled back and stretched tightly over the gums in ghoul-like grins" (p. 99). When Pete and Maggie go out together they visit "a dime museum where rows of meek freaks atonished her. She contemplated their deformities with awe and thought them a sort of chosen tribe" (p. 68). The word "grotesque" is a shorthand device for invoking the fearful, the quasicomic, and the wondrous, and for underlining the shortcomings of proletarian taste, but after a while one begins to feel that some of the grotesquerie is there for its own sake. The scene comes to a climax when a vocalist sings "The star-spangled banner" [*sic*] and the crowd voices its collective approval. The economy of the scene requires nothing more, but more is given as a fat little man "began to roar a song and to stamp back and forth before the footlights, wildly waving a glossy silk hat and throwing leers or smiles broadcast. He made his face into fantastic grimaces until he looked like a pictured devil on a Japanese kite" (p. 63). In Crane as in Norris the theatricality that appears in certain scenes, leaning now toward melodrama, now toward the grotesque, expresses a tension between irreconcilable forces. In melodrama the tension takes the form of open opposition, in the grotesque it is controlled combustion. Further examples of both modes will be discussed in future sections of this study.

This theatricality is cousin to a strain of "demonism" that emerges in some of Norris's tales and many of Bierce's. The strain is particularly evident in three major predecessors – Dickens, Balzac, and Poe. Yet there is little straining in this strain; it races forward like a power that, once released, goes on running. Perhaps it would not have developed much of a tradition at all without some prior validation of "excess," as, for example, in Wordsworth's theory of the spontaneous overflow of powerful feelings. There is in any case – both in grotesque theatricality and the demonic strain to which it is related – the phenomenon of overflow. Imagination indulges itself, producing strange things and stranger feelings: a terror with decorum, a laughter without relief. Such playing is in its very nature perspectival, an experimenting with angles of vision. What keeps these flights within bounds is precisely that they embody a mood that is provisional: This is an author who will limit a lot of things, but never his freedom to shift at will to some other thing. Crane's grotesque, in short, is one way of attaining what Kenneth Burke calls perspective-by-incongruity,[10] the difference being that Burke is operating mainly with the shifting and juxtaposition of terms, while Crane is operating mainly with the shifting and juxtaposition of characters, things, and events.

Crane's concern with the explicitly theatrical and its grotesque potential is explained in part by the fact that the theater carries out its actions in a manner somewhat independent of the performers in the play. The performers are given over to a schema of gesture, posture, and utterance from which they must not deviate however mindful they may be of its illusionary nature. To a considerable extent the same applies to the performance of social roles that have a life of their own, so much so, at times, that, in a flash of self-awareness one may look upon oneself as a spectator in a theater looks upon an actor. It is in such sudden, perspectivistic moments that we glimpse the artificiality of what we are doing and, paradoxically, its genuineness. In the perspectivistic structure of the portion of *Maggie* I am now treating, Maggie conceives of the possibility that her life could resemble what she sees on stage, and the reader conceives of the possibility that what she sees on stage could resemble her life. The relation being that of analogy and not of a mimesis or a doubling, there are differences as well as similarities. The principal difference is that the characters cannot put off their roles; here the roles play their actors. In this sense the "falsity" of appearance donned by the characters is an ultimate falsity, in contrast with that of the stage performers, whose falsity is temporary and limited. Bound by a self-perpetuating, all-powerful system, the character Maggie is unable to act in her own right, having none. The result is a series of acts that seem to happen without the mediation of an agent: "Then missles [*sic*] came to every man's hand. The place had heretofore appeared free of things to throw, but suddenly glasses and bottles went singing through the air" (p. 100). The dissociation applies even to feelings. When Pete surrenders to drink at the beginning of Chapter 18, it is not that he loses self-control – there is no self to control: "The man had arrived at that stage of drunkenness where affection is felt for the universe" (p. 150). He has become a type whose course is such that at a given stage a foreknown emotional state will exist. This inability to deviate from a line of prescribed behavior is underlined by the passive construction "is felt," which is linked to the question of posture and related patterns, at which we have so far only glanced.

POSTURES

Erwin Straus has explored the significance for human development of the upright posture, which consists in a vertical axis permitting flexibility of action (e.g., the hand, released from merely supporting the body, is freed for a variety of performances), in contrast with the horizontal or digestive axis of quadrupeds. Ludwig Binswanger probes the *Verstiegenheit* of Ibsen, the passion for vertical transcendence that causes characters (such as Solness in *The Master Builder*) to ascend either literally or figuratively; while a wider range of corporeal acts and states is examined in Merleau-Ponty's phenomenology of perception, with which a number of Bachelard's inquiries (e.g., into the imagination of air – involving flight, ascent, and other patterns; and into the imagination of water – involving descent, submergence, and the like) invite comparison.[11]

In the works we have been reading we find at one extreme the behavior of the little man, striding like "a proud grenadier" (VIII, 264), or swaggering on a mountain peak. His equivalents in *Maggie* are Pete, who "could appear to strut even while sitting still" (p. 105), and Jimmie, who stands upon a heap of gravel for the honor of Rum Alley. At the other extreme are the frozen postures in the opening scene, where the relative immobility of the woman leaning from the window is repeated in the laborers who pause, the engineer who hangs "lazily" over the railing of "a passive tugboat," and the "worm of yellow convicts" that "crawled slowly along the river's bank" (p. 5), all in contrast with the violent kinetic activity around the heap of gravel. With this in mind we see more readily what Crane is up to in the opening scene of the following chapter, where the curious postures of submission are followed by intense kinetic activity, as Jimmie battles with Maggie and the mother battles with Jimmie.

The most arresting posture is that of bending: "People leaned forward to watch her and to try to catch the words of the song . . . . An occasional man bent forward, intent upon the pink stockings" (pp. 59–60). In a subsequent passage, Maggie, returning home, confronts her mother, who "bent down and peered keenly up into the eyes of the girl" (p. 131), while children "ogled her, as if they formed the front row of a theatre" and women "bended toward each other and whispered, nodding their heads with airs of profound philosophy" (p. 132). The postures of curiosity, insofar as they are assumed both by the mother and by the outsiders, draw the former toward the latter: She looks upon her daughter as an object in the same way as those who do not belong to the family. But there is also a difference, for the curiosity of the outsiders is idle curiosity; her mother's, on the other hand, is defiant. Assuming a mock subordination, she lowers herself derisively to someone who has lowered herself socially.

A bending posture is to be found, about equally often, in what may be described as work situations. In the sweatshop Maggie sees the other women in the room as "mere mechanical contrivances sewing seams and grinding out, with heads bended over their work, tales of imagined or real girl-hood happiness, of past drunks, the baby at home, and unpaid wages" (p. 66). As she is attracted away from this situation, her submission to Pete increases; it is then that we see her, in a passage already quoted, adopt a leaning posture in relation to him. We next see her bending in an attitude that the two intervening passages I am about to discuss throw into relief.

The first displays that other fallen woman, Nell, in her own version of the posture: "She bended over and whispered in his ear. He smiled again and settled in his chair as if resolved to wait patiently" (p. 123). Here is a mocking submission, reminiscent of the attitude of Maggie's mother, but more compliant, since the woman must placate the man by leaning into her work of pleasure. The second passage occurs at the start of the succeeding chapter: "Hurrying men, bent on catching some boat or train, jostled her elbows, failing to notice her, their thoughts fixed on distant dinners" (p. 128). "Her" is the forlorn Hattie who moves but, as the result of her submission to a man who rejects her, is going nowhere. It is in the same chapter that Maggie returns home, also to be rejected, reinforcing the parallelism between herself and Hattie. These, then, are the overtones to be heard when the bending posture appears for the last time: "She hurried forward through the crowd as if intent upon reaching a distant home, bending forward in her handsome cloak . . ." (p. 145). Like Hattie, Maggie is hurrying somewhere while going nowhere.

MATTERS ECONOMIC

In his treatment of work Crane favors automatism or moments of inactivity. Thus the laborers and the tugboat engineer in the opening scene are shown "at work" but not actually working, and the labor that goes on in the sewing shop is described as the operation of a mechanism. Here Maggie works; but we never see her working. What the employees are shown to produce are not sewn goods but projections of the past (happier days or states of drunkenness) or of the future (wages to be paid) or of something absent (the baby left at home). Maggie's behavior, basically, complements the behavior of Jimmie, to which I will turn below. Her equivalent of the trance into which Jimmie typically falls is resentment-filled daydreaming: "She felt she would love to see somebody entangle their fingers in the oily beard of the fat foreigner who owned the establishment" (pp. 66–9). Ordinary work is not, for Crane, a significant activity. Essentially gestural, work is an aspect of a condition that has its roots in an attitude – again, in the sense of a state of mind or feeling as well as in the sense of a posture. Significant activity for Crane would be a struggle against the basic condition. Mere combativeness does not suffice, for combat is simply the corollary of submission – an automatism embodying a predisposition or general state. It is not by accident that when Jimmie detects the policeman rushing toward the fight with Pete, he regards this advent as an interruption. The automatism of work is similarly interrupted. In order to stand up and fight Jimmie climbs down, leaving a job of work in which he has never been, in any case, deeply involved. With the interruption nothing is essentially changed. Jimmie lives a generalized conflict, now striking out at random against the world, staring away from the things to which he ought, in performance of his job, to attend: "He fell into the habit, when starting on a long journey, of fixing his eye on a high and distant object, commanding his horses to begin, and then going into a trance of observation" (p. 36).

Earning money, where Jimmie is concerned, has more to do with attitude than need. Driving a truck, with ample time off for daydreaming and fighting, is merely a version of his earlier, more essential occupation, in which he dreamed about fighting: "Jimmie's occupation for a long time was to stand on streetcorners and watch the world go by, dreaming blood-red dreams at the passing of pretty women. He menaced mankind at the intersections of streets" (p. 33).

Crane explains the transition to the second or paying occupation by inverting the likely sequence. He might more plausibly have said, for example, that Jimmie's father died, and that Jimmie as a consequence felt obliged to work. Instead, he turns the chain of events around: "When he had a dollar in his pocket his satisfaction with existence was the greatest thing in the world. So, eventually, he felt obliged to work. His father died and his mother's years were divided up into periods of thirty days" (p. 34). The middle sentence defines the decision to work as the result of attitude, not of the historical circumstances of his father's death, which is positioned almost as an afterthought. It is not that Jimmie is obliged to work, it is just that he *feels* obliged to work. Between the felt obligation and the father's death – the attitude and the fact – there is a temporal discontinuity, the latter being a specific event at a certain time, the former being something that happened "eventually." The little "so" in the middle attempts not merely to bridge this gap, but to offer a transition from attitude to underlying fact. The fact is history, the attitude is fable, with the middle sentence falling in between: fabulous insofar as it expresses a mere feeling, historical insofar as that feeling is a concrete obligation. The fable is Jimmie's; the totality – fable and attitude, history and fact, and the transition that connects them casually – is Crane's. That is not so much a way of saying that the account is ironic, as a way of saying in what manner it is ironic. Playing one type of explanation off against the other, Crane, without doing full justice to the economic motive, yet wields that motive in a way that tends to discount the role of mere attitude. The further consequence is that, against this accomplishment, the inadequacy of his account of economic realities emerges all over again, for, while it is the author who corrects the myth, it is the author who has indulged it. Crane's understanding is, to repeat, substantially an understanding of attitude, which is by no means to imply that he accepts what Jimmie, for example, believes. The point is that this latter issue, belief, is what mainly interests Crane, and that historical facts, economic motives, and other considerations arise only in relation to that interest. In the present passage, the irony finally discounts the history even more than it discounts the fable.

Crane accepts the primacy of consciousness that Marx endeavored to dissolve. For the Crane of *Maggie,* Marx's dictum "Life is not determined by consciousness, but consciousness by life," would be accurate if reversed. If this is not quite what Jimmie's decision to work proves, Crane's emphasis does locate the flashpoint of decision in the attitude of his character rather than in "life," by which Marx understands all social and material being that is gathered by the name of world. The basis of Maggie's decision, however, is unmistakably clear. Jimmie declares, " 'Mag, I'll tell yeh dis! See? Yeh've eedder got teh go teh hell or go teh work!' Whereupon she went to work, having the feminine aversion of going to hell" (pp. 41–2). Work is the alternative to sin, as "going to hell" is called in the poems that Crane was composing at about this time. Jimmie's imperative is moral, not economic.

If Crane differs from Marx in his approach to the polarity of consciousness and "life," his approach to the living habits of his characters is very similar, in one important economic respect, to that of Crane's contemporary Max Weber. "With some over-simplification," Weber observes, "one might thus say that 'classes' are stratified according to their relations to the production and acquisition of goods; whereas 'status groups' are stratified according to the principles of their *consumption* of goods as represented by special 'styles of life.' "[12] Although Crane, as we have seen, never shows his characters actually producing but merely pictures them in producing situations, the population of the book endlessly consumes. The mother, the father, Jimmie, Pete, the gnarled old woman, the clientele of the saloons, and, in time, Maggie herself – at every opportunity someone drinks to excess. Between the extreme results – oblivion on the one hand, an outburst or a fight on the other – there is little to choose, except when the fight is more or less uncontrolled. Then there occurs an increase of excess, a phase of destruction (as in the battle of Chapter 11), which is precisely another form of consumption. In Chapter 18 Pete consumes even more excessively, guided by a ratio of prestige: The more he drinks and the more he spends (i.e., the more he wastefully consumes), the higher his "honor." To this extent his is the "purest" conspicuous consumption in the book.

I am suggesting, then, that Crane views class through the prism of status. Given his own social origins and the degree of experience he had acquired when he wrote the present work, there is no reason to suppose that he knew what his characters (more precisely, the individuals whose typical activity could serve as models) actually did at work.

Had he rendered the concrete productive activity of his characters (a surmise that presupposes his interest in the subject, which may be doubted) the book might have been even more remarkable than it is, though in a different way. That the denizens of the Bowery waste their lives by, for example, spending excessively on drink and cheap entertainment, is conventional wisdom, and easily accommodates the interest of a writer concerned with social honor or "face." One can well understand why such an author would have an eye for the type of behavior appropriate to the status group, with its devotion to consumption, and would be comparatively near-sighted about that behavior in regard to class.

MEASURE

What appears to the members of such a group as a norm appears to an outsider as an excess. Crane, however, offers an additional standard of measure that is internally based. I refer to the fact that the behavior of the Johnson family is judged negatively by other inhabitants of the Bowery. If evaluation generally takes for Crane the form of description, it takes for these creations of his the form of open denunciation. The neighbors of the Johnsons consider that the mother and the father – and eventually the daughter – all exceed the neighborhood's moral norm. From another point of view, this excess is a deficiency, a want of proportion. To use the term that Crane will later favor, the victimizers of Maggie are wanting in virtue, and virtue entails self-control, for without self-control there can never be the middle condition of classical ethics that lies "between two forms of badness, one being excess and the other deficiency . . . ." There can never be "the right measure."[13]

Crane's sense of measure manifests itself in *Maggie* as a concern with number, proportion, and rate:

> In a hilarious hall there were twenty-eight tables and twenty-eight women and a crowd of smoking men . . . . Soiled waiters ran to and fro. . . . stumbling over women's skirts and charging two prices for everything but beer, all with a swiftness that blurred the view of the cocoanut palms and dusty monstrosities painted upon the walls of the room . . . . The rate at which the piano, cornet and violins were going, seemed to impart wildness to the half-drunken crowd. (p. 117)

The specific matching by number of women and tables, set off against the nonspecific "a crowd of smoking men," creates a ratio that is its own perspective on the women. The rate of activity in the hall contributes to a misprision to which Maggie herself is prey: "Three weeks had passed since the girl had left home. The air of spaniel-like dependence had been magnified and showed its direct effect in the peculiar off-handedness and ease of Pete's ways toward her" (pp. 117–18). The length of her absence, which is here measured specifically for the first time, is placed in such a way as to suggest the reason for the proportionate adjustment of her dependence. In looking at Nell, who enters the scene shortly thereafter, Maggie sees a case of the perfect fit: "She perceived that her black dress fitted her to perfection . . . . Tan gloves were stretched over her well-shaped hands" (p. 118). Nell's own way of measuring is revealed by the fact that, in addition to knowing about Pete's friends and affairs, she "knew the amount of his salary" (p. 120).

If the excesses of Maggie's mother are judged by her peers, they are also measured, in ironic number, from outside her group and class. A magistrate declares: " 'Mary, the records of this and other courts show that you are the mother of forty-two daughters who have been ruined' " (p. 115). The woman's loss of measure is demonstrated in a passage that gains in resonance from the perfect fit of Nell:

> The mourner arose and staggered into the room. In a moment she emerged with a pair of faded baby shoes held in the hollow of her hand . . . .
>
> "Jimmie, boy, go git yer sister! Go git yer sister an' we'll put deh boots on her feets!"
>
> "Dey won't fit her now, ye damn fool," said the man.
>
> "Go git yer sister, Jimmie," shrieked the woman, confronting him fiercely. (pp. 161–2)

Although character and scene are about as finely attuned to one another as in Balzac, the harmony is differently achieved. In the environmentalism of Balzac there resides an intimacy, a fusion, which it is not completely inaccurate to call organic. In *Le Père Goriot* Madame Vauquer and her *pension*[14] seem to be the outgrowth of each other, a sentient totality composed of two symbiotic parts. Crane tends to rely on contiguity. From the diachronic point of view this involves a movement from the one, the character, to the other, the scene – a further example of Crane's shifting technique; whereas the synchronic result is a *juxtaposition* that the reader experiences as a *connection* revealing a *relation*. Such a "matching" procedure, as against the fusing procedure in Balzac, poses a challenge to the reader. *Mon semblable, mon frère,* says Crane: Connect as I connect, in a measuring way, by contiguity, juxtaposition, matching, in short, by techniques of metonymy.

Pete, of course (to turn to the character "side" of the relation), does not connect; and it is precisely his sense of measure that prevents him from detecting his true need of it: "He saw no necessity that people should lose their equilibrium merely because their sister or their daughter had stayed away from home" (p. 135). In Lawrence's "The Prussian Officer," the orderly yearns to escape into a protective "neutrality." Pete already has. What he has escaped, furthermore, is not the imposition on him of brutality, such as that from which the orderly suffers, but responsibility for imposition of brutality *by* him. The mean Pete achieves is a travesty of right measure, the moral deficiency he embodies being merely the other face of his excess.

SYMPATHY

This deficiency is a want of what Henry James calls moral sense, a concept expressing, among other things, the importance of fellow feeling or social sympathy. In general, sympathy is severely restricted in the book; in exceptional cases it takes a special form. Pete's opportunity for sexual aggression toward Maggie depends on his friendship with Jimmie, but this is framed in terms of power, as Pete is first shown asssiting Jimmie by attacking an enemy who is much smaller; Pete next offers to host the younger lad to a boxing match, a gesture of "generosity" that needs to be seen alongside his drinks-on-me performance in the penultimate chapter.

The mother in the novel may be viewed in the context of the contemporary ideals about motherhood. William James, writing in 1890, can assert that "*Parental Love* is an instinct stronger in woman than in man, at least in the early childhood of its object," before quoting from an animal psychologist who praises motherly virtue at length, but hints that the good mother is a disappearing type. "She has, in one word, transferred her entire egoism to the child, and lives only in its. Thus, at least, it is in all unspoiled, naturally-bred mothers, who, alas! seem to be growing rarer . . . ."[15] It is self-evident that by this measure the Johnson home is wanting in parental and especially in maternal love, and that such sympathy as the mother feels is introjected: "She rocked to and fro upon a chair, shedding tears and crooning miserably to the two children about their 'poor mother' and 'yer fader, damn 'is soul' " (p. 20).

The most spontaneous expression of sympathy is Maggie's:

> "Are yehs hurted much, Jimmie?" she whispered timidly.
> "Not a damn bit! See?" growled the little boy.
> "Will I wash deh blood?"
> "Naw!" (p. 18)

The more dependent on Pete Maggie becomes, the less we see of such sibling sympathy, almost her only positive tie to the family. Indeed, from this point on Crane brings out Maggie's capacity for sympathy only in one theatrical scene, and in a way that suggests that the capacity is no stronger in her than in any other member of the crowd. This he accomplishes again by creating conditions for a matching-up, describing in one chapter how "many heads were bent forward with eagerness and sympathy" (p. 62), then reporting in the following chapter that she "lost herself in sympathy with the wanderers swooning in snow storms beneath happy-hued church windows. And a choir within sang 'Joy to the World.' To Maggie and the rest of the audience this was transcendental realism" (p. 70). If this suffers in comparison with the first expression of sympathy we saw, it suffers no less in comparison with the vigor of her hate for the fat foreigner. That hate and this new form of sympathy are two poles of the same state. A socially disconnected sympathy now compensates on an imaginary plane for the inability to escape an oppressive environment. By the same process Maggie magnifies the virtues of her lover out of all proportion. Thus limited, she cannot see clearly enough, or soon enough, the difference between a concrete phenomenon and an abstract type.

It is a deficiency shared by her brother in whom there are nonetheless traces of sympathetic imagination deeper than those in the father. In Jimmie's relation to the old woman who is something like a surrogate mother, there is a spontaneous sympathy, colored, to be sure, by the ability of the one to help the other. And a little sympathy shows through when he reports Maggie's ruin; to his mother's rioting oaths he replies: " 'Here, now . . . Take a drop on yerself' " (p. 39). Learning of his sister's ruin does not in itself cause Jimmie to reject her or to see his past friend as a present enemy. He turns from her when her condition threatens the honor of Rum Alley that he had previously defended on a different front. Yet he can still experience a feeling that renders only partly true Bernard Berenson's statement that the Irish-Americans in the book "are pugnacious, brutal, utterly without self-awareness, energizing with no thought of consequences, and ending dead drunk on the dung heap. The girl Maggie, a flower of that dung heap, too delicate, too tender to live in her surroundings, does away with herself. Not even in her does mind count, and in the others there is no sign of it."[16] On the contrary, mind matters a great deal, as we have seen. "Honor" is a social system backing an idea; and the use Maggie finally makes of her body cannot be separated from the use she makes of her imagination. Even Jimmie has thoughts:

> Of course Jimmie publicly damned his sister that he might appear on a higher social plane. But, arguing with himself, stumbling about in ways that he knew not, he, once, almost came to a conclusion that his sister

> would have been more firmly good had she better known why. However, he felt that he could not hold such a view. He threw it hastily aside. (p. 115)

Such is the last phase of the perception, announced by him earlier, that " 'it ain't dessame as if – well, Maggie was diff'ent – see – she was diff'ent' " (p. 88). Regarding self-awareness as such, Berenson, then, is right. For imagination involves the ability to put oneself in the place of another, to grow in sympathy (the capacity to imagine, Shelley reminds us, being an instrument of moral good). The trouble with Maggie's brother is not so much that he completely lacks this imagination, as that he has just a little of it. This is the other face of the excess that is a peculiar Bowery deficiency.

RESTRUCTURING

After the original family of five is reduced, first by the death of the youngest child Tommie, then by the death of the father, Jimmie and his mother restructure their relationship into a cooperative pairing so as to oppose the "other" who is Maggie. Their daughter and sister must be changed into an object for those within the family as she has been changed into an object by those outside it: In the economy of the essential pair – a kind of deeper nucleus within the nuclear family – the third or remaining member is a surplus.

The restructuring that follows the crisis brought on by the rejection of Maggie involves a loss of difference, to borrow from the terminology René Girard has developed for examining the relation of social disorder, violence, and sacrifice.[17] Crisis is associated with what Girard calls mimetic desire, a desire directed toward an object already desired by another, transforming the two desiring persons into rivals and ultimately doubles. In *Maggie* something like this seems to happen when the son rallies to the cause of the mother. In Girard's terms the object of desire would here be social honor, first desired by the mother and then, in imitation, by the son; but Jimmie desires honor from the outset – literally from the opening scene. He does so because everyone is already imitating everyone else through a system of interlocking gazes in which "I watch the other watching me." The transformations Crane describes need to be understood within this system, but on Crane's very particular terms. This means recognizing that the members of the essential pair form a solidarity; they are not so much rivals as partners. Jimmie's true rival in the story is Pete, who takes note of the sister's physical charms one chapter after the brother had done the same. On the other hand, the mother has and can have no true rival. She is too outsized, too grotesque – in a word, too excessive. To align himself with her unchanging nature her son must change roles, and this he does by becoming a surrogate father. Thus situated, he functions not in competition with the mother but in concert with her. The realignment attempts to solve a problem of legitimacy. Why should the son be preserved while the daughter is sacrificed? Because the son has become the father. To put it another way, the only child with the authority to judge another child is a child who has become a parent.

The solidarity this relationship embodies is the extreme negative form of the "good" solidarity, such as it is, in the book. I refer to the relationship that exists at one time or another with Pete, the old woman, and Maggie. None lasts; and the companion on whom Jimmie leans as he prepares to fight Pete is labeled an "ally," suggesting a contractul partnership in a social order outside the family.

COLOR

Only with difficulty, and at the risk of fudging, can Crane's famous colors be categorized neatly. As a large body of criticism demonstrates, certain family resemblances may nonetheless be discerned. This section builds on what has been learned about these colors, exploring in detail how they work, and suggesting some additional ideas of my own.[18]

When a color more or less directly indicates a phenomenal base, its function is essentially reportorial. It registers the impression that such and such a phenomenon would make on a normal retina under everyday circumstances. To the extent that this type of coloration provides a rough standard against which other patterns may be measured, it can be thought of as normative, which is not to say neutral. Such is the case when "some blue policeman turned red" (p. 36), the first color registering the hue of his uniform, the second the hue of his complexion as he becomes agitated; the blue ribbons in the Johnson flat (pp. 52, 53, 85) as well as the red and green of a family quilt (p. 20) work the same way. Reportorial color can intensify an effect, as shown by "their white, gripped teeth" (p. 99), the "white, insignificant coffin" in which Timmie is buried, or the "white socks" worn by Maggie's employer (p. 67). The explanation of eerie or spectral effects, which some critics have called surrealistic, may lie in the source: The "great green-hued hall" (p. 56) houses "pale-green snow storms" (pp. 70–1) because of artificial illumination, especially stage lighting.

Any color may carry with it conventional associations. This is obviously the case in the "immaculate" whiteness of Pete's jacket (p. 137), suggesting purity in appearance only; in the "chaste black coat" (p. 141) of the man who is the first to reject Maggie on the streets; or in the black of Nell's dress (p. 118), signifying the same refined taste implied by her tan gloves, in contrast to the black of Maggie's worn dress (p. 55), where emphasis falls on humbleness.

Red and its relatives, crimson, pink, and scarlet, appear more often than any other color, and often in a reportorial vein. Like the stagey green already mentioned, or like the yellow glare to be examined in a separate section, red may be scenic, as in the "red hues" (p. 21) the fire throws across the floor in the Johnson flat. But Crane applies it more frequently to one or another aspect of a character's appearance. We see Pete with "a red puff tie" (p. 44), a performer in a scarlet dress and a male counterpart in a red wig, and a woman dances in a pink dress and pink stockings. The color can bring out, as in the case of the red-faced policemen, a temporary state: "A small ragged girl dragged a red, bawling infant along the crowded ways," or a permanent one, as in the case of the red fat of the great figure (p. 149) at the end of Chapter 17, or of Maggie's mother, with her red arms, hands, fists, and body and "crimson features" (p. 76). Through repetition the epithet becomes a leitmotiv, a kind of pervasive tone. No mere part of the mother but her very being is expressed by the color when she is called "Maggie's red mother" (p. 55). Crane brings out the choleric extremes of her character by showing her, as it were, redder than red; as occurs when her color rushes toward the blue phase of the spectrum: "The fervent red of her face turned almost to purple" (p. 21).

These visual tones illustrate the "impressionistic" use of color for which Crane is celebrated; and there is probably no color that does not contribute to the overall impression a given work makes. But impressions are expressions as well. More than mere registered sensation, they communicate through a perceiver's specific way of perceiving, which is to say that they are actively interpretative and not passively responsive. To this extent one may speak of Crane's art as being both impressionist and expressionist.[19] It would not be misleading, indeed, to term it impressionist–expressionist, though this is admittedly awkward. The very assertiveness of Crane's colors, their high pitch and emotional intensity, make his slum novel read at times like a nightmare or a hallucination. The effect can be traced in part to something that fits into no category of color, and that is the cumulative effect of repetition. A recurring leitmotiv in a piece of fiction, as in a piece of music, "says" more than a nonrecurring feature, or says it differently. In any case, the impressionist vision already tends in an expressionist direction, for the severity, starkness, and intensity that characterize expressionist vision enter by doors that impressionism opens: the concrete, isolated image, the bonding of image to raw emotion, the accentuation of the immediate, the sensational, and the fragmentary – these are what the expressionist receives and radicalizes.

Expressionist color moves away from the reportorial: "His small body was writhing in the delivery of great, crimson oaths" (p. 3). The concluding phrase registers no particular visual appearance but expresses an emotional state and an emotion-charged act. In the same way "Pete swore redly" and Jimmie can be heard "cursing blackly" (p. 78). Unlike his mother, who is red from the moment she first appears, Jimmie is associated with the color contingently: "Jimmie's occupation for a long time was to stand on street-corners and watching the world go by, dreaming blood-red dreams at the passing of pretty women" (p. 33). While the dreams could be said to possess a phenomenal base insofar as they take on the color of blood, the fact that the blood itself is imaginary makes the statement essentially expressionist. The window, on the other, stays closer to its phenomenal base, the shining light; yet the color applied to it, drawing force from conventional associations between blood and murder, is equally imaginary. One value of the comparison is to remind the reader that impression and expression, which sometimes overlap, form, like colors themselves, a continuum.

THE PECULIAR CHARACTER OF YELLOW

If Goethe's theory of color influenced Crane, as Robert L. Hough suggests, the nature of the influence remains open to debate. Goethe contends

> that general impressions produced by single colors cannot be changed, that they act specifically and must produce definite, specific states in the living organ.
>
> They likewise produce a corresponding influence on the mind. Experience teaches us that particular colors excite particular states of feeling.[20]

The proposed correlation may epitomize an eighteenth-century sense of symmetry; does it prove a natural fact? The sticking point is the concept of single color and its counterpart, the particular state of feeling. C. S. Peirce, whose life encompassed Crane's years, denies that pure colors exist or that they engender correspondingly pure, or simple, sensations. The first thing to understand "is that red, orange, yellow, and green are not pure feelings, but are generalizations of feelings." Noting that an antagonistic school of thought admits that yellow resembles red and green more than red and green resemble one another, Peirce infers that we discern some common element in red and yellow, therefore classing them together.

> They therefore fall into self-contradiction when they say that we perceive that yellow is a simple sensation. It is true that we do not see red in yellow, nor do we see green in it, but only an element of red-likeness and an element of green-likeness; and furthermore we see something

> peculiar in yellow which predominates over its red-likeness and its green-likeness. (7.376)

A pair of ironies rises to view. One is that Peirce's refutation of the notion of single colors, with its insistence on generalization, translates into modern terms something at least of what Goethe means by general impressions. A second irony is that Peirce had developed an approach that in fact comes much closer to formal Impressionist theory than Goethe's. This is not to deny Hough's assertion that in Goethe's theory Crane found a basis for Impressionism before he knew the Impressionist painters. But it is more likely that Crane got from Goethe encouragement, a sense of inspiration even, that could help him work out his own palette.

That Peirce's approach accommodates itself to the Impressionists is even clearer from another passage:

> When the ground is covered by snow on which the sun shines brightly except where shadows fall, if you ask any ordinary man what the color appears to be, he will tell you white, pure white, whiter in the sunlight, a little greyish in the shadow. But that is not what is before his eyes that he is describing; it is theory of what ought to be seen. The artist will tell him that the shadows are not grey but a dull blue and that the snow in the sunshine is of a rich yellow. That artist's observational power is what is most wanted in the study of phenomenology. (5.42)

It is also what is wanted, and supplied, in Impressionist practice. For the Impressionist eye works as the eye of Peirce's artist works, decomposing single tones into multiples and reorganizing these into a new general impression.

Like Goethe and like Crane, Peirce gives importance to yellow:

> [A]ny color when highly illuminated looks more yellow. Now since the illumination of surfaces is constantly changing, this yellowishness has to be allowed for specially in classing the color of the surface; and thus it is very natural that the peculiar character of yellow should acquire a special importance. (7.377)

Goethe is concerned to show how yellow differs in different manifestations. One of the warm colors, yellow is a welcoming tone that carries brightness with it when it appears in its purest form, but is prone to becoming impure:

> When a yellow color is communicated to dull and coarse surfaces, such as common cloth, felt, or the like, on which it does not appear with full energy, the disagreeable effect alluded to is apparent. By a slight and scarcely perceptible change, the beautiful impression of fire and gold is transformed into one not undeserving the epithet foul; and the color of honor and joy reversed to that of ignominy and aversion.

An Impressionist painter, too, might notice the changes that a color undergoes under certain circumstances. But the differences occasioned by common cloth or felt would be just that, visual differences; they would exemplify neither degeneration nor contamination. Goethe moralizes his palette, and it is just this that meets Crane's needs as well. To a literary imagination like Goethe's or Crane's, the color of the sky or of anything else, while always associated with a visual stimulus, is always something to be interpreted and not merely registered.

Further background considerations, this time from the 1890s, will furnish an additional context for Crane's use of the color with the peculiar character.

Yellow led a lively life in the 1890s. This was the decade in which the telephone yellow pages and "yellow journalism" were launched. In 1895 Pulitzer's New York *World,* the paper that in the following year published Howells's review of *Maggie,* pictured a girl in a yellow dress, hoping that this experiment in color printing would attract more readers. To boost circulation for his own New York *Journal,* William Randolph Hearst hired R. F. Outcault away from Pulitzer, whereupon the graphic artist produced the Yellow Kid, the protagonist of the first sequential comic strip employing balloon diaglogue. Meanwhile, in 1894, Aubrey Beardsley and Henry Harland, wanting to launch a trendy magazine, looked to the yellow covers in which French novels had long appeared, and transferred that hue to their own, producing *The Yellow Book.* A year earlier Crane published "Why Did the Young Clerk Swear?" the protagonist of which secretly reads a French novel; the drift of the action takes on a coyly erotic aspect as Crane transfers the traditional yellow, slightly altered, to his hero's moustache: "Soon it could have been noticed that his blond mustache [*sic*] took on a curl of enthusiasm . . ." (VIII, 34).

In the same year, at his own expense, Crane published *Maggie.* Its covers were yellow.

It is one of the first colors to appear in the novel: "Over on the island a worm of yellow convicts came from the shadow of a grey ominous building and crawled slowly along the river's bank" (p. 5). Even as these people beyond the law foreshadow Maggie's illicit future, the juxtaposition of their yellow with the dark building foreshadows the crucial juxtaposition of yellow and black in Chapter 17, to be discussed below. Whatever yellow may look like when it occurs in Goethean purity, dust is one of those dull and coarse surfaces on which the color produces the kind of effect Goethe has mind: "A wind of early autumn raised yellow dust from cobbles and swirled it against an hundred windows" (p. 12). When a little later the "rough yellow" of the face and neck of Maggie's mother "flared suddenly crimson" (p. 17), and she swills "from a yellow-brown bottle" (p. 20), we see that she belongs to the same pattern.

For some time Maggie remains apart from the pattern of contamination and degeneration. For, though she "blossomed in a mud puddle" (p. 41), she avoids being muddied: "None of the dirt of Rum Alley seemed to be in her veins. The philosophers, upstairs, downstairs, and on the same floor, puzzled over it" (p. 41).

The color with the peculiar character is associated with the feelings of Maggie and the other employees, who are "of various shades of yellow discontent" (p. 42). In its next application the color adumbrates more: The "yellow silk women" (pp. 56, 59) are professional performers who, while they do not quite belong to the painted cohorts, are associated with drink and sex and hence contamination.

On two notable occasions Crane devotes attention to yellow glare. The same kind of excessive lighting, and especially glaring effects, had drawn the attention of Poe. In "The Philosophy of Furniture" Poe condemns glare as a leading error of decoration, and denounces the American infatuation with gas and glass and "the rage for glitter," suggesting that the mirror, "potent in producing a monstrous and odious uniformity," be banned altogether.[21] Crane for his part depicts the illumination in connection with illusion. To appreciate the effect it is necessary to quote at some length.

> On a corner a glass-fronted building shed a yellow glare upon the pavements. The open mouth of a saloon called seductively to passengers to enter and annihilate sorrow or create rage.
>
> The interior of the place was papered in olive and brown tints of imitation leather. A shining bar of counterfeit massiveness extended down the side of the room. Behind it a great mahogany-imitation sideboard reached the ceiling. Upon its shelves rested pyramids of shimmering glasses that were never disturbed. Mirrors set in the face of the sideboard multiplied them. Lemons, oranges, and paper napkins, arranged with mathematical precision, sat among the glasses. Many-hued decanters of liquor perched at regular intervals on the lower shelves. A nickelplated cash-register occupied a place in the exact centre of the general effect. The elementary sense of it all seemed to be opulence and geometrical accuracy. (pp. 91–2)

The description works on a variety of levels. Like the blue of "The Blue Hotel," the yellow glare publicizes the position of the saloon, assisting in the seduction of customers by attracting their attention. The glass front that makes this possible initiates a chain that includes the shimmering glasses inside, the nickel plate of the cash register, the shining bar, and everything that is also a mere front, such as the imitation leather, the counterfeit massiveness, and even the face of the sideboard with its imaging mirrors.

Since nearly everything in the description is manufactured, from the glass to the cash register, it is tempting to attribute the illusionary effects to artifice. But the natural and the artificial, interwoven in the same color spectrum, are not easily distinguished. In the present case there are the lemons and oranges, which are cousins of the yellow in the opening paragraph. Earlier, on the lambrequin in the Johnson flat may be seen "immense sheaves of yellow wheat and red roses of equal size" (p. 85), and then there is Pete's glitter and glory at the far, "transcendental" end of the spectrum, where the artifices of his manner inspire Maggie to see in him the ultimate natural object of the world: "Swaggering Pete loomed like a golden sun" (p. 68).

The second and last yellow glare occurs at the end of Chapter 17 as Maggie finds herself beside the horrible red fat man:

> At their feet the river appeared a deathly black hue. Some hidden factory sent up a yellow glare, that lit for a moment the waters lapping oilily against the timbers. The varied sounds of life, made joyous by distance and seeming unapproachableness, came faintly and died away to a silence. (p. 149)

After the deathly black hue of the river brings attention down, up goes the yellow glare, whereupon attention comes back down once more to the waters. The concluding sentence, by contrast, works on a horizontal plane as sounds come from distant venues. Here the visual and the aural are interwoven: The black is visual; the yellow, though visual in itself, illuminates the sight and sound of lapping; while the aural dominates in the sounds that die away to silence. The significance of all this for the protagonist is not far to seek. After Maggie arrives at the final block, in the preceding paragraph, the tall buildings first appear, their eyes looking over her into the distance. Then, in the paragraph quoted above, there is a rising movement that falls in the end, followed by another rising movement that also falls in the end, followed by a sense of distance and the ultimate diminution – where sound is concerned – of silence. Here, in essence, is the structure of a dying fall. Such an effect can be heard, as often in Crane, in the structure of the clause explaining the effect of the yellow glare: "that lit for a moment the waters lapping oilily against timbers." First, móment, wáters, lápping, oílily, tímbers all have feminine endings, producing an effect of "trailing-off." Second, lapping, a surge that rises to a fall, surges once more, and once more falls, is itself a trailing-off motion. Third, "óilĭlў," that peculiar nonce formation, increases liquidity by introducing a second "l," with the same stroke increasing the falling effect: *oil,* a diphthong ending with one weak stress becomes a three-syllable term with two weak stresses.

A second office of the yellow glare, and one it shares with the various blacks, is the interweaving of concealment and revelation. Such interweaving occurs in the saloon scene as well, where illumination and illusion act as conspirators: Something is going on behind the facades, something intentionally deceptive and vaguely sinister that the text but partly discloses; and the irony is not merely that no one knows what this concealment amounts to, but that no one even knows there is one. The later passage partly reveals hidden things, the blackness of the block and the river and the oil, things with no intent to deceive and representing nothing but the nothingness that approaches. In its own way the last yellow glare, which appears for only a moment, reveals more than the first, which is more sustained, and is more conclusive than the latter. Far from breaking up the fatal atmosphere, the glare intensifies it, revealing on the river's uneven surface dark motions of matter in nonhuman time and nonhuman space.

COMING TO THE END

In a sense the novel ends twice: first when Maggie approaches death, then in the scenes of aftermath, the last of which focuses on her mother's self-pity. This relation alone would make the concluding pages of the novel somewhat problematic, at least from a strictly structural point of view, but, like the conclusions of *The Red Badge of Courage* and other works, they are problematic for other reasons as well. In the first place, there seems to be a discrepancy between Maggie's status in Chapter 17 and her fate, a circumstance that has a significant bearing on the temporality of the episode. In the second place, it is not at all clear, from the original text of 1893, what ultimately happens to her. There then remains the problem of deciding what if any larger meaning may be derived from this suite of chapters.

By giving pleasure Maggie has prospered; she wears a "handsome cloak," her feet are "well-shod" (p. 145), and she has a positive sense of the propriety of her appearance, "daintily lifting her skirts" (p. 145) as she walks. "An atmosphere of pleasure and prosperity seemed to hang over the throng, born perhaps of good clothes and of having just emerged from a place of forgetfulness" (p. 144). On this glittering avenue Maggie apparently feels at home, and there is nothing to imply that this evening is signficantly different from any other. But, despite her looks and her success, and despite the fact that the locale is fitting, she is rejected by "a tall young man," "a stout gentleman," and "a belated man" (pp. 145–6), then in a darker district by a young man in light overcoat and derby hat and "a laboring man"; "a drunken man" does not accept her "because he has no money," and after being turned down by "a man with blotched features," on the grounds of already having a date, "a ragged being with shifting, blood-shot eyes and grimey hands" (p. 148) says in effect that he is broke too. How the last of the nine men relates to Maggie will be considered after an attempt to elucidate the general pattern just described.

One may approach the pattern by asking how, if this evening is typical, Maggie's prosperity and self-assurance are to be explained. Crane's handling of the situation, it appears, will not tolerate too strict a construction. One infers that chance is a key factor, and that the chance circumstance here depicted relates in a significant way to an implied typical pattern of feeling. That is, Maggie must be supposed to experience a sense that she is superflous to the world in which she wanders. It then follows that (a) she is typically depressed when she happens to be rejected repeatedly, or (b) she happens to be depressed when she is typically rejected repeatedly. The latter interpretation lays stress on the exception, the former on the nexus of exception and rule. But it is unclear which of the two is the likelier. The problem, I think, is that the symbolic cards Crane holds are higher than the literal ones. By symbolic I mean the desire for a powerful representation morally grounded. The preceding chapters depict the previous history of Maggie, this chapter her fate.[22] As "a girl of the painted cohorts of the city" (p. 144), she has lost even the historical particularity of a name. The diachronic time in which the chapter unfolds yields to a kind of synchronic pressure, an overview that sees the present moment both *as an endless cycle and as a compressed duration.*

A second problem is what to make of the men who reject her. One may begin with their symmetry, for they come, in fairy-tale and folklore fashion, in sets of three, each set being located in its own region of the city. Their function is itself threefold. First, they reinforce the repetitiveness of Maggie's life in the way that a pairing, for example, would not have done: a pair could be taken as a doubling, such as occurs in the later parts of Crane's war novel, where the issue is the relation of the two young soldiers. The issue here is the characters' relation to Maggie, and this the tripling helps: The figure who follows a figure who follows a figure makes this a random series, conveying the brute fact of aleatory repetition. Second, the trios, by virtue of their positioning, indicate the worsening of the girl's situation. The first three appear in the glittering theater district, the second trio in "darker blocks" (p. 146), and the last, as noted in the previous section, in the gloom near the East River. Maggie's descent is intensified by the fact that one part of this district, the part associated with the horrid fat man, is even worse than the others, and more final.

The third function of the groupings is to contribute an aura of mystery or mysterious horror. Three is a noumenal number when, in religion, it represents a trinitarian structure; when it is figured as a triangle, like the circle, one of the "perfect" structures; or, more importantly for the present context, when it applies (as suggested above) to wondrous beings in a

Märchen or fairy tale. Here Crane writes "The Tale of the Three Men," times three.

This three-movement escalation in emotional intensity culminates in the portrait of a creature whom Crane does not immediately identify as a man:

> When almost to the river the girl saw a great figure. On going forward she perceived it to be a huge fat man in torn and greasy garments. His grey hair straggled down over his forehead. His small, bleared eyes, sparkling from amidst great rolls of red fat, swept eagerly over the girl's upturned face. He laughed, his brown, disordered teeth gleaming under a grey, grizzled moustache from which beer-drops dripped. His whole body gently quivered and shook like that of a dead jelly fish. Chuckling and leering, he followed the girl of the crimson legions. (pp. 148–9)

The presence of this demonic creature, and his pursuit of Maggie beside the river, could signify the last degree of her degradation, the recognition of which leads her to take her life; this is indeed a generally accepted reading. According to the Reverend Thomas de Witt Talmage, whose *Night Sides of City Life* appeared some fifteen years before Crane published *Maggie,* a fallen female soul must choose between the sewing girl's cold garret and the East River. A drawing in Charles Loring Brace's *The Dangerous Classes of New York,* preceding *Maggie* by twenty-one years, portrays a girl preparing to drown herself in the same river. By contrast, a Maggie created by the same author returns home to die, repentant over her life of sin, in the presence of forgiving parents. Crane's character is also, like Talmage's, a sewing girl, and she is also in a position to drown herself. The probability that she does so increases if one assumes that Crane is following the minister's lead. If in fact he borrowed Maggie's name from Loring he is following that lead, too, but not very far since his Maggie ends very differently.

Crane of course may be turning Brace's resolution inside out. Inasmuch as *Maggie* is a shocker, a brash book by a rather daring young man, Crane could just as easily be subverting the stereotypes of the suicide, leaving open the possibility that Maggie does not die at her own hands but at the hands of the fat man. There was literary precedent for this as well. In 1889 Edgar Fawcett's *The Evil That Men Do* depicted a lower-class girl, also the daughter of brawling drinkers, who becomes a streetwalker and is murdered in an alley by a lover.[23] Regarding Maggie as the victim of a similar act could help to satisfy those readers who have trouble reconciling Maggie's success with Maggie's suicide.[24] I have suggested above an additional way of explaining a related issue, the paradox of her prosperity as a prostitute with her repeated rejection. But finally there is no Archimedean point from which to leverage Crane's creation into one definite position or another. The conclusion has the look, as

Crane himself often does, of a mugwump. Whether this reflects his ambivalence toward the conventional fable about the fallen woman remains unclear. What is clear is that he is giving conventionality, which is to say society, a hard look. This is perhaps the final justification of the last two chapters, which incline toward the anticlimactic in Crane's usual way.

The final chapter is an exercise in moral torsion. Condemning Maggie while consoling Maggie's mother, the woman in black is a leitmotiv of self-serving conventionality. That the woman herself is a kind of moral contagion is suggested metonymically by the juxtaposition of the black in her appearance with the black in her speech:

> The woman in black came forward and again besought the mourner.
> "Yeh'll fergive her, Mary! Yeh'll fergive yer bad, bad chil'! Her life was a curse an' her days were black an' yeh'll fergive yer bad girl? She's gone where her sins will be judged." (pp. 161–2)

The wailing mother replies, " 'Oh yes, I'll fergive her! I'll fergive her!' " (p. 163). Both women, like the other characters, speak in one of the book's two languages, the language of dialect: "As in most slum novels, Crane uses dialect to an excess to characterize his slum dwellers and to indicate the paucity of their linguistic, intellectual, and emotional resources."[25] In a sense the characters belong to their language more than their language belongs to them. Each seems pulled, as by a hidden force, into an undertow of socially preconditioned, linguistically mediated behavior. It might not be unfair to call it predetermined. Crane's literary economics charts the movements of a powerful social energy. The depicted excesses – whether of swearing, fighting, or drinking – are moments of overflow within a system that prides itself on its propriety and decorum: The owner of the saloon in which Pete tends bar "insisted upon respectability of an advanced type" (p. 135), and it is to his own respectability that Pete returns after cursing and slamming the door on Maggie. Respectability is complemented in nature by sunlight: "The inevitable sunlight came streaming in at the windows and shed a ghastly cheerfulness upon the faded hues of the room" (p. 161). That first adjective gives the game away: This sunlight is inevitable in just the way that crocodiles are inevitable at critical moments in Tarzan films. Here is conventionality with a vengeance, which is to say that Crane is taking literary vengeance on the nineteenth-century funereal mode, with its chiaroscuro scenes of dark-toned grief sometimes relieved by redeeming rays of light.

Pete's respectability, like Maggie's taste in entertainment or her mother's mourning rite, belongs to the social field, more particularly, as noted above, to a strange honor system devoted to the preservation of its own equilibrium. Pete's respectability, aimed at maintaining his status in the status quo, is a set of conforming acts identical with the ones being carried out simultaneously by his peers. "The social field is full of acts with no author, of constructions without a constructor."[26] What Sartre means, and what Crane means, is that people create patterns that become self-perpetuating and practically autonomous. When a member of a group feels the gaze of the other, that member will be seen to follow whatever foreknown generic routes the situation requires. Thus in *Maggie,* on the saying of certain words, certain objects fly through the air and certain fists pound certain faces. Sartre of course insists that any situation offers some prospect of free choice, and Crane explains: "I tried to make plain that the root of Bowery life is a sort of cowardice. Perhaps I mean a lack of ambition or to willingly be knocked flat and accepting the licking."[27] This is a more negative way of making the same point as Sartre, namely, that the people in the Bowery are free after all to live differently. That Crane's novel communicates the same message is, however, questionable at best. Maggie does not do what she wants, she does what she can. If in fact she is murdered, she is even more the passive victim, and the senseless violence that launches the story comes, intensified to the extreme, full circle. If on the other hand she takes her own life, she passes upon herself, like a Kafka protagonist, the judgment that others have passed on her. Her fate becomes a parody of the golden rule: Do to yourself what others have done to you.

4

Doing Without: *George's Mother*

While it would be an exaggeration to say that Crane was in the habit of composing works in pairs, certain of his writings enjoy a conspicuously close relationship to one another. Among the New York pieces featured in this chapter, "An Experiment in Misery" and "An Experiment in Luxury" are unmistakably companion pieces. "The Veteran," a sequel to *The Red Badge of Courage,* shows the now aged Henry Fleming bravely attempting to rescue colts from his burning barn, as if to remove any doubts a reader might have about its hero. In "Regulars Get No Glory," a war dispatch, Crane develops a framework for "The Price of the Harness," one of the better stories in *Wounds in the Rain,* while "The Reluctant Voyagers," depicting the trials of two men stranded at sea, is apprentice work for "The Open Boat." Between "The Open Boat" and "The Blue Hotel" the relation is almost dialogic. To the Nebraska story of brutal violence and brooding tragedy the saga of the sea responds with an account of quiet courage and spontaneous fraternity. *A Woman without Weapons,* retitled *George's Mother,* complements *Maggie* in a related but different way as Crane tempers the jarring noise of his first slum novel with a more balanced orchestration. It has been proposed that he was looking for a manner more compatible with the realism of William Dean Howells or the veritism of a Hamlin Garland, his "literary fathers," as Crane called them.[1]

In *George's Mother,* Crane treats a bad family situation less harshly and with more attention to aspects of city life, in particular the presence of idlers, members of "the dangerous classes," who create a powerful sense of menace. To say that the city is defenceless against this menace from within is to state a proposition that applies in varying degrees to everything in the book: The city is, like George's mother, without weapons. Weapon is a trope for whatever it takes to succeed in the battle of life, and viewed in this way the principal characters are headed for defeat. After his decline George is without work, like the street people; without friends at the beginning of the novel, he is without a mother at the end. Considering how he drops in the affections of other club members when he requests a loan, and how he is later jeered by the second cohort, the street gang, just prior to his mother's death, in essence he is once more without friends even before he is without a mother. For reasons to be taken up in the second section, the most important of the extrafamilial formations, the club, is without the very solidarity it is supposed to ensure. In sum, the principal subject of this chapter is the circumstance and condition of doing without.

THE SON

> A brown young man went along the avenue. He held a tin lunch-pail under his arm in a manner that was evidently uncomfortable. He was puffing at a corn-cob pipe. His shoulders had a self-reliant poise, and the hang of his arms and the raised veins of his hands showed him to be a man who worked with his muscles.
>
> As he passed a street-corner a man in old clothes gave a shout of surprise, and rushing impetuously forward, grasped his hand. (I, 115)

It would be vain to look in *Maggie* for anything like self-reliant poise. Pete and Jimmie swagger, Mrs. Johnson staggers, and Maggie's self-reliance is mere body-relaince at best. Someone turning from *Maggie* to its sequel might be on guard, at this point, fearing that this self-reliance, with its Emersonian overtones, goeth before a fall. This suspicion would be all the more justified if the reader had perused "Coney Island's Failing Days," published in the *New York Press* the month before Crane finished *George's Mother:* "At the stand where one can throw at wooden cats and negro heads and be in danger of winning cigars, a self-reliant youth bought a whole armful of baseballs, and missed with each one" (VIII, 325). Self-reliance prevents neither the nameless youth nor the brown young man, George Kelcey, from being good at failing.

Jones, the man in old clothes, quickly establishes himself in George's present so as to define the latter's future. The bar mirror in which Jones soon sees himself reflects the state of "vast knowledge" (I, 116) the old acquaintance has attained and that Kelcey will wish to acquire by imitation. Such imitation of others becomes in fact his main mode of operation. Through Jones we learn that the Kelceys have been in the city for three years, that the four other Kelcey sons are dead, and that the father was killed in a fall. This gives a sense of historical depth that is absent from *Maggie,* which is an exercise in uncompromising immediacy. At the same time, and more importantly, the reduction of the family to mother and son puts pressure on the son to protect and cherish the mother.

George's conduct is measured by the conduct of the four who are gone. Her other boys, Mrs. Kelcey reminds her son, were not profane:

" 'I don't see where yeh ever caught this way a' swearin' out at everything,' she continued, presently. 'Fred, ner John, ner Willie never swore a bit. Ner Tom neither, except when he was real mad' " (I, 131). One difference between these four and those in the Sullivan County writings is the privileged, the almost sacred status of the Kelcey group: In the mother's memory the four are held, ineffably superior, apart and above. A second difference is that the protagonist, in contrast to the little man, does not belong to the group; nor does the text depict George's relation to his brothers when they were alive. Like castles and fortresses, the brothers belong to an anterior, heroic time that lives in the mother's present but not in the son's. Veneration for an unfallen past and its corollary – a sense of subsequent decline – are powerfully felt by Henry Fleming as well. Like a young Brooks Adams, the young soldier regrets that the great passions of the past are held in check by "firm finance" (II, 5). In his letters Crane reveals that he could not forget the glories of his own familial past: "Of course, I have never been in a battle, but I believe that I got my sense of the rage of conflict on the football field, or else fighting is a hereditary instinct, and I wrote intuitively; for the Cranes were a family of fighters in the old days, and in the Revolution every member did his duty."[2]

The Sullivan County sketches on hunting traditions appear, against this background, as experimental efforts to avoid the contamination of a past that threatens to overshadow the present and make it little. Similar efforts, carried further, create in Kelcey a character whose sensitivity to the past is no less a vacuum than his sensitivity to the present: "He was a little late in getting to Bleecker's lodging. He was delayed while his mother read aloud a letter from an old uncle, who wrote in one place: 'God bless the boy! Bring him up to be the man his father was.' Bleecker lived in an old three-storied house on a side-street" (I, 141). No reaction, no transition; that George might carry on in his father's mould simply does not occur to him. In his blankness George anticipates Camus's Meursault: "Mother died today. Or maybe yesterday – I don't know which. I received a telegram from the home: 'Mother deceased. Burial tomorrow. Sincere regrets.' That means nothing. It could have been yesterday."[3] Kelcey is not, of course, an absurd man exposed to his own lucidity, but he is thoroughly alienated in his own right: His sullenness bespeaks a resentment that is slow to break out just because it lies so deep. A sign of this depth is the apparent absence of any reaction to his mother's tacit acceptance of his uncle's admonition. The juxtaposition of the father, the subject of the last verb in the letter, and Bleecker, the subject of the first verb in the sentence following, is part of the process by which Bleecker becomes a father surrogate whom George can reject with impunity after the drunken party: "When he stared over at old Bleecker, he felt a sudden contempt and dislike for him. He considered him to be a tottering old beast. It was disgusting to perceive aged men so weak in sin" (I, 151). The connection depends upon the reader's ability to extend the original metonymic link between father and father-surrogate for some ten pages. In the same way it is the reader who must connect Blue Billie, whom George is supposed to fight, with George's father, who was also named Bill, and it is the reader who must infer a distinct though obscure intention behind the fact that the son turns from the fight to rejoin his mother. Here is a case where the importance of a relation is clearer than its significance, for the opposition between father and son is never accommodated in the same terms as that between mother and son. It is a kind of deviated opposition that keeps promising to amount to more than it ever does.

This failure is related to the nature of the work's central character:

> An indefinite woman was in all of Kelcey's dreams. As a matter of fact it was not he whom he pictured as wedding her. It was a vision of himself greater, finer, more terrible. It was himself as he expected to be. In scenes which he took mainly from pictures, this vision conducted a courtship, strutting, posing, and lying through a drama which was magnificent from flow of purple. (I, 137)

Here, as in his thinking about the gang, George's idealizations prepare the basis for defeats he will suffer in his dealings with others. He meanwhile relates to his mother by outbursts, gestures, evasions. Despite the fact that the relation between mother and son dominates the narrative, as will also be true of "His New Mittens," Crane makes no attempt to render George's consciousness of his mother as he does the consciousness of Horace in that later story. The result is, as some readers have noted, a sense of absence or lack of centering in the book, possibly because Crane was unwilling or unable to engage certain issues that the mother–son conflict was producing. To this extent the author perhaps resembles the character, who tends to turn away from confrontations. When he comes face to face with Maggie Johnson, his dream girl, "he was always overcome by the thought that the whole thing was obvious to her. He could feel the shame of it burn his face and neck. To prove to her that she was mistaken he would turn away his head or regard her with a granite stare" (I, 138). And when Mrs. Kelcey tries to waken her son he first turns his face to the wall, then rolls over and buries his head.

George's Mother has been called Crane's most personal book, and John Berryman was the first to try to say specifically why.[4] Fortunately, one does not have to subscribe to Berryman's brand of Freudianism to subscribe to the view that George's mother bears some resemblance to Stephen's, both being religious and both devoted to the cause of temperance. Stephen was also, like George, no stranger to the grape, and it is entirely possible that he too, like George, had occasion to resent his mother's attitudes or behavior. What son hasn't done likewise at some time? A treatment of such complex matters lies, however, outside the scope of this study. Equally outside its scope is the issue of Crane's apparent desire to rescue women of "low" repute, an issue that surfaces in the notorious Dora Clark affair, when Crane came to the aid of a prostitute arrested on a false charge of soliciting. What does fall within the scope of this study is the theme of rescue.

George twice imagines himself rescuing Maggie, a reiteration that works in counterpoint to the first appearance of the theme in connection, ironically, with the mother: "Later, she imagined a woman, wicked and fair, who had fascinated him and was turning his life into a bitter thing. Her mind created many wondrous influences that were swooping like green dragons at him. They were changing him to a morose man, who suffered silently. She longed to discover them, that she might go bravely to the rescue of her heroic son" (I, 133). When the scene shifts to the son, Crane devotes a long and sardonic passage to the means by which George portrays himself, *to* himself, as indeed an heroic son. He also envisages a woman and a rescue, though now the woman is the goal and not the threat. "He reflected that if he could only get a chance to rescue her from something, the whole tragedy would speedily unwind" (I, 139).

The actual tragedy, from George's perspective, is that he is without true self-reliance, and when someone happens by who is not, he is without Maggie. Looking at Pete, Kelcey knows all is lost: "the grandeur of the clothes, the fine worldly air, the experience, the self-reliance, the courage that shone in the countenance of this other young man made him suddenly sink to the depths of woe" (I, 139). Mrs. Kelcey's son cannot know what will happen to Mrs. Johnson's daughter any more than he can know the future of his own desires. An excerpt describing the vision of himself that fills his dreams reveals the problem:

> In scenes which he took mainly from pictures, this vision conducted a courtship, strutting, posing, and lying through a drama which was magnificent from glow of purple. In it he was icy, self-possessed, but she, the dream-girl, was consumed by wild, torrential passion. He went to the length of having her display it before the people. . . . It amazed them infinitely to see him remain cold before the glory of this peerless woman's love. She was to him as beseeching for affection as a pet animal, but still he controlled appearances and none knew of his deep abiding love. (I, 137)

The problem is that the vision is precisely of himself and that the woman is a prop on the stage of his self-centered imagination. George is without capacity for love; at best he is in love with the idea of being loved, and that is of course a different thing. A true lover makes sacrifices. A true lover is constant. George is neither. Even the thought of performing a sacrifice must come to him from without; thus it is by the infusion of drink that he comes to "expand with manly feeling. . . . He looked upon the beaming faces and knew that if at that instant there should come a time for a great sacrifice he would blissfully make it" (I, 129). No such sacrifice occurs; and the sole small sacrifice he makes for his mother (going with her once to prayer meeting) produces in him the type of hostility little Horace feels toward his mother in "His New Mittens": "He was resentful because she did not display more appreciation of his sacrifice" (I, 156).

George has not passed beyond the state of mere constancy that, in the view of Gabriel Marcel, provides but "the rational skeleton of fidelity." Compared with fidelity, constancy "exhibits a characteristic which is to some extent formal; it may even be said . . . that I am constant for myself, in my own regard, for my purpose, – whereas I am *present* for the other, and more precisely: for *thou.*" Constancy faces the threat of "a struggle, at first internal, then external, which can culminate in hatred and mutual aversion."[5] The son in *George's Mother* exists between these two states. Faithful in a formal way, as dictated by habit and a residual sense of duty, he exhibits constancy toward his mother; but more and more he struggles with her, at first repressing his resentment, then expressing it in proportion to the attraction he feels toward the group that appears to offer a home away from home: In the church scene we learn that "He could have assassinated her" (I, 157). What precisely is the nature of this group's remarkable attraction?

THE GROUP

When Kelcey finds in a group of friends a home away from home, he follows an American tradition. In nineteenth-century American fiction the home away from home is frequently found on water. One thinks of the solidarity Ishmael finds with Queequeg, especially in "A Squeeze of the Hand," or of the bonding of Augustus and Dirk Peters with the title character of Poe's *The Narrative of Arthur Gordon Pym;* above all, perhaps, one thinks of the raft-borne intimacy of Huck and Jim in Twain's masterpiece. Nor would it be difficult to find equivalents in land-based fiction: The list might begin with the Chingachgook and Natty Bumppo of James Fenimore Cooper. Whether directed toward water or wilderness, the desire for fraternity reflects a hope that "out there," away from responsibility and routine, circumstances will make possible, through a stronger fellow feeling, a more spontaneous and more elemental order. From a negative point of view, on the other hand, flight to fraternity can be an escape from natality, or rather an attempted escape. Partly in response to Heidegger's emphasis on mortality, Hannah

Arendt adopted the term natality to denote all the conditions of human existence that come with birth. Through natality human beings enter the realm of three great activities, labor, work, and action.

> All three activities and their corresponding conditions are intimately connected with the most general condition of human existence: birth and death, natality and mortality. Labor assures not only individual survival, but the life of the species. Work and its product, the human artifact, bestow a measure of permanence and durability upon the futility of mortal life and the fleeting character of human time. Action, in so far as it engages in founding and preserving political bodies, creates the condition for remembrance, that is, for history. . . . However, of the three, action has the closest connection with the human condition of natality; the new beginning inherent in birth can make itself felt in the world only because the newcomer possesses the capacity of beginning something anew, that is, of acting.[6]

For reasons of space, and because Twain tends to be more explicit on the issues than other writers, I will confine myself, by way of briefly illustrating the tradition in question, to his conceptions. In creating Tom and Huck and Jim, Twain imagines the possibility of escaping from conditions one never chose by choosing another one, the condition of idleness, which leaves one free merely to "live," and to do so in nature, that complex of elements and ideas that means so much more than the out-of-doors. Here each fraternal fugitive is reborn (in Huck's case several times) and each new birth is better than the old one because less blameable: That the brothers were thrown into the world without being consulted is the parents' fault – though more the mother's than the father's since she did the dirty work. If flight to fraternity is in general a flight from natality, and especially from the routine of work and the responsibility of action, it is in particular a flight from the mother.

In *George's Mother,* where Crane explores, more than in any other work, the problems of family, fraternity, and idleness, a special importance attaches to social orders, based on fraternity, that offer an alternative to the nuclear family. The first such order in Crane's canon is the group of four men in the Sullivan County tales, and the second is the street gang, which appears in *Maggie* and reappears in *George's Mother.* The third order is the club, which is founded by a group of acquaintances surrounding the figure of old Bleecker. Here is the status group of which Weber speaks, a collection of persons "stratified according to the principles of their consumption of goods as represented by special styles of life." One acquires status in the Bleecker crowd by drinking, the highest position being reserved for the host who, by furnishing everything that is consumed, is himself, ultimately, the leading consumer and, to borrow Veblen's term, the most conspicuous.[7]

The Gilded Age

> was the great age of the fraternal orders which sprang up across America in the townsman's search for some safe retreat from his daily life of competition, insecurity, and hostility. The lodges did not try to conquer that environment; rather they allowed men to escape from it into a world of pure affection, a momentary place of romance. Aside from a commitment to patriotism and a hostility to variously defined outsiders, the orders had no distinct values. . . . The private world of affection made bearable much of the townsman's life which would otherwise have been intolerable and allowed him to cling, in his public life, to the individualistic creed and the established mores.[8]

The Bleecker club's violent rejection of a drunk who stumbles in attests to its hostility toward outsiders, grounded as it is in its sense of special status. But this sense covers up the weakness that necessitates violence in the first place. The group is a collectivized little man, threatened by anything that encroaches upon its terrain. The members of the group are even prone to violence among themselves. "Old Bleecker, late that night, was violently elected president" (I, 161; *cf.* I, 128, 129).

A useful perspective on group formations is furnished by Sartre, who traces the process of consolidation by which random arrangements of persons become more organized and more complex. A queue of passengers waiting for a bus is a mere seriality, an assemblage of individuals linked only by a shared ephemeral purpose, which does not unify them, since they are basically in competition, but simply arranges them in a temporary order at once spatial and temporal (this one stands *behind* that one and boards *later*). A group-in-fusion, by contrast, is sufficiently cohesive to pursue its aims in concert but not yet sufficiently differentiated to assign particular roles on a regular basis. Although Crane does not offer a very close look at them, the dangerous loiterers who are seen in the streets are close to constituting such a formation. All they need is what the crowd that rushed to the Bastille needed in 1789: a suitable occasion. There will be more to say about these figures.

A collectivity surviving this stage may pass into the stage of the statutory group, such as Corcoran's gang or Bleecker's club, whose members commit themselves by a pledge. The power of the pledge consists in the fact that, in binding each member to every other, it defends the group against intrusion from any external other. Through the pledge the members of the group, without explicitly admitting the possibility of infidelity or disintegration, tacitly acknowledge the intimate relation between fraternity and fear:

> The origin of the pledge, in effect, is fear (both of the third party and of myself). The common object exists; indeed it is common interest in so

> far as it negates a community of destiny. But a reduction of enemy pressure while the threat persists, entails the unveiling of a new danger for everyone: that of the gradual disappearance of the common interest and the reappearance of individual antagonisms or of serial impotence.[9]

Crane elaborates no explicit theory of collectivities, and it would be idle to seek overly close correspondences between the portraits drawn by Crane and Sartre. But the pertinence of the latter's account is very evident. The excesses of the Bleecker order, with its loud gladhanding, its competitiveness, its frenzied excitement, its violent rejection of the drunk testify precisely to its fear of an urban environment in which strife reigns and security is only temporary, and to the correlative fear that the group may not have enough solidarity to prevent its own disintegration.

George's desire to display fraternal fidelity by beating the intruder cannot be distinguished from the desire of the collectivity itself, but is not for that reason any less self-serving. Egoism does not consist, according to Max Scheler, in behaving

> "as if one were alone in the world"; on the contrary, it is taken for granted that the individual is a member of society. The egoist is a man so taken up with his "social self" that he loses sight of his individual private self. It is not that he loves this social self; he is merely "taken up" with it, i.e., *lives* in it. Nor is his concern for his own values, as such (for it is only by chance that he finds them in himself); it is for *all* values, in things or in other people, but only *insofar* as they are, or might come to be *his,* or having something to do with *him.*[10] [Italics in original.]

An ironic juxtaposition reveals the inconstancy of the sympathies felt by the Bleecker group when, following his failure of courage with Maggie, and his defeat by his rival Pete, George encounters Jones and grasps his hand: "He felt now that there was some solacing friendship in space" (I, 141). But when Kelcey approaches Bleecker for a loan after losing his job, the old man rejects him. The fragile social basis of the club, its dependence on blind submission to a figure who has temporary authority because he has money, is suddenly exposed. The member of the group who wished to show his fidelity by fighting an outsider has himself become an outsider.

While establishing himself in the Bleecker fraternity, George had also become associated with the street gang, whose leader, Fidsey Corcoran, plays a mediating role analogous to Jones's role in the Bleecker group. In keeping with the fact that it lives in the streets, the gang is more aggressively idle and potentially more violent.

> They were like veterans with their wars. One lad in particular used to recount how he whipped his employer, the proprietor of a large grain and feed establishment. He described his victim's features and form and

> clothes with minute exactness. He bragged of his wealth and social position. It had been a proud moment of the lad's life. He was like a savage who had killed a great chief. (I, 163)

George is going down in the extrafamilial world insofar as that world is defined in relation to other males. But within the family he is already an outsider over against his four brothers, who have become a sacred group for which the Bleecker order is a weak surrogate: "Now that five of them had congregated it gave them happiness to speak their inmost thoughts without fear of being misunderstood" (I, 129). The five to be thought of as surrogates for the five Kelcey brothers are the two men (Jones and Bleecker) who are already in the bar when George arrives, and the two (O'Connor and a nameless companion) who come later, plus George. The subsequent rejection by Bleecker of George's request for a loan dissolves the solidarity: "In them all he saw that something had been reversed. They remained silent upon many occasions, when they might have grunted in sympathy for him" (I, 172). Crane underlines George's downward mobility by placing two critical moments – the fall from grace in the club and then in the gang – side by side in the next-to-last chapter.

CHANCE, CHARACTER, AND CIRCUMSTANCE

The three elements of concern in this section form an important nexus in Crane's canon. Although each is indispensable, one, as Orwell says, is more equal than the others. This is chance. A rising interest in this phenomenon is a notable feature in the intellectual and artistic history of the nineteenth century. Although that history is too complex to justify more than a glance here, a glance may be of interest.

Nineteenth-century science discovered, *inter alia,* that many things in the world were far less predictable than previously supposed, that many events occur or appear to occur quite at random, and that certainties can sometimes be arrived at only through probabilities, which are always calculations of the way chance-based events or entities may be expected to turn out. In literature Dickens defended his use of coincidence by suggesting that in his life coincidences happened all the time; earlier in the century the genius of Heinrich von Kleist so fastened on the role of chance that coincidences and improbabilities wilder than any imagined by Dickens fill the pages of virtually everything he wrote; Peirce was so convinced of the crucial nature of aleatory happenings that he found only three elements in the world, chance, law, and habit-taking; while in *Chance,* Crane's friend Conrad finally has Marlow hold forth on the dominance of chance throughout the preceding narrative.

The role of chance in *George's Mother* invites particular attention. One reason is that whereas character and circumstance are factors in fiction generally, chance, though often a factor, plays a larger role in Crane than in most writers. A second reason is that the nexus of chance, character, and circumstance in *George's Mother* looms larger than in Crane's earlier works. There is circumstance enough in the early tales but relatively little development of character, and though chance is a factor it is hardly the force it becomes in Crane's second novel of the city. Crane's first novel is so tightly structured and its creatures are so trapped in their own typicality that little or no room is left for the aleatory. This is far from the case in "The Open Boat," where the entire adventure is precipitated by the accidental sinking of a ship, or "The Monster," which revolves around the consequences of an accident in a laboratory, or "The Blue Hotel," in which the Swede just happens to stop in a place where he is indeed, as he fears, likely to get killed, or in "The Veteran," where the Swede accidentally starts the fire in the bar, or in *The Red Badge of Courage,* where the fact that Jim Conklin is killed and Henry Fleming is not is only one of countless illustrations of the omnipresence of chance.

Much of what happens to George Kelcey follows from a chance encounter. George's meeting with Jones, for example, is entirely fortuitous. The two have not seen each other for some time (one year by George's account, seventeen according to the boozy and forgetful Jones), neither is looking for the other and neither knows the other lives in this, the country's largest city; that they have not run into each other earlier is also a matter of chance, and it is another matter of chance that Jones is in a position to introduce George to Bleecker.

To explain away the signs of his deterioration George appropriates a chance incident: "At one time Kelcey had a friend who was struck in the head by the pole of a truck and knocked senseless. . . . Kelcey had always remembered it as a bit of curious history. When his mother cross-examined him in regard to the accident, he told this story with barely a variation. Its truthfulness was incontestable" (I, 154).

In a later scene chance, character, and circumstance converge:

> As he passed along the street near his home he perceived Fidsey Corcoran and another of the gang. They made eloquent signs. "Are yeh wid us?"
>
> He stopped and looked at them. "What's wrong with yeh?"
>
> "Are yeh wid us er not," demanded Fidsey. (I, 172)

The exchange distinguishes between two orders of speech, the *wid* of Corcoran and his companion representing Bowery dialect at its "purest," the *with* of Kelcey representing a mode of expression still colloquial, and even dialectal, but closer to standard English. If George's mother and his friend Jones also prefer George's preposition it is because these three are not Bowery natives like Corcoran but have migrated to the city from the country. The juxtaposition of speech types confirms George's marginal status just as he is being pressed to declare for or against the gang. Chance, circumstance, and character here converge. It is a matter of chance that Kelcey meets the gang under circumstances of crisis, while a characterological tendency (avoidance of confrontation) combines with a familial circumstance (his mother's illness) to shape his response. The nature of that response and its relation to a further intervention of chance will be taken up shortly.

With belongs, as noted in Chapter 1, to a family of words known as syncategorematic, "words markedly relational in that they can be employed solely in connection with other terms. According to William of Sherwood, logic consists not only of categorematic terms, deployed as subjects or predicates, but also of terms that are 'functional' in the sense that they operate only in service to those other, categorematic terms."[11] Although little attention has been paid to these terms outside of logic, Heidegger has explored their operations in poetic thinking and in poetry as such. Noticing such terms is important in the present context because of what Crane does with one of them, namely, *with*; in the following chapter we will examine his use of another, *at*.

As a device for characterizing the cityscape, *with* appears in no less than six of the first seven sentences:

> In the swirling rain that came at dusk the broad avenue glistened with that deep bluish tint which is so widely condemned when it is put into pictures. There were long rows of shops, whose fronts shone with full, golden light. . . .
>
> The lights made shadows, in which buildings loomed with a new and tremendous massiveness, like castles and fortresses. There were endless processions of people, mighty hosts, with umbrellas waving, bannerlike, over them. Horse-cars, aglitter with new paint, rumbled in steady array between the pillars that supported the elevated railroads. The whole street resounded with the tinkle of bells, the roar of iron-shod wheels on the cobbles, the ceaseless trample of the hundreds of feet. (I, 115)

With occurs in two syntactical units – clauses and phrases – and plays roles ranging from what might be called the primary to the complementary. In the first two sentences the preposition is primary, providing a link in the initial sentence between the rain and the key effect, which is the tint condemned in pictures, while in the second it links the shop fronts with the full, golden light. In sentence three its role is intermediate, serving as it does to facilitate a transition from the shadows to the castles and fortresses, and informing the reader of the size of the constructions. A complementary role is played in the next two sentences, in the first of which the prepositional phrase adds a feature to the primary nouns, processions and hosts, and in the second of which it adds a feature to the horsecars. *With* resumes a primary role in the final sentence by leading into the catalogue of sound effects.

The function of this syncategorematic, then, is to endow various represented entities with essential attributes. To put it another way, *with* provides the wherewithal without which the scene would not come to life. But in light of the issues raised at the beginning of this section, it is clear that the attributes are not the type that help in battle: They are not weapons but effects – providing here a touch of beauty, there a suggestion of the sublime – that in no wise alter the circumstance that the city, against those with weapons, is without defenses.

The convergence of chance, character, and circumstance is facilitated by Crane's term, which works in artful counterpoint to the general state of being-without that is so central to the story, while indicating (as noted above) what it actually means for the city to be endowed with certain attributes. The counterpoint also extends to two differentiations of usage. We have looked at the first, which turns on the contrast between "pure" and standard instances of the preposition. The second differentiation is between two disparate meanings. Kelcey's *with,* in "What's wrong with yeh?", means "what is the meaning of your attitude?" or "What is your problem?" But the gang members' locution bears upon a more substantive aspect of "being-with," which is the need for George to make, under the circumstance of a crisis, a decision that could be irrevocable. No longer with the Bleecker group, a least on the old terms, he could find himself without friends in the street gang as well if he does not choose as it wishes him to choose.

The final test comes in a coincidence of timing almost worthy of Kleist. The test turns on the question, already quoted, that is put to him by Corcoran: "Are yeh wid us?" The gang expects from Kelcey the same generic behavior it would expect in like circumstances from anyone wishing to belong to its brotherhood: It expects him to fight, no matter who the opponent may be, on cue. It is a matter of chance that George's prospective opponent is Blue Billie and a matter of more dramatic chance that the fight never takes place: For at the very height of tension an anonymous boy runs on stage to summon Kelcey to his mother's side, and again the behavior he exhibits is shaped by circumstance and character as well as chance. It is shaped by circumstance because the group is disposed this day to manipulate and because as a result of previous circumstances Kelcey is in a position to *be* manipulated, a position that only changes with the changed circumstance of his mother's situation. George's behavior is shaped by character, first, because it is his nature to avoid confrontation, and second, because there remains in him a dozing loyalty to his one surviving parent.

THE MOTHER

If the behavior of the street gang provides one measure of George's being, the behavior of his mother provides another. By identifying her as "a woman without weapons," the original title of the book suggested that courage was her sole endowment. The second chapter makes this clear:

> There was the flurry of a battle in this room. Through the clouded dust or steam one could see the thin figure dealing mighty blows. Always her way seemed beset. Her broom was continually poised, lancewise, at dust demons. There came clashings and clangings as she strove with her tireless foes.
>
> It was a picture of indomitable courage. And as she went on her way her voice was often raised in a long cry, a strange war-chant, a shout of battle and defiance. (I, 120)

Although the passage seems headed in the direction of Frank Norris, this woman differs from the latter's heroic women who strive to match the male hero on his own grounds, who have masculine names and who look, in short, like men in disguise. George's mother struggles, rather, with the traditional domestic enemies of the homemaker; she struggles at the same time with a vague social menace that dimly expresses to her the desperateness of her situation, a menace to be taken up below, in connection with the city. Finally, she struggles with the one person who should be her ally: "Each morning his mother went to his room, and fought a battle to arouse him. She was like a soldier" (I, 166–7).

The old woman finally gets her son to prayer meeting, but only once. Although she cannot understand his reluctance, that reluctance, and her sense of being embattled in the same way as her church, are signs of the times. In 1899 Thorstein Veblen reports "the latter-day complaint of the clergy – that the churches are losing the sympathy of the artisan classes, and are losing their hold upon them. At the same time it is currently believed that the middle class, commonly so called, is also falling away in the cordiality of support of the church, especially as regards the adult male portion of that class."[12] When George refuses to accompany his mother for a second time to a prayer meeting, "she resembled a limited funeral procession" and George "writhed under it to an extent" (I, 125). While "to an extent" suggests the limitations of George's emotional range, the clause about the mother associates her with mortality. Even as it anticipates her demise it recalls that she is without a husband and has lost all but one of her children. Such a woman, like the church at which she worships, bears much; and if her attitude is not contempt for death, there is something in her that is equally illimitable, something of whose presence George has scarcely an inkling.

The old woman's situation leads her to entreaty, pleading, supplication. Her son is her little god; her dreams, in which he appers as a king and benefactor of the poor, "shed a radiance of gold upon her long days, her sorry labor. Upon the dead altars of her life she had builded the little fires of hope for another" (I, 135). The mother in short exemplifies the fidelity of which the son knows nothing.

Before turning to the city, the topic of the final section, a word remains to be said about the manner in which the characters in this work relate to characters in other works. *George's Mother* and *Maggie* both deal with pressures that a family undergoes and the grave consequences that follow certain types of changed relations. *Maggie* concerns a family unfaithful to a child, *George's Mother* a child unfaithful to a family. In the one case hostility results in expulsion, in the other the absence of fidelity results in loss. Each line of action involves elements that are either given, as if *sui generis,* or developed – "natural" premises, if you will, that become modified by "history." In *Maggie* the mother's bondage to drink and her preoccupation with self are given, while the sexual activity that leads to Maggie's expulsion is developed. It is true that the coming of puberty is the basis for this, but most girls do not become prostitutes; the book is about the difference instigated by the particular behavior of an individual outside the family toward an individual within it. The consequence is that *the parent who stays the same lives while the child who changes dies.*

George's Mother holds a mirror to this structure. Here the given is the mother's fidelity to something other than self – principally to her family, as embodied in her child, and collaterally to the church. The activity developed in the narrative is George's drinking, a promiscuity in its own right that is mediated, as in Maggie's case, by an outsider (Jones), and that results, again as in Maggie's case, in a cleavage in the family. Then comes the inversion; for now the consequence is that *the parent who stays the same dies while the child who changes lives.*

This remarkable structural symmetry is further evidence for the need to consider certain of Crane's works as being, if not precisely paired, notably close in their relationships.

THE CITY

As she is dying, George's mother sees some terrible menace approaching: " 'Ah, there they come! There they come! Ah, look – look – loo–'. She arose to a sitting posture without the use of her arms' " (I, 177). The old woman here experiences in a personal vein the apocalyptic vision that hovers in the atmosphere of the book, especially in connection with the city. This is not to deny that the city has a certain beauty, as in "that deep bluish tint which is so widely condemned when it is put into pictures," and the "full, golden light" of the shop fronts (I, 115). But something vaguely threatening waits in the wings, the first suggestion being the sentence that concludes the paragraphs the first two sentences of which have just been quoted: "Here and there, from druggists' windows, or from the red street-lamps that indicated the positions of fire-alarm boxes, a flare of uncertain, wavering crimson was thrown upon the pavements" (I, 115). From the druggist one seeks relief from suffering; one pulls the fire alarm to ward off damage or destruction; crimson, traditionally associated with sin and blood, has an even more negative cast thanks to associations fostered by *Maggie*; and the reader is made yet more wary by the fact that this brooding hue is said to be uncertain and wavering.

One of Crane's epithets for Bleecker's party is "this strange land" (I, 147):

> A valor, barbaric and wild, began to show in their poses and in their faces, red and glistening from perspiration. The conversation resounded in a hoarse roar. The beer would not run rapidly enough for Jones, so he remained behind to tilt the keg. This caused the black shadow on the wall to retreat and advance, sinking mystically to loom forward again with sudden menace, a huge dark figure controlled, as by some unknown emotion. (I, 144)

The ironically named valor of these figures is a little thing compared to that of the loiterers in the street:

> The vast machinery of the popular law indicated to them that there were people in the world who wished to remain quiet. They awaited the moment when they could prove to them that a riotous upheaval, a cloudburst of destruction would be a delicious thing. They thought of their fingers buried in the lives of these people. They longed dimly for a time when they could run through decorous streets with crash and roar of war, an army of revenge for pleasures long possessed by others, a wild sweeping compensation for their years without crystal and gilt, women and wine. This thought slumbered in them, as the image of Rome might have lain small in the hearts of the barbarians. (I, 163)

The hero of James's *The Princess Casamassima,* bearing witness to the barbarians in England's counterpart to New York, focuses on the problem of getting rid of them. In language surprisingly harsh for Crane's countryman and friend, Hyacinth Robinson envisions the apocalyptic prospects for London: " 'What remedy but another deluge, what alchemy but annihilation?' he asked himself as he went his way; and he wondered what fate there could be in the great scheme of things for a planet overgrown with such vermin, what redemption but to be hurled against a ball of consuming fire."[13]

In *The Dangerous Classes of New York and Twenty Years' Work among Them,* Charles L. Brace offers a nonfictional complement to the notion of a potentially threatening collective presence in the city. Brace finds the varieties of life among these classes quite as picturesque as those to be found in James's London and, partly because of the mixing of nationalities, even more dangerous. For the dangerous classes mainly consist, he points out, of children born to Irish and German immigrants, giving some point to Crane's selection of names like Kelcey, Corcoran, and O'Connor, on the one hand, and Bleecker, Schmidt, and Zeusentell on the other. Thomas E. Watson is more virulent: "The scum of the earth has been dumped upon us. Some of our cities are more foreign than American. The dangerous and corrupting hordes of the Old World have invaded us. The vice and crime which they have planted in our midst are sickening and terrifying." Even a Hamlin Garland was so frightened by the menace of the city that, on approaching Chicago for the first time, he feared that he would be assaulted before he could get from the railway station to his hotel.[14] Such anxiety was not without foundation. Crane was born within a few months of the Orange riot of 1871 in which the New York militia, under orders to defend parading Protestants, may have killed as many as twenty persons; he was halfway to his fifteenth birthday at the time of the Haymarket Riot in 1886; and he was a New York reporter during the Homestead strike of 1892 and the Pullman strike of 1894. Partly from these events and partly from his own experiences as a reporter, especially in the Bowery, Crane formed his view of the "lower orders," finding them interesting and colorful but morally deficient because of their supposed unwillingness to escape their condition by courageous exertion – a notion closely related to a contemporary Christian argument, with roots going back for centuries, that poverty originates in vice rather than vice in poverty.

Crane does not see Christian soldiers marching onward; much of the agitation he describes represents the sheer movement of daily urban life. Such is not the case, however, with the army of revenge. In this army the type of resentment Maggie feels toward her sweatshop employer is intensified and collectivized; the vision of the barbarians also displays on a larger scale the figurative violence George's mother is said to have experienced: "It was as if she had survived a massacre in which all that she loved had been torn from her by the brutality of savages" (I, 167). Unable to identify a specific enemy, she peoples her surroundings with anonymous foes, an act of imagination complemented by the posture of the little chapel, to which she enjoys a synecdochic relationship. Small as it is, the chapel is a prominent feature in the urban landscape:

> In a dark street the little chapel sat humbly between towering apartment-houses. A red street-lamp stood in front. It threw a marvellous reflection upon the wet pavements. It was like the death-stain of a spirit. Farther up the brilliant lights of an avenue made a span of gold across the black street. A roar of wheels and a clangor of bells came from this point,

> interwoven into a sound emblematic of the life of the city. It seemed somehow to affront this solemn and austere little edifice. It suggested an approaching barbaric invasion. The little church, pierced, would die with a fine, illimitable scorn for its slayers. (I, 156)

The mother's later "Ah, there they come!" echoes the poem in *Black Riders* about the advent of marching mountains, and a similar motion is subtly evoked at the very outset of the novel: "There were endless processions of people, mighty hosts . . ." (I, 115). The motif of marching indicates the great city's relentless pace and purposiveness, though what its ultimate purposes may be remains undefined: "He had a vast curiosity concerning this city in whose complexities he was buried. It was an impenetrable mystery, this city. It was a blend of many enticing colors. He longed to comprehend it completely, that he might walk understandingly in its greatest marvels, its mightiest march of life, its sin" (I, 135–6). The scenic disclosure in the final chapter perpetuates the motif: "The window disclosed a fair, soft sky, like blue enamel, and a fringe of chimneys and roofs, resplendent here and there. An endless roar, the eternal trample of the marching city, came mingled with vague cries" (I, 178). Trample suggests that the marching continues to possess a destructive character and will do so forever. Whether in the city or on the battlefield or in a single soul, conflict is deemed to be endless, a fact that gives Crane's vision a somewhat fatalistic cast and explains why every fiction he writes is to some degree a story of war.

If the present text is a war novel as well as a novel of the city, there should be not one but two armies, and not surprisingly there are. The first, the army of revenge, has already been discussed. The second is the army housed in the church.

> The chandelier in the centre was the only one lighted, and far at the end of the room one could discern the pulpit swathed in gloom, solemn and mystic as a bier. It was surrounded by vague shapes of darkness on which at times was the glint of brass, or of glass that shone like steel, until one could feel there the presence of the army of the unknown, possessors of the great eternal truths, and silent listeners at this ceremony. (I, 157)

If the church were a character, it would vie to be the most appealing one in the novel on two grounds: It is heroic, as the mother is, and it is also sublime, as she is not. This state of affairs is connected with the decentered nature of the novel, as noted above, and with the problem of knowing and doing that figures in so many of the author's works. The novel is decentered because, while readers may identify with the mother, the son is the main character and it is very hard to identify with him. The problem of knowledge and action is more complex. In the first place Kelcey, without being innocent, doesn't know very much, and when in the church he gets an inkling of something that could be important to know, he shows no desire to learn what it is: "Kelcey fell to brooding concerning this indefinable presence which he felt in a church" (I, 157). But the brooding goes nowhere. As church members rise to give testimonials, he gets a second chance: "Kelcey listened closely for a time. These people filled him with a great curiosity. He was not familiar with their types" (I, 158). "For a time" echoes "to an extent" (when George is shown writhing under pressure from his mother). The inattentive George never attains true knowledge of these types, and when the minister holds forth, "the speech had no effect on Kelcey, excepting to prove to him again that he was damned" (I, 158). The action implicitly at issue is George's redemption, but his inability to learn what matters destroys any prospects he might have had.

The two armies raise the issue of knowledge and action in a different but related way. The army of the streets, though pictured prior to its assault, is in a position to act because its soldiers know their target and are filled with energy. Such knowledge and such energy are the only weapons they need. For its part the army of the church, itself unknown, is possessed of the highest knowledge, the knowledge of eternal truths. But what it knows does not prepare it to act. Essentially passive, its role is simply to be present, to possess, and to listen, and there is no sign that on its part anything more active is either immanent or imminent. Without any weapon but defiant gallantry, the church is prepared to die when the barbarians invade. For the army of the church is not of this world in the same way as its church, which is a social institution with worldly as well as spiritual offices to perform: This army's truths are for all time, not this time.

If the little chapel and the city as a whole have no weapons, the club George joined has no solidarity, and George himself has neither mother nor friends. All must live by doing without, which is also the way they will die.

Crane's shorter writings on New York City started appearing the year before he published *Maggie* and continued until a few months after the appearance of *George's Mother* in the spring of 1896. Modest in the main, yet sometimes memorable, these writings complement the tenement novels, in general confirming the vision the latter communicate while modifying it in ways that reward attention.

From the viewpoint of genre these pieces, not all of which are included in the section the Virginia edition assigns to "New York City Sketches," fall roughly into two types, with some overlapping between them. Pieces such as "The Broken-Down Van," "The 'Tenderloin' as It Really Is," and "In the Broadway Cable Cars" are studies in local color. Other pieces, such as "An Experiment in Misery," "An Experiment in Luxury," "Mr. Binks's Day Off," and "A Desertion," are sketches that, while essentially reportorial, lay stronger claim to narrative interest. Crane's instinct for storytelling was such that he teased a yarn from his materials whenever he could, or such at least is this reader's surmise.

On his beat the young reporter makes the rounds of the kind of living hell we find in *Maggie,* but he balances the ledger more than in that novel, and more even than in *George's Mother,* by also recording the brighter side of city life. The earliest sketch, "The Broken-Down Van," shows how entertaining chance can be when one adopts a bantering manner and no great issues are involved. Describing an 1890s "rear-ender" involving gaudily colorful vehicles, the sketch brings into the metropolis the breathless comic momentum alluded to in Chapter 2, where Twain's raft scene served as the model, and the coincidental "just as" and "just then" effects, in the mode of Kleist, that we have seen in *George's Mother.* Too lengthy to warrant inclusion here, a representative portion of the lively initial description is furnished in the note below.[15] While few if any of the other sketches are as effervescent, it is fair to say that as a local colorist Crane is brisk and genial. Such is not the case, typically, in the more narrative pieces, some of which are extremely grim.

An exception proving the rule is "Mr. Binks's Day Off," a pastoral that mixes humor with sentiment. Restless at the advent of spring, Mr. Binks and his family make a Sunday excursion to the New Jersey countryside only to find boredom in its peace:

> The sense of a city is battle. The Binkses were vaguely irritated and astonished at the placidity of this little town. This life spoke to them of no absorbing nor even interesting thing. There was something unbearable about it. "I should go crazy if I had to live here," said Mrs. Binks. A warrior in the flood-tide of his blood, going from the hot business of war to a place of utter quiet, might have felt that there was an insipidity in peace. And thus felt the Binkses from New York. (VII, 309)

The tranquility grows on them, however, and it is not long before they fall under the spell of nature, which is communicated, as often in Crane, by means of the musicality discussed by Pythagoras and Plato, developed by Saint Ambrose, and reworked by Whitman.[16] In Crane's story, as in much of Whitman's poetry, the music of the natural scene creates an aura of the universal and the sublime:

> This song of the trees arose in low, sighing melody into the still air. It was filled with an infinite sorrow – a sorrow for birth, slavery, death. It was a wail telling the griefs, the pains of all ages. It was the symbol of agonies. It celebrated all suffering. Each man finds in this sound the expression of his own grief. It is the universal voice raised in lamentation. (VIII, 312–13)

The main drift of this pastoral, however, is again toward an effect that may be called the sentimental sublime, something the reader also encounters in "The Men in the Storm" and in those later writings where Crane revives the spirit of his 1894 Decoration Day piece "The Gratitude of a Nation." The sentimental sublime arises in connection with the sense of what it means to be American. When Mrs. Binks has trouble climbing a steep road and her husband comes to her aid, he is reminded of their courtship: "It was a repetition of old days. Both enjoyed it because of this fact, although they subtly gave each other to understand that they disdained this emotion as an altogether un-American thing, for she, as a woman, was proud, and he had great esteem for himself as a man" (VIII, 312).

The graphic rendering that makes "An Experiment in Misery" so effective also enlivens "The Men in the Storm" which to Alan Trachtenberg is "as objective as Alfred Stieglitz's street photographs taken with a hand-held camera in the same year."[17] The men in question are waiting during a snow storm to be admitted to a soup kitchen.

> The winds seemed to grow fiercer as time wore on. Some of the gusts of snow that came down on the close collection of heads cut like knives and needles, and the men huddled, and swore, not like dark assassins, but in a sort of an American fashion, grimly and desperately, it is true, but yet with a wondrous under-effect, indefinable and mystic, as if there was some kind of humor in this catastrophe, in this situation in a night of snow-laden winds. (VIII, 319)

Despite this attempt to be as upbeat as possible, the dominant note of the sketch is one of suffering, as is even more the case in that excursion into purgatory called "An Experiment in Misery": "and all through the room could be seen the tawny hues of naked flesh, limbs thrust into the darkness, projecting beyond the cots, up-reared knees, arms hanging, long and thin, over the cot edges . . . . With the curious lockers standing all about like tombstones there was a strange effect of a graveyard, where bodies were merely flung" (VIII, 288). As in "The Men in the Storm," Crane reveals his sympathy with the downtrodden men, though in a subtler way. By continually referring to the youth's companion as the assassin, one of the author's favorite words, he echoes the menace in the two novels, but ironically; to similar effect the poor child in "An Ominous Baby" is called "the small barbarian" and "the little vandal" (VIII, 50). The child does steal a plaything, but that is because, being poor, he is without such things. Neither the assassin nor the barbarian is truly ominous.

The nightmarish atmosphere of the flophouse is epitomized by wails:

> The sound, in its high piercing beginnings that dwindled to final melancholy moans, expressed a red and grim tragedy of the unfathomable

> possibilities of the man's dreams. But to the youth these were not merely the shrieks of a vision pierced man. They were an utterance of the meaning of the room and its occupants. It was to him the protest of the wretch who feels the touch of the imperturbable granite wheels and who then cries with an impersonal eloquence, with a strength not from him, giving voice to the wail of a whole section, a class, a people. (VIII, 289)

From this apparently sincere but highly rhetorical excursus Crane shifts to another perspective on the nation, disclosing a different version of the sublime: "And in the background a multitude of buildings, of pitiless hues and sternly high, were to him emblematic of a nation forcing its regal head into the clouds, throwing no downward glances; in the sublimity of its aspirations ignoring the wretches who may flounder at its feet" (VIII, 293). In *Active Service,* Crane, once more mocking a sublimity that is nothing more than unenlightened self-interest, will send the reader up in a skyscraper for just such a glance. He also offers a downward glance in "An Experiment in Luxury" as the youth, in the residence of a millionaire, wonders at the fate that deposits him so high "when certainly there were men, equally fine perhaps, who were being blackened and mashed in the churning life of the lower places. . . . The eternal mystery of social condition exasperated him at this time" (VII, 297).

The only way the theme of doing-without can enter the scene of wealth is the way it does here, through the mediation of the visiting youth; for like "A Night at the Millionaire's Club," "An Experiment in Luxury" is a study of doing-*with.* The woman of the house is a woman with weapons, "a grim old fighter," the lines of whose face "denoted all the power of machination of a general, veteran of a hundred battles. . . . Here was a savage, a barbarian, a spear woman of the Philistines, who fought battles to excel in what are thought to be the refined and worthy things in life; here was a type of Zulu chieftainess who scuffled and scrambled for place before the white altars of social excellence" (VIII, 299). Ever interested in suffering, Crane weighs the costs of the woman's advantages and finds them to be high: She looks as worn as any woman selling apples in the street. In an atmosphere that seems more suited to Henry James, Crane produces the type of insight James himself could appreciate: "Somewhere in her expression there was terrible pride, that kind of pride which, mistaking the form for the real thing, worships itself because of its devotion to the form" (VIII, 299).

From what Crane says about wealthy mothers it seems he would have understood Veblen's view of the key role women play on the domestic front by devoting themselves to conspicuous consumption and conspicuous leisure, as well as Veblen's belief that the status of women always exemplifies the level of culture within a community or within a class in a community.

> Too, the youth thought he could see that here was the true abode of conservatism – in the mothers, in those whose ears displayed their diamonds instead of their diamonds displaying their ears, in the ancient and honorable controllers who sat in remote corners and pulled wires and respected themselves with a magnitude of respect that Heaven seldom allows on earth. (VII, 300)

If Crane and Veblen both point to aspects of the woman's role in the leisure class, Veblen thinks of her mainly as a wife while Crane, always sensitive to family dynamics from the perspective of the child, thinks of her mainly as a mother. Though this is not a corrective to Veblen, it does open up for consideration the way in which the woman, through nurture, example, and instruction within the family, furnishes a domestic continuity in support of the functions of the father and the interests of their class.

"A Detail," published in the same year as *George's Mother,* portrays a woman at the other end of the social scale from the wealthy matron. More refined in speech than any character in the tenement novels, the little old lady, without funds, goes to the streets in hopes of finding someone who will direct her to employment. Her status as a woman without weapons is contrasted with that of two fashionable young ladies, one of whom promises to be of help if she can: "The tiny old lady dictated her address, bending over to watch the girl write on a visiting card with a little silver pencil. Then she said: 'I thank you very much.' She bowed to them, and went on down the avenue" (VIII, 112). The politeness of manners contrasts with the harsh expressions and actions in the city sketches featuring "lowlife," the life Crane would appear, all things being unlikely, to enjoy covering. The language is typical of the New York City writings, on the other hand, by virtue of adding to the mosaic of Americanisms that furnishes so much interest to the pieces.

Of particular interest for the purposes of this chapter are those deriving directly from big-city life. Meetings and other encounters occur more often in places like the *Tenderloin* (VIII, 388 *et passim*), the political precinct of New York City, which the *Dictionary of American English (DAE)* describes somewhat editorially as "affording police officers luscious opportunities for graft" (*DAE* 2.a., 1887). The tenderloin is notable for the *joint,* "An illegally kept place for opium-smoking, drinking, or gambling. Later often applied to such places that are legally open" (*DAE* 3, 1883). There one may enjoy the new cocktail (*DAE,* 1894) called the *Manhattan* (VIII, 443) as well as *Whisky Slings,* which Crane is familiar with in 1894, though the *Dictionary of Americanisms (DA)* does not turn it up until 1928.

Crane likes to note any part of city life involving locomotion, such as *horsecars* (VIII, 399), for the horse-drawn railroad cars (*DAE,* 1833) that are virtually synonymous, until electrification, with *street cars* (*DAE* 1, 1862), though the latter usually run on rails and the fomrer may or may not. The paradigmatic devices for locomotion, however, are the ones that whirl you around, such as the *roller coasters* (*DAE* 2. [4], 1904) and *observation wheels* (VIII, 324) of Coney Island, the latter being, apparently, an early version of the Ferris wheel, or the *razzle-dazzle* (*OED* b., 1891) of the Jersey seaside, which "is a sort of circular swing. One gets in at some expense and by climbing up a ladder. Then the machine goes around, with a sway and swirl, like the motion of a ship. Many people are supposed to enjoy this thing, for a reason which is not evident" (VIII, 512). By far the largest cluster in the large family of kinetic terms are those involving rapid circular motion of this or a similar type. The key terms, *whirl, swirl, twirl,* and *wheel,* appear, it seems, for several reasons. On the one hand, they express the fascination with movement that is a pervasive theme in nineteenth-century literature and thought, which not only addresses drastic changes in science, technology, religion, morals, and manners but develops a self-conscious "metadiscourse" about them. Movement by technological means tends to symbolize the pattern and pact of these changes. The evidence of this in the writings of Twain and others is so abundant that it would be easier to list authors of whom the same cannot be said. A second reason for kinetic words is simply that they reflect aspects of daily life, such as the wheeling of bicycles, which were enormously popular in Crane's day, or the whirling of the roulette wheel, or the circling of the Coney Island conveyances. Third, for those caught up in its motion, whirling entails loss of orientation, hence of perspective. But at the same time the reader is often permitted to view this motion from a removed locus, and this facilitates perspective. Hence the represented motion becomes, in effect and simultaneously, both perspectivist and antiperspectivist, the latter development connecting it with another of Crane's themes, the unknown, and the former with the problematic nature of knowledge in general.

The strongest transitive sense of *whirl* occurs in "The Strong Man did indeed whirl his . . . limbs in the silver water" (VII, 96), where the issue is swift or forcible rotation or revolution (*OED* 3, 1400). This may be compared to the intransive in "the bellowing throng went whirling around . . ." (II, 31), which implies more variety of direction and an element of commotion (*OED* 1., 1290), whereas more intention enters in "the animal whirled" (VIII, 257) in that the animal itself determines the movement (*OED* 2., *trans.*, 1384). More strictly circular in the motion (5, 1698) are *wheel of fortune* (V, 99) and *turnstile* (VIII, 8).

These examples will serve to exemplify the type of motion at issue when Crane employs words from the "whirl" family; space considerations do not permit a more thorough survey. But given Crane's prepossession with this type of movement, it may be in order to take note of a formative youthful experience:

> In the old days at military school I once rode a wheel – a high one – about three miles high, I think. . . .
>
> When I wished to dismount however I found I couldn't. So I rode around the armory. Shafer, who was champion of Pennsylvania in those old high-wheel days watched me and said I did some things on that wheel which were impossible to him. (*Letters*, p. 66)

Although the vehicle could be taken for a monocycle, in Crane's day *wheel* was already the old word for bicycle, the front wheel of which was originally several times larger than the rear. *High-wheel* is evidently a coinage intended to make this clear, the point being supported by the fact that his friend was a champion in the "old" days.

In more ambitious works Crane develops episodes with more dramatic potential into pieces that verge upon being full-fledged tales. Bad parents and suffering children figure in two of the better pieces, "A Dark-Brown Dog" and "A Desertion." In "A Dark-Brown Dog," the last of three sketches about a city boy, the relation of the dog to the child provides a fraternal solidarity not found within the urban family. Like the early relationship between Jimmie and Maggie, the pairing is broken up by the father, who throws the dog out the window. The father thus plays a role analogous to Maggie's mother, the little boy's playmate being, as surrogate sibling, a surrogate object of sacrifice.

In "A Desertion" the protagonist Nell must suddenly do without her father, whose dead body she discovers on returning to their flat. Crane focuses first on her incomprehension, for she does not realize for a time that the man is dead, then on her frightened cries. He does so, however, through the mediation of the neighbors:

> "What is it?"
>
> "What's th' matter?"
>
> "He's killin' her."
>
> "Slug 'im with anythin' yeh kin lay hold of, Jack."
>
> But over all this came the shrill shrewish tones of a woman. "Ah, th' damned ol' fool, he's drivin' 'er inteh th' street – that's what he's doin'. He's drivin' 'er inteh th' street." (VIII, 81)

The exchange underlines Crane's continuing interest in threats to the integrity of the urban nuclear family; the exchange between Mary Johnson and her neighbor at the end of *Maggie* of course does the same. The difference is that the present scene focuses more sharply on the relation of the hidden and the revealed. On the one hand, the remarks of the neighbors make clear the long-range meaning of the father's behavior toward the daughter: He has indeed been driving her toward prostitution. But on the other hand, these remarks demonstrate the extent to which the true meaning of Nell's cries are hidden from the neighbors. The statements are simultaneously fact and error, true interpretation and false; and it is this discrepancy, of which the reader is made aware, that constitutes the concluding irony.

In *George's Mother* Crane looks at Maggie's past from another angle, and in "A Desertion" he seems to be doing the same with Nell. The hypothesis appears to be supported by the fact that the story was written after the publication of Crane's first novel and by Crane's tendency, discussed above, to rework materials and themes. At the beginning of the story Nell has been doing without normal parental affection, and at the end she must, as we have seen, do without a parent altogether. Although it is not easy to discern which deprivation is worse, both are bad.

The sketch reflects a growing fear that the nuclear family is greatly at risk in the tenements of the 1890s. Other pieces say the same of fraternity, though less by showing it breaking down, as in *George's Mother,* than by recording the aftermath of its demise. One seemingly positive use of the concept of brotherhood is in fact an aspect of that aftermath:

> There is a similarity in coloring and composition in a group of men about a midnight camp-fire in a forest and a group of smokers about the layout tray with its tiny light. Everything, of course, is on a smaller scale with the smoking. The flame is only an inch and a half perhaps in height and the smokers huddle closely in order that every person may smoke undisturbed. But there is something in the strong mystery of shadow at the backs of the people that brings the two scenes into some kind of artistic brotherhood. (VIII, 369)

In the first place, fraternity enters here only by analogy. Second, the analogy aims at aesthetic compensation; it is a way of getting a semblance of actual human brotherhood into the picture since one cannot have the actuality. Third, the entire sketch, entitled "Opium's Varied Dreams," concerns the techniques by which the opium smokers, though physically near one another, drift into utter isolation. The picture finally is a travesty of fraternity.

That true fraternity has become a thing of the past, at least in this modern city, is attested to by the self-conscious quotation marks Crane employs when speaking of the "Tenderloin." Two of three late sketches dealing with that district by name carry such marks, suggesting that they may have been Crane's way of recognizing that what he was describing was already a piece of history, both for himself and for the city.

> If there ever has been in a New York cafe an impulse from the really Bohemian religion of fraternity it has probably been frozen to death. (VIII, 393)

> In those days long ago there might have been freedom and fraternity. (VIII, 389)

The first quotation is from "In the 'Tenderloin' " the second from "The 'Tenderloin' as It Really Is," the two articles having been published a week apart in 1896. Both testify to Crane's sense that a way of life has evaporated that can never precipitate back into being. Nostalgia for a time when the spirit of fraternity reigned reappears in "Stephen Crane in Minetta Lane," the young reporter's last New York sketch, describing a sanctuary of violent crime. "Indeed, it is difficult to find people now who remember the old gorgeous days. . . . But after a search the reporter found three" (VIII, 401). From these black oldtimers Crane learns that the days were gorgeous because "the song of the razor" (VIII, 405) was heard more often and more people were maimed and killed. True community could be observed when Bloodthirsty wielded his razor and Black Cat the bandit made his home in the Lane. By this grotesque parody of fraternity, Crane registers a conviction that brotherhood in the city survives only in a weak aestheticized form, strong enough to suggest a kinship between a pair of scenes imagined by a detached observer, but too frail to do more. Now as in the past fraternity is something that this segment of the city, just like all the others, must ever do without.

5

Eternal Fact and Mere Locality: *The Red Badge of Courage: An Episode of the American Civil War*

ENTITLEMENT

Titles entitle in several ways. Some condense a work to its essence, and all titles do this to one degree or another. Their leading words suggest, in the case of literary works, an imaginary order to which the title itself is a first indication. Insofar as a title inheres in the work it inaugurates, it stands in a synecdochic relation to that work. Titles serve at the same time a metonymic function. Abbreviating the work as a whole by substituting a few words, or even a single word, for the many words of the work, the title starts a chain of contiguities that, by a process of association, replacement, and supplementation, comes to constitute the work in its entirety.

Titles wield onomastic power. In all of Western literature nothing illustrates this better than the title Sophocles gave to his most celebrated play. With his swollen (*poús*) foot, Oedipus is visibly the child abandoned to die, even as he is the one who knows (*oido*) not only the riddle of the foot but the meaning of the Sphinx.[1] By the names of its hero the title suggests the essential meaning of the play as a whole.

If few titles achieve such semantic saturation within a single name, many are productively "overdetermined" nonetheless. The Don Quijote of Cervantes's title is revealed to be, or at least to have been called, Quixada, Quesada, or Quixana; he becomes Quijote only in his knightly stage. This paranomasia spreads representations like a contagion, multiplying etymologies, neologisms, and undecidable ambiguities. As in the medieval tradition on which Cervantes draws, proper names generate more metonymic alternatives of themselves than common nouns, proper names being more gratuitous and mysterious, whereas common nouns are continually adjudicated and adjusted to public norms. Cervantes creates perspectivism at least as radical as Crane's, but more "linguistic," to borrow Spitzer's term: "There can be no certainty about the 'unbroken' reality of the events; the only unquestionable truth on which the reader may depend is the will of the artist who chose to break up a multivalent reality into different perspectives."[2]

In the title of his best-loved novel Henry Fielding, an admirer of Cervantes, fashions a similar, though somewhat more schematic, perspectivism. As in Oedipus, *Tom Jones* is identical with the name of the hero, who belongs to the same plain-name family as Wilkins or Mrs. Miller, in contrast to a larger family of names, some with Restoration overtones (Allworthy, Mrs. Honour), some with animal names (Partridge, Nightingale), and some with names possessing an almost Dickensian flavor (Blifil, Thwackum). Ranging across such extremes gives a sense of amplitude, suggesting that the author, at ease among differences, knows how to render their typicality.[3]

Finally, *The Scarlet Letter,* a particularly interesting case, can provide a way in to *The Red Badge of Courage.* While the phenomenal base of Hawthorne's title consists of course in the embroidered A, *The Scarlet Letter* is primarily the sign of a sign. In the A, the community has inscribed a text at once revelatory and mnemonic, reminding its members of the particular sin, but also of that congenital state of the entire species that every member knows from the "A" page of the primer: "In Adam's fall we sin all."

But Hawthorne's letter, by revealing publicly at the price of concealing privately, proves to be disjunctive. To the public the letter signifies Hester's transgression but not Dimmesdale's. Only the private community of the two lovers and, *mutatis mutandis,* of their child and the former mate, know all that the letter means. Although the correlate of Hawthorne's letter in Crane, the red badge, is only at first something wished for, the lack is figured by a trope of lettering: "Crane turns around the symbolism of Hawthorne's *The Scarlet Letter* or 'The Minister's Black Veil.' The *lack* of any mark distinguishes Henry. . . . He wished that he, too, had a wound, a red badge of courage. . . ."[4] The red badge, like the scarlet letter, operates disjunctively. Its mode of revelation is one that manages, ironically, to conceal. One person alone knows its true meaning, but in contrast with the letter, the true or private meaning is the very inverse of the public one. Whereas the letter reveals incompletely, the "revelation" represented by the badge completely conceals. In a manner foreign to Hawthorne's vision, the badge signifies by means of an act that did occur (the injury to the youth by a fellow soldier) an act that did not (courageous behavior on the part of the youth).

The titles of both novels function synecdochically. In Hawthorne we find both the letter of the *letter* and the *Letter* of the letter: The former in that the embroidered figure inheres in the entitling that informs all that the book means, the latter in that the very ability to do so depends upon the embroidered figure. Far from making *letter* and *Letter* interchangeable, this proposition recognizes the metaphorical office of entitlement, which states in effect that this, the title, is similar to that, the story as a whole. To the extent that the title may be thought of as the term to which the fabula can be reduced, a metonymic office, too, is fulfilled, the essence of all that happens being encapsulated in these three entitling words. Here, however, a qualification must be registered, for the lower-case scarlet letter, the needlework figure, already works metonymically by reducing the complexity of events and motives and feelings to its own physical compass.[5] This is a more radical reduction than the one effected by the title's metonymic function (which is subordinate), and one to which this function points as being similar but distinguishable; in other words, insofar as it points to a difference in degree, such that the two metonymic levels may only be likened, it functions for practical purposes – ironically – in a metaphorical mode.

The Red Badge of Courage: An Episode of the American Civil War is a synecdoche not only of the novel itself but of the particular war indicated in the subtitle and of war in general. This is to say that, proximally, the whole of which the title is a part is the American Civil War and at the same time the general phenomenon of war that the American Civil War instantiates. The latter's larger measure reflects Crane's belief in the universality of conflict – in conflict as condition – visible now in the Bowery, now at Chancellorsville, now in the American West.

The metonymic function consists, as in *The Scarlet Letter,* in the "reduction" of the intangible to the tangible. The bloody wound tangibly signifies courage, but, again as in *The Scarlet Letter,* the entitlement is disjunctive since the badge merely *appears* to cover a wound received in honorable action.[6] Like *The Scarlet Letter,* the title thus works differently in the public sphere from the way it works in the private; and, as in Hawthorne, the public sphere itself appears in a dual aspect. For there is the meaning of the badge for the bearer, who knows how it actually came to be; and there is the meaning both for the public within and without the novel – on the one hand, the protagonist's fellow soldiers and, on the other hand, the novel's readers. To the latter belongs the fullest knowledge since the readers know what the characters do not know.

How all this broadens the scope of the irony may be seen by comparing Crane's treatment of the badge with one by Henry James. Noting a silver cross suspended from the neck of Lord Warburton's sister, Isabel Archer asks Warburton, "Is that silver cross a badge?"

> "A badge?"
> "A sign of rank."
> Lord Warburton's glance had wandered a good deal, but at this it met

> the gaze of his neighbour. "Oh, yes," he answered in a moment; "the women go in for those things. The silver cross is worn by the eldest daughters of Viscounts." Which was his harmless revenge for having occasionally had his credulity too easily engaged in America.[7]

As in Crane's novel the badge is derealized inasmuch as it does not signify that the wearer is the eldest daughter of a viscount any more than Henry Fleming's badge signifies courage. The difference is that James conceals the opposite side, as it were, of the supposed signifier; here, in contrast to Crane's strategy, the protagonist does not have access to the meaning of the badge, or rather the nonmeaning of the nonbadge. Only the Warburtons do, and in this respect their situation parallels Henry Fleming's. It resembles the latter, too, in that the improvised fiction of daughters and viscounts hypostatizes meaning, even if that meaning is illusory. The cross becomes the badge James's protagonist had envisaged as the wound becomes the badge Crane's protagonist had envisaged.

As there is a letter of the *Letter* and a *Letter* of the letter, there is also a badge of the *Badge* and a *Badge* of the badge: a synecdochic arrangement through and through, yet a metaphoric one as well. In the first place the title invokes the principle of similarity, indicating that the badge is like the wound. In the second place the title suggests its own resemblance to the story as a whole, which, like the title, gravitates around the same central irony and displays the same disjunction between public and private that informs so much of the book.

Finally, a word concerning the title of this chapter. The entitling phrase comes from a posthumously published poem: "There exists the eternal fact of conflict / And – next – a mere sense of locality" (X, 84). Conflict for Crane, as I have already argued, is a condition inseparable from the human condition as such. An old spirit of *eris* or strife hangs over Crane's world, which is a modern world nonetheless. It is as if his eyes, though trained on the present, see through it to the past – to the achievements of his family, for example, or to things great and Greek. But the present remains present, even if its features do not become explicit. In attending-to a type of strife no longer possible, Crane attends-from a type of strife that is current. From the late 1870s through and beyond the time of the *Red Badge*'s publication, headlines blare about strikes, shootings, arson, and attempted assassinations, portraying a nation yet again at war with itself. The same *New York Tribune* that was bringing out the *Sullivan County Sketches* recounts a violent conflict, resulting in twenty deaths, between Pinkertons and strikers; a follow-up story, reporting rumors that locked-out workers were arming themselves with a cannon, appears on the same day as one of the pieces by Crane. If a military Civil War can become a social civil war, the latter can seem a variation on the theme of the former, an instance of an ever-recurring type. Crane for his part is inclined to think this way. A finder of generalities hidden in details, his imagination, as suggested in the first chapter of this study, is notably typological. In the particular it finds the general, in the contingent the necessary, in the local the eternal. To this extent the American Civil War is not less a literary myth than the myths of Greek antiquity:

> In the violent war world of *The Red Badge* Crane . . . has created an enduring myth that draws on, universalizes and puts in perspective the immediate violence of militia and Federal troops, of Pinkerton strike breakers and corporate warfare, of lynchings and the armed counterattacks of black men, of the subjugation of the Indians, entire industries shut down, cities under martial law, workers and police killed, dynamite exploding, and men either baffled and unemployed or deeply uncertain about their position in a rapidly changing urban, industrial world.[8]

Eternality and locality are, as Poe would say, intervolved: "Of course, I have never been in a battle, but I believe that I got my sense of the rage of conflict on the football field, or else fighting is a hereditary instinct, and I wrote intuitively; for the Cranes were a family of fighters in the old days, and in the Revolution every member did his duty."[9] As the eternal is to the local, heredity is to the football field. On the football field the learner learns by doing, and not by intuition, what the rage of conflict amounts to. Then there is heredity, whereby the rage of conflict descends through time, directly accessible to the inheritor who therefore needs nothing empirical like a football field; here, after all, intuition *will* do. Crane did interview veterans, did get information from a retired general, did do other research, and did produce not only a Civil War novel but *the* Civil War novel. The point to underline is that the novel indicates two further signifieds: (1) the violence-torn society of late nineteenth-century America, a localization of the eternal fact of conflict, and (2) that eternal fact itself.

This examination of entitling has obviously carried investigation of *The Red Badge* far beyond the words on the title page, and the reader, having been required, in effect, to scan forward over a good deal of the novel, will have gained some idea of where the discussion is likely to head. Let me turn now to the start of the next proper, the much-quoted opening scene.

BEGINNING

> The cold passed reluctantly from the earth and the retiring fogs revealed an army stretched out on the hills, resting. As the landscape changed from brown to green the army awakened and began to tremble with eagerness at the noise of rumors. It cast its eyes upon the roads which

> were growing from long troughs of liquid mud to proper thoroughfares. A river, amber-tinted in the shadow of its banks, purled at the army's feet and at night when the stream had become of a sorrowful blackness one could see, across, the red eye-like gleam of hostile campfires set in the low brows of distant hills. (II, 3)

Natural features of the scene are named by definite articles: *the* cold, *the* earth, *the* fogs, *the* hills; but the army is named by an indefinite article. The reason for the distinction seems clear: That entity would emerge with an already established identity, whereas the indefinite article suggests the contingency and incompleteness of something that has yet to come into its own – which is exactly the problem collectively of untried troops even as it is the problem individually of a particular untried trooper.

The process of filling in this indeterminacy begins as the army awakens. What is it that then begins to tremble? Not *an* army, but *the* army, a bit of determinacy indicating a certain growth in identity; but a good deal remains unknown. While calling the army "it" draws attention to its composite nature, the eyes with which it sees can lead in two directions: They could be a pair or they could be many eyes. The concluding sentence seems to offer a similar range, the plural "brows" existing alongside the singular "eye." This eye appears, however, by analogy, modifying the gleam that is controlled by plural "campfires," which leads in turn to the plural "brows." The plurals thus have the edge: The enemy has become a many set over against a one, who appears for the first time as an agent in the second part of the concluding sentence. Before considering that part, let us examine the sentence as a whole.

While the first clause remains within the original brief sequence ("A river . . . purled at the army's feet"), the conjunction marks a caesura between morning and night: "and at night when the stream had become of a sorrowful blackness." The second clause tells, not what is true of this particular morning, but what is generally true in the evening. The shift is not merely from day to night. It is a shift from one certain day to a composite, typical night. The shift is thus more than temporal; it is categorical. To the extent that the "one" who now appears for the first time is viewed as a discrete individual, the process of differentiation advances. Yet the term retains its base in the typical, for one could be anyone in the army who looks across the river on a typical night.

The locus that orients all this is disposed to a certain kind of discernment. Its bifocal vision trains attention both on the particular and the diachronic, on the one hand, and on the general and the synchronic, on the other. The distinction follows the one already made between the wakening that begins the passage and the wakefulness that concludes it. It thus leaves the reader, for the time being, in one of the author's favorite places, which he sometimes calls the "condition," as in "the ethics of their condition" in "The Open Boat," and sometimes by other, more or less timeless applications, such as "the eternal fact of conflict." Crane watches the condition, the eternal fact, very closely, describing both its omnipresence and, when the conflict enters the diachronic mode, its dynamics.

The temporal and categorical shifts constitute a rhythm that is itself perspectival. Each new emphasis is like a strong beat in musical time, patterned, yet different and often unforeseen. Who on a first reading can accurately predict where any sentence by Crane is going? If I may vary the musical analogy, the surprises are like modulations, in the modern sense of handling transition from one key, or mode, to another.

If rhythm is a pattern of accents, it will be helpful to look at their function in the text. The opening sentence, for example, rises to a fall. Stretched out, the revealed army is resting, a word we would not hesitate to call, in scansion, a trochee (*résting*) and at the same time a "feminine" ending. In fact this falling rhythm, with unaccented syllables following accented ones, recurs conspicuously: "Resting" echoes "retiring," which echoes "reluctantly," the rhythmic pattern being heightened by the recurrence of the prefix *re*-. "Rumors" and "thoroughfares" also contribute to this dying fall. But as the sentence approaches its climax the diminution gives way to augmentation and stronger stress, as "resting," "rumors," and "thoroughfares," the concluding words of the preceding sentences, are answered by the monosyllabic "hills," producing the only upbeat ending in the sequence. At the same time the final clause, anticipating the pounding prose rhythms of a John Hawkes, crowds in more accented beats than any comparable sequence: "the réd eýe-líke gléam of hóstile cámp-fíres śet in the lów bróws of dístant hílls." In my scansion this makes for twelve accents in only fifteen words. Even if one counts the hyphenations as individual words the number of accents is very high, and there are no less than three spondees (eýe-líke, cámp-fíres, lów bróws). All this requires of the reader a rising exertion, as in the movement from sleep to wakefulness. Crane heaps the reader further by offering, in the paragraph, three sentences of about the same length, then switching, even as he quickens the tempo of stress, to one that is more than twice its length.

In considering these matters we need to remember the shift in perspective, noted above, from morning to night, together with the commensurate shift from awakening to watching. The transition from awakening at dawn to nocturnal wakefulness cannot be separated from the transition from one particular moment, in which the army awakens, to the more generalized time in which a typical member of the army attentively stares. If one could compress all this into a single figure it would be something like an oxymoron, with the lightening revelation of morning coming into dissonant harmony with a darkened counterpart as the seen (the observed army) becomes the seer.

Being seen and seeing are modes of knowing, of revealing. But often, as here, Crane's revealing has a way of concealing. The revelation is not a disclosure *to* the army but *of* it. The seen are the known who for their part do not know or who cannot be certain of what they know. It is a state in which the youth finds himself again and again. Smoke makes it hard for him to see what lies ahead and the confusion of movements makes it hard to know forwards from backwards. Even when he can perceive something, he may not discern what is most important: "The youth could not tell . . . which color of cloth was winning" (II, 124).

The difficulty of knowing makes for difficult connections. The things one wants to know lie beyond reach; one can even be distanced from one's own knowledge or emotions, hence the disarming but typical locution about a character who only surmised concerning what he desired: "He now thought that he wished he was dead" (II, 62). Like a spell, such alienation suspends knowing contact, interrupting one's relation with oneself, the correlate of which is a state of spell-like suspension with respect to things other than the self: "The youth was in a little trance of astonishment. So they were at last going to fight" (II, 5; *cf.* II, 28).

A trance is an interruption in a state of wakefulness, a little sleep. The collective sleep that is just ending when the novel begins is also, in its own way, an interruption, and as it ends, the rhythm of waking starts, a rhythm that, synecdochically, assimilates the youth even as it assimilates the army itself. A slow rhythm, this, moving in tides of advance and retreat, of assault and flight, on a forward–rearward axis, which now accents the collective, as in the opening paragraph of Chapter 1, now the individual, as in the opening paragraph of Chapter 6: "The youth awakened slowly. He came gradually back to a position from which he could regard himself" (II, 39). "He had burned several times to enlist" (II, 5) further suggests the way that Henry's feelings fluctuate both with the oscillations of his still-forming character and with the pressures of circumstance; these oscillations having their counterpart in the rhythm of the military life, which alternately rises and falls, now ascending to peaks of effort, now descending into the "sort of eternal camp" (II, 4) with which the narrative begins.

Of at least equal importance to these preliminary matters are some meaning-making patterns that invite more attention than they have received. The patterns include position, opposition, immanence and transcendence, astonishment or wonder, direction, and the role of pairings. In the case of Crane's relation to antiquity, the role of the little, and his use of color, the topics to which this discussion now turns, and in the case of the novel's ending, with which the present chapter will itself end, we have patterns whose functions, though frequently analyzed, warrant further consideration.

NOT DISTINCTLY HOMERIC

If the youth's original attitude toward the war attests to a sense of being late on the historical scene, it attests as well to a vague hope for a return to glory, a not uncommon attitude at the time, as suggested by Brooks Adams's *The Law of Civilization and Decay,* which in 1895 could nostalgically admire the ancient bonding of poet and warrior. As Henry Adams was still making his way toward Mont St. Michel and Chartres, Charles Eliot Norton was already idealizing the Middle Ages, while others saw prospects for a return to glory through bully behavior in foreign affairs.

Crane portrays Henry's attitude in the first chapter: "Tales of great movements shook the land. They might not be distinctly Homeric, but there seemed to be much glory in them" (II, 5). Such views are little things to hold onto for their familiarity, like personal possessions that help you feel at home in strange places. That the great movements "might not be distinctly Homeric" is cautious, even a bit world-weary, in the manner of the preceding statements, but the attitude is premature; the young man's innocence is showing, and it is the same innocence that in the next breath can yet attest to a belief in much glory.

Ironically, Henry turns out to be right about glory. Just as ironically, his actions cover a wide range of what was possible in the antiquity by which Henry, like Crane, is fascinated. At one extreme are the trancelike periods of fighting. In Chapter 17 Henry fires wildly without even knowing either where the rebels are or what he is feeling: "His rifle-barrel grew so hot that, ordinarily, he could not have borne it upon his palms but he kept on stuffing cartridges into it and pounding them with his clanking, bending ram-rod" (II, 96). Later, hypnotized by the goddess-flag, Henry and his friend wrestle for it; later still each throws himself into combat with utter abandon; while in the chapter that follows, Henry experiences the "subtle fellowship and equality" (II, 112) which, together with the flag-oriented exertions of the two friends, will be taken up again below. In this and similar moments of bonding, the youth is alert to what is going on in himself and around him, and is lucid about the significance of it all. At other times and at another extreme he feels trapped, a helpless creature in a moving box, bound by the iron laws of tradition. That this sense may recur at any time is suggested by the sentence following the statement, above, on fellowship: "But the regiment was a machine run-down" (II, 112). The main line of development, despite much zigzagging, leads in any case from an archaic vision of traditional warrior values, to a more contemporary orientation that accepts the discipline of military organization, and even justifies it as a case of transcendental fraternity.

This line follows to a considerable extent the process by which the ancient Greek warrior ethic was reshaped through democratization, the two main roles falling to the *hippeus,* avatar of the heroic Homeric charioteer, and the *hoplite,* who represents the soldier as citizen.

> What counted for the *hippeus* was the individual exploit, splendid performance in single combat. In battle, a mosaic of face-to-face duels between *promachoi* [champions], military worth was asserted in the form of an *aristeia,* a wholly personal superiority. The warrior found the boldness that enabled him to perform such brilliant feats of arms in a sort of exaltation or warlike frenzy, *lyssa,* into which he was thrown, as though beside himself . . . . But the hoplite no longer engaged in individual combat; if he felt the temptation to engage in a purely individual act of valor, he was obliged to resist it.[10] [Italics in original.]

While it would be excessive to suppose that these features account for features in Crane's novel, in fact the text offers some close approximations. In the beginning Henry yearns for the type of glory that came to the ancient warrior whose *lyssa* carried him to heights of bravery, and later just such a frenzy comes upon him: Oblivious to obstacles, ignorant even of direction, he becomes a man possessed. But the old warrior ethic will not suffice. If operations are to be modern and collective, one's personal animus must be rechanneled into *sophrosyne,* the particular wisdom that is self-mastery. War now demands the discipline of the hoplite, the temperate tiller of martial fields. When each soldier's *sophrosyne* functions properly, all are attuned to *philia,* the spirit of community, military success having become a group goal rather than a personal goal. Such a spirit is, in modern and American terms, the spirit of fraternity. For Crane, possessing a flag, whether it is the ensign of one's unit or of an enemy's, signifies a success that is precisely collective. In this connection Crane underlines, just before the passage on fellowship and equality, Henry's resentment over the accusation that the men of his regiment are mule drivers. He exemplifies now the creed of one for all.

Further perspectives for consideration include the following. First, the parallels that have been noted strengthen the case, already widely accepted, that early Greek culture made a memorable impression on the young author. Second, this interpretation does not assume that Crane had direct knowledge of the post-Homeric experience here described (though it does not deny that he could have had it). He may simply have made some educated guesses about this experience – just as he made educated guesses about the American Civil War. Given Crane's unmistakable powers of imagination, he could have projected on the near past some aspects of a more remote past; or his retracing could have been aleatory. The parallels in question rest, in any case, as an intertextual basis – a basis of affinity and not necessarily of influence. For whatever reason and from whatever source, Crane actually does follow a path already followed in ancient history.

A third perspective stems from the author's relation to his family's distinguished past, which included long religious, as well as military, leadership in the American Revolutionary War; late in life Crane planned a novel on that war. A lover of horses, Crane never commanded from his mount the movements of men fighting for the nation and never carried Christian faith across the countryside like his circuit-riding ancestors. As journalist, fiction writer, and poet, Crane is the observer, ever distant from events large or little, ever shadowed, like Hawthorne, by the ancestral past. Did Crane fear with Hawthorne that his was a thin-blooded version of the flesh that lived and died to found a new world? Crane was never explicit on this topic in Hawthorne's way. I merely propose that here is another example of that recurring theme, the replacement of an old and glory-laden ethic by a new one lacking aura, and hence another possible if partial explanation for Crane's inspired guessing.

If Greek-like struggles will no longer take place, neither will anyone write an epic. A given novel or series of novels may be "epiclike," as in the case of *Tom Jones* or the Yoknapatawpha novels of Faulkner. Among the reasons why these are not true epics is that they treat of epic individuals rather than epic heroes. The epic individual appears in the novel as an agent through whose struggles the world is revealed in all its otherness: "The epic hero is, strictly speaking, never an individual, . . . for the completeness, the roundness of the value system which determines the epic cosmos creates a whole which is too organic for any part of it to become so enclosed within itself, so dependent upon itself, as to find itself as an interiority – i.e. to become a personality."[11] The protagonist of Crane's novel is just such a part and just such an interiority. It is not that the narrative steers clear of the destiny of the community it depicts; that precisely the opposite occurs will be another focus in the present chapter. But the destiny of the community is mediated through the part, the personality, the interiority – in short, the individual – the community being regarded, finally, as an aggregate of individuals.

The resulting limitation of vision can have an intensifying effect; in the case of Jim Conklin's death, it is excruciatingly intense; but this is really the epic effect turned inside out.

> Virgil had expanded Homer's view of ten or twenty years of glory . . . to include a long-lived empire encompassing the known world. Similarly, the Christian epics of Charlemagne and the crusades are described as world wars. Milton extended beyond human time and farther out than human space. Crane doubled back upon the epic vision. . . . It is

> epical in its achievement and heroic only because Crane has shown it to be the only vision possible for man that remains "bold and clear."[12]

Virgil enters discussions of Crane less often than Homer because critics have been more interested in the textual than the intertextual; that is, they have favored inquiry into Crane's demonstrated or possible knowledge of a given text over inquiry into affinities between such a text and a text by Crane, irrespective of what he had read. The latter approach, when applied in the present context, indicates that Crane is about as Virgilian in spirit as he is Homeric.

The following simile from the *Iliad* will help to illustrate the way in which Virgil departs from his Greek predecessor.

> And when the men who were moving towards each other had come to the same spot, they clashed, shield on shield, spear on spear, in bronze ferocity. . . . Then mingled the shrieks and the cheers of killer and killed, and the earth streamed with blood. As when winter rivers, flashing from their vast springs down the mountains to a glen, clash their colossal waters in the hollow ravine, and in mountains far distant a shepherd hears the tumult of their meeting, such was the roar and clamor of the soldiers as they met.

In Virgil the perspective is more personal, less omniscient, and more problematic:

> Meanwhile the howls of war confound the city. And more and more – although my father's house was far, the dread clash of battle grows. I start from sleep and climb the sloping roof above the house. I stand, alerted: just as when, with furious south winds, a fire has fallen on a wheat field, or a torrent that hurtles from a mountain stream lays low the meadows, low the happy crops, and low the labor of the oxen, dragging forests headling – and even then, bewildered and unknowing, perched upon rock, the shepherd will listen to the clamor.

The Homeric description, which has as many correlates in Crane as his novel has battle scenes, presents deadly combat in all its immediacy, with armed troops clashing and voices crying. Here too is what might be called immediate perspectivism. Like Crane, Homer offers on the one hand a general, omniscient view that nonetheless "feels" close, then, again like Crane, shifts to a distant, more limited locus. But despite the distance, there is an immediacy to the shepherd's hearing: The sounds that carry to him do so directly and unproblematically.

Virgil's more radical shift in perspective shakes the very ground of epistemology: "The action and therefore the image of the action have been internalized in such a way that this simile, unlike Homer's, is not used to intensify the pleasure, strength, and mystery of perception, but rather to emphasize what cannot be seen and to intensify the uncertainty and apprehension that can occur when something that needs to be seen cannot be seen."[13] Instead of informing, the heard sounds, as though screened by the very process that in Homer is the source of knowledge, leave the speaker bewildered and unknowing. Correlates in Crane abound. Time after time the youth and his comrades hear without knowing, see without knowing, think without knowing. That cognition does not necessarily follow from perception is suggested, both in Virgil and in Crane, by the event of wakening. At the beginning of Chapter 6, Henry, like Aeneas, starts from sleep, but, again like the latter, he is in no wise enlightened. "The red, formidable difficulties of war," he concludes, "had been vanquished" (II, 39). Here the youth repeats the experience of the army, which wakes up at the beginning of the novel, whereupon the men of Fleming's unit are immediately misled by Jim's rumor. Alertness in itself does nothing to alleviate bewilderment and unknowing.

In sum, Crane's novel resonantes with echoes both from Homer and from Virgil. On balance, however, the latter may yet be the louder. The unknowing epitomized by the shepherd boy in "Death and the Child" underscores the basic condition of Henry Fleming for most of the novel and for most participants in most wars. Uncertainty and apprehension are endemic, lack of knowledge chronic. Though it is hardly Homeric to say so, Crane implies that a man is what he knows, but little does he know.

SOME VERSIONS OF THE LITTLE

In his postepic situation, Crane focusses on all manner of little things, of which the little man is only one exemplar. In general he works "within a tightly restricted area. . . . Like the painters of the Italian Renaissance who conceived the *tondo,* a form that forced the artist to choose and manipulate his subject matter to fit a small circular canvas, Crane chose to restrict his novel to war and its impact upon the hero."[14] The novel is full of little things the young soldier knows and large things he does not know: "Each blade of the green grass was bold and clear. He thought that he was aware of every change in the thin, transparent vapor that floated idly in sheets. . . . His mind took mechanical but firm impressions, so that, afterward, everything was pictured and explained to him, save why he himself was there" (II, 105). Whitman's leaves of grass, which may serve as one measure of Crane's vision, suggest a different but related way of connecting the little and the large. For the expansive poet, everything is pictured and explained, including why he himself is there. Indeed, he occupies the foreground. To him the grass is plenitude and overdetermination. In *Song of Myself* (1891–1892) the inquiring child's hands are full of it and it is full of meaning: It is "the flag of my disposition" (1. 101); "Or I guess it is a uniform hieroglyphic" (1. 107). Unlike the Whitman persona, the Crane protagonist possesses large knowledge of the little but little knowledge of the large.

The little is so large a topic in *The Red Badge* that it must be approached selectively and by means of some basic groupings. The term *little* and its companions (*wee, small, tiny, elfin*) apply to things both inanimate and animate, to events and their interpretation, and to the protagonist. In the original manuscript "little" even characterizes the red badge of courage.

The hills that appear in the early tales and sketches, the poems, and other works take a manmade form in the novel: "During this halt, many men in the regiment began erecting tiny hills in front of them. . . . Some built comparatively large ones while others seemed content with little ones" (II, 26). Henry is astounded when ordered to leave the "little protection" thus achieved (II, 26). But elevations can provide a perspective: "He scrambled upon a wee hill and watched [the brigade] sweeping finely, keeping formation in difficult places" (II, 43). If little fields are part of the same scene, so too are "a little clump of bushes" (II, 56), a little tree to hide behind, and the "little, guarding edifices in the forest chapel."

Although little ants appear on the corpse in the same chapter, small-scale animacy inheres, for the most part, in the human realm. There are the little formations of soldiers, the "little accent of despair" in the tattered man's voice (II, 61), and, above all, Henry, who is " 'jest one little feller amongst a hull lot of others' " (II, 7).

Events undergo similar treatment. Battles, duels, combats, and shootings are little or small, and two regiments fight "little separate battles with two other regiments" (II, 122). In the rush of battle, time itself seems to be compressed: If there is a pause, it is sure to be brief. The scaling-down applies to space as well; when Jim Conklin falls to his death "The body seemed to bounce a little way from the earth" (II, 58). If this detail makes the depiction more graphic, it also, by the very minuteness of its scope, thrusts the significance of the event in a closer because contrasting view. The same may be said of the end of Chapter 7, where a distant officer "held a little carnival of joy on horseback" (II, 44).

In Henry himself we have an avatar of the little man. Littleness appears in his person as his mouth makes "a little pucker" (II, 81) and his face works "in small contortions" (II, 124). These are tokens of concentration, like his "little trance of astonishment" (II, 5), or his straining to hear "little, blistering voices of pain" (II, 72), or his various little thoughts and fears. More fundamentally, littleness in Henry is suggestive of the kind of illusions to which a child is prone, of a child's devices of defenses, of its love and dread of mature knowledge. This may be explained in part by the fact that Henry is simply younger than most of the others, and, having just been in seminary, has presumably led a relatively sheltered life.

Littleness in terms of age contributes an additional perspective. That Henry is younger than Jim, whom he has known since childhood, is one of the first things we learn. Facing combat makes Henry feel "like a babe" (II, 23); subsequently, he recalls how, as "a small thrillful boy" (II, 33), he anticipated the arrival of the circus parade. For a time his wound reduces him again to an infantile stage: "At last, with a twisting movement, he got upon his hands and knees and from thence, like a babe trying to walk, to his feet" (II, 70).

The theme of infancy goes beyond Henry. To their colonel, Fleming and Wilson are both babies; an enemy prisoner nurses a foot wound "baby-wise" (II, 130); while the lieutenant in a moment of galvanized attention lapses into the infantile: "There was something curious in this little intent pause of the lieutenant. He was like a babe which having wept its fill, raises its eyes and fixes upon a distant toy" (II, 113). Littleness in age, then, is itself a kind of condition, something that one bears through life and something to which one may always revert.

The little that plays through Henry's relation to Wilson has a large effect, little of which is to Henry's advantage. An important measure is his friend's transcendence of littleness: "He was not furious at small words that pricked his conceits. He was, no more, a loud young soldier. There was about him now a fine reliance" (II, 82). The knowledge that his friend has changed for the better makes him newly dangerous to Henry, who worries that questions will expose the truth behind his badge. Remembering "the little packet" of personal effects (II, 85) he was to send to Wilson's next of kin, Henry decides to turn its possession to his advantage. First, "He resolved not to deal the little blow. . . . It was not necessary to knock his friend on the head with the misguided packet" (II, 85). The apparent magnanimity is quickly belied as Henry's attitude takes on a hostile edge: "He now rejoiced in the possession of a small weapon with which he could prostrate his comrade at the first sign of a cross-examination. He was master" (II, 85). Henry's perspective is soon enough prettified: "Besides, a faith in himself had secretly blossomed. There was a little flower of confidence growing within him" (II, 86).

Henry invites more sympathy when he experiences, in the aftermath of a charge, what any other inexperienced soldier could be expected to experience: "The youth, in this contemplation, was smitten with a large astonishment. He discovered that the distances, as compared with the brilliant measurings of his mind, were trivial and ridiculous. . . . He wondered at the number of emotions and events that had been crowded into such little spaces" (II, 117). "Measure," both as predicate and as noun, indicates Henry's uncertainty about his capacities and his desire to evaluate them clearly. As early as the second chapter, "he continually tried to measure himself by his comrades. The tall soldier, for one, gave him some assurance. This man's serene unconcern dealt him a measure of confidence" (II, 13). Although the issue is qualitative, Henry first tries to handle it in quantitative terms: He tried to mathematically prove to himself that he would not run from a battle" (II, 9). Details such as Jim measuring a sandwich and soldiers counting miles form a background against which Henry, as a disclosing sun returns, can himself be disclosed: "He was about to be measured. . . . He seized time to look about him calculatingly" (II, 23).

Wounded, Henry's measuring attempts become less cerebral, more visceral. He even supposes "that he could measure his plight" (II, 72) by his little voices of pain, but panics when they remain silent. As the book moves on, efforts at naive measurement diminish, partly because Henry proves himself in battle and because, having done so, he can switch from shaky calculations to self-glorification.

COLOR

Reportorial color, indicating a phenomenal base in ordinary experience, appears in the opening passage where the landscape changes from brown to green, the river is amber-tinted, the night black, and the camp fires red.[15] Later, guns make "grey clouds" (II, 100) and the gray of Confederate uniforms contrasts with the Union blue; and so on. Reportorial technique, in other words, registers how a color immediately appears. Some instances turn the perceptual screw, however; such is the case with "The red sun was pasted in the sky like a wafer" (II, 58). Now, the reader has no reason to suspect that the sun was not red: Red, as a solar hue, has been accepted since Anglo-Saxon times (*OED* A.I.1.c., 450). But its location in a metonymic chain of reds tints it, as it were, so that the color of the sun takes on overtones from, say, the protagonist's red rage, or the red sickness of battle. Further from the phenomenal base are "the flashing points of yellow and red" (II, 120) that penetrate a wall of smoke. Although points of such color may well appear on a battlefield, explosions from artillery are not typically in primary colors: This yellow looks suspiciously like Goethe's paradigmatic yellow and the red looks equally pure. In general, colors in Crane combine the degrees of intensity that Peirce assigns to sense-qualities and the degrees of vividness he assigns to ideas. In particular, primary colors achieve the highest degree of intensity and vividness, which is why the famous red sun, like the afterimage of a light flashed in the eye, glows in one's memory long after the page has been turned.

The same high pitch we saw in *Maggie* makes Crane's novel read like an expansion on Bacon: "a ciuill warre is as the heate of a feuer: but an honourable forraine warre is like the heate of exercise."[16] Thus "Pete swore redly" finds its equally expressionist counterpart in an outburst from the lieutenant: " 'Come on. We'll all git killed if we stay here. We've on'y got t' go across that lot. And then – ' The remainder of his idea disappeared in a blue haze of curses" (II, 107). The concluding phrase recalls the hazes that have gone before, such as "the blue haze of evening" (II, 71), not to mention the smoke, mists, and clouds metonymically evoked. Although it also recalls the Union blue, it strains from that phenomenal base toward a more expressionist extreme, spreading to the Lieutenant insofar as he comes to epitomize the martial spirit. This metonymic supplement, that is to say, draws from the phenomenal base that bears them while pulling away from that base by the *way* it draws. In the second chapter Wilson says to Henry, " 'Yeh're gittin' blue, m' boy' " (II, 18); if this sense of the word also applies to the Lieutenant, then we have a soldier who, blue in dress, is also blue in attitude.

The movement from a phenomenal base to extremes is further illustrated by the case of the two crimsons. The first example, already discussed, is the crimson foam. The second reads: "The youth's reply was an outburst of crimson oaths" (II, 134). In the case of the foam, you will recall, the basic simile exploits a quasi-explicit likeness between the movement of the flags and the movement of waves, the modifier making the color of the foam match the color of the flags. Henry's crimson oath lacks a comparable base, no oath having a color in the way that any flag has. Rather, this crimson takes the temperature of Henry's outburst, which is hotter than that of the blue Lieutenant, giving it a register at once visual and emotional. It is not a long step from here to "Following this came a red rage" (II, 35). Though in this case there is no association as handy as bloody murder, red seems an appropriately choleric color, especially when the rage in question occurs on a battlefield.

In the following, Crane combines the reportorial with the "purely" expressive: "He was aware that these battalions . . . were woven red and startling into the gentle fabric of softened greens and browns" (II, 24). Somewhat surprisingly, we do not see blue battalions, as might have been expected; they do not bear a color determination at all. This is because Crane is attending-from the color that belongs to the uniforms to the manner in which the army relates to the landscape, signified by an outburst of color, almost a tonal cry, that expressively gathers up associations with blood and war and heated emotions. In the quotation above, red as such is not present in the scene in the same reportorial way as greens and browns, it is rather a scenic distillation, a quintessence of the way in which the battalions become an aspect of the landscape, whose actual colors, shades, and tones would presumably be numerous, but which are at the same time essentialized into just two basic colors.

A more radical hypostasis occurs when color is attributed to an entirely imaginary phenomenon. Thus, after the phenomenally based colors in the book's opening passage, Jim comes back waving his shirt: "He adopted the important air of a herald and gold" (II, 3). The colors derive, in other words, not from the depicted presence of anything visual in either the landscape or the characters but by extrapolation from attitude, as in the "yellow discontent" of *Maggie*.

On a grander scale the final chapter offers this: "Regarding his procession of memory, he felt gleeful and unregretting, for, in it, his public deeds were paraded in great and shining prominence. Those performances which had been witnessed by his fellows marched now in wide purple and gold, hiding various deflections" (II, 133). Purple and gold are generic and abstract, counterparts of the intangible qualities of great and shining, which, without this translation into color, would want concreteness. In the manner of the imaginary herald, the process recorded here is attitudinal; it expresses the way the youth feels in relation to others and in relation to himself. In contrast to the earlier passage, the marching passage runs on considerably, as if to furnish by its length a quantitative complement to the expressive "exaggeration" of purple, with its splendor vaguely royal. In response to Wilson, whose probing could expose the truth of the red badge, Henry bursts out once more in crimson oaths; he then proceeds through an elaborate, seesawing process of self-justification until in the next-to-last paragraph he pronounces himself cured of "the red sickness of battle" (II, 135), whereupon "a golden ray of sun came through the hosts of leaden rain clouds" (II, 135). If this seems less radical than the imaginary procession of purple and gold, it is because Henry is trying to affirm the bond between himself and the world. To witness the color of the sun's ray as merely his own projection is far from his purpose. The ray must be more, it must in its very naturalness and immediacy represent the brightest and the best: no room here for the homeliness of "a yellow patch like a rug laid for the feet of the coming sun" (II, 15) – not when you can have the sun itself. Ultimately it is the transcendental, futural prospects of the sun that the color of the ray suggests. Higher than yellow, more precious and numinous, gold becomes in the final passage, like a yellow raised to its highest power, the color supreme.

There remains, finally, the use of the words *color* and *colors*. The latter, a companion term to flag, helps to keep visible the association between Henry and that symbol of his unit, the army as a whole, and victory. *Color,* the more significant term, can shade into *colors,* as when we are told that the color of the cloth indicates which side is winning. By metonymy the neutral term can take on a hue to which it is contiguous: "Here and there were flags, the red in the stripes dominating. They splashed bits of warm color upon the dark lines of troops" (II, 38). More often, color is a shorthand device to record a manifold of phenomena: "A thousand details of color and form surged in his mind" (II, 33).

Color is especially effective at making vivid whatever ineffable quality we feel to be the essence of something. Discussing love, Stendhal observes: "There is a physical cause, an incipient madness, a rush of blood to the brain, a disorder of the nervous system and the cerebral centres; compare the fleeting courage shown by stags and the color of a soprano's thoughts."[17] This use of the term lifts what is most basic and ownmost toward a more general level of articulation. This is no translation of the ineffable into the lucid: We do not hear the soprano's specific notes or the tone "colors" of her voice. The technique reveals immediately, evocatively, much as a whiff or a glance or a touch reveals – if not the thing itself we get at least the gist of it.

Closer to home, Whittier lets color signify that in ourselves from which we form compelling future patterns: "The tissue of the life to be / We weave with colors all our own."[18] For the Emerson of *Nature* colors signify those features of the human being that nature mediates, expressing them back to the spectator as its own delight: "Nature always wears the colors of the spirit. To a man laboring under calamity, the heat of his own fire hath sadness in it."[19] For the Thoreau of *Walden* a soldier's virtue has an innate color that, because it cannot indefinitely be concealed, need not be displayed: "nor need the soldier be so idle as to try to paint the precise *color* of his virtue on his standard. The enemy will find it out. He may turn pale when the trial comes."[20] Henry Fleming does more than turn pale when his trial begins; he fails it, at least at first; and all the while, in his own way, he is painting on the color of his virtue, as he would have it be perceived, the better to conceal his shame.

When Crane characterizes Henry's ambitions, he makes it clear that, as important as they may be, they are susceptible to change. The crucial statement occurs in the account of Mrs. Fleming's response to her son's desire to enlist: "At last, however, he had made firm rebellion against this yellow light thrown upon the color of his ambitions" (II, 6). In their original abstract state the ambitions warrant a comparably abstract noun, color; this, being indeterminate as to any specific hue or tone, leaves the nature of the ambitions open to the influence of anything that *is* specific, in the present case yellow light. If the yellow has here the contaminating effect for which Goethe's theory seeks to account, the colors in a later scene return to the phenomenal base, which is intensified, however, by the transcendent nature of the figure to whom they are applied: "[The flag] was a woman, red and white, hating and loving, that called him with the voice of his hopes" (II, 108).

POSITION AND OPPOSITION

To know a color, or even not to know it, presupposes a concrete situation, indeed a position. The epistemological relation posits in the original sense of the term: "To put in position; to set, dispose, or situate;

to place" (*OED* v.1). Crane's novel, it will be seen, is very much a positing affair, producing a wide range of positions, placements, loci, attitudes, poses, and postures – a cartography whose coordinates provide a kind of infrastructure of the narrative. Which is not to say that the positing is static. Its function is to orient, and the orientation is itself dynamic. Furthermore, the positing transpires with and as something else transpires, something that constitutes, as in *Maggie,* a veritable language of gesture.

Position and gesture play important parts at the very outset. The first thing the retiring fogs reveal is the posture of the army as it lies stretched out on the land, resting; and the opening paragraph ends with the description of the way the camp fires positioned over there, across the river, typically appear to a view positioned over here. Then comes the language of gesture: "Once, a certain tall soldier developed virtues and went resolutely to wash a shirt. He came flying back from a brook waving his garment, banner-like. He was swelled with a tale he had heard from a reliable friend who had heard it from a truthful cavalryman who had heard it from his trustworthy brother" (II, 3). Positioning the gestures of Jim Conklin prior to his tale gives precedence to them; they matter more than the message, for in their own way they are truer because expressive of a belief.

In theory a soldier could, if he wished, adopt a heroic pose; but in fact "There was a singular absence of heroic poses. The men bending and surging in their haste and rage were in every impossible attitude . . ." (II, 36). Being forced into a position or a gesture is not something that separates the quick and dead but something they have in common: "Under foot, there were a few ghastly forms, motionless. They lay twisted in fantastic contortions. Arms were bended and heads were turned in incredible ways. It seemed that the dead men must have fallen from some great height to get into such positions" (II, 37).

The detailed perspectivism of Chapter 18 largely derives from strategic positing, beginning with the horrible spectacle of the wounded Jimmie Rogers: "He was thrashing about in the grass, twisting his shuddering body into many strange postures" (II, 99), whereupon "The youth's friend had a geographical illusion concerning a stream and he obtained permission to go for some water" (II, 99). It is on their return that the two are so placed as to become truer knowers than before. A selection from the positings in the text (II, 100) indicates the care Crane has taken to position the key perspectives.

> From their position as they faced toward the place of the fighting, they could, of course, comprehend a greater amount of the battle than when their visions had been blurred by the hurlying smoke of the line. . . .
>
> Near where they stood, shells were flip-flapping and hooting. . . .

> A moment later, the small, creaking cavalcade was directly in front of the two soldiers. Another officer, riding with the skilful abandon of a cow-boy, galloped his horse to a position directly before the general. (II, 99–100)

When the general asks for troops to repel an enemy advance, the mounted officer replies that he can best spare Henry's unit, because its members fight like mule drivers. The episode gains in perspectival complexity – and verisimilitude – when, following the report that the two soldiers give to their comrades, the locus shifts to the latter, who now witness from afar a tableau of gesture: "They caught sight of two mounted figures a short distance from them. One was the colonel of the regiment and the other was the officer who had received orders from the commander of the division. They were gesticulating at each other. The soldier pointing at them, interpreted the scene" (II, 102). Thereafter the men "settled back into reposeful attitudes" (II, 102), following which our view is directed first to the regiment as a body, drawing itself up and heaving a deep breath, then to a generalized plurality of its members: "The soldiers were bended and stooped like sprinters before a signal" (II, 102).

Indeed, as in *Maggie,* characters in *The Red Badge of Courage* are much given to bending. The posture may indicate submission or victimization, as in the case of corpses, but it may also be assertive, as is the case whenever the boxing motif occurs (since pugilists typically incline their torsos toward their opponents). Charging troops advance in a similar attitude, and bending inheres in the aiming of a rifle: "They bended their heads in aims of intent hatred behind the projected hammers of their guns" (II, 124). Bending also bespeaks attention: "He bended forward scarce breathing. The exciting clickety-click as it grew louder and louder seemed to be beating upon his soul. . . . The men in the foremost ranks craned their necks" (II, 15; *cf.* II, 36). Is there a pun lurking in that last verb? It suggests, at any rate, the posture of concentration of which the author was known to be capable, and it suggests the presence of compulsion, as noted above, bending and craning being attitudes one more or less automatically assumes under circumstances such as these. According to a tradition known to the Gawayne poet, the neck, as the bodily member joining trunk and head, is associated with will and pride.[21] Although Crane may not have known of the association, he has Henry bend before the tattered man in an attitude of shame: "He bended his head and fastened his eyes studiously upon the button as if it were a little problem" (II, 53).

One artifact in particular, the box and its metonymic partner, the pen, contributes significantly to the pattern of position. By its utilitarian nature it adds to the text a detail that helps make a scene concrete. This is the function of the cartridge-boxes that "were pulled around into various positions and adjusted with great care. It was as if seven hundred new bonnets were being tried on" (II, 33). By comparison, the cartridge-boxes that flap and bob suggest the quality of compulsion noted above, as will a passage to be quoted below. In a conative vein a horseman shouts to the colonel not to forget the box of cigars, which never in fact materializes, as far as we know. Entirely figurative, on the other hand, is the box that appears at the end of Chapter 22 as the battered regiment assumes a collective position of injured and bewildered quietude: "The lieutenant, also, was unscathed in his position to the rear. He had continued to curse but it was now with the air of a man who was using his last box of oaths" (II, 126).

Other uses border on the theatrical. For the Negro teamster a cracker-box serves as a dancing stage until he is deserted by his fellows who want to debate the merits of Jim Conklin's rumor. The theatricality intensifies in the recollection that opens Chapter 5:

> There were moments of waiting. The youth thought of the village street at home before the arrival of the circus-parade on a day in the spring. . . . He particularly remembered an old fellow who used to sit upon a cracker-box in front of the store and feign to despise such exhibitions. A thousand details of color and form surged in his mind. The old fellow upon the cracker-box appeared in middle prominence. (II, 22)

In two of the most quoted passages a third use of the box motif adds the quality of compulsion noted above. The first establishes an immanent perspective: "But instantly he saw that it would be impossible for him to escape from the regiment. It enclosed him. And there were iron laws of tradition and law on four sides. He was in a moving box" (II, 23). This soon leads, metonymically, to "The generals were idiots to send them marching into a regular pen" (II, 25), and to the " 'pretty tight box' " (II, 82) into which the Confederates appear to have been driven. In the second of these frequently quoted passages the motif is deployed from the outside; now the compulsion consists not in claustration but in an automatism guided by the law of a certain type of "productivity": "He was at a task. He was like a carpenter who had made many boxes, making still another box, only there was furious haste in his movements" (II, 35).

Position in a war novel has everything to do with opposition, to which the discussion may now turn.

Much of this novel's force consists in the circumstance of opposition as such. Gabriel de Tarde, an influential French contemporary of Crane's, proposes that the very idea of opposition was aroused by armed encounters. In a remark that could be an aside on some of Crane's Whilomville stories, C. K. Ogden observes that "even the infant faces his infant foe in single combat."[22] What might be called a corporeal axis enables us to differentiate sides (right and left) as well as positions and directions (in front of, behind; forward or backward).

> The *op* in oppono, the *gegen* in Gegensatz, goes back to a third characteristic of the human body. It not only has two sides and two ends (symmetry), but it "faces" one way (asymmetry). When, therefore, it faces itself in a mirror and confronts its enantiomorph, or when it faces another body, an enemy (enantios), that which it faces, that which is placed over against (anti–contra–ob) it is the primary opposite from which the long line of metaphor is derived. . . . It is only the dynamic, directional, aspect of the situation which enables us to generalize the term; for both individual facings and the facings of armies, or more generally the facings of all opposed forces, are directional oppositions.[23] [Italics as in original.]

In various battle scenes the face expresses *enantios*. Henry's encounter with the man who wounds him begins the moment they oppose each other face to face: "They swung around face to face. . . . [The man's] face was livid and his eyes were rolling uncontrolled" (II, 70). Even concealing one's face, as Henry's mother does in the opening chapter, can be antagonistically expressive, communicating as it does her rejection of Henry's desire to enlist.

Opposing faces sometimes appear to be just what they are: "The struggle in the smoke had pictured an exaggeration of itself on the bleached cheeks and in the eyes wild with one desire" (II, 31). Or, to return to an idea suggested in connection with *Maggie,* the opposing countenace can be a hieroglyph demanding interpretation: "The youth looked keenly at the ashen face. . . . He vaguely desired to walk around and around the body and stare; the impulse of the living to try to read in dead eyes the answer to the Question" (II, 24). Here the opposition is no longer between soldier and soldier but between the knower and the unknown.

The asymmetry of the human body, with its forward seeing and blindness to the rear, is a primary source of the soldier's anxiety about being overtaken; thus Henry's fears increase after "he had turned his back upon the fight" (II, 42). Following an exchange of words about that anxiety, Jim runs, dances, falls, taking his place among those figures of American fiction, such as Billy Budd and Bartleby, who operate at the limits of language. Conklin, at last, is reduced to pleading "Leave me be!" as, done with life, he would be done with talking, for utterances no longer communicate, they merely vocalize. This failure is inseparable from the dominance of the body and the manner in which the corporeal state is "embodied" in the face. After his friend falls, Henry's living face confronts the dead one: "He now sprang to his feet and, going closer, gazed upon the paste-like face. The mouth was open and the teeth showed in a laugh" (II, 58).

In this way of being face to face, the one visage seems to mirror the other through sympathetic identification. The irony is, first, that the one visage reflects what the intelligence "behind" it merely believes the other to have experienced, and second, that the other face reflects back what appears to be the opposite state: Agony is answered by a laugh. This constitutes in turn a third level of irony, for the laugh is the other man's agony in a misleadingly comic appearance.

INS AND OUTS

Although Crane often pictures a visage as it would appear to an opposed or "outside" observer, a face may also provide entry to the "inner" person: "He was filled with anxiety and his face was pinched and drawn in anticipation of the pain of any sudden mistake of his feet in the gloom" (II, 72). Here is a complete circuit from Henry's inner state, anxiety, to the visible condition of the face, and then back – beginning with the phrase "in anticipation" – to his orientation toward his own ongoing motion. Another description moves, contrariwise, inward through the face: "A scowl of mortification and rage was upon his face. He had thought of a fine revenge upon the officer who had referred to him and his fellows as mule-drivers." The description has then to pass back out again through the directedness of the gaze Henry projects, almost like a Proustean eye-beam: "A dagger-pointed gaze from without his blackened face was held toward the enemy but his greater hatred was rivetted upon the man who, not knowing him, had called him a mule-driver" (II, 111). At the caesura marked by the conjunction the description must double back into consciousness inasmuch as an observer who noted that the youth is looking daggers would be unable to discriminate, as Henry does, between the putative object of his resentment and the real one.

Or consider the following: "Into the youth's eyes there came a look that one can see in the orbs of a jaded horse. His neck was quivering with nervous weakness, and the muscles of his arms felt numb and bloodless. His hands, too, seemed large and awkward as if he was wearing invisible mittens. And there was great uncertainty about his knee joints" (II, 40). The first two details – the look in the eyes and the quivering of the neck – are the sort any observer might note. But an observer would not discern, in the same way, the numbness described in the second clause of sentence two. The third sentence, on the other hand, shifts from an external to an internal perspective. Although the observer might be able to see awkwardness in the hands, "seemed" points to the way the youth himself just then perceives his hands, as does the analogy of the invisible mittens. In the concluding sentence emphasis falls on the inner side of the experience. An observer would be able to see Fleming wobble or bend at the knees, but the "great uncertainty" expresses the way Fleming feels about a condition that might lead to wobbling or bending at the knees: Imminent behavior is experienced in a kind of immanence. These perspectives are situated, then, in a territory fought over by the desire to present phenomena emotionally, as they are experienced immediately, and a desire to present them neutrally, as they are perceived from a detached locus, the two desires being no more separable from one another than breathing is from exhaling: "The youth, forgetting his neat plan of getting killed, gazed spell-bound. His eyes grew wide and busy with the action of the scene. His mouth was a little ways open" (II, 28). Here Crane moves from internal to external; the main clause of the first sentence expresses what an observer could see, while the parenthetic phrase reveals again the "other" side of the gaze. In the second sentence the two perspectives tend to merge. Whereas the "inside" of the previous sentence occurs parenthetically in the middle of the statement, it is joined almost indistinguishably, in the second sentence, to the "outside." "His eyes grew wide and busy" describes a gaze visible to any observer, but such an observer could not see with equal certainty the orientation of that gaze, and it is precisely such an orientation that the double prepositional phrase "with the action of the scene" provides. Finally, the third sentence of the paragraph presents a wholly externalized perspective on the gaze.

Chapter 16 presents a skillfully orchestrated series of shifts:

> (1) "Well, don't we fight like the devil? (2) Don't we do all that men can?" demanded the youth loudly.
>
> (3) He was secretly dumb-founded at this sentiment when it came from his lips. (4) For a moment his face lost its valour and he looked guiltily about him. (5) But no one questioned his right to deal in such words, and, presently, he recovered his air of courage. (6) He went on to repeat a statement he had heard going from group to group at the camp that morning. (7) "The brigadier said he never saw a new reg'ment fight the way we fought yesterday, didn't he?"
>
> (8) "And we didn't do better than many another reg'ment, did we?"
>
> (9) "Well, then, you can't say it's the army's fault, can you?" (II, 90–1)

The locus of sentences 1 and 2 is external: The youth says something so loudly that anyone, including our hypothetical observer, can hear it. Sentence 3 presents his internal reaction to the remark. Sentence 4 shifts back to the external – the appearance of his face – then shifts again. This second shift is to one of those merged perspectives: We are told how the protagonist looks from the outside and how he feels from the inside, though in this case outside and inside are virtually interchangeable, a guilty look being something that an observer might well detect on the basis of visual data alone. Sentence 5 also presents a merged view. At first sight the statement is entirely external: It is an observable fact that no one questioned his right to deal in such words and that he recovered his air of courage (an *air* of courage being a quasi-public "appearance" of the same type as a guilty look). But an observer relying on visual data alone would not conclude that no one questioned the speaker's right: He would merely note "behavioristically" that no one responded to the speaker's remark. To say that the auditors failed, in effect, to seize the opportunity is to interpret the silence – more precisely, to see it from the speaker's locus. Sentence 6 then leads to another external phenomenon – Fleming's concluding oral statements – but is itself internal insofar as a hypothetical observer would have no way of sharing with him the origin of the story about to be depicted. Sentences 7, 8, and 9, finally, constitute the youth's public statement, paralleling sentences 1 and 2. The full pattern, then, runs as follows: Sentences 1 and 2; external; 3, internal; 4, merger of external and internal; 5, merger of external and internal; 6, internal; 7, 8, and 9, external.

In a related pattern, externalization is achieved *through* the internal. The point of departure is Henry's habit of seeing himself as if he were apart from himself. The tendency emerges, for the first time, as he remembers the way he used to regard himself: "In visions, he had seen himself in many struggles. He had imagined people secure in the shadow of his eagle-eyed prowess. But awake he had regarded battles as crimson blotches on the pages of the past" (II, 5). From this preoccupation with a past image the youth moves toward an image of himself in the future, only to discover that his imagination no longer supplies the proper pictures: "He contemplated the lurking menaces of the future and failed in an effort to see himself standing stoutly in the midst of them" (II, 10). This is a positive failure, implying that the young soldier is becoming "demythologized." A later passage, which we have examined in another context, appears to confirm this sanguine view: "The youth awakened slowly. He came gradually back to a position from which he could regard himself. For moments, he had been scrutinizing his person in a dazed way as if he had never before seen himself" (II, 38). This can also be read as implying a new birth and thus an end to Fleming's habit of flashing glorious pictures of himself on the screen of an imagined future. But the opposite happens. Instead of transcending, Henry, imagining that he has met all the challenges war has to offer, slips back into the old pattern: "He went into an ecstasy of self-satisfation. . . . Standing as if apart from himself, he viewed the last scene. He perceived that the man who had fought thus was magnificent" (II, 39).

His former pictures of himself were the projections of a lad who had never experienced war; in such projections imagination necessarily predominated. And yet, although the later Fleming has acquired experience, he is as much as ever the creature of his imagination, for it is precisely on the basis of what he has actually undergone that the youth projects himself in the posture of a sublime hero. Certain possibilities of action, certain potential states of being, are open to him, and the "pictures" of himself that he sees are the visual investiture of these actions and states. If he does not experience the pictures as projections it is because he does not know that he initiates them; such images of himself, so far as he is concerned, *are* himself. The images flash before him separately and almost statically, like those projected by the Edison Kinetograph, which became a fixture of penny arcades soon after its introduction in the early 1890s: "Swift pictures of himself, apart, yet in himself, came to him – a blue desperate figure leading lurid charges with one knee forward and a broken blade high – a blue, determined figure standing before a crimson steel assault, getting calmly killed on a high place before the eyes of all" (II, 64). The youth, in other words, can watch his own field of vision in almost the same spectatorial way in which he watches a field of battle.

In the context of literary history Crane's technique looks forward, for Sherwood Anderson will also see imagination as a space open to invasion by images and thoughts. The protagonist of *Poor White* never thinks – thoughts "come" to him. But the process has already been described by the author of *The Red Badge of Courage:* "He wished to be alone with some new thoughts that had lately come to him" (II, 4; *cf.* II, 24). Thoughts can command the imagination that made them because that imagination does not *know* that it made them. Thoughts seem autonomous things with a force of their own: "Absurd ideas took hold upon him. He thought that he did not relish the landscape" (II, 24). One finds in thoughts, then, the same gap between appearance and reality that one finds in the world: There are the intentions you actually have and, quite separate from these, the intentions you think you have. The distinction *is* evident, of course, to the reader and to Crane. Yet the reader does not have equal access to the two separated poles, the apparent and the actual. Crane gives the apparent, and withholds the actual. He shows what Fleming believes he wished, and he hints that this belief does not accord with Fleming's underlying intention; but that intention stays hidden. Beyond the vantage point of the apparent, which we know to be illusory, there is only a sense of distance.

A passage near the end of a chapter brings together several of the patterns we have been discussing. The young soldier is considering the implications, for himself, if the Union Army should be victorious:

> Again he thought that he wished he was dead. He believed that he envied a corpse. Thinking of the slain, he achieved a great contempt for some of them as if they were guilty for thus becoming lifeless. They might have been killed by lucky chances, he said, before they had had opportunities to flee or before they had been really tested. Yet they would receive laurels from tradition. He cried out bitterly that their crowns were stolen and their robes of glorious memories were shams. However, he still said that it was a great pity he was not as they. (II, 67)

Although these thoughts flash before Fleming, as they did earlier, like a series of images across a field of vision, they are not as autonomous now because we are no longer "with" Fleming. We have been invited, instead, to an unveiling of the process through which the youth talks himself into his attitudes. We see that the pictures emanate from the very imagination that watches them. At the same time Crane reveals once more the distance between apparent intentions and actual ones, though without disclosing what the latter may be: Fleming *thought* that he *wished,* he *believed* that he *envied.*

The passage concerns, in other words, operations of will and strategies of persuasion: Having willed to believe certain things, Henry then attempts to demonstrate the self-evident nature of what is believed. The object I will is over there, separate from me. It is not something I create, but something that already exists. This is true not merely of things I desire in the material world, but also of objects existing solely in consciousness: "Thinking of the slain, he achieved a great contempt for some of them. . . ." To feel contempt is to experience an emotion intimately and viscerally, but to achieve it is to overcome a distance through the exertion of will – it is to win one's way, as across a battlefield, to a specified objective. This being the case, we are able to modify the view, suggested above, that the object of desire is a separate, pre-existing state. We can do this by comparing Henry's relation to contempt with his relation to his "images" of himself. Although he makes the pictures, and although he projects them before his own gaze, he does not regard them as his own productions. To his eyes they occur in the field of vision in the same manner as trees or flags. In a similar way he hypostatizes a state, called contempt, which is then regarded as a phenomenon entirely independent of himself. The object of desire – whether an image of oneself or a state – is a stabilizing thing, something one holds onto, in moments of crisis, for security. Awakening at the start of Chapter 14, Fleming sees himself surrounded with a motionless mass of men "pallid and in strange postures. His disordered mind interpreted the hall of the forest as a charnel place. He believed for an instant that he was in the house of the dead, and he did not dare to move lest these corpses start up, squalling and squawking. In a second, however, he achieved his proper mind . . ." (II, 80). That stabilizing entity, the proper mind, is the corollary of the contempt achieved in the earlier passage. Once the object of desire has been secured, the youth immediately moves, in both passages, to the stage of persuasion. The purpose of the move is to reinforce, by a kind of rhetorical pressure, the attitude arrived at: "He swore a complicated oath at himself." Here Henry "talks to himself," the better to hold himself to the proper course of action, whereas the strategy of the earlier passage is similar but more indirect: "They might have been killed by lucky chances, he *said*. . . . He *cried out* bitterly . . . he still *said* that it was a great pity. . . ." The statements read like remarks to an audience. But the audience has no existence apart from the youth himself. He is addressing, to no one in particular, *the things he needs to hear in order to justify the belief he has willed himself to adopt*.

His problem, at this early point in the narrative, is that his imaginings are sometimes too heady; He has not yet won his way to the actual. To do that would amount to demythologizing; it would mean an end to the magnifications, such as the gigantic colonel on the gigantic horse, with which that section of the book is adorned; and it would mean a greater effort to see other human beings as human beings – to face their faces, as it were. There is, eventually, some progress on both fronts. Although Fleming continues to indulge in his magnifications, he sometimes recognizes them for what they are. His progress toward seeing other human beings as human beings is a more complex issue. When close to a group one may view it as a collection of individual faces, while from far away it may seem a composite thing. But instead of perceiving the unity of the group – its collective purpose and praxis – one may perceive only an appearance to be measured against familiar conceptual models – drawn, for example, from the animal world: "It was now like one of those moving monsters with many feet" (II, 15). On the other hand, when Henry, in flight, imagines himself once more in the midst of the "others," he feels the impact of a truly collective human gaze: "Then, as if the heads were moved by one muscle, all the faces were turned toward him with wide, derisive grins. . . . He was a slang-phrase" (II, 68).

The final development of this pattern is direct, individual interpretation; gazing at a Confederate captive, "The youth could detect no expression that would allow him to believe that the other was giving a thought to his narrowed future, the pictured dungeons, perhaps, and starvations and brutalities, liable to the imagination. All to be seen was shame for captivity and regret for the right to antagonize" (II, 131). If this were the only pattern of development one could say that the youth had progressed from a "mythological," pseudoreligious view of things to a more naturalistic, more "human" conception. But the pattern is more complex than that. For the Henry Fleming who appears late in the book, between the moment when he sees the enemy's collective face and the face of the individual captive, is as mythically minded as the Henry Fleming of the opening chapters: As they fight, the soldiers are "like strange and ugly fiends jigging heavily in the smoke" (II, 124; *cf.* II, 129), and the eagle is seen to shed its static, heraldic quality and come alive in the flag, invigorating the young soldier's spirit and drawing him forward to conquest.

Later, Fleming's imagining begins to work in a different way; instead of giving form to his fears, his thoughts now help him to fight:

> The youth had centered the gaze of his soul upon that other flag. Its possession would be high pride. It would express bloody minglings, near blows. He had a gigantic hatred for those who made great difficulties and complications. They caused it to be as a craved treasure of mythology, hung amid tasks and contrivances of danger.
>
> He plunged like a mad horse at it. . . . It seemed there would shortly be an encounter of strange beaks and claws, as of eagles. (II, 129)

The difference between the two patterns of mythmaking springs from the difference between the Fleming who fights with himself early in the novel and the Fleming who fights the enemy later on. Although the imagination is much the same, its direction and its management are different; its mythmaking tendencies, entering into the service of fighting, have finally become vocational.

ASTONISHMENT

The relative brevity of Crane's chapters, sentences, and scenes is a corollary of his emphasis on the flash of astonishment, itself an aspect of his stress on sudden contrasts and shifts. His *unit of composition,* in other words, may be said to contribute as much to his impressionism and his expressionism as his use of colors or physical details. The small unit registers an immediate sharp imprint in a way that longer units (such as the sentences in Faulkner) do not. The moment of astonishment, by deepening this imprint, produces tableaux of wonder, of which the scene of the little man alone on the heights of the mesmeric mountain is an eminent example. In *The Red Badge of Courage* a tableau of this type occurs just after Henry flees the tattered man, another when he begins to get an overview of the war: "As he gazed around him, the youth felt a flash of astonishment at the blue, pure sky and the sun-gleamings on the trees and fields. It was surprising that nature had gone tranquilly on with her golden processes in the midst of so much devilment" (II, 38). The tableau, with a subtle force, records a particular brief state to be carried over into the next unit, where our sense of that state will be strengthened or qualified.

Crane weaves these moments of astonishment into a complex rhythm.

The youth first feels amazed, then the tattered man, "filled with wonder at the tall soldier" (II, 57), looks on "in gaping amazement" (II, 61); Henry, imagining the amazement another might feel, later feels amazement himself; amazement is then felt by a friend, but instead of rotating back to Henry it passes on to another man, then to a group: "During this moment of leisure they seemed all to be engaged in staring with astonishment at him" (II, 96; *cf.* II, 101).

Astonishment can become an all-absorbing, almost hypnotic state: "Awakening from his trance of observation, he turned and beheld the loud soldier" (II, 28). It is not memories that freeze you in this immobile dream-like state, it is the waking world of events, which take possession of you in two basic ways. If you identify with them, you get swept up – not until the events are over do you come to know your role in them. But if you do not identify with others – if the astonishing things always happen to someone else – you become a prisoner of your own detachment.

Within the preceding passage, the trance and the moment of awakening are brought into a single sentence, while later they are stretched out between the end of one chapter and the beginning of another. Thus, at the end of Chapter 5 Fleming feels his flash of astonishment at the blue, pure sky, but does not wake up until the beginning of the next chapter: "The youth awakened slowly. . . . So it was all over at last. The supreme trial had passed" (II, 39). Henry does not "wake," in other words, to a new awareness, but merely enters another phase of illusion.

Much later Henry is astonished, for example, at the illusory ideas in his own mind and later still he believes the regiment's efforts will "spread consternation and amazement for miles" (II, 128). Astonishment is also a quality "out there" in the world: There is amazement in the regiment as a whole, in the speed with which the sound of artillery spreads or the men get dirty, in the feelings of an enemy prisoner toward his own wound. The "sharing" of astonishment and amazement, then, is one of the paths Henry follows on his journey from isolation to fraternity. In the same connection, he wakes up to those around him; then, although in the battle heroics of Chapter 17 he forgets himself without remembering his comrades, he later feels a solidarity with the rest of his regiment. This process, frequently interrupted as it is, may be described as an irregular rhythm in which awareness advances, then recedes. It is not merely that the youth must become aware; he must become aware again and again, for between the moments of awareness come periods of oblivion: "By this struggle, he had over-come obstacles which he had admitted to be mountains. . . . And he had not been aware of the process. He had slept and, awakening, found himself a knight" (II, 97). Although the awakening ends this particular battle trance, in a sense it begins another one, for Henry's comfort in the gaze of the others is too full of prideful ease; it is less difficult to wake up than to stay awake – to meet an astonishing world with unclouded eyes – and that is one of the reasons why the astonishment-driving process of coming to awareness occurs so often in the book.

DIRECTION

Any positing is in principle directional, as is any opposition. An attacking unit moves its position toward the position of the defending unit, which directs itself in turn toward the attacking unit; if the former repulses the latter it may then take up the attack, forcing the attacker to reverse direction. The rhythm of Crane's novel largely consists in just such seesaws of attack, counterattack, and retreat; the contrast between movement and immobility; and in movements so random as to seem directionless.

If the revelation that occurs at the opening of the book derives from the directionality of withdrawal, as the cold passes away and the fogs retire, a pattern of reverse direction is established immediately thereafter as Jim Conklin goes off in one direction only to come directly back. Crane's ironic economy is such that the purport of the message Jim carries is not only directional but wrongly directional: The army will not go way up the river, cut across, and come around behind the army, as he proposes. Revealing the error of the message is itself a reversal of direction, for that matter, since the truth is that the army is not to move, for now, in any direction.

As soon as Henry has heard the debate over Jim's rumor he himself withdraws; temporally, his ensuing reflections then move in two rhythmic waves, first toward the past, with its memories of home, then toward the future. These approximate a miniature of impending battle scenes in which neither of the previous temporal directions dominates; yet neither does a sense of the present: "As his imagination went forward to a fight, he saw hideous possibilities. He contemplated the lurking menaces of the future and failed in an effort to see himself standing stoutly in the midst of them. He re-called his visions of broken-bladed glory but, in the shadow of the impending tumult, he suspected them to be impossible pictures" (II, 10). The early tension in the story comes, of course, from Henry's worry that fear will drive him in the direction of retreat: " 'Did you ever think you might run yourself, Jim?' " (II, 12). The youth does not take the direction he fears, however, until he has been thoroughly schooled in confusion: "For a moment, in the great clamor, he was like a proverbial chicken. He lost the direction of safety. Destruction threatened him from all points" (II, 41). The scene in the forest chapel, after Henry has indeed taken the direction of defeat, furnishes a respite that suddenly turns into a confrontation with death.

Terrified by the sight of a corpse, the youth retreats in such a way as to invoke a correlative theme, pursuit: "The dead man and the living man exchanged a long look. Then, the youth cautiously put one hand behind him and brought it against a tree. Leaning upon this, he retreated, step by step, with his face still toward the thing. He feared that if he turned his back, the body might spring up and stealthily pursue him" (II, 48).

The imagination of pursuit produces a fear of being overtaken that foreshadows the fear that the mortally wounded Conklin will express: "So he displayed the zeal of an insane sprinter in his purpose to keep them in the rear. There was a race" (II, 42). Henry's relation to the tattered man is itself a kind of slow race, with Henry trying at first to pull away from the man, only to find himself following the wounded Conklin; soon Jim is running, followed by both Henry and the tattered man, who has overtaken him: "He and the tattered man began a pursuit. There was a singular race" (II, 56). The direction of the race and its destination, called simply "the place for which he had struggled" (II, 57), are determined by death, which speaks, as we have seen, in gesture. But when Henry turns in rage in the direction of the battlefield and shakes his fist, life speaks in gesture, too:

> The youth turned, with sudden, livid rage, toward the battlefield. He shook his fist. He seemed about to deliver a philippic.
>
> "Hell – "
>
> The red sun was pasted in the sky like a wafer. (II, 58)

Anticlimactically, and yet dramatically, the wafer makes its appearance after the action has ceased, and on a plane that transcends. This color in the sky is what Henry does not know, but what exactly *is* there to know?

Osborn was the first to uncover the apposite passage in Kipling: "The fog was driven apart for a moment, and the sun shone, a blood-red wafer, on the water." Colbert found two similar passages in which the sun strikes a puddle and steel, respectively, producing red discs on each surface. Marlowe discovered that a wafer was a type of artillery primer used in the Civil War; meanwhile Cazemajou proposed that Crane had intuitively come up with the same symbol for sacrifice that the Aztecs employed.[24]

In analyzing Crane's image, Osborn points to the old practice of sealing envelopes with a wafer of wax. Stallman responds that the sealant was glue (in which case we have pasted glue). More importantly, of course, Stallman identifies Crane's image as the wafer of Communion, setting off a chain of reactions, negative in the main, that may never end. La France, rejecting this sacramental reading, states that "the use of 'wafer' and 'pasted' implies the seal at the end of a legal document and thus suggests completion, finality. . . ."[25] Further meanings emerge when additional features are taken into account, such as the relation of the final sentence to Henry. As suggested above, this color in the sky combines with other instances of the same color to form a metonymic chain. In the present case, the closest red, in feeling, is probably Henry's red rage, though his red sickness of battle may contribute to the resonance. A second feature is the relation between the dynamic that informs most of the chapter and the stasis that concludes it. Henry walks in the same direction with Jim, then Jim runs and Henry runs after him with the tattered man, then Jim performs his dance of death. Turning in the direction of the battlefield, Henry proceeds to gesture and cry out his word, then finally appears the sun, which goes nowhere, heads in no direction, a shift in perspective that suddenly terminates the directional dynamics.

This is the kind of tension that the Expressionists understood. Set to music, it would consist in a torsion of rhythmic accents: *crescendo, decrescendo, fortissimo, sforzando-piano*. For a visual equivalent, a Paul Klee might send one limning arrow zigging up just before sending it zagging down; this is what in his *Pedagogical Sketchbook* he calls an angry line (resembling a drawing of jagged peaks). The effect Crane achieves, temporally, is disjunctive. Carried forward at a rapid pace through movement after movement, in a continuous line of time, the narrative suddenly turns dissynchronous. When the sun appears, already pasted, an anterior time overtakes the events. In dynamics the effect resembles the moment in Wordsworth's *The Prelude* when the skater, suddenly braking, feels the universe overtake him. The difference is that Wordsworth shows the connectedness between his protagonist and the universe: He feels all things in his very being and knows that he feels; skater and universe are going the same direction. Crane by contrast presents what his protagonist does not know. If there is a connection between him and the wafer sun, it is made through the metonymic process discussed above, which is to say through that always present agent, the reader. Other agencies come and go, and what fascinates here is the manner of their coming and going. As the chapter nears its end, Henry becomes the principal agent, replacing Jim. It is Henry who turns his attention in the direction of the battlefield, it is Henry who shakes his fist and seems about to deliver a philippic; and if it is Henry who then fails to, it is because he is now no more an agent. With the final sentence a new agency appears – that is to say, whatever power was great enough to paste the very sun in the sky – and as quickly disappears. As though to take away what has scarcely been given, the passive construction "was pasted" barely hints at the nature of the agency before shifting attention to the wafer.

The power of the crux consists in the fact that there is no obvious ground for excluding any of the meanings presented here, just as there is none for fixing on only one. The legitimacy of multiple meanings is supported by current theories of overdetermination, polyphony or polysemy, which in essence recognize that discourse has a right to its own richness. The interpreter has at least two rights: to decide which construings are intelligible, and to posit that such and such a meaning is stronger than some other. The latter procedure of course is no better than the criterion on which it leans (e.g., by the criterion of influence Osborn's recourse to Kipling is stronger than Cazemajou's to the Aztecs). When no hierarchy can be established, when the only thing is to stir the ingredients and savor their blending, we arrive at undecidability. Thus Derrida lays out a series of ways in which to understand *pharmakon* and cognate terms, elucidating each in detail but without deciding for the primacy of any.

It is fair to ask at this point whether Crane's ensemble of meanings aims as a whole at some larger meaning. Emblazoned in the text as the sun is emblazoned in the sky, *mutatis mutandis,* Crane's conceit is in its own way not only arresting but arrested. As in his use of the preposition "at," the last topic in this section, Crane refuses to satisfy the reader's desire for something simple to grasp. He tells the reader what the character does not know without telling the reader what to do with that knowledge. In the chapter itself, as we have seen, doing has effectively ceased. Henry's word is past, there is no philippic, and the sun itself is entirely passive.

But there is still the wafer, to whose specific nature we may now return. Significantly, all the candidates for the wafer's material correlate have something important in common, and that is a flat surface. On the same roster belongs the red badge itself, insofar as it signifies a bandage; Crane was also familiar with the red-patch insignia worn by troops under General Kearney.[26] Now a surface is, as it were, two-faced. One face is a blank, a flat and "superficial" thing that one does not penetrate because nothing lies behind it. Yet the other face of the surface looks precisely in that direction, toward the deep and the hidden: How do we know that a surface is flat, a mere integument, if we do not experience it as "other" than depth or hiddenness? A surface is an oxymoron, a both/and whose function is to reveal concealingly or to conceal revealingly. That earlier perspectivist Søren Kierkegaard deploys the both/and as an instrument of irony, a dialectical pairing that, without the *Aufhebung* of faith, leads nowhere. This is basically what Crane does too. Like a sublime version of a creature known for fence-sitting, it turns its mug toward a larger meaning and its wump towards undecidability.

A different kind of unknowing is experienced in battle, where confusion reigns: "Presently, men were running hither and thither, in all ways. The artillery bouncing, forward, rearward, and on the flank made jumble of ideas of direction" (II, 70). For Henry worse is yet to come, and the wound is the reason. He receives it in quest of knowledge, not intelligence about this or that direction but something more fundamental: The question he puts to the man who strikes him with a rifle is simply "Why – why – " (II, 70). Experience reduces to absurdity all his attempts to reason, and, fittingly, he takes his wound in that supposed seat of reason, the head. If there was much he did not know before, there is even more now. His very relation to the earth is in doubt: "He did not know the direction of the ground" (II, 95). In their open boat four men could be comparably ignorant, it would seem: None of them knew the color of the sky. Yet none of them needed to. In an open boat the color of the sky is a grand irrelevance, whereas knowing the direction of the ground is of first importance to Henry, as his sudden loss of balance attests. It is only when he regains his sense of its direction that he can proceed to safety.

It is largely through the lieutenant that Henry knows which direction is which, the officer being often the point of reference by which Henry orients this or that position and action: "The youth's eyes had instantly turned in the direction of the awakened and agitated lieutenant and he had seen the haze of treachery disclosing a body of soldiers of the enemy" (II, 113). Leaping at, springing at, and pulling at now lead to the achievement of goals. The men do get over the fences and, climactically, the youth not only pulls at the flag he desires but takes possession of it, setting an example for Wilson's efforts a little later. The object of desire is no longer, as if by definition, something remote and withheld, it is something one can actually reach.

PAIRINGS

The contrasts, juxtapositions, and reversals in Crane's war novel shape a symmetrical structure one is tempted to term architectonic.[27] Structure is also, to use a more dynamic term, a rhythm of expectations and resolutions that come and go with a certain, though rarely predictable, regularity. Crucial to this is Crane's use of pairings, which can be divided into those involving relations between enemy soldiers, on the one hand, and relations between soldiers who are on the same side, on the other hand. In point of fact, just as there are friendly relations between soldiers on opposing sides, so are there antagonistic relations between soldiers on the same side. Where the latter are concerned, nevertheless, a pattern of struggles between fellow fighters gradually gives way to such struggles against the enemy as facilitate the bonding of fellow fighters into a more or less spontaneous fraternity.[28]

In this respect, Crane's war novel represents an advance over *George's Mother,* where there bonding always feels forced. The gatherings presided over by Bleecker are neither spontaneous nor particularly brotherly, except in the gladhanding vein. In *The Red Badge of Courage,* by contrast, bondings are as genuinely fraternal as they are spontaneous. Military purpose and military organization help to explain why. When fighting for your life and the lives of those beside you, acting in concert is an obligation to be met on the instant. But military purpose and organization don't explain everything. There is also the question of the author's own desire for fraternity, or at least of his willingness to test fraternal ideas against the pressure of actualities. This is clearly a recurring theme in the early tales and sketches, in the Bowery novels, in pieces like "An Experiment in Misery," in the later, major tales, in the letters, and in his saga of the Civil War. How the testing comes about in the latter is itself a long tale.

It will not be necessary to review here the entire sequence of pairings between enemy soldiers, beginning with the implicit conflict of the opening scene. As prominent as these are, they do not contribute to the unfolding of the protagonist's character to the same degree as his relations to his comrades. An exception is the competitive pairing of the youth with the color-sergeant and with the rival color-bearer; but the key moments of contacts are so intimately bound up with the relations that prevail just then between the youth and Wilson, and to the relations of both to the lieutenant, that it would be more profitable to consider them in the latter context.

The initial pairing of the youth and his older friend Jim provides a norm by which to measure the former. It is not that Jim does very much in a strictly military vein; his moral stature, rather, accounts for the dynamic in his pairing with his younger friend. Between their initial pairing and their reunion Henry's pairing with the dead man in the forest chapel is interposed: "He was being looked at by a dead man who was seated with his back against a column-like tree. The corpse was dressed in a uniform that once had been blue but was now faded to a melancholy shade of green. The eyes, staring at the youth, had changed to the dull hue to be seen on the side of a dead fish" (II, 47). That this confrontation occurs in "a forest chapel," and that Henry flees from it in adumbration of the flight that becomes one of his chief moral burdens, makes all the more central the renewal of Henry's pairing with Jim as the latter dies. Crucial too is the pairing of the youth and the tattered man:

> After a time, he turned to the youth. "Where yeh hit, ol' boy?" he asked in a brotherly tone.
>
> The youth felt instant panic at this question although at first its full import was not borne in upon him.
>
> "What?" he asked.
>
> "Where yeh hit?" repeated the tattered man.
>
> "Why," began the youth, "I – I – that is – why – I – "

> He turned away suddenly and slid through the crowd. His brow was heavily flushed, and his fingers were picking nervously at one of his buttons. He bended his head and fastened his eyes studiously upon the button as if it were a little problem.
>
> The tattered man looked after him in astonishment. (II, 53)

The scene of Jim's death, witnessed as it is by his friend and by the tattered man, may be viewed as an overlapping of pairings, with Henry as the connecting figure. The point is that Henry's bonding with Jim, combined with the guilty feelings the tattered man has exacerbated, turn the screw of emotional pressure about as far as it can go. Hence the almost grotesque intensity of Crane's detailed description, reminiscent of sensational effects in the Gothic novel, but also reminiscent of the preoccupation with bodily death in medieval accounts.

Although the chapter break relieves the pressure briefly, it resumes in the pages that follow as Crane, working repetitive structure for all it's worth, sets the tattered man on the path to death, accompanied by thoughts of the latter's friend, Tom Jamieson. Thinking Henry is Tom, the tattered man says: " 'Look-a-here, now, Tom Jamieson – now – it ain't – ' " but "The youth went on. Turning at a distance he saw the tattered man wandering about helpless in the fields" (II, 62). The other key pairings are the youth and Wilson, the youth and the regimental color-sergeant, the youth and the enemy color-bearer, Wilson and the enemy color-bearer, the youth and the lieutenant, and Wilson and the lieutenant.

The pairing of the youth and the loud soldier is at first antagonistic. When the latter doubts that he himself will run from battle, and Henry retorts that his friend is not the bravest man in the world, Wilson stalks off in a huff; the youth "felt alone in space when his injured comrade had disappeared. . . . He was a mental out-cast" (II, 20). Later, reconsidering his friend's character, he concludes, as we have seen, that Wilson has developed confidence, a development that could hardly stand in sharper contrast to the state of the protagonist. In Chapter 15, Henry, paired with his friend for the third time, savors the advantage that the possession of Wilson's packet of personal effects can offer, should the latter ask dangerous questions. "The youth felt immensely superior to his friend but he inclined to condescension. He adopted toward him an air of patronizing good-humour" (II, 86). Having finally returned the packet, having failed to lord it over his friend only because he can think of nothing clever to say, Henry leaves strategic matters behind so as to reconstitute his being on a higher plane: "After this incident, and as he reviewed the battle-pictures he had seen, he felt quite competent to return home and make the hearts of the people glow with stories of war" (II, 87).

Henry's pairing with the tattered man, then more briefly with the cheery-voiced man, makes the renewed pairing with Wilson a tough test, especially since the latter has grown so much in stature. It is a test that Henry, in a failure of fraternity, is unable at the present juncture to pass.

At this stage of his career, evidently – and in this novel, certainly – Crane is intrigued by the distance between acting and thinking. As thinker, Henry can scarely deliberate on anything but himself, and when he thinks of others he thinks of them in relation to himself and his problems. What enables the thinker to become active is, ironically, military discipline, and in particular the compulsion represented by command. Like his comrades, the youthful soldier acts, forgetful of himself, when compelled to follow orders that immediately trigger behavior. The state that the actor then enters borders upon, if it does not pass over into, a state of possession not unlike the Dionysian state that Crane's contemporary Nietzsche had begun to explore in *The Birth of Tragedy out of the Spirit of Music,* first published the year after the American's birth. If I have shifted from speaking of action to speaking of behavior, it is because the distinction falls into an area of ambiguity that would seem in principle, in Burke's terms, unresolvable (or, in Derrida's, undecidable).

The pairing of the youth and his comrade is meanwhile taking a more affirmative turn: "The youth and his friend had a small scuffle over the flag. 'Give it t'me." 'No – let me keep it.' Each felt satisfied with the other's possession of it but each felt bound to declare by an offer to carry the emblem, his willingness to further risk himself" (II, 110). Near the end of Chapter 23 Crane positions the term "rival" before the enemy color-bearer whose chief antagonist is not Fleming but Wilson: The fraternal bonding has now reached the point that Henry can be replaced by his friend. "The youth's friend went over the obstruction in a tumbling heap and sprang at the flag as a panther at prey. He jerked it, and wrenching it free, swung up its red brilliancy with a mad cry of exultation even as the color-bearer, gasping, lurched over in a final throe and stiffening convulsively turned his dead face to the ground" (II, 130).

Chapter 20 widens the canvas, presenting a more general picture of conflictual pairings, though the presentation still depends on the centrality of Henry's perspective; and even a general picture may be expressed in particularities: "The two bodies of troops exchanged blows in the manner of a pair of boxers" (II, 114). Boxing suggests the formality of a game whose participants play arbitrary and inflexible roles. Soldiers play similar roles insofar as the rules they play under force them into very restricted kinds of behavior. They are not, however, the rules of the players themselves, but the rules of the game, and what the game amounts to is something that no one on the board, so to speak, can know. The soldiers in the ranks and their superiors may be pieces whose moves are directed by players called generals, or by gods, or by chance. But what we see of generals in the novel does not demonstrate their power to control; and ubiquitous chance is the player that no other player can control. None of these considerations speaks immediately, of course, to the implied analogy between the military fight and a prizefight. But the latter looms against the entire background of war, which is inscrutable not because no one plays by the rules but because no one knows what they are. In the chapter that follows, participants in the battle bring their perspectives to bear on what has occurred:

> The youth spoke soothingly to his comrade: "Well, we both did good. I'd like to see the fool what'd say we both didn't do as good as we could."
>
> " 'A course, we did," declared the friend stoutly. "An' I'd break th' feller's neck if he was as big as a church. But we're all right, anyhow, for I heared one feller say that we two fit th' best in th' reg'ment an' they had a great argument 'bout it." (II, 119)

In this bonding of the two friends the lieutenant plays a crucial role. When Chapter 19 enters a state of suspension, as the men of the regiment confront each other face to face, effectively hypnotized, it is the lieutenant who rouses them and, interestingly, it is Henry's friend who is credited with first responding: "The friend of the youth aroused. Lurching suddenly forward and dropping to his knees, he fired an angry shot at the persistent woods" (II, 106–7). In this way Wilson becomes, in a way that he had never been, a role model for Henry while serving as an exemplar of prowess for the lieutenant.

The subsequent pairing of the lieutenant and Henry is more intense, more protracted, and for a time more hostile. Seizing the youth by the arm, the lieutenant roars at him to advance, just before his intention disappears in the blue haze of curses.

> The private felt a sudden unspeakable indignation against his officer. He wrenched fiercely and shook him off.
>
> "Come on yourself, then," he yelled. There was a bitter challenge in his voice. (II, 108)

Ignoring the insubordination, the lieutenant accepts the challenge and the antagonists are suddenly paired shoulder to shoulder against the enemy. Even more significantly, they are joined by Wilson, with whom they form a threesome of leadership whose combined voices now command in lieu of the voice of their commander.

Henry has, of course, his own peculiar reasons for fighting with abandon: The man who had called the soldiers of his regiment mule drivers. Throughout the battles, this antagonistic side of motivation provides a background, usually implicit, while emphasis falls on the formative, fraternal side. Perhaps the crux occurs when Henry puts his resentment behind him and embraces all that his pairing with the lieutenant promises: "Between him and the lieutenant, scolding and near to losing his mind with rage, there was felt a subtle fellowship and equality. They supported each other in all manner of hoarse, howling protests" (II, 111–12).

There are at least three ways, all closely related, of putting into perspective the pairings with the lieutenant. First, the value structure of military command is assimilated to that of martial valor, which is to say that the narrative stresses not so much the officer's rank as his particular way of being human in a battlefield context. By his example of courage and determination he inspires others; that rank alone does not suffice is indicated by his recourse to argument, swearing, shouting, and wrestling. Second, the initial, vertical relation of officer to men becomes horizontal. By the rules of military organization the officer stands at the apex of a triangle of which Fleming and Wilson are poles of the base; but by Crane's rules of pairing the triangle tips over onto its side as the three men – Henry, Wilson, and Hasbrouck – unite in a common front of leadership. A third perspective discerns in the pairings with the lieutenant a signal instance of fraternity. If only for a time, Henry Fleming forgets himself, and the same may presumably be said of the lieutenant and Wilson. Essentially undifferentiated, the three men are equalized in the manner of warriors in ancient Greece. On the authority of Hesiod, "all rivalry, all *eris,* presupposes a relationship of equality: Competition can take place only among peers."[29] If any of the three men in Crane's alignment are to be deemed first among equals, the honor would probably go to the enlisted men, each of whom takes possession of that symbolic grand prize, a flag.

ENDINGS

American fictions are slightly notorious for their endings. Famously and problematically, *The Scarlet Letter* leaves it to the reader to decide what has truly happened, while *Adventures of Huckleberry Finn* drifts into tedious comedy and moral confusion. Ambrose Bierce's "An Occurrence at Owl Creek Bridge" reveals that the escape with which it appears to end is an illusion, the protagonist having just died. American fictions favor closures that seem reluctant to close; like the manifest destiny of Robert Frost's "The Gift Outright," they claim the privilege of "vaguely realizing westward," and if possible might do so forever. Such open endings suggest a kind of negative capability. For the fine abstinence of an imagination that can dispense with "irritable reaching after fact and reason," the reward must be uncertainties, mysteries, and doubts. Such an imagination lays claim thereby to the positive of this negative, which is a sense of freedom.

That the conclusion of *The Red Badge of Courage* is somehow problematic has become a commonplace of criticism, and for good reason. It is, for one thing, anticlimactic.[30] The main action having transpired, the final chapter once more explores Henry's reflections on what has happened and what may yet happen. The chapter also illustrates Crane's fascination with repetition. At the outset of the novel he presents a scene of waiting; in the conclusion he presents another. While it is true that movements occur in the latter, they are casual and remote, details of the battle's aftermath. The essence of the scene is summed up in an early sentence: "They waited, watching" (II, 132). Repetition takes another form as the unit heads back in the direction of the river, going the way they have just come. Repetitive, too, is the drift of Henry's reflections, which also begin in a manner reminiscent of the opening scene: "Gradually his brain emerged from the clogged clouds and at last he was enabled to more closely comprehend himself and circumstance" (II, 133).

As he remembers his flight from battle and the tattered man, Henry's conscience sends him on twists and turns, but he manages in the end to exonerate himself, prompting the reader to wonder how much progress the private has made. The original manuscript indicates frequent relapses and overall regression, whereas the Appleton text, which most editors have favored, often gives Henry the benefit of the doubt. Rejecting the Appleton version, Henry Binder revivifies the original manuscript, arguing for the effect that their inclusion produces.[31] It will suffice here to record that first-stage cuts in the manuscript involve interior monologues in which Henry inveighs against various cosmic powers such as nature and fate and God. Second-stage deletions also remove interior monologues and newly positive reflections on the world: "There was a slowly developeing [*sic*] conviction that in all his red speeches he had been ridiculously mistaken. Nature was a fine thing moving with a magnificent justice. The world was fair and wide and glorious. The sky was kind, and smiled tenderly, full of encouragement, upon him" (II, 308).

A weightier issue for an editor is what to do with Chapter 12, which the editor of the Virginia edition relegates to an appendix. In Chapter 10 Henry, who has just witnessed the death of Jim, hears the tattered man speak of his own lost friend, Tom Jamieson, thinking Henry, as we have seen, is that friend. Fear of exposure dominates the chapter that follows, which ends with Henry imagining that everyone will regard him as a slang-phrase. Chapter 12, which surpasses the final chapter in the length of the meditations it contains, serves two main purposes. One is to round off the preceding chapters, producing a symmetry of twelve chapters to match that of the succeeding twelve. The second office of Chapter 12 is to foreshadow what Henry amounts to in the end; the chapter is, in other words, an early "conclusion" of which the actual conclusion thus became a kind of sequel.

The first conclusion underlines Henry's egotism:

> It was always clear to the youth that he was entirely different from other men; that his mind had been cast in a unique mold. Hence laws that might be just to the ordinary man, were, when applied to him, peculiar and galling outrages. Minds, he said, were not made all with one stamp and colored green. He was of no general pattern. It was not right to measure his acts by a world-wide standard. (II, 139)

On the other hand, the youth is capable of insight. In the forest chapel he had grossly misread what he saw, deriving reassurance from things that he took for signs but were simply things. Now, like the correspondent in "The Open Boat," he knows the color of nature's intentions: There are none. Intentionality is a human faculty. Thus Henry can think: "He still distinctly felt that he was arrayed against the universe but he believed now that there was no malice in the vast breasts of his space-filling foes. It was merely law, not merciful to the individual; but just, to a system" (II, 139). The tenor of this thinking is echoed in the manuscript version of the final chapter after Henry tries again, in thought, to escape from his guilt: "But the sky would forget. It was true, he admitted, that in the world it was the habit to cry devil at persons who refused to trust what they could not trust, but he thought that perhaps the stars dealt differently. The imperturbable sun shines on insult and worship" (II, 107). The Appleton text then reads: "A spectre of reproach came to him," omitting the introductory clause in the manuscript: "As the youth was thus fraternizing with nature" (II, 378). The sardonic force of the clause throws a skeptical light on the reasoning. It is not that Henry errs in deeming nature to be a system unto itself, it is simply that this is another rationalization.

The two versions of the final chapter differ most with respect to Jimmie Rogers, the friend who had been stricken at the beginning of Chapter 18. "When their eyes first encountered him there was a sudden halt as if they feared to go near. He was thrashing about in the grass, twisting his shuddering body into many strange postures. He was screaming loudly. This instant's hesitation seemed to fill him with a tremendous, fantastic contempt and he damned them in shrieked sentences" (II, 99).

A family resemblance based on interconnecting names brings together Henry's friend Jim, who is a "jim-dandy" (II, 59, 60); the tattered man's friend Jamieson; Jim, the friend of Henry; Jack, the friend of the tattered man; and Jimmie Rogers, the friend of both Henry and Henry's friend Wilson. Seven chapters after Jimmie is wounded, as the manuscript version of the novel proceeds through its final phase, Jimmie makes his last appearance. Since Appleton omits the passage, it will be unfamiliar to many readers. It occurs just after Henry watches the procession of his marshaled acts:

> His friend, too, seemed engaged with some retrospection for he suddenly gestured and said: "Good Lord!"
>
> "What?" asked the youth.
>
> "Good Lord!" repeated his friend. "Yeh know Jimmie Rogers? Well, he – gods, when he was hurt I started t' git some water fer'im an', thunder, I aint seen 'im from that time 'til this. I clean forgot what I – say, has anybody seen Jimmie Rogers?"
>
> "Seen 'im? No! He's dead," they told him.

Wilson's reaction to this news recalls Henry's reaction to the death of Jim: "His friend swore" (II, 313). The passage that follows then makes a pointed distinction between the attitudes of Wilson and Fleming. Following "His friend swore," we read: "But the youth, regarding his procession of memory, felt gleeful and unregretting, for, in it, his public deeds were paraded in great and shining prominence. . . . He spent delightful minutes viewing the gilded images of memory" (II, 133–4). A mere juxtaposition between Wilson's caring and Fleming's indifference would have shown well enough that fraternity, where the latter is concerned, has faded. But attributing to the youth glee, pleasure, and delight makes the indifference more repugnant. That could be why the passage about Rogers does not appear in the Appleton text and why the original twelfth chapter doesn't either – Crane may simply have thought he was handling his hero too roughly. In any case, other passages in the original manuscript operate in the same circular way, following the routes of rationalization that the protagonist has taken in Chapter 12. One passage, however, only the first sentence of which appears in the Appleton text, works to Henry's advantage:

> Yet gradually he mustered force to put the sin at a distance. And then he regarded it with what he thought to be great calmness. At last, he concluded that he saw in it quaint uses. He exclaimed that its importance in the aftertime would be great to him if it even succeeded in hindering the workings of his egotism. It would make a sobering balance. . . . He would be a man.
>
> This plan for the utilization of a sin did not give him complete joy but it was the best sentiment he could formulate under the circumstances and when it was combined with his successes, or public deeds, he knew that he was quite contented. (II, 135)

The second paragraph is at once cautious and detached, perhaps too much so; omitting it scarcely diminishes the narrative, especially when one considers that later passages, while still conveying a sense of restraint, do the same job with greater verve. Consider the following, in which Henry makes his second emergence: "He was emerged from his struggles, with a large sympathy for the machinery of the universe. With his new eyes, he could see that the secret and open blows which were being dealt about the world with such heavenly lavishness were in truth blessings. It was a deity laying about him with bludgeon of correction" (II, 135). The implicit analogy between the world of war and the wrathful god of the Old Testament is not earned, it is merely hypostatized: Henry sounds here like the seminary student he just was, ready to tidy up the chaos of war in the same way that he tidies up his personal failings. There evidently remains the task of yoking this new philosophical position to his previously established attitude toward nature. But the task cannot be done. In accordance with Henry's putative growth in stature, the role of nature must be construed anew, notwithstanding that the new position does not jibe either with the previous position or with the image of the bludgeoning deity: "He beheld that he was tiny but not inconsequent to the sun" (II, 13).

These passages are hard on Henry. Chapter 12 portrays an egotist who will justify his ways at any cost and the conclusion suggests that while the private has made some progress he may not be much better tomorrow than he is today. In the last analysis, excluding Chapter 12 from the published text may not detract much, however, from the reader's experience. The chapter is more abstract than is usual in Crane and also more static. Though it does tell us something about the protagonist, we probably know him well enough from the pages that were not held back from publication. The issue, finally, is one of degree; how much if at all does the chapter improve the novel? In my judgment it does not improve it enough to warrant inclusion.

The manuscript version of the conclusion is another matter, for the passage contrasting Henry's reaction to the death of Jimmie Rogers to Wilson's reaction makes a difference. Leaving it out puts Henry in a much better light, a situation that his editors may well have desired and that Crane could have. But its omission makes the ending of the novel even more equivocal, and it is already equivocal enough. Moreover, leaving the passage out eliminates a dramatic contrast between Henry's reaction to the death of the first Jim and his reaction to the death of the second.

In any case some of the passages that help to close the chapter in both versions are strong in their own right and deserving of attention:

> (1) So it came to pass that as he trudged from the place of blood and wrath, his soul changed. (2) He came from hot ploughshares to prospects of clover tranquility and it was as if hot ploughshares were not. (3) Scars faded as flowers. (II, 135)

Circularity of structure is reinforced by (1), which embodies the same basic design as a sentence in the opening chapter: "Once a certain tall soldier developed virtues and went resolutely to wash a shirt" (II, 3).

Although "once" recalls the "Once upon a time" of fairy tales, just as "So it came to pass" recalls the Bible, the main task of both sentences is to telescope time radically: In an instant a soldier develops virtues, when in fact such development would normally be very protracted, and just as suddenly the soul of another soldier changes. This is what Aristotle means by "a thing improbable and yet possible," as against "a probable impossibility," which he holds to be preferable in art (*Poetics,* XXV). While it is possible that the soul of Henry Fleming changed in the manner indicated, the context makes it not only improbable but highly improbable; any other assumption undercuts the irony, which the sentences that follow carefully reinforce. The future moves into the foreground in (2) as Henry envisages not tranquility but prospects of tranquility. The second clause, however, does not depend on that temporal orientation. Entirely hypothetical, it applies neither to the present nor to the past. It does not apply to the past because no one can reasonably deny that hot ploughshares did exist in the form of battling swords. It does not apply to the present because it has no power to derealize their existence, which is just what it tries to do. The "as if" says more about Henry's present state, in other words, than it does about the world in which it transpires.

With (3) the circularity of the paragraph itself becomes manifest, for only a temporality that permits a soul to change quickly permits scars to fade quickly too, in the manner of flowers. This telescoping of time reduplicates on a smaller scale the design of the opening sentence and fairly exemplifies Crane's penchant for anticlimax.

> It rained. The procession of weary soldiers became a bedraggled train, despondent and muttering, marching with churning effort, in a trough of liquid brown mud under a low, wretched sky. Yet the youth smiled, for he saw that the world was a world for him though many discovered it to be made of oaths and walking-sticks. He had rid himself of the red sickness of battle. The sultry night-mare was in the past. He had been an animal blistered and sweating in the heat and pain of war. He turned now with a lover's thirst to images of tranquil skies, fresh meadows, cool brooks; an existence of soft and eternal peace.
>
> Over the river a golden ray of sun came through the hosts of leaden rain clouds. (II, 135)

Sentence three was originally the last. Oaths, of which the novel is full, suggest that for some the hard facts of life are too hard – all these "many" can do is expostulate, possibly brandishing their walking-sticks, which are dispensable props for the likes of the world-accepting Henry. A connection between the lieutenant and walking-sticks disappears from the Appleton text. This could reflect a desire to avoid confusion, since Henry has followed the lieutenant's leadership, whereas walking-sticks now are reduced to furnishing the world that the "many" discover. The omission of the final one-sentence paragraph means that the "second" ending of the novel coincided with what stands in Appleton as the penultimate paragraph. This paragraph deserves a closer look.

As the rain falls and the soldiers move, the scene comes to resemble the opening of the novel, with "long troughs of liquid mud"; "procession" echoes the procession of memory earlier in the chapter; the marching men remind the reader of the marching of Henry's remembered "performances"; while "tranquil skies" metonymically follows through on clover tranquility. From near the middle of the paragraph to the end of the text the youth attempts to synthesize various perspectives into a harmonious and reassuring whole. He meets with some success: Coming to terms with the world in the manner indicated is an accomplishment. And it is accurate to hold that battle is behind him. But battle lies before him, too, and this he cannot permit himself to know. To be properly soothing, the future must be more than a time of promise, it must be, in effect, transtemporal, an imagined and welcoming ideal. In fact it is even more remote than an ideal, it is that ideal's representation, and the representation itself has a remoteness: The vision does not deliver tranquil skies and fresh meadows and cool brooks but only images of these; the images; moreover, are not said to be possessed, they are simply that to which the youth turns his attention. The reference to thirst removes any doubt that the satisfaction of desire is more an aim than an achievement.

There remains the problem of the "third" ending: "Over the river a golden ray of sun came through the hosts of leaden rain clouds." This crowd-pleaser may have resulted from the Appleton editor's desire for something more positive than what Crane had already provided. But the positioning of the sentence, coming as it does after the last long paragraph, makes it easy enough to discount. By tracing the process of Henry's thinking, the concluding sentence of that paragraph offers a helpfully proleptic view of the last sentence of all. It says that this youth is a dreamer whose eyes are at least partly open. The relegation of skies, meadows, and brooks to the status of mere images, themselves objects of desire and not of actual possession, is a sufficient signal to the reader that anything the color of gold should be assayed with care.

6

The Mysteries of Heroism and the Aesthetics of War: Army Tales and Other War Writings

Crane's attitude toward war in general and heroism in particular is reminiscent of the little man's attitude toward the mountain. War and heroism all but mesmerize. To behold a specific heroic deed, or a tissue of collectively heroic deeds, is to be captive to awe, and what inspires awe is mystery. The source of inspiration is not normally charisma, so far as this term implies personal leaderhsip of an ostensibly inspired nature. With some exceptions Crane's military heroes are followers more than leaders, and when they lead, as in the case of young Henry in *The Red Badge of Courage* and old Henry in "The Veteran," they do so in a manner at once spontaneous and nonhierarchical. For Crane as for Garland, the ordinary fighting man is a type: "The common soldier of the American volunteer army had returned. His war with the South was over, and his fight, his daily running fight, with nature and against the injustice of his fellow men was begun again. In the dusk of that far-off valley his figure looms vast, his personal peculiarities fade away, he rises into a magnificent type."[1]

Larger than life, such types invite an evocative, admiring treatment, the texture and tenor of which we find subsumed within an aesthetics of war.

MIGHTY SPIRIT

Many years after his own return, the common soldier who became a brave color-bearer occupies a position of respect in his hometown, the setting of "The Veteran." " 'Mr. Fleming,' said the grocer. His deferential voice expressed somehow the old man's exact social weight. 'Mr. Fleming, you never was frightened much in them battles, was you?' " (VI, 82). The grocer poses a retrospective version of the questions Fleming asked himself when preparing for his first battle. By admitting (as he soon and freely does) that he panicked and ran, the veteran distinguishes himself from the recruit who existed in a world distorted by self-aggrandizing imagination. The long view of the veteran enables him to see that world in a focus that neither unduly extends nor unduly foreshortens his own role. At the same time, this focus is broad enough to draw in circumstances hidden to his younger self.

> "That was at Chancellorsville. Of course, afterward I got kind of used to it. A man does. Lots of men, though, seem to feel all right from the start. I did, as soon as I 'got on to it,' as they say now, but at first I was pretty flustered. Now, there was young Jim Conklin, old Si Conklin's son – that used to keep the tannery – you none of you recollect him – well, he went into it from the start just as if he was born to it. But with me it was different. I had to get used to it." (VI, 83)

While this statement and the confession about running both aim at an audience of townspeople, the attention paid to his grandson Jimmie just afterward reveals that the boy is the crucial point of impact. The status of grandfather situates the veteran, from the standpoint of the boy, in a past more legendary than historical, a time closer to that of Fleming the recruit than of Fleming the veteran. It is a time of happenings wonderful and strange, of figures larger than life. When Jimmie learns that his grandfather is not larger than life after all, he does not realize that from this fall the old man will rise to a mysterious apotheosis.

The crucial rescue occurs in two phases. Summoned to a fire in his barn by a hired hand – a frightened Swede resembling, as often noted, the Swede of "The Blue Hotel" – the veteran leads to safety several horses and cows, one of which knocks down the Swede, who "had been running to and fro babbling" (VI, 85). With the Swede's announcement that the old man has forgotten the colts, Fleming enters a second phase of exertion. The new demand takes its measure of his courage by asking more of him than anyone could reasonably expect, as the townspeople recognize by declaring that it would be suicide to go back into the fire. Absentmindedly intent, like the little man before the mesmeric mountain, the veteran goes anyway, leaving the people to wonder at the mystery of heroism. His movement – "He rushed into the barn" (VI, 86) – is one of those outbursts so familiar in Crane but one which, in contrast to many others that we have seen, suggests a transcendence of self in a spirit of sacrifice.

This gives Crane the chance to eulogize – something that the ending of *The Red Badge of Courage* permitted only in part. As a late nineteenth-century author, he can no longer draw readily upon a tradition in which the heroic is conveyed by *topoi* of inexpressibility, such as "the whole earth sings his praise." His solution is, in part, to plunge at the effect anyway, without transition, in a panegyric that is like an authorial version of his character's burst of movement: "When the roof fell in, a great funnel of smoke swarmed toward the sky, as if the old man's mighty spirit, released from its body – a little bottle – had swelled like the genie of fable. The smoke was tinted rose-hue from the flames, and perhaps the unutterable midnights of the universe will have no power to daunt the color of this soul" (VI, 86). "Rose-hue" combines the prospect of new dawning with the overtones of the process of revivification reposed in the myth of flame and phoenix. Finally, what is left of the tradition of inexpressibility finds voice in the "unutterable" of the last sentence. To say any more about the difficulty of expression, to try to utter the unutterable, would detract from what is otherwise expressed, and lessen the mystery of the veteran's heroics. To say more would threaten to dissolve the mystery of the midnights, which Crane seems bound to preserve. The color of Old Henry's soul, for its part, carries the same general force that we have seen in other works where Crane eschews any specifications of tint and hue so as to concentrate, almost to distill, the essence that color, as noun, is taken to express.

The old soldier, again heroic, rises again into a magnificent type.

PERSPECTIVES ON A MYSTERY

"A Mystery of Heroism" is a study in perspectives played off against one another, repeated, and interwoven.

> The dark uniforms of the men were so coated with dust from the incessant wrestling of the two armies that the regiment almost seemed a part of the clay bank which shielded them from the shells. On the top of the hill a battery was arguing in tremendous roars with some other guns and to the eye of the infantry, the artillerymen, the guns, the caissons, the horses, were distinctly outlined upon the blue sky. (VI, 48)

The perspectives in this story are largely confined – as in these opening sentences – to the experience of the Union soldiers. Only by means of these experiences – seeing a shell explode, watching a rider fall from a bullet – is the presence of the enemy constituted. The same applies to the constituting of the presence which the Union soldiers manifest to themselves. For example, when "the infantry" look up in sentence two, it is their own artillerymen they observe. These are significant considerations, for, as I shall now try to show, the narrative is to be understood precisely against the horizon of this perceiving, experiencing community.

The perspective is near in that everything is seen through the eyes of the regiment; it is far because it presents the regiment viewed, as through a field glass, from a locus shared by author and reader but inaccessible to the members of the regiment. There is a temporal distance as well, for the reference to the wrestling of the two armies is a miniature history of how the regiment came to be all but indistinguishable from the clay bank.

In the second sentence Crane invokes anew the motif of the figure outlined against the sky, but collectivized, as artillerymen, guns, caissons, horses all rise plurally and simultaneously "upon the blue sky." There is even a collectivization of the perceiver, for the outlined figures appear not to an individual vision, such as Henry Fleming's, but to the collective "eye of the infantry." The technique is employed again, with a significant variation, at the beginning of paragraph three: "As the eyes of half the regiment swept in one machine-like movement, there was an instant's picture of a horse in a great convulsive leap of a death-wound and a rider leaning back with a crooked arm and spread fingers before his face" (VI, 48). Like "half-Rome" in Browning's *The Ring and the Book,* Crane's half-regiment is an attempt to locate a "type" that can somehow reduce a multiplicity of particulars without becoming reductive. Browning's solution draws the type away from its phenomenal base: To present the thoughts of many persons, one must essentialize, as a playwright does when letting a single voice speak for a crowd. One does not imply thereby that the crowd ever expressed itself precisely as this voice does, but only that the things it says are typical. In Crane's situation the typical is given in the multiplicity. Since half the regiment sees the same thing at the same time, the author has only to say so. We might therefore be tempted to assert that Browning essentializes while Crane describes. yet Crane's description relies once more on a sense of the typical, and the typical expresses a concept of what is essential.

That sense arises in the present story from the image the men see, an image that is itself a type, defined in part by the immediate context and in part by previous ones. The horse and rider frozen here in a moment's vision can only be understood in relation to the role of the horse throughout the story. For the horse is not only the indispensable complement of the rider, but a participant in a wider fraternity of martial experience:

> And at that interval to the rear, where it is the business of battery horses to stand with their noses to the fight awaiting the command to drag their guns out of the destruction or into it or wheresoever these incomprehensible humans demanded with whip and spur . . . in this rank of brute-soldiers there had been relentless and hideous carnage. From the ruck of bleeding and prostrate horses, the men of the infanty could see one animal raising its stricken body with its fore-legs and turning its nose with mystic and profound eloquence toward the sky. (VI, 50)

This sympathy for the horse – more explicit than any sympathy for the men – recalls the strategy adopted about a year before in the newspaper sketch "In the Depths of a Coal Mine," where Crane eulogizes a donkey, and anticipates the treatment of horses in "The Price of the Harness": "As the infantry moved along the road, some of the battery horses turned at the noise of trampling feet and surveyed the men with eyes deep as wells, serene, mournful, generous eyes, lit heartbreakingly with something that was akin to a philosophy, a religion of self-sacrifice – of gallant, gallant horses!" (VI, 102). Crane's problem, evidently, is how to praise the fighting men without slipping into sentimentality; the solution is to displace the energy of the encomium in two moves. The first move directs attention to the officer and his ideal, and when the rhetorical temperature starts rising Crane cools things off, in the last two sentences of the description, with irony. Having done this, he is freer, in the second move, to lavish on the horses an exclamation that could have sounded excessive if applied to the human beings themselves.

In the principal human being of the story, Private Collins, we encounter a representative Crane type, though one with distinctive attributes. Through a process started by himself, Collins becomes a version of the little man, truculent, inclined to outbursts – even, at first, potentially comic. "There was a quarrel in A Company. Collins was shaking his fist in the faces of some laughing comrades. 'Dern yeh! I ain't afraid t' go. If yeh say much, I will go!' " (VI, 51). Once launched on his mission, Collins lives literally in the gaze of the others (VI, 52), playing for his audience the role he has rashly assumed, for it is only through the mediation of the other men that his "heroism" is initiated and brought to an end. Even on the verge of his exploit, Collins is viewed by them no longer as an oddity but as a source of genuine mystery: "When they inspected him carefully it was somewhat like the examination that grooms give a horse before a race; and they were amazed, staggered, by the whole affair" (VI, 52).

As he runs, Collins is like a dreamer for whom the world gradually becomes real: "As he neared the house, each detail of the scene became vivid to him. He was aware of some bricks of the vanished chimney lying on the soil. There was a door which hung by one hinge" (VI, 54). But there is little Collins can do about the things he perceives. He just perceives them and heads on down the inclined plane of an act that has lost all volitional meaning. If Henry Fleming is the prisoner of his perspectives, Fred Collins is the prisoner of his acts. The very manner in which his body moves catches the manner in which he is, as it were, situationally bound: "In running with a filled bucket, a man can adopt but one kind of gait" (VI, 55).

The protagonist is not without a margin of freedom in his situation, however, compounded as it is of the relation between circumstances and character combined with an element of chance in the person of the officer who happens to be shot from his horse in the path that Collins happens to choose. When the officer asks the running soldier to give him a drink of water, " 'I can't,' he screamed, and in this reply was a full description of his quaking apprehension" (VI, 56). But he can, or at least he can try. Terrified, Collins dashes back to the fallen man. "Collins tried to hold the bucket steadily, but his shaking caused the water to splash all over the face of the dying man. Then he jerked it away and ran on" (VI, 56).

What happens here exhibits a distinctive structure reflecting on everything that occurs in the story. The scenario runs on the following lines: *A man carried water across a battlefield and a dying man asked for a drink. "I cannot stop!" the first man cried, but ran back, giving drink; but the water splashed upon the dying man's face.* Through the double negation that this construction brings out, we see Collins's courage and at the same time his fear: Despite his misgivings he comes back; despite his efforts to hold the bucket steadily, he is so frightened that he spills the water.

The risk he takes by returning to the wounded officer lifts his enterprise to a second and higher level. His quest for water is limited by the nature of the desired object, which is marginally needed, and by the nature of his acts, which are carried out in consequence of a personal desire and of the "moving box" into which his rash statements have placed him. But his effort in behalf of the officer responds to the desire experienced by another; it is an act beyond self.[2] To be sure, his inability to control the bucket undercuts his technical competence as hero, but in no way does it diminish the essence of his act. That is why his spilling of water, while regrettable, is not finally wasteful.[3]

The ultimate spilling is another matter, assuming that one is clear about who does it and how. According to La France, "Collins spilled the water *en route,* and thus he risked his life to bring back an empty bucket."[4] But this is surely not what the text relates. Although the captain tells Collins to give the water to the men,

> the two genial, sky-larking lieutenants were the first to gain possession of it. They played over it in their fashion.
>
> When one tried to drink the other teasily knocked his elbow. "Don't, Billie! You'll make me spill it," said the one. The other laughed.
>
> Suddenly there was an oath, the thud of wood on the ground, and a swift murmur of astonishment from the ranks. The two lieutenants glared at each other. The bucket lay on the ground empty. (VI, 56)

In a struggle without risk the officers cause the loss of that for which Collins has risked his very life. Whatever the merit of the impulse that results in the vessel's safe arrival, that vessel has acquired, like a wound, a distinctive value, even a certain sanctity. Thus the genuine sense of loss, and the sense that in the very act of losing, what is lost seems somehow the more precious. The essence of a thing is sometimes revealed – to develop an idea of Heidegger's – more through the loss of it than through its normal use. With a certain thing I hit and pound, scarcely regarding it as more than the extension of my arm. Then it snaps and is disclosed: It is a broken *hammer.* In its sudden failure its being "stands out" for me. The contents of the spilled vessel stand out in a similar way.

In the absence of the treasure the treasure is suddenly present: The value of its springs up in and through its loss.

Like one of the negations in Crane's verse, the moment reverses an expectation. A poem on the episode might have said: *The brave man came back with water, but there were two whose joy was to spill it on the ground.* The object to which Collins's act has lent a value disappears, while the meaning of his act remains a mystery, peculiar to a moment of time that, being past, no later time can either affect or properly interpret.

THE BALLAD OF PRIVATE NOLAN

If war is hell, as General Sherman said, it is also hard work. Unified by discipline in their harness of blue, the fighting men of "The Price of the Harness" are first and last workers, and the rhythm of their work pulsates through the story (as does a collateral rhythm of music, to be taken up below):

> Twenty-five men were making a road out of a path up the hillside. . . . The men worked like gardeners, and a road was growing from the old pack-animal trail. Trees arched from a field of guinea-grass which resembled young wild corn. The day was still and dry. The men working were dressed in the consistent blue of United States regulars. They looked indifferent, almost stolid, despite the heat and the labor. (VI, 97)

Like the red badge, the harness is a measure of a man's "virtue in war" (to borrow the title of another tale of the Cuban campaign). Taken on voluntarily, the harness grows on the regular until it is part of him. Remembering the connection between horse and soldier in "A Mystery of Heroism," one notes that a harness suits that animal no less than a man. Associating these two types of being is a habit of Crane's, as shown by the action of "One Dash – Horses," "The Veteran," and a number of other writings. It is not coincidental, then, that the description quoted above shifts near the end from the men to the animals on which they depend: "From time to time a government pack-train, led by a sleek-sided tender bell-mare, came from one way or the other way, and the men stood aside as the strong, hard, black-and-tan animals crowded eagerly after their curious little feminine leader" (VI, 97).

A harness is a pledge to continue on "active service," and if Robert Frost caught something of this when he lauded the American capacity for feeling "easy in the harness," Crane pursues the implications even further by considering, for example, why it is that the men feel easier when they get to the fighting phase of their work:

> All impatience, all rebellious feeling, had passed out of the men as soon as they had been allowed to use their weapons against the enemy. They now were absorbed in this business of hitting something, and all the

> long training at rifle ranges, all the pride of the marksman which had been so long alive in them, made them forget for the time everything but shooting. They were as deliberate and exact as so many watchmakers. (VI, 110)

Their new "sense of safety" (VI, 110), of being sheltered in their work, contrasts with the anxiety caused, in "A Mystery of Heroism," by the postponement of battle. Like Fleming and Collins, Michael Nolan, the man who pays for his harness the price of his life, wonders how long he can contain himself: " 'My gawd,' said Nolan, squirming on his belly in the grass, 'I can't stand this much longer' " (VI, 109). What fighting provides is the relief of automatism, the complex of acts-without-actors that Crane likes to render in mechanical terms:

> The line now sounded like a great machine set to running frantically in the open air . . . to the prut of the magazine rifles was added the under-chorus of the clicking mechanism, steady and swift as if the hand of one operator was controlling it all. It reminds one always of a loom, a great grand steel loom, clinking, clanking, plunking, plinking, to weave a woof of thin red threads, the cloth of death. (VI, 109)

Nolan's friend Martin is sorely tested: Besides being wounded, he contracts fever. What is asked of Nolan, on the other hand, is life itself, for in the end it is Martin who survives and Nolan who dies. This development, nearly as unexpected as the death of the oiler in "The Open Boat," is only slightly foreshadowed. We are told that "with his heavy roll of blanket and the half of a shelter-tent crossing his right shoulder and under his left arm, each man presented the appearance of being clasped from behind, wrestler-fashion, by a pair of thick white arms" (VI, 100). This arresting image is related to the fear of being overtaken by some force that is unknown and thus a mystery, something that comes from behind and takes one by surprise, as happens not only in "Death and the Child" and "The Clan of No-Name" but, as we have seen, in *The Red Badge of Courage*. When we read at the start of part two of the present text that Nolan was "well gripped by his shelter-tent, his blanket and his cartridge-belt" (VI, 99), we have a hint that he will be made to pay the ultimate price of the harness.

Nolan is capable of forgetting about Martin's injury when forced to dive for cover; but this is only to say that there are times when a soldier must think of himself. There are equally times when the same soldier, through the same sense of duty and of "battle brotherhood" with which it is merged, sees himself pre-eminently, willingly, almost religiously, a member of the group:

> Something fine, soft, gentle, touched his heart as he ran. He had loved the regiment, the army, because the regiment, the army, was his life. He had no other outlook; and now these men, his comrades, were

> performing his dream-scenes for him. They were doing as he had ordained in his visions. It is curious that in this charge he considered himself as rather unworthy. Although he himself was in the assault with the rest of them, it seemed to him that his comrades were dazzlingly courageous. His part, to his mind, was merely that of a man who was going along with the crowd. (VI, 110)

If Collins stands out, Nolan blends, performing no act that makes him mysterious in the gaze of the others. Collins begins to feel the palpable presence of the others only as he moves back into their orbit following his mission, whereupon the story ends. But in Nolan's case the presence of the others is a constant if tacit given. There is no time when he is not within the collective orbit, and so there is no occasion for him to "stand out" before it. His relation to his comrades, moreover, is qualitatively different from Collins's. Nolan's mode of being is a "being-with." It is not that he has no ego; it is just that his ego, this notional projection that lets others perform *his* dreams, is in fact the mediating link between his individuality and the collectivity. Nolan has it both ways. It is as if he were to say, The others make my vision come true: They do what I could never do alone, and so I am a part of "them," of their fraternal unity.

As a final illustration of the difference between this pair of characters we may note that Nolan does his job just as he is supposed to do it. He works on the road and then he fights, and he does both in a way that benefits the group: He has discipline. But Collins breaks discipline. His act is out of keeping and in a sense pointless – he has neither harmed the enemy nor helped his friends. Although he gains somewhat in status, he does so in a self-directed way that does little or nothing for the group. The officers in that story are also reckless. Thinking only of their immediate pleasure, they destroy the emblem of Collins's foolhardy but daring enterprise. The officers in "The Price of the Harness," by contrast, are closer to being idealized types, and closer to laying claim to charisma; if they do not it is because they are socially and not divinely commissioned, a circumstance of which the regulars are quite aware: "The whole scene would have spoken to the private soldiers of ambushes, sudden flank attacks, terrible disasters if it were not for those cool gentlemen with shoulder-straps and swords who, the private soldiers knew, were of another world and omnipotent for the business" (VI, 100). The relation of officer to men, Crane suggests, resembles the relation of parents to children:

> A lieutenant . . . was talking in soothing parental tones.
>
> "Now don't get rattled. We're all right here. Just as safe as being in church. . . . They're all going high. Don't mind them. . . . Don't mind them. . . . They're all going high. We've got them rattled and they can't shoot straight. Don't mind them." (VI, 104–5)

If the most fully developed archetype of the ideal officer is Lt. Hasbrouck in *The Red Badge of Courage,* an officer Crane singles out in the Cuban campaign is the exemplary type in "The Price of the Harness":

> A man of this kind might be stupid; it is conceivable that in remote cases certain bumps on his head might be composed entirely of wood; but those traditions of fidelity and courage which have been handed to him from generation to generation, and which he has tenaciously preserved despite the persecution of legislators and the indifference of his country, make it incredible that in battle he should ever fail to give his best blood and his best thought for his general, for his men and for himself. And so this young officer in the shapeless hat and the torn and dirty shirt failed to heed the wails of the wounded man, even as the pilgrim fails to heed the world as he raises his illumined face toward his purpose – rightly or wrongly his purpose – his sky of the ideal of duty; and the wonderful part of it is that he is guided by an ideal which he has himself created, and has alone protected from attack. The young man was merely an officer in the United States regular army. (VI, 101–2)

To regard the officer's idealism as solipsistic, as Crane here allows himself to do, is at least partly to miss the crucial presupposition, underlying the entire account, of the unity of public behavior and private feeling. The ideal he sustains is a received ideal, a social formation built up through many years; Crane himself points to generation after generation of tradition. To save Crane from a naive individualism one would have to read the penultimate sentence as a more subtle statement than it appears to be. On this reckoning Crane is saying something like: The officer's *cogito,* if you will, is grounded equally in himself and the social world, as exemplified by military tradition. On this reckoning, to know your duty is to know what you expect of yourself in relation to what others expect of you. My suspicion is that such a reading, defensible as it is, makes Crane a more sophisticated social theorist than he probably was. If anything, the passage speaks to Crane's own idealism, with its sacrificial aesthetic cast that nonetheless leaves an almost ironic aftertaste. Nameless, faceless, the young officer embodies an ethical norm in unusually pure form. He is not this particular soldier of this particular rank but a noun with an indefinite article. The fact that he is a staff officer, and therefore more remote from engagements than a line officer, may account for the abstract aura of the portrait, though something of the same aura hovers around Manolo Prat, the protagonist of "The Clan of No-Name," as well. In both cases, it would seem, Crane found an opportunity to put his ideas about officers and duty into a particular form with a generalizing force. Crane also saw a chance to talk up his subject, to sound out ringing words in a manner vaguely grand. The problem for him, here, as in "A Mystery of Heroism," is how to reconcile this inclination with his reiterated opposition to "eloquence."

In Nolan we see a more satisfactory blending of the private and the public, the individual and the collective, than in the officer. It is more satisfactory, I think, not because Crane avoids eloquence, but because, by gradually inducing the reader to identify with Nolan, he gives his vision a concreteness lacking in his portrait of the idealized officer. The public aspect is the soldier's sense of the battle as an historic event; the private aspect is his sense of his own place in it:

> Here, then, was one of those dread and lurid situations which in a nation's history stand out in crimson letters, becoming a tale of blood to stir generation after generation. And he was in it and unharmed. If he lived through the battle, he would be a hero of the desperate fight at – and here he wondered for a second what fate would be pleased to bestow as a name for this battle. (VI, 105)

Nolan's participation in the historic battle is projected into the future as a function of the heroic endeavors of all. Because he has his individual way of seeing himself, no one else in the battalion (we are told) is thinking such thoughts. Yet there are several respects in which individualizing characteristics tend toward generality. First, his way of thinking is itself general, or rather, is general at certain times. Just as he allows every man his ego, so Crane allows every man his dream of glory; it is merely that the army, in its role of moving box, limits the expression of the dream, the assertion of the ego. There is, to put it another way, a little of Henry Fleming in every soldier.

The uniqueness of Nolan's thoughts is relative: At the present time, Crane goes on to say, "hardly" another man is having thoughts just like these. Secondly, as time passes the thoughts do too, and Nolan is finally no more attentive to historical dimensions of the combat than anyone else; the next time we see him he is squirming on the grass, itching to fight. Thirdly, the sense of history is, like the officer's ideal of duty, a notional, generalizing phenomenon. It is an idea in a man's head that is also in the heads of other men. Furthermore, the very positing of an historical dimension expresses a reciprocity between the private sphere and the public sphere, or to give the pattern its broadest name, the one and the many. Fourthly, the limitation of knowledge that is applied to the weaker members of the group applies as well to the other members, including Nolan. There is always something, and often an important something, that none of them know. Even in the present instance the limitation extends beyond the weak, for no one, not even Nolan, knows for sure that the battle will be famous forever. Crane says that the weak would behave better in light of a knowledge they do not have, but the presupposition seems to be that such knowledge is simply not to be had, either by the weak or anyone else.

Equally interesting is the specific handling of Nolan's ignorance. Like the rowers in the open boat, Nolan is so intent on his work "that he did not know of new orders until he saw the men about him scrambling to their feet" (VI, 110). The section concludes:

> Grierson seemed to be afraid of Nolan's agitation, and so he slipped a hand under the prostrate man, and presently withdrew it covered with blood. "Yes," he said, hiding his hand carefully from Nolan's eyes, "you were right, Jimmie."
>
> "Of course I was," said Nolan, contentedly closing his eyes. . . .
>
> He did not know that he was dying. He thought he was holding an argument on the condition of the turf. (VI, 112)

The authorial locus, by contrast, is omniscient in a way that one is inclined to call omnitemporal. In the very course of an event the aftermath is already known: "By the men's shoulders under their eager hands dropped continually the yellow empty shells, spinning into the crushed grass blades to remain there and mark for the belated eye the line of a battalion's fight" (VI, 109–10). Or the locus shows the contrast between a past "then," equivalent to the time of the historical event as it is now happening, and a "now" more or less equivalent to the present in which the author is recollecting or reconstructing. When a stranger asks the wounded Martin to help carry another wounded soldier, Martin rejects the offer with weary words: "This answer, which rings now so inhuman, pitiless, did not affect the other men" (VI, 108). This now-and-later vision applies equally to the physical scene: "The road taken by this battalion as it followed other battalions is something less than a mile long in its journey across a heavily wooded plain. It is greatly changed now; in fact it was metamorphosed in two days; but at that time it was a mere track through dense shrubbery from which rose great dignified arching trees" (VI, 103).

When this shifting from tense to tense occurs in Balzac, who uses the technique frequently, it takes its resonance from a direct historical context. In Balzac a statement concerning "a battle that would be famous forever" would likely lead to another statement identifying the battle and, as often as not, the war as well. By taking the opposing tack of withholding what he knows, Crane achieves an effect that has less to do with the historical as such than with the broadly, temporally essential. It is as if he were to say, Don't worry over the why or wherefore of it, worry over what it is. There is an almost platonic streak in Crane which leads him to feel that all those facts, those names and places and dates and miscellaneous details are, notwithstanding their specificity, not entirely relevant to the essence of the matter. All the context the reader really needs is the context built into the story – the nexus of elements essential to an event or to a particular way of seeing it. If Crane expatiates upon, say, a national trait, as he does at the end of this story, the reason will be found within the story:

> Thereafter there was silence in the fever tent save for the noise made by a man over in the corner, a kind of man always found in an American crowd, a heroic, implacable comedian and patriot, of a humor that has bitterness and ferocity and love in it, and he was wringing from the situation a grim meaning by singing The Star-Spangled Banner with all the ardor which could be procured from his fever-stricken body. (VI, 113)

To the other dimensions of the tale – the historical, the quasi-religious, and that of the individual and the group – Crane thus adds a distinctly national dimension.

The group presented at the end of the story, like most groups in Crane, lacks a permanent structure: It will endure only as long as it takes the men to recover. But there is something about it that makes it in another sense not so different from the group the battle has broken up. This something is the men themselves, or perhaps better – taking into account Crane's tendency to give priority to essence rather than accidence – something ineffable within them, which is theirs but not exclusively theirs. This is, quite simply, the ability to take it, the capacity to absorb all the punishment that life can bring without, as F. Scott Fitzgerald would have said, cracking-up. Crane shows often that the capacity is grounded in courage. "The Price of the Harness" enriches that conceptualization by demonstrating that, in these men, courage has become routine. Only a brave man wears the harness and the harness keeps him brave.

Another main pulse in the story, that of music, is early audible in the cry of " 'Ay–ee! Ay–ee! Madre mia! Madre mia!' " A Cuban soldier, Crane reports, "sang this bitter ballad into the ears of at least three thousand men" (VI, 101). Later, against a background furnished by "the under-chorus of the clicking mechanism" (VI, 109), bullets "make the faint note of a vibrant string touched elusively, half dreamily" (VI, 103). Hence "at the front the battle-sound, as if it were simply music, was beginning to swell and swell until the volleys rolled like a surf" (VI, 103). In the end, as suggested by the passage on the fever tent, ballad turns to anthem, an anthem – to employ the term associated above with the office – of "duty": "But he ran on, because it was his duty, and because he would be shamed before men if he did not do his duty, and because he was desolate out there all alone in the fields with death" (VI, 127).

Such a code is in one respect abstract – like the sky of the ideal of duty – but in another it has a concrete resonance by virtue of the almost fatalistic self-control it requires:

> He knew that he was thrusting himself into a trap whose door, once closed, opened only when the black hand knocked, and every part of him seemed to be in panic-stricken revolt. But something controlled him; something moved him inexorably in one direction; he perfectly understood, but he was only sad, sad with a serene dignity, with the countenance of a mournful young prince. He was of a kind – that seemed to be it – and the men of his kind, on peak or plain, from the dark northern ice-fields to the hot wet jungles, through all wine and want, through all lies and unfamiliar truth, dark or light, the men of his kind were governed by their gods, and each man knew the law and yet could not give tongue to it; but it was the law, and if the spirits of the men of his kind were all sitting in critical judgment upon him even then in the sky, he could not have bettered his conduct; he needs must obey the law, and always with the law there is only one way. (VI, 131)

In the second sentence Crane starts a characteristic shift, such that the reader is no longer thinking with the protagonist but looking at him. In the process of following a prince he has become one, his conduct in the light of an ideal illuminating his very being. The status thus acquired is not unique but typical. The officer is a member of a community one might hesitate to call by that name were it not for its ideal nature. As Crane repeatedly suggests, one has to be a member of a most distinct elite, a man of a certain generic, almost genetic category: "His glance caught the staring eye of the wounded soldier, and he smiled at him quietly. The man – simple doomed peasant – was not of his kind, but the law of fidelity was clear" (II, 168).

Although a certain class consciousness enters here, the cleavage between the two kinds of men is not primarily social or political or economic; it is ontological. The two men belong to different orders of being, which accounts for the perhaps unwitting condescension of "simple doomed peasant." How, we ask, can Crane endorse such an attitude? How, in the light of his concern for fraternity and his sometime egalitarianism, can he set one man so much higher than another? The answer in both cases is that he does not do so unequivocally. There is something of Quijote in a man with the countenance of a mournful prince who sacrifices all for an ideal; and where Quijote enters, irony enters, too. The second question must be answered in two parts. First, Crane's egalitarianism is, as I have already implied, intermittent, and it is also vague and largely negative. On the one hand he is skeptical about the upper classes in general, and critical of anyone, especially society matrons, who are insensitive in the treatment of their "inferiors." On the other hand he is against the downtrodden for being downtrodden; for Crane, the root of Bowery misery, we recall, was cowardice. Crane seems to be saying in his own way, with Orwell, that some of us are more equal than others;

that one becomes more equal – superior – by brave conduct; that the opportunities for such conduct are more plentiful in military than in civilian life; and that the officer, by virtue of his nearer contemplations of the ideal, plays a special role in relation to the private soldier.

It is, in a word, a mediating role. The private soldier, for his part, identifies with his group. Its members are equals pledged to a common purpose. (This applies also to the noncommissioned officer, who enjoys a higher status with the enlisted-man group: No private soldier regards his sergeant as a cool gentleman from another world.) In relation to the officer, the situation is a little different. The men continue in their solidarity, but a new element is added; a being-with-*toward*. It is in relation to the officer the men take on directedness. Among themselves, as members of a group in which each member sees himself in the other, they stand shoulder to shoulder with their faces toward the leader. For his part the leader relates in two directions: toward his men and toward the sky of the ideal of duty that keeps him on a course of conduct determined by traditional if unwritten laws.

All of which is a way of talking about a mystery of heroism. One must also speak, however, about something closely related, which is the question of being itself, a question posed pointedly in "Death and the Child."

A MYSTERY OF BEING

The main character of this tale of the Greco–Turkish War seeks what the correspondent Vernall refers to in "War Memories" as "the real thing." Much as the Swede strives to participate in the life of the American West or Kelcey in the life of New York City, the journalist Peza strives to participate in the life of war. Crane suggests what the real thing "is" in terms of what it is "like," employing an almost Homeric analogy: "It was as if fear was a river, and this horde had simply been caught in the torrent, man tumbling over beast, beast over man, as helpless in it as the logs that fall and shoulder grindingly through the gorges of a lumber country" (V, 121). But with his eye on the supposed real thing, Peza remains stuck in the gluey medium of language: "Peza was chattering a question at every one. In the way, pushed aside, or in the way again, he continued to repeat it. 'Can they take the position? Can they take the position? Can they take the position? Can they take the position?' " (V, 137).

War is a mystery for the child in the story as well as for Peza. Familiar only with the life of grazing, the child tries to translate the unknown into familiar terms: "He reproduced, to a degree, any movements which he accounted rational to this theory of sheepherding, the business of men, the traditional and exalted living of his father" (V, 128). In the panic of war, the child has become literally fatherless in his fatherland. The problematic identity of Peza – clearly, in this respect, the boy's older counterpart – also hinges on a paternal relation: " 'I came here merely because my father was a Greek, and for his sake I thought of Greece – I loved Greece. But I did not dream – ' " (V, 122). The child defines his situation in terms of his own and his father's vocation, while Peza defines his situation in terms of his father and his own, apparently different, vocation.

For Peza, however, as for Henry Fleming, the basic ontological question, the question of what one amounts to as a man, is posed by battle. Although at first the war appears to Peza in a visual perspective, which is also how it appears to the child, eventually it dissolves into a medium in which, as in water, he becomes immersed: "It was as if Peza was a corpse walking on the bottom of the sea, and finding there fields of grain, groves, weeds, the faces of men, voices" (V, 129). Analogies with bodies of water – rivers, streams, seas – suggest forces that overwhelm the human capacity to maintain an ordered and ordering perspective. The loss of that perspective takes the form of a declining sense of measure, as the fleeing peasants fail to note their missing possessions; the little boy's parents fail even to note their missing son. At its most mundane level, measure embraces the "apparently horizontal course" (V, 133) followed by a shell, a voice "calling out the calculation of the distance to the enemy, the readjustment of the sights" (V, 140), the manner in which a road "seemed to lead into the apex of an angle formed by the two defensive lines of the Greeks" (V, 129).

This near–far axis (exemplified by the long-range vistas of the child) has its complement in a high–low axis through which Crane envisages the relation between immediate, "ground-level" experience and that less definable realm we have in mind when we speak of things *sub specie aeternitatis*. The latter is expressed, on the one hand, in the following way: "The firing was full, complete, a roar of cataracts, and this pealing of connected volleys was adjusted to the grandeur of the far-off range of snowy mountains. Peza, breathless, pale, felt that he had been set upon a pillar and was surveying mankind, the world" (V, 136). The passage forms a bridge toward the second, more sublime way of expressing the high–low axis:

> From a land toward which their faces were bent came a continuous boom of artillery fire. It was sounding in regular measures like the beating of a colossal clock – a clock that was counting the seconds in the lives of the stars, and men had time to die between the ticks. Solemn, oracular, inexorable, the great seconds tolled over the hills as if God fronted this dial rimmed by the horizon. (V, 123)

At this point it is impossible to say where measure ceases and perspective begins, for the scene Crane describes takes so much in while leaving so much unresolved. If the scene is cosmic in the same way that the experience of the men in "The Open Boat" is cosmic, it is because the description constitutes a statement, built into the very physics of the setting, about the relationship of God, human beings, and the universe. The fullest statement of that relationship comes as early as the second paragraph of the story:

> The blue bay with its pointed ships, and the white town lay below them, distant, flat, serene. There was upon this vista a peace that a bird knows when high in air it surveys the world, a great calm thing rolling noiselessly toward the end of mystery. Here on the height one felt the existence of the universe scornfully defining the pain in ten thousand minds. The sky was an arch of stolid sapphire. Even to the mountains raising their mighty shapes from the valley, this headlong rush of the fugitives was too minute. The sea, the sky, and the hills combined in their grandeur to term this misery inconsequent. (V, 121–2)

What is most at issue, however, is the existence of one man and the definition of his personal pain. Revealing his background, his relation to his father, his education, his vocation, his experience of art, and his motive for coming to the front, Peza provides a biography with more temporal depth than one is accustomed to find in a Crane story. As Peza enters a society like no other he has known, all the received social forms he displays – the bows, the verbal formulae, the calling card – become incongruous: "He bowed again majestically; the lieutenant bowed. They flung a shadow of manners, of capering tinsel ceremony across a land that groaned, and it satisfied something within themselves completely" (V, 124).

If Peza, like Coleman, never achieves fraternal solidarity with the men he meets, he does experience what is called, in "The Five White Mice," a sense of equality. For in contemplating these others he contemplates himself. Puzzled by their indifference and stolidity, "Peza tried to define them. Perhaps during the fight they had reached the limit of their mental storage, their capacity for excitement, for tragedy, and then simply come away" (V, 129). Peza finds an analogy in a visit he once made to an art gallery, where the riot of color and shapes had fairly overwhelmed his sensibility: "Peza no longer was torn with sorrow at the sight of wounded men. Evidently he found that pity had a numerical limit, and when this was passed the emotion became another thing" (V, 130). In contrast with the men in "The Price of the Harness" and his fellow wordsmith, the correspondent in "The Open Boat," Peza steers an essentially egotistical course, like the one pursued by the hero of *Active Service*. Though arguably "like" the other men, Peza is never "with" them. The soldiers stand to him in the relation of mediators, but what they mediate is sense of self: "A part of himself was appealing through the medium of these grim shapes. It was plucking at his sleeve and pointing, telling him to beware, and so it had come to pass that he cared for the implacable misery of these soldiers only as he would have cared for the harms of broken dolls. His whole vision was focussed upon his own chance" (V, 130).

Peza is a little man who never grows large, strive as he may to put off childish associations: "Instantly, for some reason of cadence, the noise was irritating, silly, infantile. This uproar was childish. It forced the nerves to object, to protest against this racket which was idle as the din of a lad with a drum" (V, 123–4). What this really tells us is that the correspondent cannot find a way to measure this harsh new rhythm. His reaction, moreover, is similar to that of the child, whose hovering presence is suggested by the analogy of the lad with a drum: "He was solitary; engrossed in his own pursuits, it was seldom that he lifted his head to inquire of the world why it made so much noise. The stick in his hand was much larger to him than was an army corps of the distance. It was too childish for the mind of the child" (V, 128). The perspectives, in other words, are relative: How you read the world depends on your position in it. The resemblance between Peza's view and the child's implies that he is in an early stage of development in the life-world of war. He appears, in time, to advance from this stage; for one thing he comes to know his own inadequacy: "He felt ridiculous, and also he felt awed, aghast, at these men who could turn their faces from the ominous front and debate his clothes, his business. There was an element which was new born into his theory of war" (V, 127). This comes in the aftermath of his humiliation by the lieutenant, who cannot tolerate the newcomer's sentimentality; but this too is relative since only a portion of his egotism leaves him.

The fact is that despite all the changes he undergoes, Peza remains childlike, isolated, self-concerned. Unlike Henry Fleming, he never ceases to focus on his own chance. This is not to say that he learns nothing of importance. He learns from observation, for example, that the soldiers are "actuated principally by some universal childish desire for a spectator of their fine things" (V, 135). If Peza's spectatorial perspective does not last it is because – as the shift from the visual to the tactile, discussed above, has shown – Peza is plunged into the sea of the conflict to become its victim. To this extent "Death and the Child" is, like *George's Mother,* a story about defeat, though it is not, like the earlier work, a story about degeneration. Peza does not get worse, he just doesn't get very much better. The extent of his capacity for genuine growth remains problematic; what is certain is that he hasn't the time or the opportunity given the circumstances – by these he is simply overpowered. Thus, at the time that he finds himself submerged, he finds himself also held, as in a mysterious grip. The moment recalls the image of the moving box surrounding Henry Fleming, though the constraint experienced by Peza seems more personal. It is also, like the grip that holds the soldiers in "The Price of the Harness," tighter. It is, indeed, the harness itself that grips: "each man presented the appearance of being clasped from behind, wrestler fashion, by a pair of thick white arms" (VI, 100). In "Death and the Child" Crane modifies the equipment but the effect is the same: "Peza, having crossed the long cartridge-belt on his breast, felt that the dead man had flung his two arms around him. . . . The bandoleer gripped him tighter; he wished to raise his hands to his throat, like a man who is choking" (V, 138–9).

Peza's condition is meanwhile being defined on an abstract level as well. We have already seen his effort to define the soldiers, and his conclusion that they had simply reached the limit of their mental storage; we have also seen the way in which the universe defines the pain in 10,000 minds. We may now consider more closely Peza's manner of defining himself. The crucial passage occurs, significantly, just after his long speech about his past and his motives for coming to the front: "Eager, passionate, profoundly moved, his first words while facing the procession of fugitives had been an active definition of his own dimension, his personal relation to men, geography, life. Throughout he had preserved the fiery dignity of a tragedian" (V, 122–3). In a broad sense, then, Peza defines himself through the mediation of language. This does not mean he is in control of everything he says. On the contrary, his words sometimes assume, as in the case of Collins in "A Mystery of Heroism," an autonomous force: " 'Yes, I am a Greek. I wish to fight.' Peza's voice surprised him by coming from his lips in even and deliberate tones" (V, 133). Language becomes detached from the things it is meant to express. The names of the nations cited by the officers in their conversation with Peza are, like Peza's own mannered verbalizations, mere words, a linguistic equivalent of the chivalric manners cast like a shadow across the groaning land. But these reservations, too, are relative, for in another sense language is all there is. Nature itself is a kind of speaker; the sea, the sky, and the hills combined, we recall, to *term* the human misery inconsequent, just as later "A breeze made all this verdure gently rustle and speak in long silken sighs" (V, 127). Even more important – because of their strategic placement at the end of the story – are the words with which the child confronts the mystery of the being that comes toward him.

> The child heard a rattle of loose stones on the hill-side, and facing the sound, saw a moment later a man drag himself up to the crest of the hill and fall panting. Forgetting his mother and his hunger, filled with calm interest, the child walked forward and stood over the heaving form. His

> eyes, too, were now large and inscrutably wise and sad, like those of the animal in the house.
>
> After a silence, he spoke inquiringly: "Are you a man?" (V, 140–1)

War, a mystery of doing, gives way to a mystery of being. Is this crawling creature a man? Yes, if a man (or so it can be argued), is excitable and self-centered, an outsider, and a bit of a fool. But the creature is not a man (it can equally be argued) if a man is a being who meets each new challenge on its own terms, who has an instinct for the proper decorum in a novel situation, and who lives for some good held in common with others. Or one could put aside both lines of argument, as I am inclined to do, and understand the story in a larger sense as a statement about human mutability. The story reminds the reader that everyone dies and that a man in the time of his dying may feel most deeply the meaning of life; and that the meaning of life is, for Crane, like the heroism that may be its highest manifestation, an ultimate mystery. The irony of the question, as it is put by this particular character, is that it is posed in words – words, the things that defined him for us – and that words are now beyond his capacity. How then is his misery to be expressed? "Palsied, windless, and abject, he confronted the primitive courage, the sovereign child, the brother of the mountains, the sky and the sea, and he knew that the definition of his misery could be written on a wee grass-blade" (V, 141). The word "written" expands the dimension of the irony not merely by pointing again at the wordlessness of the dying man, but by reminding us that definitions are made and miseries "termed" by things beyond him – by sea, sky, hills, by the cosmos itself, which, if it can define the pain in 10,000 minds, can certainly define it in one. The statement connects this perspective, finally, with the concern for measure, for the statement is also a comment on the "scale" of a man's condition. Blake makes a similar move when he places eternity in a grain of sand, but Crane's compression serves a different end. Blake helps us see the large through the little: Looking at the grain, we behold its eternity. Crane's achievement is to concentrate meaning in the minute particular: When we look at the grass-blade we see the misery of the individual human, the ultimate nature of whose being remains a mystery.

THE AESTHETICS OF WAR

In his writings on the Greco–Turkish War in 1897 and on the Spanish–American War in 1898, Crane brings to his portrayal an aestheticism that is the complement of his fascination with irony and the grotesque:

> The roll of musketry was tremendous. From a distance it was like tearing a cloth; nearer, it sounded like rain on a tin roof and close up it

> was just a long crash after a crash. It was a beautiful sound – beautiful as I had never dreamed. It was more impressive than the roar of Niagara and finer than thunder or avalanche – because it had the wonder of human tragedy in it. It was the most beautiful sound of my experience, barring no symphony. The crash of it was ideal.
>
> This is one point of view. Another might be taken from the men who died there. (IX, 19–20)

The dispatches are full of such shifts. Now the manner is detached and cool, now florid and rhetorical; now Crane decries and compliments, now mocks and praises.

In a later dispatch he writes: "Even friendly armies can but destroy the more subtle effects of nature, although they substitute a wilder beauty of their own creation" (IX, 31). This wilder beauty, which Crane creates in the preceding passage as well, fairly typifies what may be called the military sublime. Now, the aesthetic dimension of military life already enjoys a central place in Kant's *Critique of Judgment,* together with the concept of the sublime. Noting the "special reverence" enjoyed by the soldier, Kant suggests that this fearless, undaunted, virile, and hard-working figure is more appealing aesthetically than the peaceful politician. "War itself, provided it is conducted with order and a sacred respect for the rights of civilians, has something of the sublime about it, and gives nations that carry it on in such a manner a stamp of mind only the more sublime the more numerous the dangers to which they are exposed, and which they are able to meet with fortitude."[5] This is the close indeed to Crane's attitude toward the fighting men in "The Price of the Harness"; Crane also resembles Kant when invoking the roar of Niagara, thunder, and avalanche: "Bold, overhanging, and, as it were, threatening rocks, thunderclouds piled up the vault of heaven, borne along with flashes and peals . . . the high waterfall of some mighty river, and the like, make our power of resistance of trifling moment in comparison with their might."[6] Little in comparison with such might, possessing no sensuous standard by which to measure these phenomena, human beings nonetheless transcend them; for they comprehend that such things claim no dominion over them even as they discern in themselves an innate nonsensuous standard, a standard so superior that even nature's infinity may be measured by it and in comparison with which each thing in nature is but a little thing.

Of this discernment there seems to be no precise equivalent in Crane. Crane is Kantian, however, insofar as the human agency on which he reports in both passages is transcendent: As impressive as Niagara and the other natural forces may be, battles fought by human beings are more impressive; nor would it take much ingenuity to argue that such a view does after all approximate the superior standard proposed by Kant.

In two respects, on the other hand, Crane's sublime differs from Kant's. In the first place, whereas the beautiful and the sublime are distinct modes in the Kantian aesthetic, they coalesce in Crane. What is tremendous and therefore sublime is precisely what is beautiful, as further attested in passages too numerous to quote. In the second place, Kant's orientation toward mighty effects is specular and distanced. The locus of apprehension that leads to aesthetic appreciation in the sublime mode is implicitly that of a spectator who remains at a distance from forces that would overwhelm if too closely approached. What intrigues Crane, on the contrary, is precisely the fact of being overwhelmed: "It was more impressive . . . because it had the wonder of human tragedy in it." Thus Kantian transcendence and distance are replaced by immanence and immersion.

It is also worth considering how Crane's aesthetic resembles and differs from that of a contemporary, Walter Pater. Pater's claim that all arts aspire to the condition of music is a strong way of positing musicality as ultimate aesthetic measure. No formal aesthetician, Crane admittedly makes no equivalent statement, but as several passages in the present study combine to show, Crane employs musical terminology and analogy throughout his writings (and to a greater extent, incidentally, than those pertaining to painting, on which critics typically concentrate). Music embodies principles, such as beauty and ideality and transcendence, to which Crane's aesthetic constantly hews. Being the most difficult of the arts to translate into anything like verbal counterparts, music also suggests the inaccessibility of mystery. If that does not suffice to confirm the eminence of music, Crane's aural–oral criterion for ultimate beauty does: "It was the most beautiful sound of my experience, barring no symphony. The crash of it was ideal." From among all the arts Crane makes the choice Pater could be expected to make in similar circumstances, the point being that if music is an ultimate measure in the aesthetic realm, as we frequently think it to be, another type of sound may make a still higher claim, in effect enlarging the aesthetic realm. The music of musketry is simply a particular instance of a general aesthetics of war.

Crane neither states nor implies that the men who are doing the shooting appreciate it in the same way as a correspondent. They are as short on knowledge as the men in the open boat: They know neither their reason for fighting, nor precisely where they are, nor even, for that matter, whether they are winning. In this respect they are truly in the same boat as a correspondent, who, despite his role as professional observer, achieves no comprehensive overview; the phrase "I don't know" weaves through these writings like a refrain.

Such ignorance can be an advantage to a sensibility that thrives on wonder and mystery. Thus Crane does not write of war in historical contexts put together from patiently gathered information about political, social, economic, or strategic motives; he writes, rather, of particular persons and scenes sufficiently close to observed phenomena to appear lifelike yet so representative of broad human patterns that they insist on their typicality. On the comparatively rare occasions when he does turn historically specific, Crane relies on satire, irony, and the grotesque. In discussing "The Eastern Question," for example, he reduces Turkey and the Concert of Great Powers to caricatures:

> One could hardly have the temerity to observe the emotions of this gigantic creature, the Concert, at this particular hour. It would be an intrusion too grievous. Nor would one dare to scan the colossal countenance, broken with surprise and pain. It no doubt feels itself to be an immense and hideous bit of nonsense. It went into a thing with a great deal of solemnity and kow-towing and salaaming on all sides and with a loud declaration to do its own will in a certain matter and there rose up from the dark East a little man in a red fez who took it by the hair and mopped the world with it. (IX, 79–80)

For Crane this figure, modeled on the merchant in the bazaar who gulls his customers into buying dear, *is* the historical issue and the historical issue is essentially a game: "In fact the Turk is nothing if not the Eastern question. . . . It has been his business for a long time to mystify and seduce and trick his neighbors and he does it with the skill that comes from perfect devotion to the game" (IX, 76). If the game analogy is not profound, neither is it trivial. Crane repeatedly underlines the gratuitous element in war and the crucial role of chance; in this his dispatches resemble his fiction. The games he describes are often comic or quasi-comic: "Filibustering was once such a simple game. It was managed blandly by gentle captains and smooth and undisturbed gentlemen who at other times dealt in the law, soap, medicine, and bananas. . . . And yet the game is not obsolete; it is still played by the wise and the silent – men whose names are not display-typed and blathered from one end of the country to the other" (V, 94).

Crane thinks differently when the context is military: "Scattered fragments [of squadrons] slid slowly back, leaving the plain black with wounded and dead men and horses. From a distance it was like a game. There was no blood, no expression, no horror to be seen" (IX, 20). The implicit trope is a theater as the curtains part: Crane uses the same sliding trope in describing the sea vista in an earlier dispatch; and a variant reading of the present passage contains a reference to "the movements of tiny doll tragedy" (IX, 628). The correspondent here seems quietly astonished by his own indifference. While he does not perhaps feel the guilt of a man with a "survivor complex," being an outsider places a burden upon him that is not unlike those who do know the guilt of being spared when others are not. Soldiers bleed and die; correspondents watch. Crane's fraternization with the fighting man may thus attempt to compensate for whatever indifference he may feel when playing his professionally spectatorial role. He comes closest to a "fraternal, fusing feeling," to borrow Ishamel's phrase, when he contemplates groups: "This hospital was a spectacle of heroism. The doctor, gentle and calm, moved among the men without the common-senseless bullying of the ordinary ward. It was a sort of fraternal game. They were all in it, and of it, helping each other" (IX, 145).

Crane shows the difference between a near, sympathetic view and a far, detached one in the dispatch headlines "The Red Badge of Courage Was His Wig-Wag Flag." The observer feels detached because of the distance separating him from the object of his attention, and because the object is the enemy: "Now began one of the most extraordinary games ever played in war. The skirmish suddenly turned into something that was like a grim and frightful field sport. It did not appear so then – for many reasons – but when one reflects, it was trap-shooting" (IX, 140). Conversely, the near view develops – as in *The Red Badge of Courage* – when the men you watch are yours and you are close enough to see their faces. The game *these* men play is one of existential commitment: "One could note the prevalence of a curious expression – something dreamy, the symbol of minds striving to tear aside the screen of the future and perhaps expose the ambush of death. It was not fear in the least. It was simply a moment in the lives of men who have staked themselves and have come to wonder which wins – red or black?" (IX, 135).

The general predominance of types over individuals is a corollary of Crane's interest in the theme and motif of the game and is related in turn to his interest in the figure (a special case of typicality to which I will turn below). In a game the individual loses individuality in performing certain typical functions (e.g., shuffling, dealing, receiving cards, bidding, and so on) that the other players also perform. If a player wants to be "individual," and wants to show a unique human "personality," it must be done within the rules of the game, but ironically, this too means "typing" oneself – as, for example, the bluffer, the poker face, or, as in the case of the cowboy, in "The Blue Hotel," the board-whacker. In the game of war the pattern presents itself on a larger scale, which means a greater abundance of types and also of figures. The type tends to be transparent; we "see through" it toward the object for which it stands. The figure, on the other hand, tends to be opaque; it is something we just see, like a color or a physical thing in a visual field. Let us examine briefly some passages in which the two phenomena, the figure and the type, appear.

Crane ends "A Fragment of Velestino" with a scene dominated by a group of mountaineers: "They were curious figures in the evening light, perfectly romantic if it were not for the modernity of the rifles and the shining lines of cartridges. With the plain a sea of shadow below, and the vague blue troops of Greece about them in the trenches, these men sang softly the wild minor ballads of their hills" (IX, 44). The scene takes place on a height, and in the paragraph preceding this one we see a colonel of infantry sitting on a rock criticizing his line officers. Had Crane left it at that, the description might have recalled the scene in *The Red Badge of Courage* in which Henry views the colonel looming against the sky on a horse. By including the mountaineers, Crane adds a quality that, though rare in the earlier work, is common in the war dispatches. The quality is not easily described, but involves a close sympathetic attention to admirable human properties rendered with sensory vividness. Here, as in the passage discussed above, Crane is on the watch for beauty, except that the beauty in this case resides unmediated, in human beings. If there was less attention to admirable properties in *The Red Badge of Courage,* that was perhaps because it centered on a character who was, to a large extent, alienated from the events in which he was involved. The correspondent does not feel alienated in the same way, though it is clear enough that he often feels removed. This is especially the case when there is no particular urgency in a scene. At such times one can describe things more or less as they meet the eye. Crane does that in the scene we have been discussing, but for a different reason. Here urgency unquestionably exists. The problem is that Crane is too remote from the historical situation to feel it. The deputy who tries in the present dispatch to approach the king remains therefore a type and a figure. The things he says to the crowd are the things that any disgruntled political leader would say in a similar situation – the typical things; the only explicit remark he makes is "I wish to see the king" (IX, 71). The scene is practically in pantomine: The crowd waits; the man arrives and is greeted tumultuously; he makes his way to the palace and is turned away, only to be cheered by the crowd. Meanwhile, on the steps of the palace, a guard – another figure – picks up a handful of pebbles and flings them contemptuously "straight into the upturned faces of the Athenians" (IX, 71). The deputy's complementary gesture, as he leaves the arena, is the lifting of "his tall white hat" (IX, 72).

History, for Crane, is largely a costume affair. In this sense he continues the tradition of Hawthorne. In *The Scarlet Letter* the climactic events of the narrative occur on a festive occasion in commemoration of the founding of the colony. Although the occasion is historical, in the sense that it looks back to a significant public event, Hawthorne is largely interested in what happens to his four principal characters as they stand framed against a background of pageantry; relishing spectacle, he dwells at length on the colorful clothing worn by the members of the community. Similarly, in his description of a procession during the New Orleans campaign in *Great Battles of the World* Crane can write: "Here tossed the bonnets of a fierce battalion of Highlanders; here marched a bottle-green regiment, the officers wearing furred cloaks and crimson sashes; here was a steady line of blazing red coats. . . . It was like a grand review" (IX, 283). The scene with the mountaineers likewise depends for much of its effect on their clothing; and no reader of Crane needs to be reminded how frequently, both in the fiction and in the war dispatches, he calls attention to details of military dress. When Crane singles out the white hat in the Athenian scene, to which we may briefly return, he continues this pattern. Here he reverts to the technique of "the Eastern Question," in which he essentializes the historical antagonists into figures in a comic myth. The mythical figure in the present sketch is the hat itself:

> It was the hat of violence. It was the hat of insurrection. It proclaimed terror. In New York this hat would foreshadow the cessation of the cable-car, the disappearance of the postman, the subterranean concealment of the cook, the supreme elevation of the price of beer – all the horrors of municipal war. . . . If you study the history of the famous revolutions you will be taught to tremble at this hat. (IX, 70)

Crane's attitude toward the U.S. Marine signalmen is much closer to his attitude toward the mountaineers. Crane can understand the human urgency in a situation that exposes a man to a barrage of enemy fire. Here, consequently, is a figure with whom he can identify. Crane provides a background for this piece, published in 1899, in the dispatch "The Red Badge of Courage Was His Wig-Wag Flag," which shows how the fighting man stakes his life in the game, invoking a "sinister" forewarning "of certain tragedy, not the tragedy of a street accident, but foreseen, inexorable, invincible tragedy" (IX, 136). After devoting two paragraphs to the noise of bullets, Crane lifts his eyes to the top of a hill:

> And – mark you – a spruce young sargeant of marines, erect, his back to the showering bullets, solemnly and intently wig-wagging to the distant *Dolphin!*
>
> It was necessary that this man should stand at the very top of the ridge in order that his flag might appear in relief against the sky, and the Spaniards must have concentrated a fire of at least twenty rifles upon him. (IX, 138)

In "Marine Signalling under Fire at Guantanamo" Crane uses similar techniques to heighten our sense of the signalman's peril, but, having more time for composition, he goes further. Dividing the story into two sections, he presents the exploits of the signalmen in a cumulative series, concluding with a dramatic picture of one of the men, a St. John H. Quick, still wigwagging against the sky. Moreover, he emphasizes (perhaps reaching back to the Sullivan County writings and "The Open Boat") that these signalmen constituted a group of four. He focuses, however, on two of them. The first is at once a type and a figure. To establish the type Crane employs the epithet "A red-headed 'mick,' " then remarks, "I think his name was Clancy, at any rate, it will do to call him Clancy" (VI, 198). It is the job of this typical-Irishman-cum-typical Marine to stake his life at ever-escalating odds. The ship he signals can't see him the first time, so he "had to return to the top of the ridge and outline himself and his flag against the sky" (VI, 198). If Quick's heroism seems even more palpable, this is evidently by design. First, we have already seen Clancy perform, and we know the risks. Second, Clancy survived, and we wonder how much longer the odds will hold. Third, Quick is seen at closer range: Crane is so near we can study the soldier's face, and this humanizes him. Finally, Quick's exploit is the last one in the account, and for this reason climactic: "I watched his face, and it was as grave and serene as that of a man writing in his own library. . . . He stood there amid the animal-like babble of the Cubans, the crack of rifles, and the whistling snarl of the bullets, and wigwagged whatever he had to wigwag without heeding anything but his business" (IX, 199–200).

At the end of the dispatch "Stephen Crane at the Front for the World" Crane presents a type based on geopolitical identity:

> "Say, doctor, this ain't much of a wound. I reckon I can go now back to my troop," said Arizona.
>
> "Thanks, awfully, doctor. Awfully kind of you. I dare say I shall be all right in a moment," said New York. (IX, 145)

These remarks serve as a reminder that the trait or quality Crane aestheticizes, though relatively faceless and generalized, is rarely altogether stereotyped. A stereotype replaces the field of individuals for which it ostensibly stands, while types, as Crane designs them, truly represent the field. A stereotype draws attention to itself; one cannot see through the figure to anything beyond. A type, on the other hand, mediates, connecting with the field. A steretotype is an abstract composite of traits, a type a lived embodiment. With a truly typical soldier, therefore, it is easy to identify:

> There was a soldier there among the ten of a type I know. In the photograph galleries in Athens there are many portraits of bearded gentlemen, in kilts festooned with 500 yards of cartridge belt and gripping their Gras rifles ferociously. By the Athenians they are supposed to be away killing battalion after battalion of Turks. I know that type too, and I have never seen them do anything. Generally speaking, they are a pack of humpty-dumpties. But this brown-faced quiet lad with his lamb-like eyes and gentle, considerate ways, I know him too, and he will stick to a trench, and stick and stick and go without water and food

> and fight long and still stick until the usual orders come to fall back. Barring the genuine euzone, this gentle lad is the best man in Greece, even if he does wear the regulation uniform. (IX, 67)

Crane presents the good type first, but before describing the lad who "belongs" to it, he takes time to satirize the bad. This type is cousin to the mystifying Turk in "The Eastern Question" and the ridiculous man in the white hat, the endless cartridge belt being the equivalent of the deputy's omnipotent headdress. The noble lad, framed between the two references to the bad type, becomes a kind of Billy Budd, meek and gentle and, by virtue of being the best man in Greece, transcendent.

One may compare this individual to the dead young Greek whose body Crane regards after an engagement:

> As for the clothes . . . they were cut after a common London style. Beside the body lay a black hat. It was what one would have to call a Derby, although from the short crown there was an inclination to apply the old name of dicer. There was a rather high straight collar and a little four-in-hand scarf of flowered green and a pin with a little pink stone in it.
>
> This dead young Greek had nothing particularly noble in his face. There was expressed in this thing none of the higher thrills to incite, for instance, a company of romantic poets. This lad was of a common enough type. The whole episode was almost obvious. He was of people in comfortable circumstances; he bought his own equipment, of course. Then one morning news sped to the town that the Turks were beating. And then he came to the war on the smoke, so to speak, of the new fires of patriotism which had been immediately kindled in the village place, around the tables in front of the cafe. He had been perhaps a little inclined to misgiving, but withal anxious to see everything anyhow, and usually convinced of his ability to kill any number of Turks. He had come to this height, and fought with these swarthy, hard-muscled men in the trench, and, soon or late, got his ball through the chest. Then they had lifted the body and laid it to the rear in order to get it out of the way. (IX, 39)

Although Crane uses the familiar image of the upturned face to debunk, the main interest of the description is his imaginary reconstruction of the young volunteer's life just preceding the battle. The colorful civilian clothes are an advantage over a uniform, from which Crane could have inferred only that the soldier was an enlisted man or an officer, and that he had been recently introduced to the field of action. The clothing enables Crane to deduce and reconstruct. At first glance the point of departure is the fifth sentence of paragraph two: "He was of people in comfortable circumstances. . . ." But the reconstruction is imminent, as it were, even in the preceding paragraph, where "one" would have to call the hat a Derby, and where "there was an inclination." The pronoun and the clause both refer, despite the grammatical depersonalization, to the correspondent, whose imagination goes beyond the immediate data of the scene.

The story he reconstructs is the story of a Greek Henry Fleming; the assumptions Crane makes are like the assumptions he would have made if he had been a Civil War correspondent and had found Fleming's body in civilian dress. In keeping with the attitude expressed throughout the war dispatches, this description is an implicit eulogy. Looking down from the top of the ridge, where the dead soldier fought with his comrades, "one" sees a "great" plain and a "great" map of the plain of Thessaly; there are "natural splendours," and the distances are "magnificent" (IX, 38). The description is there partly for contrast; as in other war writings Crane shifts quickly from the beauty of the scene to its horror. But it is also there to add an aura to the account of the young volunteer's heroism – to the valor of his life and the poignancy of his death. Later we shall see how Crane uses such techniques and attitudes in the composition of fictional works.

In "War Memories," which has attracted relatively little notice, Crane combines a number of motifs to form a work that contributes significantly to his aesthetics of war.[7] Largely episodic in structure, this blend of fiction and journalism is organized around scenes in which key figure-types are represented as sublime or ironic, or both. An officer described by Vernall, the correspondent who records the memories, appears at first to be in for sublime treatment: "The scene on the top of the ridge was very wild, but there was only one truly romantic figure. This was a Cuban officer who held in one hand a great glittering machete and in the other a cocked revolver. He posed like a statue of victory. Afterwards he confessed to me that he alone had been responsible for the winning of the fight" (VI, 231). With that confession the portrayal turns suddenly and conclusively ironic. On a hilltop Vernall later attains a different perspective as distance diminishes the sighted figure while at the same time lending it an aura of enchantment:

> In truth, there was a man in a Panama hat strolling to and fro behind one of the Spanish trenches, gesticulating at times with a walking-stick. A man in a Panama hat, walking with a stick! That was the strangest sight of my life – that symbol, that quaint figure of Mars. The battle, the thunderous row, was his possession. He was the master. He mystified us all with his infernal Panama hat and his wretched walking stick. (VI, 244–5)

Confronted with this figure, so reminiscent of the man in the white hat, Crane's imagination again turns spectatorial and mythopoeic – even if the resulting myth is small and wreathed in irony. Like the man in the white hat, the figure is drawn away from the realm of historical, motivated acts toward the gratuitous and the mysterious. Indeed, the wonder Crane attributes to the innocent girl in "Three Miraculous Soldiers" is not unlike his own wonder at the way the figure, like those soldiers, suddenly disappears:

> Later, the American guns shelled the trenches and a block-house near them, and Mars vanished. It could not have been death. One cannot kill Mars. But there was one other figure, which rose to symbolic dignity. The balloon of our signal corps had swung over the tops of the jungle's trees toward the Spanish trenches. Whereat the balloon and the man in the Panama hat and with a walking-stick – whereat these two waged tremendous battle.
>
> Suddenly the conflict became a human thing. A little group of blue figures appeared on the green of the terrible hillside. It was some of our infantry. The *attaché* of a great empire was at my shoulder. . . . "Why they're trying to take the position," he cried. . . . And – good fellow that he was – he began to grieve and wail over a useless sacrifice of gallant men. (VI, 245)

The shift in feeling from the single small figure to the many small ones illustrates Crane's preference for the soldier over the civilian and for the American soldier over all others, and his preference for praising, wherever possible, by indirection. This can be accomplished through the use of a mediator such as "one" or "you," or by stressing the unpretentious simplicity of an heroic act or attitude. In the paragraph that follows, Crane does both: "One's senses seemed to demand that these men should cry out. But you could really find wounded men who exhibited all the signs of a pleased and contented mood. . . . 'Well, this ain't exactly what I enlisted for, boys. If I'd been told about this in Tampa, I'd have been resigned from the army' " (VI, 245–6).

Crane discovers in these war scenes patterns of behavior resembling patterns he had discovered in the Bowery. The mixture of self-mocking irony and stoicism in the passage above recalls "The Men in the Storm," who swore in their semihumorous American way. The difference between this and the war scene lies partly in the circumstances and partly in Crane. The city reporter is a little more detached than the correspondent, first, because he does not feel the same urgency that the latter feels on confronting a gravely wounded man. Although his civilians are desperate enough in their own way, their lives are not directly in jeopardy. A soldier with a red badge, on the other hand, has come face to face with death; above all, he has staked life itself in the interest of a cause, the existence of which leads us to a second distinction, namely, that the civilian men are members of a seriality while their military counterparts are members of a group. There is a wholeness to a group – a sense of collective purpose – that, though not explicitly referred to, tends to validate its attitudes and acts. Third, the military group constitutes, as it were, more of a good thing. If the men in the soup line behave occasionally "in a sort of American fashion," soldiers, in Crane's eyes, do it all the time and on the grandest scale: In war, the typical national qualities that Crane seeks out in "The Men in the Storm" and other Bowery sketches finds a permanent institutional form.

The contrasting roles played by solitary figures suggest a further difference between the two types of sketches. "In the brilliantly lighted space appeared the figure of a man. He was rather stout and very well clothed. His beard was fashioned charmingly after that of the Prince of Wales. He stood in an attitude of magnificent reflection. He slowly stroked his moustasche with a certain grandeur of manner, and looked down at the snow-encrusted mob" (XI, 43). The relation between the figure and the rest of the men, as this scene from "The Men in the Storm" goes on to show, is antagonistic, as the men call attention to him, bait him, and force him at last to leave. Compare that picture with Crane's treatment of Admiral Sampson in "War Memories":

> Admiral Sampson is to me the most interesting personality of the war. I would not know how to sketch him for your even if I could pretend to sufficient material. Anyhow, imagine, first of all, a marble block of impassivity out of which is carved the figure of an old man. Endow this with life, and you've just begun. Then you must discard all your pictures of bluff, red-faced old gentlemen who roar against the gale, and understand that the quiet old man is a sailor and an admiral. This will be difficult; if I told you he was anything else it would be easy. He resembles other types; it is his distinction not to resemble the preconceived type of his standing. (IV, 239)

The passage illustrates the direct colloquial style one finds on every page of "War Memories" and in many of the dispatches. The form is almost conversational, not only in diction and tone but in strategy; the conversational quality is suggested also by the use of dashes, which occur often in the dispatches, giving a sense of thought in process and of a voice hesitating – "For my part, an impressive thing of the war is the absolute devotion to Admiral Sampson's person – no, to his judgment and wisdom" (VI, 239) – or of a voice pausing rhetorically before the enunciation of a crucial word: "But finally I saw that it was all manner, that hidden in his indifferent, even apathetic, manner there was the alert, sure, fine mind of the best sea-captain that America has produced since – since Farragut? I don't know. I think – since Hull" (VI, 239). Crane strives to make the admiral bigger than life and at the same time lifelike by stressing the "everyday" nature of the man's appearance and behavior – a corollary of his attempt to explode any romantic notions about the way an admiral ought to look or act. In order to reveal the man as a type, in the highest sense, it must be demonstrated that he is not merely a stereotype. Thus Crane heightens the verisimilitude by imitating Sampson's own speech patterns: "Once, afterward, they called upon him to avenge himself upon a rival – they were there and they would have to say – but he said no-o-o, he guessed it – wouldn't do – any – g-o-oo-o-d to the – service" (VI, 239–40). Having turned a national hero into a personal presence – having contracted him, as it were, to believable size – Crane then expands him again. The tone, as before, is casual, even laconic, but the feeling seems to be intense: "No bunting, no arches, nor fireworks; nothing but the perfect management of a big fleet. That is a record for you. No trumpets, no cheers of the populace. Just plain, pure, unsauced accomplishment. But ultimately he will reap his reward in – in what? In text-books on sea campaigns. No more" (VI, 240).

In the sketch of Sampson there are two kinds of subordinates: The naval officers under the admiral's command, and Crane, whose admiration for Sampson brings him, in effect, into a similar relationship. If the charismatic leader knows much and is self-complete, the subordinate is dependent and knows little. As Crane's area of knowledge is literary, so his self-effacement takes a literary form: "I would not know how to sketch him for you even if I could pretend to sufficient material." This confession of ignorance has its counterpart in other sections of "War Memories" and in those dispatches in which, as I have already pointed out, Crane repeatedly declares, literally or in effect, "I don't know." Here his aim is to identify with "the men," who also don't know, and to preserve the air of mystery that for Crane surrounds the obedient performance of service to a higher power: "The fine thing about 'the men' is that you can't explain them. I mean when you take them collectively. They do a thing, and afterward you find that they have done it because they have done it" (VI, 230).

The things the correspondent learns tend to be small and late in coming. He pictures himself repeatedly as a man in a dream experiencing brief interludes of reality that, far from providing an overview of his situation, merely tell him about his immediate physical state. A situation becomes comprehensible only later, when he has time to reflect. One result of writing these "memories" at some remove from the event is a mixed temporal perspective – a new kind of shifting in which the imagination shuttles back and forth between poles of knowledge and ignorance:

> I was in a dream, but I kept my eye on the guide and halted to listen when he halted to listen and ambled onward when he ambled onward. Sometimes he turned and pantomimed as ably and fiercely as a man being stung by a thousand hornets. Then we knew that the situation was extremely delicate. . . . The bay was white in the sun, and the great black-hulled armored cruisers were impressive in a dignity massive yet

> graceful. We did not know that they were doomed ships, soon to go out to a swift death. My friend drew maps and things while I devoted myself to complete rest. . . . We did not know that we were the last Americans to view them alive, and unhurt, and at peace. Then we retraced our way, at the same noiseless canter. I did not understand my condition until I considered that we were well through the Spanish lines and practically out of danger. Then I discovered that I was a dead man. The nervous force having evaporated I was a mere corpse. . . . But just at this time we were discovered by a Spanish patrol, and I ascertained that I was not dead at all. (VI, 237)

The first knowledge Crane acquires here is a form of news: The gestures of the guide reveal the essence of the situation. So far, both knowledge and ignorance are confined within the frame of the event as originally experienced. But the second piece of knowledge is earned outside the frame and after the event; not until much later will he learn that the ships he saw were to be sunk, and that he and his companions were the last Americans to see them "alive." The third advent of knowledge, like the first, is confined to the event as originally experienced: Crane realizes his physical condition immediately after the period of exertion comes to a close. The last moment of enlightenment, in contrast with the earlier ones, is a masquerade. In the statement "I ascertained that I was not dead at all," the verb of the independent clause points not to something learned but to something done; or more precisely, it points to a thing done under the guise of a thing learned. The real "ascertaining" is done in the first half of the sentence, when the Spanish patrol discovers them. Crane learns, in other words, that the Spanish are upon them; decides to flee; and presents that act in the ironic guise (through the use of the word "ascertained") as a purely epistemological event.

The last isolated, noumenal figure in the work appears in the church scene:

> The interior of the church was too cave-like in its gloom for the eyes of the operating surgeons, so they had had the altar-table carried to the doorway, where there was a bright light. Framed then in the black archway was the altar-table with the figure of a man upon it. He was naked save for a breach-clout, and so close, so clear was the ecclesiastic suggestion, that one's mind leaped to a fantasy that his thin, pale figure had just been torn down from a cross. The flash of the impression was like light, and for this instant it illumined all the dark recesses of one's remotest idea of sacrilege, ghastly and wanton. (VI, 254)[8]

The difference between this scene and Henry Fleming's forest-chapel scene, with which it invites comparison, is threefold. First, this chapel is literal, a given in an historical scene, while the forest chapel is figurative. Second, the latter is mediated by a consciousness unaware of the nature of his own interpreting. The Cuban scene, by contrast, is mediated by a consciousness entirely aware of its own operations. We experience the described event both as happening in the phenomenal world and as a perceptual process, meanwhile holding onto our sense of the boundaries of consciousness through the mediation of consciousness itself. Third, the religious element in the Cuban scene, unlike the religious element in Fleming's scene has, so to speak, no meaning. The aim of giving the ecclesiastic suggestion is, in effect, to take it away. That sudden deprivation, that stripping away of all significance, gives the episode a peculiar negative force. There is nothing left but the tension of a feeling that cannot discharge itself – a sense that the scene is utterly meaningless and at the same time "overwhelming, crushing, monstrous" (VI, 254).

A similar tension can be felt in the following account, devoted to the exchange of Lt. Hobson and the other captured men of the *Merrimac*. After a long wait, the prisoners appear:

> Then the men of the regular army did a thing. They arose *en masse* and came to "Attention." Then the men of the regular army did another thing. They slowly lifted every weather-beaten hat and drooped it until it touched the knee. Then there was a magnificent silence. . . .
>
> Then suddenly the whole scene went to rubbish. Before he reached the bottom of the Hill, Hobson was bowing to right and left like another Boulanger, and, above the thunder of the massed bands, one could hear the venerable outbreak, "Mr. Hobson, I'd like to shake the hand of the man who – " But the real welcome was that welcome of silence. However, one could thrill again when the tail of the procession appeared – an army wagon containing the blue-jackets of the *Merrimac* adventure. . . . And the army spoke to the navy. "Well, Jackie, how does it feel?" and the navy up and answered: "Great! Much obliged to you fellers for comin' here." . . . Here was no rubbish. Here was the mere exchange of language between men. (VI, 258)

If the opposing poles of interpretation are made explicit in the chapel scene, here they can be felt in the tug and pull of the language. The issue is whether to thrill or not to thrill, and the crucial section is in the second paragraph where (sentences three and four) Crane piles one negative conjunction on top of another, the "but" of sentence three turning attention way from the rejected features of the event to prior accepted ones, while the "however" of sentence four swings to a new acceptable feature in the immediate scene. The latter negates, in other words, the turning-back in time; and beyond this the word has no negative force. The sentence could as easily have begun: "And the real welcome . . ."

The fundamental problem, therefore, is not how to describe or react to this or that feature, but how to relate the description or reaction to the feature. A partial solution is the use of repetition. Having affirmed, at the end of the paragraph quoted above, that "Here was no rubbish," he remarks, at the end of the next paragraph: "They had no sense of excellence. Here was no rubbish" (VI, 259). He then turns once more to the mode of indirect, tight-lipped congratulation which he favors in his descriptions of "the men." The types he invokes in the process – the "army" and the "navy" – are representative, however, in a new way. In his quest for the typical, Crane normally presents an individual who embodies qualities shared by many others. Even when the individual is a composite, as in "The Price of the Harness," he still possesses a variety of unique features. The types invoked in the present passage, by contrast, lack individualization. They are faceless spokesmen for a group from which they never really emerge.

Crane works a variation on the technique in the concluding section of "War Memories":

> Men are always good men. And at any rate, most of the people were in worse condition than I – poor bandaged chaps looking sadly down at the waves. In a way I knew the kind. First lieutenants at forty years of age, captains at fifty, majors at 102, lieutenant-colonels at 620, full colonels at 1,000, and brigadiers at 9,768,295 plus. A man had to live two billion years to gain eminent rank in the regular army at that time. (VI, 261)

The lightness of the passage accords with Crane's manner throughout the first part of the sketch, an expanded version of a dispatch called "The Private's Story" in which Crane assumes the first-person persona of a homeward-bound enlisted man. The dispatch shifts midway from an ironic mode to a mode of seriousness, then back again to a kind of sentimental seriousness, then back again to irony. In the pivotal scene the private sees a little woman in an approaching launch. Some black soldiers stir themselves and hurry to bring their colonel to the rail where he cries "Alice," at which the little woman – much as Henry Fleming's mother had done at her son's departure – covers her face: "She made no outcry: it was all in this simple, swift gesture, but we – we knew them. It told us. It told us the other part. And in a vision we all saw our own harbor lights. That is to say, those of us who had harbor lights" (IX, 197). The two figures remain anonymous because the narrating private is typical and a typical private in that situation would not have been able to identify them. As a consequence they stand in the scene, like the private himself, as types.

Describing the same scene in "War Memories," where he does not adopt the persona of a type, Crane reveals the knowledge he had withheld in the earlier piece:

> There was a little woman in the launch, and she kept looking and looking and looking. Our ship was so high that she could see only those

> who hung at the rail, but she kept looking and looking. It was plain enough – it was all plain enough – but my heart sank with the fear that she was not going to find him. But presently there was a commotion among some black dough-boys of the Twenty-fourth Infantry, and two of them ran aft to Colonel Liscum, its gallant commander. Their faces were wreathed in darkey grins of delight. "Kunnel, ain't dat Mis' Liscum, Kunnel?" "What?" said the old man. He got up quickly and appeared at the rail, his arm in a sling. He cried, "Alice!" The little woman saw him, and instantly she covered up her face with hands as if blinded with a flash of white fire. She made no outcry; it was all in this simply swift gesture, but we – we knew them. It told us. It told us the other part. And in a vision we all saw our own harbor-lights. That is to say, those of us who had harbor-lights. (VI, 261–2)

The repetitions near the conclusion of the passage, though not unprecedented in Crane's earlier work, are prominent features of his descriptions of the Spanish–American War. The repetition following Alice's gesture ("but we – we knew them") attempts to capture the spontaneity of these oral communications. The correspondent is not merely a man writing but, to the extent that his medium will allow the illusion, a man speaking.

One finds orality also in the earlier works: The adjectives, adverbs, and colloquial expressions, which might look like "fillers" in the prose of another writer, give the sense of a voice caught, on the page, in a flow of speech. Side by side with this pattern appear snatches of talk by characters, where Crane tries, as above, to capture the redundancy of actual utterance, as in this exchange from *The Red Badge of Courage:*

> "Who is it? Who is it?"
> "It's Jimmie Rogers. Jimmie Rogers." (II, 99)

The correspondent often finds himself in a passionate state that he attempts to communicate through balladlike repetition: "The spray of the chatter whirled against them and they were bronze, bronze men going to bury their dead" (IX, 175); "The sad, sad, slow voice of the bugle called out over the grave" (IX, 176). Such effects are not the result of hasty composition in the field. The account of Hobson's exchange, for example, was written many months after the event. Moreover, Crane turns to balladlike repetition when the pace of action slows and one can see the shape of events against a long-range temporal horizon. Crane often turns balladeer when the scene is not martial at all, but domestic. One need only consider, in this connection, the description of separated lovers, above, or a dispatch in which Crane observes that "all the circumlocution and bulwarks and clever football interference and trouble and delay and protracted agony and duennas count for nothing, count for nothing against the tides of human life, which are in Cuba or Omaha controlled by the same moon" (IX, 205).

Crane's rhythms are not less controlled for appearing spontaneous, as can be seen by comparing a passage in "The Private's Story," which was written under deadline pressure, and the successor to the passage in "War Memories." Both works describe a procession of wounded men. In "The Private's Story" we read:

> When that load passed the hotel, there was a noise made by a crowd which brought me up trembling. Perhaps it was a moan, perhaps it was a sob – but, no, it was something far beyond a moan or a sob. Anyhow, the sound of women weeping was in it, for I saw many of those fine ladies with wet cheeks when that gang of bandaged, dirty, ragged, emaciated, half starved cripples went by in review. (IX, 197–8)

In the later version of the passage, Crane no longer employs a string of adjectives to drag the emotion in: "When that crowd began to pass the hotel the banks of flowers made a noise which could make one tremble. Perhaps it was a moan, perhaps it was a sob – but no, it was something beyond either a moan or a sob. Anyhow, the sound of women weeping was in it. – The sound of women weeping" (VI, 263). In this version, the tough word "load" is replaced by the soft word "crowd," and the word "crowd" in the original version (referring there to the female spectators) gives way to "banks of flowers." There is, at the same time, a break in the flow of language, as if the speaker were searching for the properly expressive word, and a shift from piled-up adjectives to the repetition of the most feeling-laden phrase, "the sound of women weeping." It is through these techniques that the correspondent earns the right to conclude the work with the rhythmical, poetic lines: "The episode was closed. And you can depend upon it that I have told you nothing at all, nothing at all, nothing at all" (VI, 263).

7

Community and Crisis: "The Monster," *Tales of Whilomville*, "The Blue Hotel," "The Bride Comes to Yellow Sky"

In Crane's slum novels the primary community facing crisis is the nuclear family; the nuclear family also plays a role in *The Third Violet* and *Active Service*. Family relations are so interwoven with relations to a larger community, in each of these works, that is is hard to say where one set ends and another begins. The same applies to the works in this chapter, "The Monster," "The Blue Hotel," "The Bride Comes to Yellow Sky," and *Tales of Whilomville*. In the first, the rescue of an only child leads to disruptions affecting not merely the family but the entire neighboring population. The second work turns largely on the manner in which a father and son deal with one stranger who is difficult and another who is diffident. In the third work the family, in the form of the newlywed couple, comes into being in a way that will alter forever the community that has existed up till now. Finally, *Tales of Whilomville* portrays crises not only within particular families but within communities of peers who are mainly children and mainly males. In all these respects the writings considered here differ from a number of other works in which crises are experienced by spontaneous, small, and temporary groups in a way that directly addresses the question of fraternity.

"Now, 'The Blue Hotel' goes in neatly with 'The Monster' and together they make 32,000" (*Letters,* p. 172). This statement by Crane presumably reflects the kind of considerations spelled out above. It may also reflect a sense of congruence between the two works on some other grounds, a sense that rests on their general drift and tragic tenor. Both narratives descend to darkness and they do so with little of the equivocation that so often marks the end of a Crane story.

"The Bride Comes to Yellow Sky" is considered here not only because it addresses community and crisis from a family perspective but because it does so from an angle that is interesting in its own right; because the relative brightness of the vision it embodies adds an element of variety; and because, like the other two works, it is a story about a town. *Tales of*

Whilomville, which will be given more attention than it usually receives, also warrants consideration on some or all of the grounds mentioned above.

THE USES OF AUTHORITY

The principal authority figure of Crane's Whilomville novel makes his first appearance mowing his lawn and dealing with his son Jimmie when the latter accidentally destroys a flower.[1] The scene is a quick portrait of Dr. Trescott in his dual role of caring parent and wise dispenser of justice. As parental authority, Trescott occupies a hierarchical relation to his son, in contrast to the fraternal relation between Jimmie and Henry. As father, Trescott creates in the child a biological counterpart of Henry Johnson, on whom the doctor confers new life. While both creations are social in a broad sense, the second is professional and public, the act of a man practicing in a community the care for which he has been trained. It is not a case of the type absorbing the individual, for the doctor's care expresses the kind of man he personally elects to be. Given the authority he enjoys as a professional man, he chooses to save the life of the man who saved the life of his son. In contributing this capacity to the power to authorize – as I think the story invites us to do – we may recall that authority has long been understood as a power that creates, that "authorizes" because it "fathers."[2]

As a public man the doctor cares for his property, the significance of which is suggested by a pairing of details: "The doctor was shaving this lawn as if it were a priest's chin" (VII, 9). Later, Henry, who is not yet his ward, exercises a care of his own that expands on the analogy of the priest: "After Johnson had taken his supper in the kitchen, he went to his loft in the carriage-house and dressed himself with much care. No belle of a court circle could bestow more mind on a toilet than did Johnson. On second thought, he was more like a priest arraying himself for some parade of the church" (VII, 13). A variation on the theme is provided in barber Reifsnyder's professional care. The effect of these parallels is cumulative, and is one of the reasons why the tale, despite its shortness, has the amplitude of a full-length novel.

In the exercise of his authority the doctor displays wisdom, a faculty whose loss, according to Walter Benjamin, is strongly felt in modern literature.[3] No longer is it possible for storytelling to convey to an audience ideas or epithets helpful in the business of living, as that office often managed to do in more traditionally oriented societies. In allowing the doctor to act as he does, Crane at least gives wisdom an individualized embodied life. Trescott, however, is more than a symbol because wisdom here is more than an attribute; it consists in conrete acts – in treating

Jimmie's carelessness with patience and restraint, for example, and in caring for Henry in the face of mounting opposition.

When a wise one decides what course of action should be taken, he delivers a judgment: "The father reflected again. 'Well, Jimmie,' he said, slowly, 'I guess you had better not play train any more to-day. Do you think you had better?' " (VII, 10). The relation to authority represented here, in which wisdom exercises care in the form of restriction, befits the parent–child structure in the same way as the exchange in which Trescott later explains to Jimmie the implications of the games the boy and his friends have been playing around the oblivious Henry. That questions of judgment shade into questions of justice becomes apparent in Jimmie's relation to Henry, as drawn in Chapter 2, where the type of blamable situation the boy has just experienced is experienced in turn by Henry: "Whenever Henry dwelt for a time in sackcloth, Jimmie did not patronize him at all. This was the justice of his age, his condition. He did not know" (VII, 11–12).

While Henry and Jimmie are friends, Henry, having lived longer, occasionally plays the role of authority figure. Because his race limits his authoritative reach, Henry's behavior appears like a shadow cast by the father – imitative but fitful and overdrawn:

> Henry, with the elasticity of his race, could usually produce a sin to place himself on a footing with the disgraced one. . . . On the other hand, Henry would sometimes choose to absolutely repudiate this idea, and when Jimmie appeared in his shame would bully him most virtuously, preaching with assurance the precepts of the doctor's creed, and pointing out to Jimmie all his abominations. (VII, 11)

In the chapters describing Henry's rescue mission in the Trescotts' burning house and the subsequent rescue of Henry himself, the two types of authority converge. Henry becomes literally the substitute of Jimmie's father – in the absence of the father he does what the father would do. Rescue here constitutes – as in Conrad – an image for authority.[4] Rescue is an act of caring, a protective act in the highest degree. For protection occurs when the danger is such that defense alone is required, rescue when the danger is such that the threatened person must be actually removed. The themes of protection and rescue, which fascinated Crane, take a variety of forms in his canon. In "A Mystery of Heroism," Collins carries a drink of water back to a dying officer, performing an act that is essentially a protective gesture, whereas the rescue that provides the central interest of *Active Service* is lengthy and literal. Thus can Berryman stress Crane's preoccupation with the rescue of fallen women. In "The Monster," in any case, the substitution of one authority figure for another is not complete. I refer to the fact that Henry transports Jimmie to a point from which his father can remove him in safety, so that the father ends what Henry, a kind of counter-authority-figure, begins. When the bystanders then prevent Trescott from reentering the fire to save Henry himself, the ground is laid for the crucial and ironic possibility of saving Henry *after* the fire.

The question of authority and care is broached from the beginning of Henry's rescue attempt insofar as it is Mrs. Trescott who calls upon him to save Jimmie. But the question turns immediately into a complex study in perspective. In the first place, by the time Mrs. Trescott calls, Henry has already plunged into the flames. It is not therefore that Henry obeys an order; he acts from the same unquestioning sense of duty that sends that other, white Henry into a burning barn. In the second place, while the Trescott house is succumbing to the flames, there is this ironic counterpoint: "Doctor Trescott had been driving homeward, slowly smoking a cigar, and feeling glad that this last case was now in complete obedience to him, like a wild animal that he had subdued, when he heard the long whistle" (VII, 25). The mosaic pattern of this motif is made the more intricate by the barbershop scene, earlier in the chapter, in which Reifsnyder, who thinks an approaching figure is not Henry, submits to the viewpoint of his customers, who think it is. " 'Oh, vell,' said Reifsnyder, returning to his business, 'if you think so! Oh, vell!' He implied that he was submitting for the sake of amiability" (VII, 15).

This scene before Henry's rescue attempt combines with the scene of the returning doctor to frame the process of submission and assertion through which Henry struggles. Henry's rescue attempt at first seems doomed to defeat:

> He was submitting, submitting because of his fathers, bending his mind in a most perfect slavery to this conflagration. . . .
>
> Suddenly he remembered a little private staircase which led from a bedroom to an apartment which the doctor had fitted up as a laboratory and work-house. . . .
>
> When Johnson recalled this stairway the submission to the blaze departed instantly. He had been perfectly familiar with it, but his confusion had destroyed the memory of it.
>
> In his sudden momentary apathy there had been little that resembled fear, but now, as a way of safety came to him, the old frantic terror caught him. He was no longer creature to the flames, and he was afraid of the battle with them. It was a singular and swift set of alternations in which he feared twice without submission, and submitted once without fear. (VII, 23)

As so often in Crane, the ordeal is the joint product not only of character but of circumstance and chance. The circumstance is that the disfiguring phase of Henry's mission takes place in the laboratory–workshop where Trescott conducts his experiments, so that the ensuing episode is to this extent historically grounded. At the same time the catastrophe transpires by chance; like the barn fire in "The Veteran," or the simultaneous arrival in "The Blue Hotel" of the Swede, the cowboy and the Easterner, it is something that just happens. Though such a distinction is a matter of degree, degree is no small matter, as may be seen by considering that Dr. Trescott's historical pattern of existence – his being a doctor – often takes him away from home, but that fire has never before broken out in that home. It is by chance that it occurs at a time when he is not at home, as it is by chance that Henry, who just happens also to be away, just happens to return in time to attempt a rescue.

The nexus of chance and circumstance, then, enables Henry to display his own manner of being historical, which amounts at first sight to being submissive. Yet, as we have seen, he submits only once while asserting himself twice. What is more, by fighting he ceases to be a slave to the conflagration, breaking with the habit with which the history of his people has supposedly imbued him. That the community subsequently rejects him makes us the more aware of what Crane does not attempt to do. Crane does not imagine for us a black man's revolt against subordination in a society dominated by another race. The historical dimension that offers itself to Crane's imagination is not that of the present but that of the past; thus Henry's submission reflects an earlier rather than the current status of his race. In the past there was slavery, a categorical, collective status; in the present there is this individual man, who insists upon his freedom, though only within a limited field. The dominant figure of the episode, in other words, is not a black man who represents his race, but this particular man who happens to be black. At issue, then, is a peculiar kind of individualization, shaped by the convergence to which I have referred, and complementary to the peculiar abstraction of the remark that "It was a singular and swift set of alternations in which he feared twice without submission, and submitted once without fear." To make this remark Crane has had to pull back from his character, to see him from a distance, endowed with a historicity all his own; for Crane gives us here a little chronicle of the phases through which his character has just been going, placing in perspective the fact which, significantly, immediately precedes it – the fact that Henry refuses to be the slave of the flames. It is as if Crane were surprised by the sudden independence of this character, this Henry Johnson who seems for a time no longer to be the obedient creature of his pen.

THE SAPPHIRE LADY

> There was an explosion at one side, and suddenly before him there reared a delicate, trembling sapphire shape like a fairy lady. With a quiet

> smile she blocked his path and doomed him and Jimmie. Johnson shrieked, and then ducked in the manner of his race in fights. He aimed to pass under the guard of the sapphire lady. But she was swifter than eagles, and her talons caught in him as he plunged past her. (VII, 24)

This is lapidary writing, a writing of "effects." Yet the verbal excesses will seem earned if one allows that the very situation is excessive: Two lives are, after all, in balance; the one made the more precious by heroism, the other by helplessness. And while the igniting of chemicals in a room is sufficiently rare, this is how a room full of ignited chemicals might well look. As for the matter of intensity, it appears that Crane's imaginative engagement grows as the fire grows, such an engagement being itself a form of submission in that Crane yields to a fascination with a power of its own. This is not of course to deny that he designs the event; it is to suggest that the event he designs is one that not only validates but almost compels – given Crane's interest in all manifestations of fire and flame. Had this not been the case, it is hard to imagine how Crane could have prevented this myriad of components – the colors, the animal analogies, the jewel metaphor, the mixture of delicacy and brutality in the fairy lady – from becoming a mere mosaic of sensationalistic detail. That consequence would have been still likelier had Crane persisted in the mode of abstraction that characterizes his remarks about fear and submission.

A similar myriad may be seen in the disfiguring of Johnson, a process that is all the more horrible because informed with visual beauty:

> Suddenly the glass splintered, and a ruby-red snakelike thing poured its thick length out upon the top of the old desk. It coiled and hesitated, and then began to swim a languorous way down the mahogany slant. At the angle it waved its sizzling molten head to and fro over the closed eyes of the man beneath it. Then, in a moment, with mystic impulse, it moved again, and the red snake flowed directly down into Johnson's upturned face. (VII, 24).

But if these graphic and colorful passages are fairly typical of Crane's manner in general, it may be doubted that they are typical of "The Monster." As Berryman points out, "Details of the exceptional, the colored, the fantastic, the cursory, will indeed be found; but on the whole he attacks his subject directly, and the change is great."[5] As vivid as the sapphire lady may be, she is less representative of "The Monster" than her victim, who also, at first, presents a resplendent appearance, only to be transformed into something so grotesque that he becomes an outsider even to the outsider-community which is the black neighborhood. How this happens can only be comprehended in relation to the question of race.

THE QUESTION OF RACE

One avenue by which the question may be approached is the use of animal imagery. Bella, the girl Henry courts, is said to gallop like a horse while Bella, her mother, and Henry are together likened to an animal with which the white mind has often associated blacks: "They bowed and smiled and imitated until a late hour, and if they had been the occupants of the most gorgeous salon in the world they could not have been more like three monkeys" (VII, 16). Similar behavior is attributed to the entire black "colony" (VII, 185) in a Whilomville tale entitled "The Knife." On the other hand, Jimmie Trescott has a bawl like that of a calf and little Willie, another white child, is said "to buck and fume like a mustang" (VII, 19). Later, when Jake Winter turns against Trescott for protecting Henry, "Winter stood on the porch, still yelping. He was like a little dog" (VII, 59). These latter instances indicate that the attribution of animal traits does not in itself, for Crane, characterize race.

What does characterize race is a broader, familiar range of traits, attitudes, and actions. Alek Williams "indulged in a shuffling movement that was really a dance" (VII, 42); then "he burst out again in song and pantomimic celebration of his estate" (VII, 42). When Johnson visits the Farraguts, this scene takes place:

> Henry's face showed like a reflector as he bowed and bowed, bending almost from his head to his ankles. "Good-evenin', Mis' F'gut; good-evenin'. How is you dis evenin'? Is all you' folks well, Mis' Fa'gut?"
>
> After a great deal of kowtow, they were planted in two chairs opposite each other in the living-room. Here they exchanged the most tremendous civilities, until Miss Bella swept into the room, when there was more kowtow on all sides, and a smiling show of teeth that was like an illumination. (VII, 16)

With his lavender trousers and the silk band on his hat, Henry is a being of brightness as he walks through town, streetlights appearing on page after page to bring details forward. But when Trescott escorts the disfigured Johnson to the home of Alek Williams, illumination performs an almost sinister role: "Trescott had taken the silent shape by the arm and led it forward into the full revelation of the light. . . . 'Whee!' shrieked Mrs. Williams. She almost achieved a back somersault. Six members of the tribe of Williams made simultaneous plunge [*sic*] for a position behind the stove, and formed a wailing heap" (VII, 34–5). The illumination reveals an all-too-clear distinction between the uncontrolled, exaggerated, and submissive behavior of the black characters and the restraint of the white doctor, whose behavior is measured and authoritative.

The contrast Crane draws when Henry pays court to Bella in Watermelon Alley is less simple and less racial, consisting as it does in the opposition between, on the one hand, Johnson's elegant manners and his monstrous appearance, and, on the other, between those manners and the exaggerated, animalistic behavior of the Farraguts: "The girl cast a miserable glance behind her. She was still crawling away. On the ground beside the porch young Sim raised a strange bleat, which expressed both his fright and his lack of wind. Presently the monster, with a fashionable amble, ascended the steps after the girl" (VII, 47). Although the scene seems at first glance remote from the fire scene, the placement of Henry in relation to Bella is analogous to the placement of the sapphire lady in relation to Henry. Each functions as an impediment to the other's desire for escape from an intolerable situation. Secondly, if the effect of the fire was to reduce Johnson to the level of a creature, as denoted by the pronoun "it," the effect of Johnson's encounter with the Farraguts is to reduce them to a comparable level: Bella moves about on all fours while her brother bleats.

The racial dimensions of the scene emerge less from any distinction drawn within it than from a distinction that emerges by metonymic position. Thus the exaggerated antics of the black characters immediately follow the scene in which Johnson frightens the children at a white girl's party:

> Hearing a noise behind her at the window, one little girl turned to face it. Instantly she screamed and sprang away, covering her face with her hands. . . . At once they all faced the imperturbable window, and for a moment there was a silence. An astute lad made an immediate census of the other lads. The prank of slipping out and looming spectrally at a window was too venerable. But the little boys were all present and astonished.
>
> As they recovered their minds they uttered warlike cries, and through a side door sallied rapidly out against the terror. They vied with each other in daring. (VII, 46)

Such bravado is the stuff of which boyish adventure is made in such Whilomville tales as " 'Showin' Off,' " "The Fight," and "The City Urchin and the Chaste Villagers," and is innocent enough. Indeed, even when the boys egg each other on to taunt Henry, they remind us more of the scallawags of the tales than of their adult counterparts: "The foolishness and destructiveness of children are but a pale reflection of adults' stupidity and savagery."[6]

The difference between the boys in the tales and the boys in "The Monster" is that the latter's mock-heroic performances have racial overtones in a way that the former do not. The blacks in the tales are effectively segregated, being principal characters only in "The Knife." But their conspicuous presence in "The Monster" alerts the reader to contrasts even when Crane does not make them explicit. Thus the predominance of the mock-heroic among the little white boys throws into relief the absence of even that mode of exertion among the general black population, where the root from which actions grow is fear. In these scenes no one is really assertive, not even the monster, who is going mindlessly through the formalities. The two males who figure in settings invaded by Johnson – Sim Farragut and Alek Williams – are shaken by fear; Alek's one moment of assertiveness takes a venal form, as he entreats Judge Hagenthorpe to pay him more for taking care of Henry. Like their white counterparts, black female characters show a special susceptibility to fear, but there is no counterpart among the white females for the wailing of Bella Farragut. Wailing is presented as a racially distinct type of utterance. Thus the Williams children form a wailing heap, being members of a "tribe" whose synchronized behavior suggests some powerful reflex to which they must submit. The same applies *mutatis mutandis* to Henry, who twice cries out "in the negro wail that had in it the sadness of the swamps" (VII, 24). That Henry resists the temptation to submit and performs a selfless heroic act makes all the more pathetic his reduction to the status of an intruder whose presence instigates the very type of feeling Henry himself was able to overcome.

The force that tries to pull Henry down in the fire is not, it should be noted, a biological one. It is historical: "He was submitting, submitting because of his fathers, bending his mind in a most perfect slavery to the conflagration" (VII, 23). The fathers embody the force of example, not the force of biological determinism as we find it, say, in Norris's account of Vandover's submission to the future inscribed in his genetic make-up. Henry follows the example of his forbears, situated as they were in a condition of bondage more social, political, and economic than biological. On the other hand, it cannot be said that Johnson submits to his situation on the same terms as the hero Hamlin Garland describes in "A Branch Road." Will Hannan is trapped in the life of a marginal farmer, a life so demanding, both physically and spiritually, that he lacks the resolve to escape. Henry, by contrast, attempts not only an escape but a rescue. The worst bondage Will can imagine is the one that already possesses him, and that is coterminous with his own life. But the worst bondage Henry can imagine belongs to a time preceding his own life. Because that bondage persists as an example, and because of the coercive nature of the situation in which he now finds himself, there is a risk of regression, but it is, again, an historical regression. If he thus faces a danger denied to Will, who simply cannot progress, he also faces a greater possibility. Henry can cease to submit and start to fight. The fear he then feels is not the apparently irresistible impulse that controls the other black characters, for Henry enjoys what is for Crane the highest form of freedom, the freedom to be brave. That Henry has this capacity does not erase Crane's reliance elsewhere on racial stereotypes, even touching Henry himself. This capacity is, rather, a counterforce, a capacity belonging to this man as man, irrespective of claims on him as a representative of his race. Crane's typically American solution is, then, the affirmation of the sovereign power of the individual. In Crane's view, although the capacity for self-determination may be highly restricted from the standpoint of the group (in the present case, blacks), this is not a decisive factor for the individual, who is free to assert himself or herself through a determinate act of will.

Equally significant is Crane's way of defining what is influential, historically, for such an individual. Crane does not specify the role of *masters* in the slave past; it is *fathers* that count: Having established the primacy of the individual, Crane can stretch his historical imagination, at least in the present instance, as far as the familial, but no further. The advantage of this limitation lies in its compatibility with the paternalistic arrangement that protects Johnson from the hostility of the community. For Dr. Trescott is doubly a father – once as the actual parent of Jimmie, then as the surrogate parent of Henry, who emerges under the doctor's care as a second-order creation. In the words of Judge Hagenthorpe: "He will be your creation, you understand. He is purely your creation. Nature has evidently given him up. He is dead. You are restoring him to life. You are making him, and he will be a monster, and with no mind" (VII, 32). Refusing to submit to the seduction of such logic just as Henry refused to submit to the seduction of fear, the doctor accepts an arrangement that both resembles and differs from those we find in other works, such as "The Open Boat" and "The Price of the Harness." It resembles these other arrangements in that one man freely assumes responsibility for another, not out of legal obligation or formal necessity, but out of a fraternal solidarity that arises when character, chance, and circumstance converge in a particular way. Yet, although the person Trescott decides to protect is another man, that man is less a brother than a child. One reason is the white habit of fixing the black man at the developmental level of the child, so that it seems natural to speak of Henry and Jimmie as "pals" (VII, 11). Another reason is that the fire which enables Henry to assume a protective role also reduces him to a helplessness in which he must himself be protected. Thus the doctor can reassert paternal authority not only over his son, but over the man who for a time took his own place. The arrangement obviates resentment, Henry being already "punished," but it leaves at least a residue of guilt. For the fact that Johnson was there when Trescott was not, the only proper compensation is the caring relationship adumbrated so early in the book. The surrogate-father becomes a surrogate-child through the restoration of the real father. As a consequence, Henry enters, ironically, a state of confinement more restrictive than before, and more like the condition of his forebears than the condition of a paid employee. The disagreeable implications of this regression from the racial point of view are overcome, in a measure, by the professionalization of the relation between the two men. I allude to the fact that the man who is practically the doctor's creation is at the same time actually the doctor's patient. The doctor, for his part, is punished doubly – economically by the fact that he continues to support his worker after he has ceased to work and socially by the ostracism from the community that he and his family undergo.

Between the racial polarities of black and white are situated those characters who have been assimilated by the white majority, yet are subtly set apart by marks of ethnic particularity. When Johnson invades Watermelon Alley "an Irish girl threw a fit" (VII, 48), an observation that relates her to the black female characters both by the parallel in behavior and by the allusion to her ethnic status. The logic that identifies a character by ethnic or national origin is the same logic that applies the term "race" exclusively to black characters. The race of white characters is unspecified because unrecognized; the black race, by contrast, stands out, distinguished as the collective embodiment of some essential principle for which, among the whites, there is simply no visible counterpart. The ethnic particularity of Reifsnyder, already intimated by his name, consists partly in his accent and partly in his attitudes. Reifsnyder's Germanic speech habits make him the only nonblack character who does not speak "general English," the status of linguistic outsider paralleling that of Henry and the other blacks, who speak in "Negro" dialect. In his attitudes Reifsnyder reveals a further affinity with the black experience, first by submitting to the will of his customers in the dispute over the identity of the figure approaching his barbershop, then by sympathizing, more than his customers, with the plight of Henry: " 'How can you let a man die when he has done so much for you?' " (VII, 40). Finally, Reifsnyder's attitude is connected with his occupation in a way that underlines the role of work in relation to social stratification. While Henry cares for horses and Dr. Trescott cares for patients, Reifsnyder cares for the human head, a fact whose ironic implications are heightened when a customer remarks that if losing face should become popular, the barber would go out of business.

MARGINALITY

Although Henry's employer performs a service more nearly resembling that of Reifsnyder than that of Johnson, the doctor, as suggested above, functions on a higher social level than Reifsnyder, which is to say that he, like the judge, has received more formal training and enjoys greater prestige. As a doctor, Trescott belongs to a profession which, with the spread into the United States of the new medicine made possible in Europe by research into micro-organisms, was beginning to come into its own in the 1890s.[7] Trescott is a comparatively young man (judging from the age of his little boy) who supplements his daily medical practice with scientific research, suggesting that he should also be numbered among those physicians who were delivering comparatively sophisticated medical care to American towns and smaller cities as well as to the main urban centers. With such considerations in mind we gain a fuller sense of the community's loss when it succumbs to the emotional contagion spreading from the doctor's regeneration of a being whose presence it regards as intolerable.

As he approaches the limits of what the community deems acceptable the doctor becomes increasingly marginal. In response to a request from a colleague, Trescott visits a girl who is supposedly traumatized by the sight of Henry, only to be turned away by the father; thus the doctor's professional good will is repaid by personal bad will. With this, Crane's handling of Trescott's dilemma rejoins his handling of two other characters who share with him, though from different premises, the status of outsiders. Alek Williams, a friend of Johnson's, agrees to harbor the monster for money; but on learning what it means to keep in his home a man with no face and no mind, he attempts a redefinition of the terms of the contract which is his own adaptation to the community's redefinition of Henry. To maintain a man, a boarding arrangement suffices, but to maintain a monster Williams requires a "Salary" (VII, 38). If the request is self-serving, it is hardly more objectionable than the behavior of the whites, and thus may be said to give him, in the words of "Five White Mice," an "equality" with them. Yet this is a dubious equality suggesting a parallel between physical and ethical patterns in the way blacks live, as though there existed an automatism of excessive greed as well as an automatism of fear.

As if in confirmation, Williams next appears as the stereotyped black: "he burst out again in song and pantomimic celebration of his estate. His feet moved in prancing steps" (VII, 42). The conversation between Williams and the judge is an exercise of opposing powers – that of the tenant who, by performing a disagreeable service, has the leverage to request a higher reward, and that of an authority figure. But there is something a little inhuman in the way the judge exercises his authority. Having taken Henry into his home after the fire, thus aiding in the preservation of his life, the judge can yet argue, as a matter of principle, that the man ought to die.

> The judge retreated to the cold manner of the bench. "Perhaps we may not talk with propriety of this kind of action, but I am induced to say that you are performing a questionable charity in preserving this negro's life. As near as I can understand, he will hereafter be a monster, a perfect

> monster, and probably with an affected brain. No man can observe you as I have observed you and not know that it was a matter of conscience with you but I am afraid, my friend, that it is one of the blunders of virtue." (VII, 31–2)

The principle by which the judge guides himself consists in a fusion of the abstract and the expedient. The more fraternal principle by which Trescott guides himself is more concrete, more bound by that convergence whose reality dissolves under the cool gaze of the judge. While the judge decides the "case" from a fidelity to society in the abstract, the fidelity that is decisive for Trescott is to society in its most concrete form – the relation of one human being to another: "He saved my boy's life." To this distinction Crane adds an historical dimension by revealing that the judge has never married, as a consequence of which his occupational role in society dominates his identity in a way that is not true of Trescott. The former is typically "the judge," the latter is typically "Trescott," a reminder that the latter's identity, though largely defined by his occupational role, is not swallowed up in it.

The last character who may be usefully termed an outsider is the spinster Martha Goodwin, who "performed nearly all the house-work in exchange for the privilege of existence. Every one tacitly recognized her labor as a form of penance for the early end of her betrothed, who had died of small-pox, which he had not caught from her" (VII, 49). Economically dependent on her sister and her brother-in-law, Martha's servitude is a version of slavery. In contrast to Henry and Alek Williams, who are paid in money for their services, Martha is paid in the intolerable coin of tolerance. It is not extravagant to discern here a hint of the Hegelian master–slave relation wherein the latter's very right to be requires the assent of the former and, *mutatis mutandis,* the former's right to be, the assent of the latter. The concluding statement, with its subtle cruelty, does not express the actual meaning of Martha's contract with the family, but a cosy moralism based on guilt and compensation. The inhumanity of the situation to which the woman submits is exacerbated by the imputed infidelity of her betrothed, and by the willingness of "every one" to convert her exploitation into her expiation.

Martha's submission, however, is the beginning of her story rather than the end. Like Henry Johnson, she fights back against the enemy, which indicates, as well, her sisterhood with George's mother: "But despite the strenuous and unceasing workaday of her life, she was a woman of great mind. She had adamantine opinions upon the situation in Armenia, the condition of women in China, the flirtation between Mrs. Minster of Niagara Avenue and young Griscom, the conflict in the Bible class of the Baptist Sunday-school, the duty of the United States toward the Cuban insurgents, and many other colossal matters" (VII, 50). Rather than a penitent fidelity to the memory of her betrothed, Martha exhibits a militant fidelity to contemporary social causes, aided both by what James would have called her moral sense and by sheer intellectual force. If there is something in her of Isabel Archer, there is something as well of Hawthorne's Zenobia and Hester Prynne. She is, on a limited scale, a heroine and a feminist, her ability to develop in the latter role being less limited than Hester's but more limited than Zenobia's. The "mental tyranny" (VII, 60) she exercises refers to her power to influence:

> Martha made definitions, but she devoted them entirely to the Armenians and Griscom and the Chinese and other subjects. Her dreams, which in early days had been of love of meadows and the shade of trees, of the face of a man, were now involved otherwise, and they were companioned in the kitchen curiously, Cuba, the hot-water kettle, Armenia, the washing of the dishes, and the whole thing being jumbled. In regard to social misdemeanors, she who was simply the mausoleum of a dead passion was probably the most savage critic in town. This unknown woman, hidden in a kitchen as in a well, was sure to have a considerable effect of the one kind or the other in the life of the town. Every time it moved a yard, she had personally contributed an inch. (VII, 51)

Among Crane's female characters, Martha Goodwin is unique in the range of her influence. George's mother, who resembles Martha in moral strength, cannot modify the behavior of her son, let alone her neighborhood or the city beyond the neighborhood. But Martha eventually affects the entire community, a capacity that Crane would not have granted her if he had not decided to explore on a broad front the problems of community in crisis. That Martha is not the last female character whose presence has such an effect will be shown in my discussion of "The Bride Comes to Yellow Sky."

In their attitudes toward the focus of the crisis, the spinster critic and the bachelor judge could not be further apart. It is the judge who, in the essentially abstract manner I have described, confers on Johnson the identity of monster. Martha refuses to accept the identity, as a result of which she faces an opposition which is surpassed only by the opposition facing Trescott:

> "Well, you can't go against the whole town," answered Carrie, in sudden sharp defiance.
>
> "No, Martha, you can't go against the whole town," piped Kate, following her leader rapidly.
>
> " 'The whole town,' " cried Martha. "I'd like to know what you call

> 'the whole town.' Do you call these silly people who are scared of Henry Johnson 'the whole town'? (VII, 60)

THE LITTLE CITY

La France, quoting from a letter by Crane, reminds us that Whilomville is based on the Port Jervis the author knew in his childhood. "I suppose that Port Jervis entered my head while I was writing it but I particularly dont [*sic*] wish them to think so because people get very sensitive and I would not scold away freely if I thought the eye of your glorious public was upon me."[8] It would indeed be remarkable if Crane had not made some use of a town he knew so well. But note the limitation: "I suppose that Port Jervis entered my head" hardly implies that he employed the town as a binding model. However one interprets the letter, it is still a particular communication on a particular occasion and should not be deemed a definitive statement about the relation between the actual town and the fictional one, especially when it is beyond question that in certain important respects the two diverge. Crane lived in the small town of Port Jervis from 1878 to 1882, but this is not the period in which "The Monster" is set, a fact which it is one of Martha Goodwin's functions to make clear: Martha would have the United States support the Cuban insurgents; as for Armenia, she would have the Turks "pushed into the sea and drowned" (VII, 50); she is also concerned with the Chinese. Now it was in 1895 that Jose Martí began a well-publicized insurgency movement in Cuba. In the same year the Turks were carrying out the systematic extermination of Armenians initiated a year earlier while China was becoming enmeshed in a war with Japan. Further, Martha's humanitarian impulses would lead her to identify with the Cubans and the Armenians, as she does explicitly, and with the Chinese, as she does implicitly. Thus Crane's story is not set in a community of the late seventies and early eighties, but in a community of the midnineties. Nor does Crane depict a "small town," as that term is usually understood. Whilomville is large enough to be divided into districts and to possess no less than six hose companies as well as a hook and ladder company. It has an indefinite number of schoolhouses and churches, including a Methodist Church and a Baptist Church, in addition to the Valley Church four miles away among the surrounding farms. Besides its own post office, the city can claim a little theater at which, in imitation of New York City, *East Lynne* is to be performed. Extensively electrified, Whilomville boasts arc-lamps in the principal streets, a signal box (presumably one of several) from which to give alarms, and "electric light" even on a "narrow side street" (VII, 15); the city even has its own electric street-car system. The impact of the railway is suggested in a general way by the distribution of mail from New York and Rochester and in a particular way by the brakeman who lives on a rear street near the Trescotts and who pulls Johnson from the fire. There is also mention of an engineer, and the opening scene portrays Jimmie in the role of an engine at full speed. As we shall see more fully in "The Bride Comes to Yellow Sky," the railway is associated in Crane's fiction – as it was associated in historical fact – with forms of change that include urbanization and industrialization, and that may be grouped for convenience under the rubric of modernization. As the accident in the initial scene and the role of the brakeman suggest, Crane also associates the railway with chance, understanding this concept as referring to all phenomena associated with the spread of a technology that emphasizes speed, increases intercourse between localities, and multiplies contact between individuals and groups.

The fire reinforces our awareness of Whilomville's up-to-date, urbanized status in two other ways, for its existence is also signaled by blasts from a whistle at a city factory, and its consequences are reported, not in the weekly newspaper that one expects of a small town, but in the local *daily* newspaper *The Morning Tribune*. In addition to the factory there are "new engines on the hill pumping water into the reservoir" (VII, 17). More significant for the theme of care is the fact that the city boasts no less than ten physicians. Finally, Whilomville is large enough and modern enough for Crane to allude twice to its suburbs. In short, there is good reason for Crane to call Whilomville "the little city" (VII, 27). If critics consistently refer to it as a town, they are not necessarily in error, however. In the first place, it is not obvious where a little city begins and a large town leaves off. In the second place, Crane focuses at close range, bringing to life, for example, the barbershop, the park, the Negro colony, and particular homes, such as the Trescotts' and the Farraguts', which gives the community something of that "feel" of a town which Whilomville enjoys in the tales, where nothing has much of the urban look.

While Whilomville may be more established and rspectable than the Fort Romper of "The Blue Hotel," the way it responds to crisis in the aftermath of the fire is unsettling. The community is all on edge, almost in a state of panic, over an outsider whose presence is like that of the *pharmakos* hero in a Greek tragedy. Indeed, this man who was literally a hero is now literally a scapegoat, soon to be joined by another in the person of the doctor. The nervousness that has been spoken of as a common phenomenon in nineteenth-century America shows itself in the overly energetic back-slapping and xenophobia of the Bleecker club in *George's Mother*. It shows itself on a larger scale as well. At the time Crane was writing, many American communities were undergoing crises of identity and self-confidence. A leading source of anxiety was the fear that small-scale enterprise was being outpaced by rapidly growing corporations and monopolies; another was the fear that too much political and economic power was passing too quickly from the hands of a predominantly Anglo-Saxon citizenry into the hands of rising immigrant interests; conventional wisdom, meanwhile, bemoaned the shrinking of the Western frontier, that horizon of open-ended possibility which had once seemed all but endless.

In the face of these and like pressures, some communities, nervously alert for internal signs that might augur their decline, attempted to assert their unity and purity, now by prohibiting drink, now by displaying patriotism, now by strengthening barriers against alien elements, including those black-skinned persons who were, after all, a type of immigrant.[9] "To some degree almost all whites found the Negro's presence both disturbing and convenient. In a loose, ostensibly egalitarian society, who could tell where the Negro might try to wander, how he might upset the order of things? At the same time, that diffuse society with its blurred hierarchies placed inordinate importance upon all visible distinctions."[10] If this meant keeping certain people on the other side of a color line, it also meant sundry strategies of social combination, as in farmers' alliances, temperance unions, labor organizations, and patriotically or "fraternally" oriented clubs. A generalized anxiety, exacerbated by the increasing visibility of non-Anglo-Saxon ethnic constituencies and of mass popular movements, achieved expression in Theodore Roosevelt's suggestion that Populist troublemakers be lined up against a wall and shot.

With this background in mind, Crane's portrait of Whilomville takes on a more specific historical coloring. Disturbed by an alien presence which has become in its view a social menace, the community unites to preserve its collective purity, the judge providing the concept – that of the "monster" – which justifies the process while bringing the citizens together into a united front. By making the disfigured Johnson the sole responsibility of Dr. Trescott, the jurist enables the citizens to seek the removal of the monster without having to reconcile the discrepancy between the attitude that formerly saw him as a hero and the attitude that now sees him as a thing. In this process the community projects into view the long-standing if tacit assumption that such a man, even under normal circumstances, is somehow a lesser order of being, which is to say that in making a monster Whilomville finally makes a monster of itself. In thus restating a conclusion reached by other readers, I am suggesting that emphasis be shifted away from the notion that Crane is dealing with the essential nature of small-town behavior or that he is drawing from personal memory. Surely he is doing both, but it is important to see that the work is also a timely exploration of tensions being experienced in the society of his day. Once the text is situated in such a context, it becomes easier to see how Crane departs from contemporary patterns, which amounts to seeing what is distinctive about his approach. It becomes apparent that Crane wants to have it both ways – to connect the hollowness of a respectable, self-centered community, dominated by whites, with the racial question, but at the same time to neutralize that question so as to make the issue more "general."

In order to establish the true identity of the community – to say what it really is – he focuses on the identity of two individuals, and in very different ways. The difference consists in the way that each man, Johnson and Trescott, relates to a possible or actual opposition. Initially Johnson's status is that of a black man in a society with a white majority, suffering the range of disadvantages typical of his time, as may be indicated for the sake of brevity as an opposition between black and white. But through the agency of the fire this is replaced by a new opposition on a lower level: Johnson is now a monster in contrast with a man, and it is here that Trescott meets his challenge. This he does by denying the opposition: To the doctor, Johnson is not a monster, which is to say that Trescott overcomes the possible opposition, in his own life, between his role as doctor and his role as man; for the doctor could emulate the judge, denying Henry's humanity and thereby his own. By doing the converse Trescott brings the two roles together in a unity implicitly contrasted with the morally hollow solidarity of the community.

Because the problem of Johnson is defined for Trescott on the second level rather than the first, the ultimate significance of the fact that Johnson is black is never clarified. It merely persists, and it is because it persists, I think, that Crane offers his readers the peculiar split-decision by which the crucial white character relates to the crucial black character at once fraternally and paternally. Accepting his responsibility for a fellow human being, a brother in the broad sense, the doctor (as we have seen) becomes a father to his patient – who then becomes a child. In his own way Crane is thinking about those anxieties of the American community, occasioned by its sense of what is alien or "other," both in a mild, ethnic form (Reifsnyder) and in a radical, racial form (Johnson), but he is not quite sure what he thinks. To this extent the central resolution in the story may be likened to the resolution offered at the end of *The Red Badge of Courage* or "The Blue Hotel." That is, there remains at issue something essentially problematic, something that Crane does not handle decisively but which at any rate – and this is no small thing – he was able to reach. In each case resolution contains an element of irresolution. In *The Red Badge of Courage* it is not settled that Henry Fleming has grown to the extent that the ending seems to imply. In "The Blue Hotel" it is not settled that the Easterner's concluding speech adequately addresses the central conflict. In "The Monster" what remains unsettled is the ultimate function of the racial theme which becomes submerged but never disappears.

As in the other works just mentioned, supreme weight rests on the solitary character who carries, in behalf of the story, some burden of proof not otherwise discharged. The difference is that in "The Monster" Crane does not try to offer the proof, as he does in the works just named, with a summary statement. Doctor Trescott's solution is distinctly and importantly individual: He alone decides what to do and does it; but he carries out his plan on a day-by-day, protracted basis, making arrangements, paying money, arguing. This totally individual enterprise, enmeshed as it is in a complex social web, is in effect his "statement." It is not theoretical, like the pronouncements of Henry Fleming or the Easterner; it is theory and practice in one. It therefore differs profoundly from anything that Whilomville can offer, for the little city's theory has nothing to do with its practice. Theoretically the community cares for the welfare of Johnson and his protector: As the wealthy John Twelve tells Trescott, he is concerned only with the harm the doctor may be doing himself. But practically, the community cares only for its own placidity. Thus Trescott answers contradiction with unity, collective schism with individual fusion.

Given Johnson's initial status as a black man and his subsequent status as a nonman, Trescott's pairing with him cannot, however, be fully fraternal. Between the two there can be nothing of the camaraderie that a military organization, for example, makes possible for soldiers in war, as there obviously can be nothing of the interpersonal access available at least in principle to persons of the same race or social standing. Under the circumstances that prevail in "The Monster" the closest thing to the needed structure of equality is the provision of basics, of food and a place to sleep, that the doctor supplies. Since there is no reason to think the doctor will give up the arrangement, and since the crisis in the community must therefore be regarded as continuing, the story must end inconclusively. But this is appropriate. In the fifteen cups that are never used because Mrs. Trescott's friends shun her tea party, Crane furnishes a glimpse into a future of definite suffering indefinitely. Like the wee blade of grass at the end of "Death and the Child," it is a small thing that says much, suggesting as it does the painful process which it is left for the Trescotts to live and for the reader to imagine.

TRAVAILS OF YOUTH

If each Whilomville tale is in its own way a story of a community in crisis, just about everything in that story is on a reduced scale. The protagonists are little, being young children in every piece but "The

Knife"; the community in which something critical happens is itself small – a household, a gang of boys, a neighborhood, three friends on a hunt; the center of interest is smaller still, being in most cases an individual boy; and the crisis itself is on a reduced scale as well: in "The Stove" the burning of turnips that produces a dreadful stench, in "Lynx-Hunting" the accidental shooting of old Henry Fleming's cow, in "A Little Pilgrim" the lack of funds for the church's Christmas tree, in "The Fight" the arrival in town of a new boy, in "Making an Orator" Jimmie's inability to recite "The Charge of the Light Brigade."

In asserting the superiority of an eye that is innocent because young, Emerson calls the child "the fool of his senses" and "the curly dimpled lunatic," applies the term "sweet" to children's pranks, and describes a typical child's typical day as "continual pretty madness."[11] Although the upshot of the passage is to praise the child's sense of wonder, the phrases all carry a sting, suggesting that the innocence of the child is not unalloyed. Emerson perceives the craziness, to which he twice refers, but he tolerates it. Crane perceives it, too, and he too is tolerant. No matter what mischief is afoot, Crane never seems to stop smiling. In the same passage, Emerson insists that the way in which the child is deceived by experience is benign, being the model by which everyone is ultimately guided. Emerson's example of something experienced is a toy, while Crane, paradoxically, makes a more "Emersonian" choice by turning to nature:

> Each boy had, I am sure, a conviction that some day the wilderness was to give forth to them a marvelous secret. They felt that the hills and the forest knew much and they heard a voice of it in the silence. It was vague, thrilling, fearful and altogether fabulous. The grown folk seemed to regard these wastes merely as so much distance between one place and another or as rabbit cover, or as a district to be judged according to the value of the timber; but to the boys it spoke some great inspiriting word which they knew even as those who pace the shore know the enigmatic speech of the surf. (VII, 139)

The boys' conviction is not endorsed. While they may "know" some great inspiriting word, they know it only as do those others to whom the surf is enigmatic, such knowing is reminiscent of the attitude of the survivors in "The Open Boat," who merely *feel* that they are capable of interpreting. Knowledge and feeling of this kind may well entail the kind of deceit of which Emerson speaks; Crane, like Emerson, appears in any case to regard it as ultimately benign.

This passage from "Lynx-Hunting" is anything but typical, however. Most of the tales deal with conflict, envy, hostility, cruelty, shame, and in several cases outright violence. In "Shame" Jimmie is ridiculed by other children when he goes to a picnic carrying his lunch in a pail; in

"The Trial, Burial and Execution of Homer Phelps" the protagonist endures painful mock versions of the three processes in the title; and bloody battles are the focus both of "The Fight" and "The City Urchin and the Chaste Villagers." Crane seems to be reminiscing about experiences much as Mark Twain does in *The Adventures of Tom Sawyer*. Here, from the vantage point of distance in time and space, a nostalgia keeps telling itself it should know better. It should know better because all that these curly dimpled lunatics lose as they age is their baby fat; but what their pranks lose is precisely their sweetness. Flaring out less readily with age, the darker impulses spread through the social system like an undiagnosed disease, permanently infecting even the most genteel of rites, the tea-party:

> On the fatal afternoon a small picked company of latent enemies would meet. There would be a fanfare of affectionate greetings during which everybody would measure to an inch the importance of what everybody else was wearing. Those who wore old dresses would wish then that they had not come and those who saw that, in the company, they were well clad would be pleased or exalted or filled with the joys of cruelty. (VII, 199)

That Crane here aims his sharpest barbs at the women of Whilomville – as he does again in "The Knife" – may be further evidence of his resentment toward his mother. In any event Horace, the hero of "His New Mittens," is manifestly resentful. Horace's mother insists that he keep his new mittens dry, an assignment that turns him into an outcast: " 'A-fray-ed of his mit-tens! A-fray-ed of his mit-tens!' They sang these lines to cruel and monotonous music which is as old perhaps as American childhood and which it is the privilege of the emancipated adult to completely forget" (VII, 83). As a consequence Horace's sense of his own masculinity is displaced to "the trunk of one of the great maple trees" with "the rough and virile bark" (VII, 83). Unable to bear the taunts, Horace gets his mittens wet in a snowball fight, precipitating a household crisis that earns him the silent treatment from his mother and his aunt. Although this is about all his punishment amounts to, his hostility is intense:

> His heart was black with hatred. He painted in his mind scenes of deadly retribution. His mother would be taught that he was not one to endure persecution meekly, without raising an arm in his defense. And so his dreams were of a slaughter of feelings, and near the end of them his mother was pictured as coming, bowed with pain, to his feet. Weeping, she implored his charity. Would he forgive her? No; his once tender heart had been turned to stone by her injustice. He could not forgive her. She must pay the inexorable penalty. (VII, 89)

With a start like this Horace could easily grow up to be a George Kelcey, whose behavior toward the indefinite woman in his dreams betrays a similar self-importance, desire for domination, and insistence on the woman's submission. Horace might grow into a Henry Johnson too, insofar as the latter refuses submission in the fire scene. Horace's refusal is cast in terms that apply to the Whilomville tales as a whole: "All in him was conquered save the enigmatical childish ideal of form, manner. This principle still held out, and it was the only thing between him and submission. When he surrendered, he must surrender in a way that deferred to the undefined code" (VII, 91).

Like nearly everything else in the collection, Horace's attitude is scaled-down. He does not face a crisis in which submission means death; it only means the demise of self-esteem, a little death from which he will soon enough recover. But the long logic beneath the tales as a whole depends importantly on "the enigmatical childish ideal of form, manner." Form and manner are what Lean and the adjutant search for in "The Upturned Face"; form and manner guide the officers and men of other war tales in times of crisis, the sheriff and the rowdy in "The Bride Comes to Yellow Sky," and the four men in the open boat. The difference between these works and the Whilomville tales is that the principal characters in the latter rely more on utterance: "It was another instance of the power of eloquence upon the human mind. There was only one boy who was not thrilled by this oration, and he was a boy whose favorite reading had been of the road-agents and gun-fighters of the great West" (VII, 179; *cf.* VII, 201).

The world of Whilomville, like the world of Tom Sawyer, is densely "literary." For one thing, Crane not only writes against the background of a particular American genre, the boyhood novel, but against the genre itself, which tends to portray youth "as a time of hopeful beginning; Crane's autumnal boy stories prefigure a pessimistic end."[12] How deliberate Crane is being is hard to say, but he is unusually self-conscious, speaking at times in an authorial first person: "I had almost said that he was of national reputation" (VII, 129); and at one point he reverts to the manner of Fielding: "It now becomes the duty of the unfortunate writer to exhibit these children to their fond parents" (VII, 134). Like *The Third Violet* and *Active Service, Tales of Whilomville* embraces other literary genres, including parody and burlesque, mock-epic, and above all mock-romance. When his friends play the parts of heroes from the American West, Homer Phelps can only "cast a wistful eye at the romantic scene" (VII, 213). Earlier, the boy who plays an Indian chief "was always trying to bring off these little romantic affairs and it seemed, after all, that the only boy who could ever really help him was Jimmie Trescott" (VII, 212).

At one juncture literary language is employed to suggest, in effect, that truth is stranger than fiction: "His face was set in a truer expression of horror than any of the romances descrie upon the features of a man flung into a moat, a man shot in the breast with an arrow, a man cleft in the neck with a battle axe" (VII, 146).

Echoes of previous works by Crane weave a kind of subtext through the tales. We have already seen one example in the passage echoing the end of "The Open Boat." "A thousand, aye, ten thousand" (VII, 90) and "he rose upon them. Yes, he rose upon them" (VII, 229) take on resonance from the numerous other places, especially in the poems, when Crane uses this expletive and, more particularly, the last lines of "A man saw a ball of gold": "It was a ball of gold. Aye, by the heavens, it was a ball of gold" (X, 20). "He seemed about to say something classic" (VII, 206) reminds us of Henry Fleming when he is about to deliver a philippic, just as "It came to pass that a certain half-dime blood-and-thunder pamphlet had a great vogue" reminds us that the same Biblical phrase appears near the end of *The Red Badge of Courage*.

Onomastically, the tales are low-keyed. As a wielder of names, Crane follows several courses. On one course he uses generic or "type" names, the most frequent being Bill and its variants, followed by Jim. A second course goes to the other extreme, usually producing comic or satiric effects: Good Grief, Wrinkles, Little Nell, Colonel Sponge, Countess Chess, which contrast with such historical names as Theodore Roosevelt, Ralph Waldo Emerson, Nathaniel Hawthorne, and Alexander Hamilton. Ethnic names span history and typology insofar as they point to members of actual populations but in a way that lets them stand for the members generally: Flanagan, Kelcey, Riley, Nolan, Clancy, Mulligan, O'Connor, are some of the Irish examples; German names include Zeusentell, Reifsnyder, and Plock; while names of additional ethnic individuals and groups may be found scattered in other writings. Place names are often actual, ranging from Asbury Park to New York but with too many stops in between to tabulate here. Fanciful place names include Fort Romper, Tin Can, and War Post, which flash with local color but by no means exaggerate the graphic and imaginative tendencies of those who gave actual Western places their names (one has only to think of Rough and Ready, California, or Rotting Buzzard, Montana).

Less colorful and more in accord with human names in Whilomville are Levelville and Handyville, middle-of-the-road names that might be spotted on any U.S. map. The human names in Whilomville are cut from the same cloth: Jimmie Trescott, Johnnie Hedge, Willie Dalzel, Homer Phelps, Ella Early, Alek Williams, Peter Washington. These are not generic names in the way that Bill or Jim are, and neither are they comic. If such a town as Whilomville existed, Crane seems to say, these would not be the actual names of its residents but their *types* of names, just as Hogan is the type of name a street would have and the "higher-sounding" Niagara is the type of name that would be more suitable for an avenue.

As regards the point of departure for this chapter, community and crisis, a word is in order with respect to two remaining stories. The most obvious question to ask about "The Knife," the only story that is not about children, is why Crane includes it in *Tales of Whilomville*. The answer, I believe, lies in the relation of the child and the adult as mediated by the black. As generally conceived by a white-majority culture, the black adult is a kind of grown child, a person lacking in the maturity enjoyed by white counterparts of comparable age, as the latter attest by saying *boy* when referring to the adult black male. Crane seems to accept the majority conception just as he accepts the black as comic stereotype. Thus Peter Washington can think of no higher goal than being a dude, and of no better exploit than stealing a watermelon – from a white man, of course. And Crane is capable of writing that, after a visit from philanthropic white ladies, the shantytown population "would preserve a comic air of rectitude for two days and then relapse again to the genial irresponsibility of a crew of monkeys" (VII, 185). On the other hand, Crane refers to the white boys as "jackal-creatures" (VII, 221) and reports that "it was the fashion among tiny Whilomville belligerents to fight much in the manner of little bear-cubs" (VII, 224). That animality is a leading trait of many characters in Crane, a trait that simply becomes more conspicuous when fighting breaks out, scarcely needs further emphasis. Crane takes the black man's passion for granted, but expresses it through a social interchange in which it is also taken for granted that the stereotype is to be approached self-consciously: "The effete joke in regard to an American negro's fondness for water-melons was still an admirable pleasantry to them and this was not the first time they had engaged in badinage over it" (VII, 184–5).

More to the point is the end of the tale, in which farmer Bryant pressures Alek Williams to identify the owner of the knife Bryant discovered in his watermelon patch. Alek lies, saying that it belongs to someone other than Peter and himself. Stallman writes: "To lie is to be saved. In "The Knife" Alek saves Peter, the betrayer, by lying to the white man, Bryant. This Judas is outwitted by the all-saving lie. White against black, the Negro's salvation lies in fidelity."[13] As far as it goes, this statement is valid. American history having made the two men adversaries, Alek rallies against the white man in solidarity with the other black man. Benign in this regard, his deceit has a less positive side, however. In the watermelon patch the little community of two black men faced a crisis when they confronted one another, both having come in order to steal a melon. Thanks to his quick wit and self-assurance, Peter immediately assumed the role of moral enforcer, Alek the role of thief. Having released Alek on his own recognizance, as it were, Peter now has Alek in his power, and the latter's awareness of this fact must be considered as an important motive for lying to the white man. The failure of fraternity between the black men springs from the fact that in the crisis Peter spontaneously takes on the part, not of his counterpart in race, but of the white owner.

This spontaneous changing of allegiance, the converse of the impulse to assocation described by Huizinga, is independent of race, if "A Little Pilgrim" is taken into account. In this, the final story in the collection, Jimmie deserts the Presbyterian Church because funds for a Christmas tree are dispatched for earthquake relief. In the Sunday-School of the Big Progressive Church, which Jimmie assumes will have the usual tree, an atmosphere of sanctity and spirituality reigns: "the man on the platform . . . was an ideal Sunday-School superintendent – one who had never felt hunger or thirst or the wound of the challenge of dishonor" (VII, 237), and who beats time "with a white and graceful hand" as "the obedient throng" sings a hymn. But, as in "The Knife," personal interest is decisive. To general consternation the ideal superintendent announces that his congregation will also have to forgo a Christmas tree. A repeat of the one that brought on his desertion, this new crisis breaks Jimmie's bond with this alternative community: "If he remembered Sunday-School at all, it was to remember that he did not like it" (VII, 239).

A GREATER TRAGEDY

The way in which "The Blue Hotel" portrays a community in crisis raises questions one is tempted to call ontological – questions, that is to say, about the very foundations of being. I believe it is to such matters that Crane is referring when he speaks in the story of "a tragedy greater than the tragedy of action."

The Red Badge of Courage opens, as we have seen, with a gradual revelation keyed to the rising of the sun, "The Open Boat" with a contrast between what the men know (the colors of the sea) and what they do not know (the color of the sky); "The Bride Comes to Yellow Sky," to be considered below, stresses movement toward a distant horizon. Nature is related in every case to a human group – armies, four men in a boat, passengers on a train – and in every case there is something foreboding in what the group sees. The Union Army looks with trembling eagerness across a dark river at hostile camp-fires. In "The Open Boat" foreboding is suggested by a horizon with an edge "jagged with waves that seemed thrust up in points like rocks." Equally ominous is the precipice–horizon that waits the train carrying the sheriff and his bride.

"The Blue Hotel" also begins with a juxtaposition between the human and the natural: "The Palace Hotel at Fort Romper was painted a light blue, a shade that is on the legs of a kind of heron, causing the bird to declare its position against any background. The Palace Hotel, then, was always screaming and howling in a way that made the dazzling winter landscape of Nebraska seem only a gray swampish hush" (V, 143). The hotel is not only a collective creation, an artifact made by sundry hands, but a piece of privately owned property, its singular appearance suggesting that identification of property and person characteristic of a social order sustained by profit seeking.[14] The color of paint selected by Patrick Scully, parent, citizen, and entrepreneur, is a self-assertion; the building is his presence architecturalized, the color his declaration of how he "stands":

> Pat Scully, the proprietor, had proved himself a master of strategy when he chose his paints. It is true that on clear days, when the great trans-continental expresses, long lines of swaying Pullmans, swept through Fort Romper, passengers were overcome at the sight, and the cult that knows the brown-reds and the subdivisions of the dark greens of the East expressed shame, pity, horror, in a laugh. But to the citizens of this prairie town, and to the people who would naturally stop there, Pat Scully had performed a feat. With his opulence and splendor, these creeds, classes, egotisms, that streamed through Romper on the rails day after day, they had no color in common. (V, 142)

As here employed, the color blue is more indicative than allusive. Blue, of course, is a prominent color in other works, such as "Blue Battalions" or *The Red Badge of Courage*. In the latter, however, the color has its phenomenal base in the Union Army uniform, and the color in the title of the poem also appears to allude to that base, or at least to validate its presence by association. If the present work is allusive in this way, there is, as far as I can see, no evidence of the fact. When I suggest that the color blue is on the contrary indicative, I mean that Crane supplies us, here and now, with all we need to understand what he has put before us. In the first place, the color of the hotel is a certain *shade* of blue, which is to say that, besides standing out in contrast to other colors, it stands out even in relation to other blues. So unusual is this shade that one has to reach a long way for another example of it – all the way to a species of bird belonging in tropical or subtropical zones, certainly not in the hard winter landscape of the North American central plains. In this sense, too, the color stands out. But it should also be borne in mind that the heron feeds alone, stalking its prey, and is frequently represented in picturesque isolation, thus suggesting an analogy with Scully as he goes off alone to prey upon prospective clients.

All of these considerations reinforce the connection between color and position to which I have already referred. The blue hotel is so positioned in its isolation as to be assertive, even aggressive; if it were not located where it is, Scully could not capture visitors before they can get to the main part of town. The hotel's position and color together evoke a feeling similar to the sense of threat conveyed in the opening of other works, as noted above, but one that is achieved by distinctive means. Surprisingly, the particular background – the winter landscape – does not seem immediately menacing when compared with the initial background of, say, "The Bride Comes to Yellow Sky." There the train seems headed for something threatening just over the waiting precipice; only as the narrative unfolds do we see that it is the passengers who are moving headlong, this movement contrasting with an initial impression that the landscape is moving while the passengers are remaining still. The blue hotel makes possible a related but different "illusion of reversal." Set in the immensity of the plain, the little building ought to be overwhelmed, but Crane implies the opposite. The landscape is alliterated into a sluggish inertia, "a swampi*sh* hu*sh,*" while the hotel gets the type of lively participle – "screaming" and "howling" – that we will find in "The Bride Comes to Yellow Sky." Here is the theme to which Wallace Stevens turns in "Anecdote of the Jar," where the "slovenly wilderness" of Tennessee is brought within the influence of human creation. Equally assertive, the hotel creates an environment of its own in which at the same time the more purely social modes of domination and submission, which Crane explores in "The Monster," are brought to new stages of manifestation.

It is not that Scully has created in the hotel a world totally apart from the main community. From the fate that the Swede meets in the saloon it is clear that life does not become another thing in the space of 200 yards. The blue hotel stands out from the rest of the town because its proprietor wants to stand out from others in the community. The color of the hotel indicates that the proprietor has his own way of achieving his goals, not that his goals are different from those of his fellow townspeople; the hotelkeeper is not less concerned with income than the gambler in the saloon, he simply goes about his job in a different way. It is a question of strategy, and it is therefore of this that Scully is said to be a master.

> One morning . . . Scully performed the marvel of catching three men. One was a shaky and quick-eyed Swede, with a great shining cheap valise; one was a tall bronzed cowboy, who was on his way to a ranch near the Dakota line; one was a little silent man from the East, who didn't look it, and didn't announce it. Scully practically made them prisoners. . . . He wore a heavy fur cap squeezed tightly down on his head. It caused his two red ears to stick out stiffly, as if they were made of tin. (V, 132–43)

The secret of the arresting detail at the end does not lie, I think, in any metallic symbolism but, again, in indicativeness. Tin ears are incongruous on a man as a shade of blue on the legs of a heron in incongruous on the prairies of Nebraska. That they protrude so conspicuously is another, more comic way of showing how Scully sticks out, while the fact that they are red indicates his reaction to the cold. He is out in the cold, however, because he is the kind of man he is, which is to say that the contingent aspect of his appearance (redness caused by weather) cannot be dissociated from the constitutive aspect (the position of his ears). In short, Scully so far looks as he is and is as he does.

As Scully steers his prisoners into hospitable captivity, the focus, having shifted from hotel to owner, now shifts back to the hotel. There is, immediately, the stove that "glowed yellow from the heat" (V, 143); and a little later, the cowboy and the Easterner "burnished themselves fiery red with this water, until it seemd to be some kind of metal polish" (V, 143); and later still, Johnnie and the Swede exchange "hot and steely" glances (V, 156) as their anger mounts. That the water used by the cowboy and the Easterner is "the coldest water in the world" (V, 143) links the interior of the hotel with the wintry nature that surrounds it. Nonetheless, the dominant influence in this internal environment is man and, especially, at this point, Scully. It is Scully who "destroyed the game of cards" (V, 143) being played by his son and a farmer, and it is Scully who assails his daughters with "officious clamor" (V, 143). Hospitality is something to be displayed: "It was notable that throughout this series of small ceremonies the three travelers were made to feel that Scully was very benevolent. . . . He handed the towel from one to the other with an air of philanthropic impulse" (V, 143). Hospitality is simply another way of standing out, generous gestures being the disguised expression of acquisitive impulse: All assertions by the proprietor on behalf of others are really assertions *for* the proprietor, who is in competition with the rest of the town. Such assertion shades into aggression, which shades in turn into violence.

A "dramatistic" analysis as practiced by Kenneth Burke[15] would show this last form of assertion to be, at this stage of the narrative, scenically present in the stove that hums "with godlike violence" (V, 143). Yet the scene derives its qualities partly from the agents who act in it, and these are now both the parent–proprietor and his son – bearing in mind that we are noting motives for the antagonistic tension that constitutes the peculiar atmosphere of the hotel. Johnnie's role is that of the troublemaker. The first action following the reference to the violence of the stove is his quarrel with the old farmer, while the first climax in the second section of the story is a repetition of the episode with heightened intensity: "The play of Johnnie and the gray-beard was suddenly ended by another quarrel. The old man arose while casting a look of heated scorn at his adversary" (V, 145). The implication is that violence is scenically present because there is violence in the agents, that term applying not only to the human beings but to nonhuman material elements, in particular the stove, which has its own way of standing out. For, in relation to the room it stands in, the stove is large; and in relation to the fiercely cold weather that it enables the occupants of the room to survive, it burns quite prodigiously. Complementing this relativistic aspect of the object is its absolute aspect – the impression that the room is its "proper temple" (V, 143) and that its violence is "godlike" (V, 143). This absolute aspect is not superhuman, however, but is a scenic expression of human agency. The text states simply that the room "seemed" (V, 143) to be a temple, meaning that it looked this way to a human perspective. Any divinity imputed to the scene needs to be interpreted, as I am suggesting, from the bottom up – not as an extrahuman presence but as an attribute of human presence, or more precisely of human action. For the scene that unfolds before the reader unfolds naturally *and* humanly – because of the influence upon it of the position of the hotel and the weather, and because of the influence upon it of the human beings who converge there.

Most readers agree that the role of Scully's son is critical, since his cheating occasions the fight with the Swede that follows Johnnie's preliminary, not quite openly violent matches with the old farmer. The second of these matches is launched in the following way: "Johnnie, son of Scully, in a tone which defined his opinion of his ability as a card-player, challenged the old farmer of both gray and sandy whiskers to a game of High-Five" (V, 144). The phrase "son of Scully," coming at just this moment of assertion, hints that father and son resemble one another in some crucial way. In fact both yearn for honor, the father for that honor of being a perfect host which is a requisite of successful hotel management, and the son for the honor of the victor. Even their strategies are more alike than first appears, for as each stands out, so does each conceal. Behind the generosity of the host, behind the sportsmanship of the friendly opponent, is the will of one who yearns to succeed.

But similarity is not sameness. Johnnie's desire is so strong, his aggressiveness so intense, that he can hardly contain himself. While the father admits "his responsibility for the Swede's new viewpoint" (V, 155), Johnnie is rebellious: "Why don't you license somebody to kick you downstairs?' " (V, 155). Further, it is the younger Scully who, by wishing that his father would throw the Swede out, first raises the issue of force. Although the cowboy is increasingly hostile toward the Swede, and although he also wants to win, he remains the child of the plains, ingenuous and impulsive: "The cowboy was a board-whacker. Every time that he held superior cards he whanged them, one by one, with exceeding force, down upon the improvised table, and took the tricks with a glowing air of prowess and pride that sent thrills of indignation into the hearts of his opponents" (V, 145).

It is the son of Scully who brings the conflict to the flashpoint by defending the honor his own behavior has called into question:

> Then suddenly there was a great cessation. It was as if each man had paused for breath, and although the room was still lighted with the anger of men, it could be seen that there was no danger of immediate conflict, and at once Johnnie, shouldering his way forward, almost succeeded in confronting the Swede. "What did you say I cheated for? What did you say I cheated for? I don't cheat and I won't let no man say I do!" (V, 157)

It would have been equally plausible to have begun the final clause of the long second sentence with a negative conjunction: "but at once Johnnie . . . " Since it has just been established that a lull has set in, and since Johnnie then reverses the situation, this alternative is arguably superior from a logical point of view. Crane's choice of conjunction enables the reader to slide over this turn of events, so that the action appears smoothly continuous. But what this innocent-looking "and" really says is that Johnnie will exonerate his honor at any price. It says that his destiny is determined not by any outside force but by his being the kind of man he is.

On a casual reading one might summarize the moment of outburst by saying that the Swede accuses Johnnie of cheating and that Johnnie denies the act. But this is only partly the case, for the Swede's specific accusation is not specifically answered. Johnnie never denies what might be called the contingent charge that he has just cheated in this particular game. For him the accusation has a more general or constitutive bearing, the Swede's charge being perceived in the form, *You are a cheater.* In his reply Johnnie does not repudiate the accusation, but addresses himself to what he takes to be an ontological condemnation. Declaring, in effect, *I am not that kind of man,* he turns the accusation against the accuser, implying that only a bad sort like the Swede would make such an allegation. Johnnie's choice of words is revealing. Five times he declares that no man can *say* he cheated. Alternatively interrogative and declarative, the assertion is always the same, always self-protective, like his father's repeated representation, to the frightened Swede, of Scully's respectability. The Swede's fear of being killed in the hotel has for the elder Scully a force comparable to the force that the accusation of cheating has for the son: It is an attack to be met by insisting on the honor of the house, as well as on the respectability of the town.

Significantly, it is when Johnnie's honor comes into question that Scully aligns himself with his son:

> A change had come over the Celtic visage of the old man. He now seemed all eagerness; his eyes glowed.
>
> "We'll let them fight," he answered stalwartly. "I can't put up with it any longer. I've stood this damned Swede till I'm sick. We'll let them fight." (V, 158)

Through the agency of the Swede, Scully has measured his own limits of endurance, with the ironic consequence that he now stands grouped with the others against the man he had previously befriended. Having been responsible for a peace, Scully now becomes responsible for a war, the fight being something "which he himself had permitted and arranged" (V, 160).

At this point we may look more closely at the character whose interaction with others brings on the conflict, first in the hotel and later in the town. In the Swede, Crane brings together in exaggerated form the tendency to sudden transformation of attitude that one finds in the New York Kid, who passes in an instant from a state of fear to a state of rage, and the inclination to mockery and other modes of hostility one finds in the Sullivan County writings. Closer still, as commentators have noted, is the resemblance between the Swede of "The Blue Hotel" and the Swede of "The Veteran." When fire breaks out in the barn, old Fleming "could hear the voice of the Swede, screaming and blubbering. He pushed the wooden button, and, as the door flew open, the Swede, a maniac, stumbled inward chattering, weeping, still screaming" (VI, 84). The kinetic effect wrought by these participles also makes the Swede resemble a fearsome version of Scratchy Wilson – or Wilson, a less dangerous version of this Swede.

The reason is that Crane, constantly experimenting, borrows elements from one character for use in another, creating new possibilities through new combinations. In "A Freight Car Incident," Crane presents a character who anticipates both Wilson and the Swede. A narrator tells a railroading story of a man mysteriously marked for death: " 'It seems that there was a fellow around there that a good many people wanted to kill, and they said they were going to kill him that day at the sale, too' " (VIII, 105). The phrase "a good many people" is as characteristic of Crane as the observation that many a man ought to have a bathtub larger than the open boat in which survivors of a shipwreck ride; more to the point, it closely resembles the Swede's observation " 'I suppose there have been a good many men killed in this room' " (V, 145–6). Like

Scratchy Wilson, the protagonist of the railroad sketch prowls about with a loaded gun in each hand, eager to fight. But the extremity of his situation is closer to that of the Swede. As the Swede anticipates being killed after he enters the presence of the other men, the marked man of the earlier story anticipates being killed on stepping outside of the railway car into the presence of his enemies. Though no one is waiting for him after all, the narrator reveals that the man was killed in the end, like the Swede, in a saloon. In the Swede there is also something of the drummer in "The Bride Comes to Yellow Sky": That man hails from the East and is preoccupied with the possibility of being killed; and there is something in him too of the protagonist of "Death and the Child," a newcomer to war who finds himself standing anxiously about, asking questions of the veterans. All of this underlines the continuing fascination for Crane of the outsider – the "stranger in the community," in Alfred Schutz's phrase – and to suggest that in the Swede the outsider or stranger as a type reaches a particular culmination.

When a stranger approaches a group in its own surroundings,

> the pattern of the approached group does not guarantee an objective chance for success but rather a pure subjective likelihood which has to be checked step by step, that is, he has to make sure that the solution suggested by the new scheme will also produce the desired effect for him in his special position as outsider and newcomer who has not brought within his grasp the whole system of the cultural pattern but who is rather puzzled by its inconsistency, incoherence, and lack of clarity.

Mistaking the performance of typical social in-group functions for singular acts by unique individuals, and conversely mistaking the latter for the former, a stranger to a community

> constructs a social world of pseudo-anonymity, pseudo-intimacy, and pseudo-typicality. Therefore, he cannot integrate the personal types constructed by him into a coherent picture of the approached group and cannot rely on his expectation of their response. And even less can the stranger himself adopt those typical and anonymous attitudes which a member of the in-group is entitled to expect from a partner in a typical situation. Hence the stranger's lack of feeling for distance, his oscillating between remoteness and intimacy, his hesitation and uncertainty, and his distrust . . .[16]

Uncertain and distrustful at first, the stranger in the community of the hotel gradually convinces himself that he will be permitted to play more than a marginal role. That is, through the mediation of the proprietor he arrives at the stage of "pseudorelations" at which, in his own perception, he attains full membership in the approached group. But his insensitivity leads him to overplay his role, making the limited degree of his assimilation all the more pronounced. Stated another way, he identifies with the members of the group to the point that, instead of oscillating between poles, he goes with swift finality from one pole to its opposite, from uncertainty to overconfidence. The Swede first acts, then, as if he were afraid; and later, as if he were not afraid. Far from being contradictory, his behavior is a unitary process: The Swede's behavior, motivated by fear, produces hostility, which in turn feeds his fear until his pretense of bravery gives way to a phase in which his actual anxiety stands revealed.

The logic of his being goes something like this. Within him there is a conflict between fear and rage – his personal version of conflict as condition. If in this state the answer to his question is yes, then his anxiety is justified, and will serve as a constraint on his rage. If, on the other hand, the West is not wild, the constraint disappears, freeing the wildness within and leading to the isolation he achieves after felling Johnnie: "There was a splendor of isolation in his situation at this time which the Easterner felt once when, lifting his eyes from the man on the ground, he beheld that mysterious and lonely figure, waiting" (V, 161).

The splendor remains with the Swede as he makes his way from the hotel to the saloon in the main part of town. He is isolated not only in the sense that for the first time in the story we see him alone, but because he is alone in a setting suddenly larger than the landscape:

> He might have been in a deserted village. We picture the world as thick with conquering and elate humanity, but here, with the bugles of the tempest pealing, it was hard to imagine a peopled earth. One viewed the existence of man then as a marvel, and conceded a glamour of wonder to these lice which were caused to cling to a whirling, fire-smote, ice-locked, disease-stricken, space-lost bulb. The conceit of man was explained by this storm to be the very engine of life. One was a coxcomb not to die in it. However, the Swede found a saloon. (V, 165)

The same adjectives that modify humanity modify the Swede. Flushed with victory, he is both conquering and elate; at the other end of the scale, "conceit of man" and "coxcomb" fit, too. Thus the Swede is defined simultaneously as individual and as type. The near-admiration felt by the Easterner has shifted into an attitude of skepticism informed with a sense of fascination, but also with something like quiet exasperation. The glamour that appears is something to be conceded rather than welcomed. But what drives the passage, mainly, is the power of amazement. If the Swede is not as comic as Scratchy Wilson or as sympathetic as Jack Potter, if he is merely this overbearing outsider, he nonetheless shares with these other beings the capacity to excite feelings for which "interest" is too mild a term. It is because this capacity stands out so remarkably that Crane deploys in the passage all the verbal magic he can muster. For Crane, the indispensable aspect of a human experience is the sheer marvel of our being-there, a phenomenon gratuitous and extreme of which the Swede is not, after all, an inappropriate representative. Unlike most people, the Swede motivates himself, and nothing is inherently more gratuitous than total self-motivation, nor potentially more extreme, there being no necessary limit to the movement of a being that autotelically moves itself.

The mediator who makes possible the initial phase of the Swede's emergence is Scully, who plies him with liquor and, perhaps more dangerously, with words and images. For Romper is represented as a kind of Whilomville West: " 'And,' said Scully, 'there's a new railroad goin' to be built down from Broken Arm to here. Not to mintion the four churches and the smashin' big brick school-house. Then there's the big factory, too. Why, in two years Romper'll be a met-ro-*pol*-is' " (V, 149–50). As a consequence of Scully's persuasion and Scully's liquor, the Swede "fizzed like a fire wheel" (V, 154), slapping the proprietor roughly on the back, nearly harpooning the Easterner's hand, and whacking the card table in emulation of the cowboy.

Led on by Scully, the Swede, twice accused of madness, moves at a pace that accelerates with the inevitability of a ball rolling down an inclined plane. It is this sense of inevitability that later suggests to the Easterner that there exists, in the prelude to the fight in the snow, "a tragedy greater than the tragedy of action" (V, 159). The further the Swede goes in his excesses, the nearer comes the danger he represents to the others. It is as if Crane, sharing Goethe's notion of crisis as a kind of sickness, wanted to create a character who, without quite embodying crisis, would bring to a head whatever "critical" possibilities existed in a given situation. That such possibilities exist in the blue hotel is shown by the opposition between humanity and nature indicated by the setting, by the opposition between the blue hotel and the rest of the community, and by the hostility that permeates the very atmosphere of its small community. This being the case, the entire environment, and not merely the Swede, may be considered contagious. Like a community afflicted with a monster or with a plague – Artaud's metaphor for total crisis – the community of the blue hotel is in a crisis which only its members can resolve.

Now, one common form of resolution is confinement, wherein the madman, the outsider, is held apart. But the situation of the blue hotel is such that all the actors are confined together. The alternative strategy of exclusion is ruled out by the Swede's host, who sees the professional danger to himself of the failure to assimilate the stranger: " 'I keep a hotel,' he shouted. 'A hotel, do you mind? A guest under my roof has sacred privileges. He is to be intimidated by none' " (V, 154). The Swede carries to such an extreme the tendency toward excess, exemplified by Crane in the outburst, that from the things he does and says there emanates, from the standpoint of the other characters, an aura of unreality. By his excesses the Swede increases this aura to the point of appearing to belong to another dimension: "The Swede domineered the whole feast, and he gave it the appearance of a cruel bacchanal. He seemed to have grown suddenly taller; he gazed, brutally disdainful, into every face" (V, 154). If there is something of the epic in this picture, there is at least as much of the dramatic. Indeed, the story resembles a drama in short scenes, as do so many of the tales of Crane's friend Henry James.

Where epic narrative is typically extensive, the drama is typically intensive, which is to say that the drama mainly presents. Showing rather than describing, embodying rather than explaining, the drama not only permits but encourages the gratuitous and the extreme. This is to suggest that a character who is both gratuitous and extreme is more than incidentally theatrical. His strangeness arises from the persistence with which he carries out the premises of his own mode of being or personal logic. In the view of the Expressionist George Kaiser, drama means thinking a thought through to its conclusion, a generalization equally applicable to gratuitous and extreme characters.

> What *is* character? Suffice it here that it is something that, in life, can rationally be regarded as a bad thing. . . . [According to Sandor Ferenczi] "Character is . . . a sort of abnormality, a kind of mechanization of a particular way of reacting." Literature has not taken its "characters" to be only this, but such interpretations do help us remember to what a degree character even in literature is only an idea of a man. Such ideas follow set patterns, conform to conventions. When we speak of "a very well-drawn character" we are bestowing an accolade for a new performance of an old routine. Even the slang sense of the word, as in "He's quite a character!" contains the implication of artifice: it is as if such a man were not alive but came out of a play.[17]

The characterization works as well as it does because the short story falls generically between the extensiveness of the novel and the intensiveness of drama. The very fact that it is short means that it must have something of a play's concentration, but not so much that it ceases to be a chronicle of events. "The short story is the most purely artistic form; it expresses the ultimate meaning of all artistic creation as *mood*. . . ."[18] If one could imagine a character as mood the Swede could be that character. Which is not to say that this character–mood is a monolith. On the contrary, it is a kind of moving matrix: A matrix insofar as his personality is a place where this or that tendency is bred up and eventually expressed; a moving matrix insofar as this breeding-place modifies what it generates as circumstances change. In other words, if the basic mood is darksome, it is also mercurial, though over the long run it is the dark undertow of the Swede's being that does most to decide his destiny.

If the emergence of the Swede as aggressor precipitates crisis, the blame rests partly on Scully, who shifts from his pairing with the outsider to a pairing with his son. Early on, father and son seem far apart, even antagonistic. Scully breaks up Johnnie's card game with vehemence and guards against the possibility that Johnny will steal his liquor. When the Swede expresses his fear of being harmed, Scully behaves as if there might be something to the Swede's allegations, and is treated disrespectfully in return. But then the fight brings Scully and Johnnie together. As the Swede and Johnnie struggle, the cowboy calls the younger Scully by name for the first time and the elder Scully soon after calls the cowboy by his first name – Bill – also for the first time. Thus familiarly does each man reach out to the other; the Swede meanwhile remains anonymous – literally without a name – as if to acknowledge his inability to belong. "Stranger," the title Scully confers on him at the end of the fight, defines his role exactly, underlining the fact that the pairing of father and son has expanded into a larger grouping in which all the spectators stand over against the Swede. When Johnnie is defeated, it is a loss for "our side."

The characters in the story are also distinguished according to family status and region. Pat and Johnnie Scully are members of a family that includes several daughters, while the cowboy, the Easterner, and the Swede are, as far as one can tell, unattached. On the other hand, Pat, Johnnie, and the cowboy are all Westerners, while the Easterner and the Swede are not. This makes for an apparent structural asymmetry of two versus three in terms of the first distinction, and of three versus two in terms of the second distinction, indicating the presence, as an addition to each pairing, of an "extra" mediating character. That character is the cowboy, who is the only figure counting both as a single individual and as a Westerner, and who thus occupies a crucial in-between status. The presence of the cowboy tilts the balance of narrative dynamics in favor of the familial, Western alignment. The cowboy belongs to what Crane at one point calls "the country": " 'It's my opinion,' replied the cowboy deliberately, 'he's some kind of a Dutchman.' It was a venerable custom of the country to entitle as Swedes all light-haired men who spoke with a heavy tongue. In consequence the idea of the cowboy was not without its daring. 'Yes, sir,' he repeated. 'It's my opinion this feller is some kind of a Dutchman' " (V, 151–2). The cowboy puts the Swede at a further remove of strangeness even as he increases the familiarity between himself and Johnnie by calling the latter by his first name.

These considerations reveal that the cowboy plays a central role on the verbal front, meaning that dimension of the story brought into being by the characters' speech and including, in particular, the pronouncements of the Easterner, who is paired in the concluding section, significantly, with the cowboy. Through the pairing (to which I will return below) the character most consistently associated with the culture of the East interacts with the character most consistently associated with the culture of the West. This serves to remind us that the Scullys, too, have migrated from the East, just as the Swede and the Easterner are doing, while the cowboy – a child of the plains – is apparently indigenous to the region. This places on the cowboy a burden of representativeness; he is the nearest thing to the "real West," to which the Swede wants so much to be assimilated and which at the same time he so much fears. During the fight he does give voice to the violence endemic to the West of the Swede's imagination: " 'Kill him, Johnnie! Kill him! Kill him! Kill him!' The cowboy's face was contorted like one of those agony-masks in museums" (V, 60). But when the "mad Swede" is about to pounce on the fallen Johnnie, it is the cowboy who restrains him. Having expressed, after the fight, his own desire to battle the stranger, he nonetheless recognizes the justice of Scully's observation that such an act at this point would be unfair, and restrains himself. The cowboy and the hotel proprietor – the native Westerner and the adoptive Westerner, as it were – have their code of honor after all; and it is the same code. Because of it, the outburst the two indulge in after the fight is, so to speak, merely linguistic, their words expressing a desire which they have no power to implement. This makes the things they say, despite their explosiveness, somehow comic:

> The old man burst into sudden brogue. "I'd loike to take that Swede," he wailed, "and hould 'im down on a shtone flure and bate 'im to a jelly wid a shtick!"
>
> The cowboy groaned in sympathy. "I'd like to git him by the neck and ha-ammer him" – he brought his hand down on a chair with a noise like a pistol-shot – "hammer that there Dutchman until he couldn't tell himself from a dead coyote!"
>
> "I'd bate 'im until he – "
>
> "I'd show *him* some things – "
>
> And then together they raised a yearning fanatic cry. "Oh-o-oh! if we only could – "
>
> "Yes!"
>
> "Yes!"
>
> "And then I'd – "
>
> "O-o-oh!" (V, 164)

The final series of pairings at which we need to look connects the Easterner with, in turn, the Swede, Johnnie, and the cowboy. Each of the two card games involving these four characters finds the cowboy throwing in his lot with Johnnie, forming a partnership of Westerners and leaving Blanc and the Swede paired as Easterners. The latter two react similarly to the playing habits of the cowboy: "The countenances of the

Easterner and the Swede were miserable whenever the cowboy thundered down his aces and kings" (V, 145). In the exchange following the Swede's remark about men killed in the room, Blanc has his first chance to come to the aid of his beleaguered partner: "Apparently it seemed to the Swede that he was formidably menaced. He shivered and turned white near the corners of his mouth. He sent an appealing glance in the direction of the little Easterner. . . . The latter answered after prolonged and cautious reflection. 'I don't understand you,' he said impassively" (V, 146). Though the Easterner has a second chance to intervene when the Swede accuses Johnnie of cheating, he limits himself instead to ineffectual vocal cautions. All the while, of course, the reader who is following these events for the first time does not know that the Easterner has also seen the young Scully cheating. Only the little man's final speech to the cowboy will reveal the implications of his silence, whereupon all the previous hints fall retrospectively into place: Scully's distrust of his son, the farmer's anger, Johnnie's cockiness about his prowess at cards, his display of a "curiously instinctive care for the cards and the board" (V, 156), and the fact that the Swede's allegations against him were never directly denied. The developments that ensue come to seem less inevitable, as the reader feels something of the backlash the Easterner must have experienced on examining his own moral failure. By holding back the revelation Crane makes us comprehend what *might* have occurred at the very moment that we comprehend what actually *did*.

As in "The Open Boat" we are given access to the Easterner's linking locus only after the other characters have become involved in the action at several levels. The point of entry to this consciousness is Section 6, when the fight is about to begin:

> During this pause, the Easterner's mind, like a film, took lasting impressions of three men – the iron-nerved master of the ceremony; the Swede, pale, motionless, terrible; and Johnnie, serene yet ferocious, brutish yet heroic. The entire prelude had in it a tragedy greater than the tragedy of action, and this aspect was accentuated by the long mellow cry of the blizzard, as it sped the rumbling and wailing flakes into the black abyss of the south. (V, 159)

The passage offers the heaviest concentration of theatrically oriented language in the story – "master of the ceremony," "prelude," and "tragedy" – while terms like "heroic" and "action," radiating from the same cluster, may suggest something beyond theatricality. Through the perception of this most passive character, the other three actors lose, for a moment, their capacity to perform; act turns to pose as the present is assimilated to a future that is already forming beyond the fight – which, ironically, has yet to occur. If the immediate scene is prelude, the future scene is postlude, or epilogue: Even before the culmination of the crisis, the event is becoming less specifically situated. On the one hand, it is turning into the disposition of a particular mind, an individualized residue in consciousness which, when the epilogic moment comes, will express itself as the Easterner's moral crisis.

On the other hand, the event points to a realm of meaning – or only, perhaps, of possible meaning – in which the particular situation becomes something like a general condition. The Easterner sees a world that, like the landscape at the start of "The Bride Comes to Yellow Sky," drops off into the unknown. This one is in every way, however, a more somber picture. The East–West axis that dominates that gentler story as the axis of historical movement figures significantly in the present story as well, but is crossed by a North–South axis that is essentially natural. The basis of the latter is the movement of winter weather from North to South (much as Crane reported it in the newspaper piece "Nebraskans' Bitter Fight," written in the winter of 1894–1895). In "The Blue Hotel" the wintry weather permeates as well as surrounds; as Scully opens the door so all four men can go out into the snow, the very stove in the room is "in midcurrent of the blast" (V, 158). After the fight, "The Easterner was startled to find that they were out in a wind that seemed to come direct from the shadowed arctic floes. He heard again the wail of the snow as it was flung to its grave in the south. He knew now that all this time the cold had been sinking into him deeper and deeper, and he wondered that he had not perished. He felt indifferent to the condition of the vanquished man" (V, 162). The interplay between the private fatalism and the interpersonal conflict has a peculiar effect. Without losing its dynamic immediacy, the conflict tends to merge with the scene. It is not that the scene takes the initiative away from the actors; what happens is that the intimacy of action and scene permits the emergence of a sense of a general condition or state.

The mediation of the Easterner suggests that the tragedy greater than the tragedy of action is a tragedy of being. At issue is a question about the ethics of their condition, to borrow a phrase from "The Open Boat." Present as it is in all members of the species, that condition is, in Montaigne's all-embracing sense, human. But in the story it is doubly particularized – by the convergence that makes the events that happen unique and concrete, and by the locus of the Easterner whose orientation shows that there is more than one way of being human, or, if you will, of achieving what is at least in part an *in*human condition. The impression taken by the Easterner confirms the position he assumes when he fails to rally to the Swede. The Easterner is already indifferent, already emotionally cold; the wind from the arctic floes merely permits this condition to stand out.

If the landscape Crane describes resembles the landscape in the Nebraska sketch to which I referred, the writer who creates Fort Romper offers no equivalent to the affirmative vision recorded by the reporter working in a room with a temperature of one degree below zero. Faced with conditions that make it almost imperative that they move, the afflicted residents of the prairie yet remain:

> They had become rooted in this soil, which so seldom failed them in compensation for their untiring and persistent toil. They could not move all the complexities of their social life and their laboring life. The magic of home held them from traveling toward the promise of other lands. . . . [Winter] was a supreme battle to which to look forward. It required the profound and dogged courage of the American peoples who have come into the West to carve farms, railroads, towns, cities, in the heart of a world fortified by enormous distances. (VIII, 411)

"The Blue Hotel" provides its own versicns of these American patterns of migration and ethnicity, the latter being suggested by Crane's choice of the plural "peoples," and exemplified in the short story by the Irish Scullys, the Swede, and the Easterner, whose surname Blanc implies French descent. Story and report both show a sense of locality and a respect for the sheer struggle to survive under hostile circumstances. But nowhere in the report can one find the equivalent of the gratuitous violence and the social disintegration that are presented in the saloon in Fort Romper. To be sure, Crane reports some cupidity in the mishandling of emergency supplies, and the gambler in the saloon engages in sharp practice at the card table. But the gambler's senseless murder of the Swede suggests that by the time Crane wrote the story he could not accept the dichotomy he had drawn, less than nine months after his Nebraska sojourn, between the "detestable superficial culture which I think is the real barbarism," meaning the culture of the East, and the more homespun, more honest culture of the West. "Culture in it's [*sic*] true sense, I take it," Crane said in the same letter, "is a comprehension of the man at one's shoulder," and the man at one's shoulder sounded, then, like Scratchy Wilson: "Damn the east! I fell in love with the straight out-and-out, sometimes-hideous, often-braggart westerners because I thought them to be the truer men and, by the living piper, we will see in the next fifty years what the west will do" (*Letters,* pp. 69–70).

To an extent, Crane redeemed this optimism by writing "Moonlight on the Snow," in which Wilson appears as Potter's deputy and arrests a gambler for murder, demonstrating that Western ruffians can be regenerated. But what does "The Blue Hotel" demonstrate if not the utter *lack* of comprehension of the man at one's shoulder? The civilization of Fort Romper, embodied in such social and legal institutions as its district attorney and a fraternal association (the Pollywog Club) and in its status as a railway stop, warrants the charge of barbarism more than the East, at least on the terms Crane was employing in 1895. Whereas the dishonesty existing in the blue hotel remained unknown to the elder Scully and the cowboy, and unacknowledged by the Easterner, the dishonesty of "this thieving card-player" (V, 167) in the saloon is common knowledge:

> Beyond an occasional unwary traveler, who came by rail, this gambler was supposed to prey solely upon reckless and senile farmers, who, when flush with good crops, drove into town in all the pride and confidence of an absolutely invulnerable stupidity. Hearing at times in circuitous fashion of the despoilment of such a farmer, the important men of Romper invariably laughed in contempt of the victim, and if they thought of the wolf at all, it was with a kind of pride at the knowledge that he would never dare think of attacking their wisdom and courage. (V, 167)

The extent of the gambler's assimilation to the inner circles of respectability is indicated by the fact that the men seated with the gambler are two prominent businessmen and the district attorney. The gambler, we are also told, was "of the kind known as 'square' " (VII, 166), a word employed proleptically in several passages. The farmer and Johnnie "sat close to the stove, and squared their knees under a wide board" (V, 144) and all four players "formed a square with the little board on their knees" (V, 155). Prior to the latter game the Swede shows his familiarity with Western terminology by exclaiming to Scully, " 'Well, old boy, that was a good square meal' " (V, 155). The pairing of the terms "square" and "little," in the first of the two crucial card games involving the Swede, echoes the description in the Nebraska report of buildings with "little square false-fronts" (VII, 415), a description informed with Crane's sense of the fragility of these prairie habitations, made of light wood, isolated, exposed to the elements, standing out square and little in vast space. Fort Romper is a collection of such objects, with the blue hotel in a position of prominence as an edifice that is even more isolated than its counterparts and that plays the role, as we have seen, of standing out conspicuously. The paint that heightens this quality is a phenomenon of the outside that is nonetheless evocative of depth. The point is that Crane is encouraging the interaction of appearance and reality in a manner intimately connected with his experience both of material civilization and of human culture.

The buildings are what they are because of the mobility of the people, who had to travel from afar to build them and who had to use materials comparatively easy to transport. An exception is the sod-house construction built of immediately available dirt, but Crane, significantly, does not incorporate these into any of the stories of this period. What interests him are the wooden structures representative of vernacular American architecture and dominant in the West, structures of the balloon-frame type which could be built without elaborate joining techniques.[19] They interest him because they are integral elements in the social mobility that largely accounts for the dynamics of "The Blue Hotel" as well as "The Bride Comes to Yellow Sky" (not to mention their Western "sequels," "Twelve O'Clock" and "Moonlight on the Snow"). These are stories of people on the move, people meeting, fighting, cooperating in a series of social formations now more or less spontaneous (as in the groupings that radiate from the card games), now more settled (as in the elder Scully's contracting or expanding recognition of family bonds). While such formations are broadly characteristic of the American social scene overall, the American West exhibited them in a more dramatic form. It is a question, again, of pace; in the West, Crane could see movement in all its aspects against an immediate physical horizon and against a more remote but recognizable national horizon as well.

Using the same building techniques and the same light, portable materials, Western buildings tend to look alike, presenting to the eye, typically, unadorned planes. Commercial establishments, being competitive and needing to stand out, could then resort to facades or "fronts," suggesting a size and configuration that the hidden portion of their structure belied. The facades were at the same time legitimate architectural images, providing surfaces on which a given establishment could declare its individuality. To an Easterner like Crane, the configuration was notable; everywhere he observed these objects that were, by the city standards to which he was accustomed, very small and very consistent in their rectangularity – in a word, little and square. The term "little," is at once, as elsewhere, physical and ethical. "Little" are the windows in the public room of the hotel, the room itself, Scully and the Easterner, the tree the Swede rests against after the fight, the trees the Swede walks beside between the hotel and the saloon, the ranch to which the cowboy and the Easterner repair, the gambler, and the den in which the conflict between the Swede and Johnnie comes to a head: "Such scenes often prove that there can be little of dramatic import in environment. Any room can present a tragic front, any room can be comic. This little den was now hideous as a torture-chamber. The new faces of the men themselves had changed it upon the instant" (V, 156). The change reflects the interaction of the universal and the concrete. On the one hand, any quality whatever may dominate any room whatever, but on the other hand, whatever quality dominates must be this particular quality, realized contingently, through convergence.

The interaction of appearance and reality takes place on two levels. On the immediate level – what we might call the evidential level – what appears is what really is: The little room looks hideous because it is. On another level, however, there is a reality that does not come readily into appearance. This is the reality of the dishonesty that occasions the transformation of the room, a reality that is not hidden by the evidential but is simply, for the time, unknowable. By permitting this to remain unknowable until the final section, Crane creates a disjunction between appearance and reality that is dynamic, sudden, and intense. All at once the measured, balanced, diplomatic role of the Easterner is seen in all its ethical disproportion. The Easterner emerges in his complicity as a little man who belongs in the company of all the other little men, Pat Scully and the gambler. I do not imply that the three are to be equated; the complicity involves an orchestration of roles, each contributory in its own way; what Crane envisages is something like a continuum of responsibility.

The scene in the saloon simply gives a particular force to a pattern of disproportion that appears as early as the initial scene in the hotel, where the animosity of the atmosphere contradicts the friendliness of the proprietor, which perpetuates itself in the expansiveness of the Swede, and which becomes more explicit in the peroration of the Easterner at the end. The difference between the saloon and the hotel emerges from simple juxtaposition more than from specific comparisons. Despite the hostility shown to the Swede and despite the escalation of his aggressiveness, the conflict in the hotel is resolved in a man-to-man fight according to rules of fair play. The participants never lose control, being guided by a sense of proportion.

> "What? You won't drink with me, you little dude. I'll make you then! I'll make you!" The Swede had grasped the gambler frenziedly at the throat, and was dragging him from his chair. The other men sprang up. The barkeeper dashed around the corner of his bar. There was a great tumult, and then was seen a long blade in the hand of the gambler. It shot forward, and a human body, this citadel of virtue, wisdom, power, was pierced as easily as if it had been a melon. (V, 168–9)

If the challenge is excessive the response is more so; but a difference of degree, when it is such a difference, is everything: By comparison with the boisterous elder Scully and the dishonest younger one, this professional cheater who fights no more honestly than he deals is a menace to the community. Such retrospection is called for by the fact that this episode gathers strands of words and events into an action that, with its ongoing dramatic pace and unity, marks the culmination of the main narrative.

The passage that concludes this section brandishes the proverbial sting in the tail: "the corpse of the Swede, alone in the saloon, had its eyes fixed upon a dreadful legend that dwelt a-top of the cash-machine. 'This registers the amount of your purchase' " (V, 169). If the previous reference to the cash register indicated the price the Swede had to pay for his drink, this reference indicates the greater price paid for a greater exchange. The words of the legend, not to mention the very designation of "legend," shift attention from the economic to the ethical, from financial to moral and vital expense. The implication is that the larger meaning of what occurs consists in a realm beyond the realm of everyday, material values. It is not that Crane devalues the material – his description of the Swede's knifed body keeps corporeality and movement palpably present. But there is more to the Swede's demise than the movements that bring it to pass. The gambler's countermovement is excessive: Provoked he may be, but he cannot fairly claim that he kills the other man in self-defense. Moreover, he does not rely on the traditional revolver, a weapon given legitimacy in popular iconography because of its comparatively public, "fair-and-square" nature. In this context the knife is a nonchivalric secret weapon with which a man who usually steals other men's money can unusually steal another man's life.

We have seen the centrality, throughout the story, of the spoken word. Scully uses such words to capture travelers stepping off the train, the Swede to express his fear of getting killed and, when this is allayed, to express his aggressive impulses. Once the Swede has departed, Scully and the cowboy take retrospective vengeance with an outburst of vocal violence; while the Swede's path to the saloon is paved once again by the things he says and the peculiar way he says them. And finally, we have the conversation between the final pair, the Easterner and the cowboy.

Learning that the gambler has been sentenced to three years in prison, the Easterner states that the tragedy might have been avoided " 'if everything had been square' " (V, 170). The cowboy's inability to comprehend this remark enrages the Easterner, who then reveals for the first time that Johnnie was cheating. The cowboy cannot accept the allegation since the game was played for fun.

> "Fun or not," said the Easterner, "Johnnie was cheating. I saw him. I know it. I saw him. And I refused to stand up and be a man. I let the Swede fight it out alone. And you – you were simply puffing around the place and wanting to fight. And then old Scully himself! We are all in it! This poor gambler isn't even a noun. He is a kind of an adverb. Every sin is the result of a collaboration. We, five of us, have collaborated in the murder of this Swede. Usually there are from a dozen to forty women really involved in every murder, but in this case it seems to be only five men – you, I, Johnnie, old Scully, and that fool of an unfortunate gambler came merely as a culmination, the apex of a human movement, and gets all the punishment."
>
> The cowboy, injured and rebellious, cried out blindly into this fog of mysterious theory, "Well, I didn't do anythin', did I?" (V, 170)

Making the murder of the Swede collaborative has the obvious tactical advantage, for the Easterner, of spreading the blame. But the speech is too speechy, these are words living on words, in a kind of verbal cannibalism; and the cowboy is not wholly off the mark in regarding the statement as foggy and mysterious. Not wholly, since there is after all something to what the suddenly long-winded Easterner has to say. There has been collaboration, first, in the way that chance, character, and circumstance come together to shape a destiny, and, second, in the way that the other characters come together against the Swede. Translated into the more optimistic terms of "The Open Boat," the story could have concluded: "He felt he could then be an interpreter." Crane goes further than that here, or rather, he goes in a different direction, producing an interpretation that is even more problematic. The Easterner hits the mark insofar as he points to a collective aspect in the sequence of events, but he misses insofar as he makes all the actors seem equally guilty when it was he, and he alone, who held the power of validating the Swede's position.

When Crane gives his ending this problematic turn, he causes it to stand out from the rest of the narrative, an ecstasis heightened by the formal division between the final and the preceding sections and by the distance in time separating the conversation between the cowboy and the Easterner from the time of the main narrative.[20] This may be compared with the technique employed in the Chaucerian *envoi,* which enables the author to emerge with the last word, or in the concluding phase of "Lycidas," where Milton displays himself in the role of poet by means of an epilogue that suddenly draws the reader toward an overview. By contrast, Crane withholds his authorial presence, preferring to let the ending do its own displaying, as it were, through the Easterner's reconstruction of events, like a coda. The final section, by heightening, reprises the pattern that begins with the first appearance of the hotel, with its standout color and its standout proprietor. But something may stand out without being self-evident in purpose or in meaning, or even clear, as is the case with the ending of "The Blue Hotel." The ending is problematic at least in part because it offers a kind of mimetic interpretation, an interpretation resembling and to some extent repeating what it interprets. For if the main happenings are complex, compromised, and contingent, so is the concluding overview. At the same time the interpreter joins the company of those who have previously, in effect, imitated the Swede, a company including every other major character, each of whom finally, like the Swede, turns antagonistic and goes on the attack. Suddenly the Easterner turns antagonistic too, attacking everyone, even himself. Each and every person is to blame, not excluding the gambler, for whom the Easterner feels sorry, but who is nonetheless a "fool" (V, 171).

A derivative of the Latin term for "bellow," *fool* formerly designated what we would today call a "windbag," an ironically misplaced term for the gambler and an apt one for everyone else – for the Scullys and the cowboy, who blow loud and early, for the Swede, who blows too loud and too long, and for the Easterner, who blows too loud and too late. If this makes everyone look the same, that consequence accords with the views of the Easterner, who discerns indifference in the motives and acts of all the collaborators. Here is another resemblance, another repetition. Confronted by "a monotony of unchangeable fighting," "confused mingling" that "was eternal to his sense" (V, 160), "He felt indifferent to the condition of the vanquished man" (V, 162). This is the Easterner, of course, as he stands out in the driving arctic wind because earlier he failed to stand up. Such a wind may blow where it listeth, just as any of the men in it may be as windy or as wordy, or as silent, as they wish. But one gets the sense here, so far as one is aligned with the locus of this little man, that what one does or does not do may ultimately make no difference, that human beings are lost on their whirling, fire-smote, ice-locked, disease-stricken, space-lost bulb, around which the winds indifferently sweep, tearing away those lesser winds, which are the words of Scully and "the remainder of the sentence" spoken by the Swede (V, 159).

If the Easterner is unique in sympathizing with the Swede as well as the gambler, and if he comes to resemble the Swede, who already claims to be different, then the Easterner is different too, in which case his theory of indifference might as well be gone with the wind along with those previously mentioned. For the fact is that where responsibility is concerned, the Easterner is more equal than the other so-called collaborators. He held the power of the word, the power to speak a truth the wind would be powerless to tear away; and he did not speak.

In his moment of crisis, knowing and doing and being intersect. Because of what he knows, the Easterner can, by doing what he ought to do, be the man he ought to be. But he does not and so he is not. Another part of the tragedy greater than the tragedy of action, then, and possibly the final part, is that having failed to make the difference he could have made, he blames others for not doing what he alone was positioned to help them do. What this means for the nexus of crisis and community is just this: In his windily wordy oration there is both a true crisis and a false community. The crisis is what we have been considering – the chance to act on what he knows and his ultimate failure to do so. The community is the one that supposedly consists of those equally responsible for the fate of the Swede. The crisis is true because it is a genuine turning point and measure. The community is false because it is not an ensemble of properly judged persons, but, as his vocabulary suggests, a mere tissue of words, as easy to see through as the truth it would mask is hard to forget.

THIS FOREIGN CONDITION

Like most authors, Crane usually draws on nouns for his titles, and when verb titles do occur, as in "Regulars Get No Glory," they usually belong to news reports or dispatches, the headlines for which are normally the responsibility of an editor. The one major piece of fiction with a verb title is "The Bride Comes to Yellow Sky." Here nouns have their office to fill as well, the first identifying a character, the second a setting, but it is the connection between these through the predicate that seizes our attention and stays in our memory. Crane's title is like an abbreviated version of newspaper headline that, in the format Crane knew well, might have read:

BRIDE COMES TO YELLOW SKY
SHOOT-OUT FIZZLES
ROWDY ROUTED BY GUNLESS LAWMAN

This story of crisis and community is first of all a story of movement, itself a form of what one critic calls "becoming," a fitting term for a work that by common agreement focuses on change:[21] "The great Pullman was whirling onward with such dignity of motion that a glance from the window seemed simply to prove that the plains of Texas were pouring eastward. Vast flats of green grass, dull-hued spaces of mesquite and cactus, little groups of frame houses, woods of light and tender trees, all were sweeping into the east, sweeping over the horizon, a precipice" (V, 109). Wherever it occurs in Crane's fiction, the advent of the train is associated, as it so often was in his century, with challenge and change. It is a train that carries the characters in *The Third Violet* back and forth between town and country – a movement that makes it possible for protagonist Hawker to assume a vocation and to attempt to alter his marital status – and it is by train that Easterners arrive at Fort Roper. In "The Monster" the train figures as a premonition of catastrophic change as well as an instrument of "progress," by which Whilomville has grown from a town to a little city.

The movement of the train at the beginning of "The Bride Comes to Yellow Sky" occasions a correlative movement in Potter: "To the left, miles down a long purple slope, was a little ribbon of mist where moved the keening Rio Grande. The train was approaching it at an angle, and the apex was Yellow Sky. Presently it was apparent that as the distance from Yellow Sky grew shorter, the husband became commensurately restless. His brick-red hands were more insistent in their prominence" (V, 111). That "commensurately" signifies that the journey is measured as much in the man as on the land, as the passage that follows signifies the relation between physical position and mental attitude; for with the approach to the town, Potter begins to project his movements through the streets: "He resolved that he would use all the devices of speed and plains-craft in making the journey from the station to his house. Once within that safe citadel, he could issue some sort of vocal bulletin, and then not go among the citizens until they had time to wear off a little of their enthusiasm" (V, 112). Crane implies a congruence between imagination and world: Both here and in his projection of his flight through town, Potter is sensitive to speed and is really speeding. What is more, his imagined action comes true, in part. Sheriff and bride take flight as soon as they arrive, and when they reappear in Part 4 they are walking "sheepishly and with speed" (V, 118). Yet events prove that the congruence goes only so far; between the immediate future that Potter imagines and the immediate future that actually occurs there is precisely incongruence. By the terms of his own understanding of his social role, the sheriff has lost his bearings: In San Antonio he "had gone headlong over all the social hedges" (V, 111). Swift to act and slow to understand, he resembles Scratchy Wilson, despite opposing him. Both imagine that the sheriff should be a man with a gun rather than a wife, which is to say that both imagine that Yellow Sky is what it was. The irony is not only that the sheriff is himself furthering the development of the town, as any reader can see, but that the very possibility of his doing so presupposes a collective readiness that he must have sensed yet cannot fully see.

The movement of the train, undeviating and direct, contrasts dramatically with the movements of Wilson, which are animalistic (he creeps like a cat), and impulsive: "He then turned his back contemptuously upon [the Weary Gentleman saloon], and walking to the opposite side of the street, and spinning there on his heel quickly and lithely, fired at the bit of paper" (V, 118). The point is not Wilson's incompetence (he remains a good shot despite being drunk), but the disintegrative nature of the movements he performs on such occasions. Shooting at a dog, Wilson drives the creature now one direction, now another, while as a result of his appearance the two Mexican sheepherders in the saloon deposit their glasses and depart. As in "The Monster," this crisis of the community disperses and divides: Wilson's shooting and the dog's howling "instantly removed a bond from the men in the darkened saloon" (V, 116). Wilson is a caricature of the individualist, able to relate to others singly, serially and oppositionally, but not cooperatively. Stated another way, the one social function that gives him continuity creates discontinuity in the community.

To do justice to the technique with which Crane renders movements of various types, one must look more closely at his language. The second sentence of the opening passage, for example, exhibits strongly rhythmic units. "Vást fláts ŏf gréen gráss" amounts to a spondee followed by an unaccented beat and a second spondee, while the last phrases in the series of nominal landscape objects are trochaic, with an elided final foot: "wóods ŏf líght aňd téndĕr trées." Alliteration by consonant produces "*g*reen *g*rass," "*t*ender *t*rees"; alliteration by vowels gives "v*a*st fl*a*ts"; "sw*ee*ping," "sw*ee*ping." Generally, the closer one listens to the vowels, the more one hears; the second phrase in the sentence offers variations on sounds revolving around "u": "d*u*ll-h*u*ed," "cact*u*s."

If we then compare this group of words with the preceding group on an accentual basis, we discover a different but related organizing principle. The opening phrase is charged with even beats: "Vást fláts ŏf gréen gráss." But the second group is relatively broken: "dúll-húed spácĕs ŏf mésquĭte aňd cáctŭs." The third group is more regular again, and the fourth has, as we saw, a distinctive lilt. In the remaining groups, finally, the rhythm is elongated through the repeated predicates and prepositional phrases. Binding all the elements together is a principle of organization that, while it is not Crane's own, is developed by him to an unusual extent. This principle involves a precise use of syllabic measure as a quantitative complement to abundance and variety. The first two groups, we note, consist respectively of words totaling five syllables and ten syllables. The next two consist of words totaling seven and seven; the two after that are eight and eight; and the final group, "a precipice," halves this to four. The sequence 5, 10, 7, 7, 8, 8, 4 involves, then, two kinds of doubling: a doubling of increase whereby the number of syllables is made either twice or half as great, and a doubling of repetition whereby the number occurs two times in succession. At the end, inverting the procedure with which the sequence began, Crane cuts the last repeated number in half. But he prevents this highly measured rhythm from becoming mechanical by shifting: Thus, though the repetitions are unrelenting, the same number of syllables is never used more than twice. Taken as a whole, the effect is of a movement that, like the movement of the train across the landscape, combines striking regular rhythm with striking rhythmic variety.

The same passage initiates a verb form typical of the story: "was whirling," "were pouring," "were sweeping," "sweeping." The first time Potter appears, his hands "were constantly performing in a most conscious fashion" (V, 109); a moment later he is "smiling with delight" (V, 109), and as the train "was approaching" the Rio Grande, Potter "was beginning to find the shadow of a dead weight like a leaden slab," since "he was now bringing his bride before an innocent and unsuspecting community" (V, 111). It is clear from these instances that the participial form, covering everything from the physical to the mental, aims to capture the process, the very flow, of action. The "news value" of the narrative depends upon this rendering of immediacy (as further suggested by the fact that newscaster Lowell Thomas relied throughout his career on "-ing" forms, on the theory that they create a sense, not of past events, but of something happening right now).

That Crane's participial forms are past progressives, in contrast to the present progressives of Thomas, suggests a compromise between the demands of a conventionally remote fictional past and Crane's interest in contemporary crisis and change. One effect of the "-ing" forms, in any case, is to heighten the more kinetic phases of the story. Scratchy Wilson is a man whose cries go "shrilly flying," whose eyes are "rolling," a man "wheeling," "laughing," "walking," "spinning," "playing," "chanting Apache scalp-music" "taking up a strategic position," "mingling" epithets with challenges, and "churning himself into deepest rage over the immobility of a house" (V, 116–18). The description renders Wilson both kinesthetically and judgmentally. That is, we experience his movements physically, as activities in space, but in relation to other types of movements – for example, the great Pullman's dignity of motion; and this is one source of the perspectivism in the story.

Another source is the relation between the movements I have described and the formal divisions of the narrative. Each of the four divisions presents one setting and one character or group of characters: 1, train (bride and groom); 2, saloon (men inside); 3, street (Wilson); 4, street (Potter, bride, and Wilson). In each section, we realize, there is something that the characters do not know. In Section 1, bride and groom do not know what they are headed for in town. In 2, the men in the saloon do not know that the sheriff is on his way home. Wilson in 3 does not know, first, that Potter is away, then that he is returning; least of all does he know about the bride. Only in the fourth and final section do the characters meet in a *peripeteia* in which, supposedly, all is revealed. But the truth, as so often in Crane, is less tidy than that. Potter advises Wilson: " 'If you're goin' to shoot me up, you better begin now. You'll never get a chance like this again' " (V, 119). He will never get that chance because Potter has no intention of being caught like this again. Thus he immediately regrets that he is unarmed: " 'And if I'd thought there was going to be any galoots like you prowling around when I brought my wife home, I'd had a gun, and don't you forget it' " (V, 119–20). As if to underline the fact that Potter does not fully comprehend what is happening historically, it is Wilson, not Potter, who announces that the fight is off, with all that this implies for the future:

> "Well," said Wilson at last, slowly, "I s'pose it's all off now."
> "It's all off if you say so, Scratchy. You know I didn't make the trouble." (V, 120)

Wilson's submission requires a concurrence that Potter can furnish because a vision of the Pullman, embodying "all the glory of the marriage, the environment of the new estate" (V, 119), presents itself to him at the height of the crisis. The sheriff knows that he must defeat his antagonist on new, nonviolent grounds, but out of habit responds by threatening to return to the gun. It is a question, in other words, of a dual pace: the pace of change being brought about by the advent of the honeymooners and the slower pace of Potter's comprehension. Potter stands firm, literally: "His heels had not moved an inch backward" (V, 119). To retreat in space would be to retreat in time, to resume the old ways. But it is still in terms of the old ways that Potter speaks when he warns Wilson that he will not again be caught in the same situation. The truth, of course, is that he will not be caught again like this because in the new estate there will be no occasion for such a confrontation to occur. Acting against the old order, Potter yet speaks its language, and therefore, as I have pointed out, it is not he but Wilson who first articulates an awareness of the end, the sheriff then completing the initiative. Hence one of the significant ironies of the story is that the sheriff does not himself understand the very message the advent of the new estate embodies. If he did, he would not be so mistaken in his ideas about the reaction of the town to his marriage:

> Of course, people in Yellow Sky married as it pleased them in accordance with a general custom; but such was Potter's thought of his duty to his friends, or of their idea of his duty, or an unspoken form which does not control men in these matters, that he felt he was heinous. He had committed an extraordinary crime. . . . At San Antonio he was like a man hidden in the dark. A knife to sever any friendly duty, any form, was easy to his hand in that remote city. (V, 111)

The story's impact derives, as has been suggested, from the implication that Potter's absurd conception of the social requirements of his position in the town also collapses with the Wild West ritual: Potter's illusions could have arisen only from a code of manners that made provision for the ritual gunfight.

Potter belongs to a line of characters including Henry Fleming, Collins, and the children of the Whilomville tales. Like them, the lawman sees himself in the gaze of others – through his vision of their vision of him. The difference is that in those other stories the code by which they are tested is sound, or at least viable, but the characters do not always, or fully, measure up to it. Potter, by contrast, measures up, but the code is dubious. The trouble with the Wild West is that everyone wants to be his own man. The criterion of social success is individual superiority, a kind of Hobbesian sudden glory achieved through personal prowess. The community plays the role of spectator, its streets providing a stage for figures who are, in a cogent sense, performers. As Chicago-school sociologists have shown, we are all performers to the extent that we all play social roles. Furthermore, we all know moments when an everyday situation appears theatrical, dreamlike, or simply unreal; one's first entry into the world of work is such a time, as are the experiences of being hospitalized or imprisoned.[22] One becomes aware of the behavior of others – and of one's own behavior – through something close to theatrical acting, just as one becomes aware of the unfamiliar setting as something very like a theatrical scene. Such theatricality, as we have seen, is a recurring feature in Crane from early writings to late.

The theatricality of the showdown in Yellow Sky, however, is not experienced by the characters, but by the reader. It is the reader who measures their performance against popular Wild West conceptions, and it is the reader who savors the parody. But the very fact that the confrontation works as parody depends upon its plausibility: In moments of crisis such as Crane depicts, Potters and Wilsons must have met in more or less this way. Like their predecessors, Crane's characters see crisis in community as serious business; if they did not, they would not be funny.

Although the code of the West is supposed to require that actions speak louder than words, the confrontation scene suggests that words have the more powerful voice, or at least that this is to be the trend. For the standoff in the street is a showdown in speech: " 'Married?' said Scratchy. Seemingly for the first time he saw the drooping drowning woman at the other man's side. 'No!' he said. he was like a creature allowed a glimpse of another world. He moved a pace backward, and his arm with the revolver dropped to his side. 'Is this – is this the lady?' he asked" (V, 120). If the horizon of consciousness is important here, it is just as important that the presence of the bride is brought over that horizon by words. It is not until the sheriff interprets her being there – " 'I'm married,' said Potter" (V, 120) – that Wilson can give her recognition. Spoken language is augmented by the silent language of gesture, understanding this term as a broad designation for physical expression. Wilson at first moves his pistol forward, then advances his entire body, lashing his weapon until, on recognizing the advent of a new estate, "He moved a pace backward" (V, 120), confirming that the community has entered an era in which a man talks rather than shoots.

Details of Wilson's appearance are also relevant: "A man in a maroon-colored flannel shirt, which had been purchased for the purposes of decoration and made principally by some Jewish women on the east side of New York, rounded a corner and walked into the middle of the main street of Yellow Sky" (V, 116). If San Antonio is the first instance of urbanization to the East, this is the paradigmatic one insofar as it connects Yellow Sky to the nation's largest city. A similar axis connects Fort Romper to the East as well. But a North–South axis intersects the latter in the form of the arctic wind, the passage of which suggests that nature is on its own, more primordial track, which it will follow as it always has, indifferent to those in its way. Nature in that mode is notably absent from the present story, where the critical track is, first, the one on which the Southern Railway runs its California Express, and then the one made by Wilson after he realizes the meaning for his community of the crisis at hand. " 'Married!' He was not a student of chivalry; he was a simple child of the earlier plains. He picked up his starboard revolver, and placing both weapons in their holsters, he went away. His feet made funnel-shaped tracks in the heavy sand" (V, 120).

Here the pairing of rivals in relation to a third person departs from the model of *The Red Badge of Courage*. There the lieutenant plays the role of third, being the model of superior behavior on which Henry and his friend can both pattern themselves. True, one could argue that the bride stands for superior behavior as well, since she initiates a pattern that will be the communal norm. But the dynamics are different here because the orientations of the rivals are different. Henry, his friend, and the lieutenant unite in pursuit of a shared ideal; so do the sheriff and his bride, whose namelessness underlines her functionality; but Wilson's ideal is precisely the one the bride replaces. Secondly, the bond between groom and bride is legal and written, meaning, significantly, that it is more like the contract between the sheriff and the community than the one, traditional and oral, connecting the sheriff and Wilson. Opposing the latter contrast, this bond affirms the former, prospectively substituting the head of a family – a fathering authority – for the bachelor sheriff. With the taking of a bride, the sheriff of Yellow Sky helps prepare for a new generation of children living within the law and supplanting the last of the "kids" who tried to live without it.

In the stories previously examined in this chapter, the presence of a foreign condition that triggers a crisis in the community is a recurrent pattern as well. Its first embodiment is the Swede, who happens to be of actual foreign extraction. It then appears in the person of a man who is racially foreign before becoming foreign to the canons of acceptable human appearance. On a milder note the foreign condition in the *Tales of Whilomville* is present in the new boy on the block, a figure who appears in three of these works. Each presence is characterized by marginality and each story by the crisis it precipitates in the community. The difference is that in "The Bride Comes to Yellow Sky" the marginal man does not want what his counterparts want. They want to be accepted, to have their foreignness domesticated; Scratchy Wilson wants "this foreign condition" to stay foreign, and so he makes tracks.

Looking back at the opening paragraph from the vantage point of the story's last sentence, George W. Johnson observes, "two roles have been momentarily juxtaposed before going over the edge. For what the confrontation shows us is that there is no ultimate meaning in either role, and that under a yellow sky men and their traditions make but passing indentations in the sands of time."[23]

Perhaps only water is a more ephemeral medium than sand for the preservation of historical traces. The inevitable disappearance of the tracks is, in any case, the final stage of a movement that contrasts with the movement with which the story begins. It is, in fact, everything that the initial movement of train and passengers is not. It is a movement-away, not movement-toward. It is a movement of resignation, not of assertion. It is a private, isolated movement, not a collective movement. In another sense Scratchy's movement is not a negation but a culmination. For if the foreign condition is to be domesticated, the movement of advent with which the story begins must be completed by a corresponding movement of departure. This Wilson provides. He provides it, moreover, with something closer to graciousness than one might expect from one who is not a student of chivalry: He simply withdraws. He makes his departure, finally, in a way that the Scully who declared a position would understand: It is just that Scully makes his mark with paints and Wilson with tracks.

8

The Ethics of Their Condition and the Unreal Real: "The Open Boat," "The Five White Mice"

THE GROUP

In throwing together the four men in "The Open Boat" chance plays a larger role than in Crane's other major tales, with the possible exception of "The Five White Mice." This group is not spontaneous in Huizinga's sense, however, for it remains importantly connected, as Crane's small groups tend to be, with a larger collectivity. As in *The Red Badge of Courage* and most of the other war writings, that collectivity is an organization. Strongly structured though it may be, an organization is susceptible to local breaking up, and when the conditions are right it can dissolve into mere seriality. In Crane's war novel the best illustration is the military unit in rout, when it is "every man for himself." In the present story the dissolving coincides with the foundering of the ship.

The central organization in "The Open Boat" is that of the ship's company, the most detailed picture of which is furnished in "Stephen Crane's Own Story," the newspaper version of the incidents later reworked into the published tale. That version also offers details of action missing from the latter, such as the panicky behavior of the "colored stoker" (IX, 93) and the seven men waiting for death on the stern of the *Commodore*. Indeed, Crane as correspondent devotes most of his energies to the moments of dissolution and chaos, limiting his account of the four men in the boat to two paragraphs and an additional sentence: "And then by the men on the ten-foot dingy were words said that were still not words, something far beyond words" (IX, 94). "The Open Boat," in which Crane tries to articulate those words and their "beyond," picks up the story after the chaos of the sinking, when the dissolution into seriality has itself dissolved, as it were, to be replaced by an ad hoc formation consisting of three members of the ship's company and the passenger whose status changes quickly from that of outsider to that of insider. In this formation aspects of the original organizational structure remain: The captain gives orders and the others obey them; at the same time the oiler, whose job it was to help keep the ship's motive power in working order, now helps in a similar way, though at a "lower" level of technology. In this re-forming of the original organization, the correspondent becomes a member of the company in the new vessel, while the cook, remaining subordinate with the others, is effectively unemployed, having no food to prepare, and apparently being unable or unwilling to assist in the rowing.

If organization carries over from ship to boat, at least in a partial way, it still leaves room for a degree of spontaneous and fraternal association, which is precisely what the pairing of the correspondent and the oiler represents. It is not, of course, that the organizational structure requires this, but simply that it is one of the conditions in terms of which the fraternalizing can come about.

The emphasis thus far has fallen, in effect, on doing, with which Crane's newspaper version of the adventure is almost exclusively concerned. But when Crane rethought and reshaped his experiences, concentrating on the fate of the boat rather than the fate of the ship, doing once more turned out to be inseparable from the question of knowing and the question of being. Such, at least, is what is implied at every important juncture, including the famous opening description.

THE COLOR OF THE SKY

> None of them knew the color of the sky. Their eyes glanced level, and were fastened upon the waves that swept toward them. These waves were of the hue of slate, save for the tops, which were of foaming white, and all of the men knew the colors of the sea. The horizon narrowed and widened, and dipped and rose, and at all times its edge was jagged with waves that seemed thrust up in points like rocks.
>
> Many a man ought to have a bath-tub larger than the boat which here rode upon the sea. These waves were most wrongfully and barbarously abrupt and tall, and each froth-top was a problem in small boat navigation. (V, 68)

I would like to reinforce some features of the readings to which these famous lines have been submitted, and to add some of my own.[1] The level perspective of the men's gaze recalls, in its own way, the placement of the little man in "Killing His Bear": "The dying sun created a dim purple and flame-colored tumult on the horizon's edge and then sank until level crimson beams struck the trees" (VIII, 249). The description tells us that the little man knows *mutatis mutandis* more than the men in the open boat. If the little man can, for example, take in the specific colors of the scene, it is because his situation requires him to be alert to the landscape and also provides him with time for observations, whereas the men in the open boat, being obliged to labor for their lives, have time for nothing else.

Describing the various ways in which people at sea perceive nature, Lucretius observes: "To sailors at sea it is as if the sun rises from the waves, and in the waves sets and buries its light. This is because nothing else but sea and sky meets their view; so you must not rashly assume that the evidence of our senses is wholly unreliable."[2] Like the generalized sailors in Lucretius, Crane's particularized sailors know what they are in a position to know and the knowledge they have is genuine; but it is a limited, situated, and therefore a perspectival knowledge.

Now perception in "The Open Boat" is not the same as perception in *The Red Badge of Courage.* Crane often concerns himself in the earlier work with phenomena that hide behind appearance. There, reality is a potential illumination concealed by a veil – a veil of circumstance and chance (as in the case of smoke or fog) or of character (as in the case of Henry Fleming's projection of false appearances). "The Open Boat," on the other hand, deals mainly with circumstantial veiling. The men in the boat want to get the facts straight, not in the interest of uncovering some hidden light, but in the interest of getting on with their task. This does not spare them the effort of interpretation. On the contrary, we are constantly being told how things "seemed" or "appeared." But the seeming and the appearing have to do with the relation between the act of perception and the perceived phenomenon, and not with the relation between the phenomenon and something behind it. In "The Open Boat" there *is* nothing behind the thing you see. Consider for example the proposition that the waves "seemed thrust up in points like rocks": That describes the appearance of the waves, but it does not incite curiosity about their reality. All the reality they have is *in* their appearance. "Seemed" simply acknowledges that the analogy *is* an analogy; it qualifies the statement much as if the author were to say: I know that waves aren't really like rocks, but if you had seen the way these were thrusting up, you too might have been struck by much the same resemblance.

The question of color, around which so much gravitates, is raised in different but related ways. "The color of the sky" suggests the presence of some particular hue or of some combination of such, this being the second *OED* definition of the noun *color.* At the same time something more general could be at issue if the first sense, "the quality or attribute in virtue of which objects present different aspects to the eye," is also implied. In behalf of the latter possibility, which in the final analysis may be undecidable, there is the direct association with the sky, which, as will be shown below, Crane connects with ultimate epistemological and ontological questions.

After this strong if problematic start, particular colors immediately appear and are recognized by the men, since the former belong to the waves and these are what the latter are looking at. With "the colors of the sea" the second sense is unmistakably signified, the key noun standing now as a general term for the shades of slate and white.

The brilliant primary colors of Crane's early works, colors that one might almost attribute to unaided imagination, hardly figure in "The Open Boat," where the closest thing to red is "roseate" and to blue is "bluish" (V, 86). Crane's palette has grown subtler and more precise because his imagination now hews not to conjectured event but to remembered experience. This is not to say that "The Open Boat" is colorless. We find "carmine and gold" (V, 87), "emerald-green" (V, 70), "amber" (V, 70), "green" (V, 91), and the delicate "saffron" (V, 81). But mainly we find the no-color colors, black and white and their intermediary, gray: There are "the tall black waves that swept forward in a most sinister silence" (V, 81) and the tiny house that "was blocked out black upon the sky" (V, 76), to choose only two examples. The reader has the sense that something is being recorded in process, and sometimes the process becomes explicit: "from a black line it became a line of black and a line of white – trees and sand"; "and sometimes they could see only the white lip of a wave as it spun up the beach" (V, 75–76). Whites and blacks like these, while not directly symbolic, have an elemental quality, and seem to serve, within the spectrum of coloration, as a kind of ultimate measure or delimitation. The case of gray looks a little different. By implication, gray is associated with uncertainty and expectation, which, like the hue itself, falls between extremes. It first appears in nature: "and this captain had on him the stern impression of a scene in the grays of dawn of seven upturned faces" (V, 69), and later in an artifact: "Southward, the slim light-house lifted its little gray length" (V, 76). The two instances are indirectly connected. In the first the metonymic closeness between the color and the faces foreshadows the humanizing that gray will undergo, while the second links the color to littleness, which, given the vast scope into which the narrative frequently widens out, implies fragility and hence vulnerability. There is added resonance, therefore, when Crane says of the rowers, "Gray-faced and bowed forward, they mechanically, turn by turn, plied the leaden oars" (V, 81) and, of the lighthouse, "It has now almost assumed color, and appeared like a little gray shadow on the sky" (V, 74).

The constant presence of the sky is comparably resonant from various associations in Crane's corpus. Some are from the many silhouettes against the sky, images that function like diacritical marks, adding force to a given nexus without delivering a determinate meaning. Though the pasted red wafer is not a silhouette, its positioning in the sky is similarly suggestive, as is the smoky skyward soaring of soul in old Henry Fleming's apotheosis. The sky is also an expanse by which to measure and be measured, as in the case of the young officer who fails to heed the cries of the wounded "even as the pilgrim fails to heed the world as he raises his illumined face toward his purpose . . . his sky of the ideal of duty" (V, 102).

A more directly relevant nexus appears in "Flanagan and His Short Filibustering Expedition," concerning the same kind of adventure that lands the correspondent in the open boat: "The captain knew that it requires sky to give a man courage. He went for a stoker and talked to him on the bridge. The man, standing under the sky, instantly and shamefacedly denied all knowledge of the business" (V, 97). Here the sky is both motive and measure. It is motive in that it furnishes a man with the resolve necessary for the act in question. It is measure in that it tests the degree to which the appropriate motivation is operative. Moreover, as in "The Open Boat," the human relation to the sky is expressed in terms of knowledge, though here the terms are more judgmental. That the men in the boat do not know the color of the sky but do know the colors of the sea are facts that stand as stated, make of them what you will. In "Flanagan and His Short Filibustering Expedition," by contrast, a man is put on trial for what he knows and is. The premise, framed as knowledge possessed by the captain, is that sky gives a man courage, from which it follows that someone called before its court can be either found competent in this regard, or wanting. When the stoker then denies all knowledge, he admits in effect that the sky's dose of courage has not "taken," a failing underlined by the haste and shame of his reply.

"None of them knew the color of the sky" and the echoic "all of the men knew the colors of the sea" exemplify the regularity of rhythm that is one of the features of the story, even as it is one of the features of the sea. But the story, like the sea, displays uneven movements too. One has only to consider the two clauses quoted above, each of which exhibits four accents, with the varied rhythm of the clauses and phrases that come between them. The second sentence, for example, starts off with an even feel and strong accentuation (four stresses in four words), only to be interrupted by a caesura at the comma, after which the rhythm stretches out in a lapping way, with only five accents in ten words. By comparison, the sentence that follows is a series of interruptions, being divided into an opening and a closing independent clause separated by "save for the tops, which were of foaming white"; all of the units differ from one another in rhythm, producing an effect of choppiness and unexpectedness, two additional features of experience at sea. This irregularity is highlighted, of course, by the echoic familiarity of the concluding clause, "and all of the men knew the colors of the sea," which reintroduces regularity. Contrast carries over into the final sentence in the paragraph, which moves with a rolling regularity until an abrupt break: "and at all times its edge was jagged with waves that seemed thrust up in points like rocks." This is very choppy and strung out – long-winded even, coming as it does so late, and with none of the pauses provided by the previous portion of the sentence. The most striking feature, however, is the amount of emphasis: "wáves that seémed thrúst úp in poínts like rócks." Such accentual confrontation forces the words on the reader with something of the waves' own unrelenting insistence. The forceful "thrust up," I might add, is very apt for the pointing motion, which is likewise strong and sudden; even the guttural vowels contribute, inasmuch as their deep pitch is raised semantically by the predicate, as though in imitation of the shaping energy in the thrusting-up itself.

MANY A MAN

Of the many arresting statements in "The Open Boat" one of the most conspicuous is "Many a man ought to have a bath-tub larger than the boat which here rode upon the sea." Crane is very fond of the locution that launches the statement, and uses it in a variety of ways in a variety of contexts. He is not, of course, without predecessors. Dickens observes: "But many a man who would have stood within a home dismantled, strong in his passion and design of vengeance, has had the firmness of his nature conquered by the razing of an air-built castle."[3] Dickens's "many a man" expresses a conviction about the behavior one can expect from a certain type of person, given the attributes of character associated with that type. Such a view may be compared with a statement in the Sullivan County sketch "Two Men and a Bear": "The bear then has a bad quarter of an hour, but many of the dogs must weep and wail and gnash their teeth, for the bear crunches them and crushes them as if they were papier-mâché images" (VII, 248). Crane's statement is, one might say, conative; his "must" is a way of construing what ought to have happened, given the typicality of the situation. The laconic "bad quarter of an hour" and the papier-mâché analogy are a tough guy's way of reporting or, to state the matter more decorously, of constructively describing. For Crane does little to render any direct connection between himself and the scene, despite the use of the present tense. Here that tense gives the action, to be sure, a certain vividness, but it also produces a timeless, almost fatalistic quality, balancing the force of the immediate situation with the force of typicality.

For further comparison we may turn to Gloucester's exclamation in *Henry VI, Part 2:*

> The gates made fast! Brother, I like not this;
> For many men that stumble at the threshold
> Are well foretold that danger lurks within. (IV.vii.10–12)

The statement is Gloucester's attempt to support his sense of foreboding with prudential wisdom; his remark is like an improvised folk saying, keyed to a new situation. When Thoreau makes his famous observation that "Most men lead lives of quiet desperation," he also, in his own way, expresses the voice of wisdom, as though to urge upon the reader his belief that the observation is not only true but also possibly new, at least to those listening to a different (or less well, to the same) drummer. It is, in short, the voice of the sage.

Crane's uses of the same phrase are sometimes interpretative: "But presently he could see that many of the men in grey did not intend to abide the blow" (II, 128). When the Swede says " 'I suppose there have been a good many men killed in this room' " (V, 145–6), he is not interpreting so much as he is testing his hypothesis about the West. Henry Fleming, on the other hand, tries to infer the existence of a plurality, his membership in which will protect his own self-image: "Thus, many men of courage, he considered, would be obliged to desert the colors and scurry like chickens" (II, 66).

Let us now compare the pregnant function of the phrase in the bathtub sentence with its function in the newspaper version of the sinking of the *Commodore:* "Many of the men who were to sail upon her had many intimates in the old Southern town" (IX, 85). Here is the correspondent reporting an observed circumstance, and nothing more. "Many a man ought to have a bathtub" is much more venturesome. The locus from which the observation is made is better placed for making generalizations than are the men in the boat, or, for that matter, the author of "Stephen Crane's Own Story," which does not go beyond what the reportorial eye directly witnesses. In "The Open Boat" we hear a voice saying what the men cannot say because it knows what they cannot know, or knows at least that of which they are not for the moment aware. Shifting from the plane of the particular to that of the general, the voice makes a deontological statement, an expression of what ought to be, that is at once forceful and restrained: forceful because uttered in behalf of good men in a bad situation, restrained because it falls short of being categorically imperative. The justice it calls for would be a justice for a goodly number but not for all men, a concept anticipating what Crane will later have to say about the "condition" in which the men in the open boat are situated. For now it suffices to underline the contrast between the condition described in the opening paragraph and the "ought" condition spoken of in the second paragraph, and to note that the bathtub analogy, combined with the "many a man" construction, links the two conditions in a perspective by incongruity. One justification of that analogy is, to be sure, the similarity of a bathtub and this particular boat. But mention of a bathtub also brings up life on land, making us all the more aware of isolation on the sea. The bathtub, furthermore, is something you put water into, an absurd prospect to men whose fear of swamping is epitomized by the cook, who stares "with both eyes at the six inches of gunwale which separated him from the ocean" (V, 68).[4]

THE ETHICS OF THEIR CONDITION

The statement following "many a man" – "These waves were most wrongfully and barbarously abrupt and tall" – is not so much deontological as flatly evaluative. The feeling in the words expresses the author's implicit identification with the condition of the men, linked by remembrance, as it must have been, with his own experience. *Condition* has a wide range of meaning in the story. It can refer to someone's immediate, physical state: "The correspondent arrived in water that reached only to his waist, but his condition did not enable him to stand for more than a moment" (V, 91). Condition of this kind is central. It may well be the oiler's weakened condition – brought on by a double work shift on the steamer and his heroic labors in the open boat – that leads to his drowning. But there is another condition that while implicitly including a notion of physical state, goes beyond it, and that bears not merely upon the individual but upon the entire group: "To express any particular optimism at this time they felt to be childish and stupid, but they all doubtless possessed this sense of the situation in their mind. A young man thinks doggedly at such times. On the other hand, the ethics of their condition was decidedly against any open suggestion of hopelessness. So they were silent" (V, 71).

The nouns in that sternly beautiful phrase, "the ethics of their condition" suggest not only the plight of these particular men but the more general plight that Montaigne came to call, with eloquent simplicity, the human condition. When André Malraux titles his novel *La Condition humaine,* he invites readers to consider from the beginning precisely that larger – indeed, from the human point of view, that largest – context. Because "The Open Boat" invites readers to consider the same context, Crane also deals with the intense decorum of men struggling together for their very lives. Malraux, of course, examines a complex historical situation in a way that his American predecessor does not; for even if Crane's story is "intended after the fact," as the subtitle indicates, the adventure is no chronicle of conrete political or economic events. Whereas Malraux, with his interest in just such events, investigates persons and groups with violently contrasting desires, cultures, and ideologies, Crane centers on a single, closely knit group of men with the same cultural background, a common desire, and no interest whatever – at least for now – in ideology.

The most immediately relevant context for "the ethics of their condition" is provided by Crane's repeated use of that last term. When in the

1899 story "A Self-Made Man: An Example of Success That Anyone Can Follow" Crane notes the distressed "financial condition" (VIII, 124) of his protagonist, he makes a straightforward reference to his state of indebtedness. A similar sense is invoked, in a more tongue-in-cheek manner, by his reference in an 1895 newspaper sketch to the fact that the cheapness of drink in Mexico would be regarded by New York tipplers as "a profoundly ideal condition" (VII, 458). Crane extends the concept when he alludes to "the true condition of affairs" (VIII, 57) in "A Dark-Brown Dog," by which he means the nexus of character, chance, and circumstance embodied in the father's drunken violence as well as the danger this poses to the dog. In "Seen at Hot Springs," a Western sketch, the concept carries a more collective weight, as Crane moves from a description of the "purely cosmopolitan" nature of the main street of Hot Springs, with its mixture of little prairie-style stores and Eastern-style business blocks, of bright and dull colors, of poverty and wealth, of courtesy and impertinence, to the generalization: "An advantage of this condition is that no man need feel strange here. He may assure himself that there are men of his kind present" (VIII, 421).

From serving as a vehicle for characterizing an urban, cosmopolitan situation, the concept shifts to a higher level of generalization in "An Experiment in Luxury," an already quoted excerpt from which deserves a second look. The protagonist

> was beginning to see a vast wonder in it that they two lay sleepily chatting with no more apparent responsibility than rabbits, when certainly there were men, equally fine perhaps, who were being blackened and mashed in the churning life of the lower places. And all this had merely happened; the great secret hand had guided them here and had guided others there. The eternal mystery of social condition exasperated him at this time. He wondered if incomprehensible justice were the sister of open wrong. (VII, 297)

In an 1896 sketch Crane distinguishes between this type of socially specific condition, which he sees as something everpresent, and a more limited type employed by persons who define a notorious section of New York City "as a certain condition of affairs in a metropolitan district" when "probably it is something more dim, an emotion – something superior to the influences of politics or geographies, a thing unchangeable" (VIII, 389). If that first, more limited concept of condition recalls the description of Hot Springs, the second, vaguer, but more comprehensive concept amplifies the observations put forward in "An Experiment in Luxury." At the same time it parallels, as noted in the preceding chapter, the concept of a "foreign condition" and a new "estate" in "The Bride Comes to Yellow Sky," and that all but cosmic sense of a tragic condition that informs "The Blue Hotel."

BY ANALOGY

Crane's perspectivism often works by analogy. In "The Open Boat," as in *Moby-Dick* a key analogy associates land and sea:

> Canton-flannel gulls flew near and far. Sometimes they sat down on the sea, near patches of brown sea-weed that rolled over the waves with a movement like carpets on a line in a gale. The birds sat comfortably in groups, and they were envied by some in the dinghey, for the wrath of the sea was not more to them than it was to a covey of prairie chickens a thousand miles inland. (V, 71)

Reading Melville, one feels somehow that land and sea, despite their differences, enjoy some subtle consonance. You feel, also, that Melville, without quite rejecting the phenomenal world, is striving to see through it, as through a transparency, into something beyond. Crane achieves a different effect. The descriptions in "The Open Boat" ask you to take the phenomenal world on its own merits, as something that is "just there." By the same logic, one is evidently supposed to take the shore–sea analogies discretely, as they come, without trying to see what they hide. They hide nothing.

> A seat in this boat was not unlike a seat upon a bucking broncho, and by the same token, a broncho is not much smaller. The craft pranced and reared, and plunged like an animal. As each wave came, and she rose for it, she seemed like a horse making at a fence outrageously high. (V, 69)

> By the very last star of truth, it is easier to steal eggs from under a hen than it was to change seats in the dinghey. First the man in the stern slid his hand along the thwart and moved with care, as if he were of Sèvres. Then the man in the rowing seat slid his hand along the other thwart. It was all done with the most extraordinary care. (V, 72)

The shore–sea analogies seem to result as much from Crane's interest in his audience as from his interest in verisimilitude. To a professional sailor the movements of the dinghey are not like the movements of a bucking broncho; they are like the movements of a dinghey. Changing seats in a dinghey does not mean that you must be as careful as if you were stealing eggs; it means that you must be as careful as if you were changing seats in a dinghey. The point is that the sailor knows the sea, as a landsman does not; a landsman has to be shown, and in terms that he can understand. Consequently, existence at sea is contrasted throughout the story, both explicitly and implicitly, with existence on land, which the reader is more likely to know. The strategy enables Crane to establish perspectives in which the land-based reader sees the men, and perspectives in which he or she sees *with* them. An example of the latter occurs early in the second section: "The crest of each of these waves was a hill, from the top of which the men surveyed, for a moment, a broad tumultuous expanse, shining and wind-riven" (V, 70). In the preceding section we find this example of the former type of perspective: "In the wan light, the faces of the men must have been gray. Their eyes must have glinted in strange ways as they gazed steadily astern. Viewed from a balcony, the whole thing would doubtlessly have been weirdly picturesque" (V, 69).

THE CORRESPONDENT, THE OILER, AND THE SOLDIER

The fraternal solidarity uniting the men in the boat is an attribute of those who, on an elemental level, are essentially equal, each being as susceptible to dying as any other. Within the ethics of their condition each nonetheless relates to the situation in general and to one another in particular in very distinct ways. The cook, no longer able to perform his role of food preparer, is to this degree incapacitated. In the social hierarchy that persists, and probably because of limitations in his character, he is the lowest personage; and it is not coincidental that he comes closer than the others to providing comic relief. As the highest figure in that hierarchy, the captain continues to play in the boat the role of authority that he played on the ship, though by being physically incapacitated through injury he cannot participate – "democratically," as it were – in the rowing. The comparative closeness of the oiler and the correspondent, by contrast, is embodied, as often remarked, in their cooperative labor. If the term were not so hard on the ear, we could say that whereas the other two men are more or less incapacitated, the oiler and the correspondent are "capacitated." The oiler remains crucially involved in the practical, hands-on operation of the vessel, his contact with machine tools being replaced by contact with a more elemental tool, the oar. As if to bring out this capacitation yet more clearly, Crane stresses the oiler's ability to row exceptionally despite having served a double shift before the ship went down.

The oiler's main partner in rowing participates in the life of the boat far more than he could ever have participated in the life of the ship, on which he was merely a passenger. There is at the same time a deepening of his professional role, the interpreter of public events becoming an interpreter on a more fundamental level. This is a difficult task, not least because of the burden of ignorance he shares with the other men:

> It is fair to say here that there was not a life-saving station within twenty miles in either direction; but the men did not know this fact. (V, 76)

> The correspondent did not know all that transpired afterward. (V, 72)

The correspondent, as mediator, actualizes perceptions and attitudes that are potential in the others. Thus it is not the correspondent alone who "knew that it was a long journey" (V, 90) to the shore, but, implicitly, every man in the open boat. A mediator, in general, facilitates and connects, being a "way" from here to there. The correspondent is a particular type of mediator, a combination of the spokesperson and the interlocutor. He becomes an interlocutor by participating in a dialogue with something "beyond," something elusive, indeterminate; it may be nature, or fate, or a large emptiness. The dialogue, moreover, is one-sided, for the beyond never, as far as we can tell, responds: "If I am going to be drowned – if I am going to be drowned – if I am going to be drowned, why, in the name of the seven mad gods who rule the sea, was I allowed to come thus far and contemplate sand and trees?" The correspondent is a spokesman because the statement, half question and half assertion, brings into the open something that is in the heart of every man in the boat.

The representativeness of the correspondent's attitude is confirmed in two ways. First, by a shift in grammatical subject: It is not the correspondent who is thinking, in these paragraphs, but "a man": "When it occurs to a man that nature does not regard him as important, and that she feels she would not maim the universe by disposing of him, he at first wishes to throw bricks at the temple, and he hates deeply the fact that there are no bricks and no temples" (V, 85). *A* man is in the first place the man who is reflecting on these problems at the moment; he is also the other men, who are not reflecting so "audibly," but are capable of doing so. Finally, the indefinite article brings out what is generic in the noun: *A* man is equally *any* man. The representativeness of the reflections is underlined, secondly, by the straightforward statement: "The men in the dinghey had not discussed these matters, but each had, no doubt, reflected upon them in silence and according to his mind" (V, 85). The question to be asked at this point is why the correspondent has been singled out for a mediating role.

The same question may be asked about the writer Bernard in *The Waves*. Woolf's novel presents in its six characters a constellation of persons who relate to one another like the petals of a flower; the book is about a kind of togetherness and also about the way that togetherness is gradually undone. When the time comes, near the end of the novel, to salvage what unity remains, the job falls to this professional man of words who attempts to bring things together in a vision that is at once personal and interpersonal. "The Open Boat" is also about a small group of closely related persons, and in its later parts too there is a shift of focus from the group toward another writer, the correspondent. But while Woolf's character must strain for a new unity to replace the old one, for Crane's correspondent there is an immediate unity of which he is inextricably a part, and which exists from the beginning of the narrative to the end. Nonetheless, the correspondent is, like Bernard, a professional wielder of words. The point is important, for language, and especially aesthetic language, plays a central role in the story.

Part 6 begins with the refrain, "If I am going to be drowned," leading to the four paragraphs on "a man," and to the paragraph, quoted above, in which we see the other men in a state of reflection. Its concluding sentence, not quoted above, states: "Speech was devoted to the business of the boat" (V, 85). Significantly, the individual words of this speech, which is doubtless very businesslike, are not recorded. Crane gives us, as an alternative to the thoughts of these men, the thoughts of the mediator, the correspondent.

> To chime the notes of his emotion, a verse mysteriously entered the correspondent's head. He had even forgotten that he had forgotten this verse, but it suddenly was in his mind.
>
> A soldier of the Legion lay dying in Algiers,
> There was lack of woman's nursing, there was dearth of woman's tears;
> But a comrade stood beside him, and he took that comrade's hand,
> And he said, "I never more shall see my own, my native land."
>
> (V, 85)

Compare this attitude toward the work of art with the attitude expressed through Henry Fleming in *The Red Badge of Courage*. There the "literary" view of warfare romanticizes its falsities as the youthful soldier enters the lists like a latter-day Quijote, his head full of glorious visions of himself as hero. Hence *The Red Badge of Courage* presents a dichotomy between the immediate experience of war, which is "real," and the mediated, aesthetic experience that communicates the real. The opposite is the case in "The Open Boat." "Now, however, it quaintly came to him as a human, living thing. It was no longer merely a picture of a few throes in the breast of a poet, meanwhile drinking tea and warming his feet at the grate; it was an actuality – stern, mournful, and fine" (V, 85). The experience brings the correspondent a concrete visual perspective: He sees the soldier, though against a distant background, bodily before him. Henry Fleming, too, achieves perspectives as a result of images that "came" to him. The difference is that Henry generates his own images and that these, as often as not, reinforce his tendency to retreat from community into a world of private vision. But the picture the correspondent sees is given to him; it is a made thing, known to others, and created by a human being, who, like himself, is an artful user of words. Art – the poem – is a mediating agency drawing its audience, the correspondent, to a higher order of experience.

Crane makes the resulting perspective very sharp and clear:

> The correspondent plainly saw the soldier. He lay on the sand with his feet out straight and still. While his pale left hand was upon his chest in an attempt to thwart the going of his life, the blood came between his fingers. In the far Algerian distance, a city of low square forms was set against a sky that was faint with the last sunset hues. The correspon-

> dent, plying the oars and dreaming of the slow and slower movements of the lips of the soldier, was moved by a profound and perfectly impersonal comprehension. He was sorry for the soldier of the Legion who lay dying in Algiers. (V, 86)

The pairing of "movements" and "moved" reinforces the correspondent's identification with the soldier. But the striking thing is the way Crane follows through on the aesthetic aspect of the mediating experience. Having established the sense of actuality that the art work conveys, he then emphasizes precisely its artiness. Instead of concealing the artifice he reveals it, saying, in effect, "Isn't the entire business, after all, a show? Here is the stage set, here the inevitable sky with the inevitable sunset hues. Isn't it sentimental? But isn't it also, in a strange way, beautiful and true?" Crane accepts the poem, as he accepts the sunset hues, because they bring about a good thing. If the poem is sentimental, no matter; it still communicates an image of the human condition – a picture in which this man can recognize himself, and in himself, all humanity. Through the mediation of art, a vision comes to meet his vision.

MEANING

The other men in the boat are also, in their different ways, users of words and interpreters of meaning: Besides the speech devoted to the business of the boat, the correspondent and the oiler hold "a short conversation" (V, 87) and the correspondent and the cook exchange "disjointed sentences" (V, 70). Against this foreground of speech there hovers a background of meaning shrouded in mystery. Referring to the captain, Crane observes: "Thereafter there was something strange in his voice. Although steady, it was deep with mourning, and of a quality beyond oration or tears" (V, 69). The mystery of heroism finds a complement here in the mystery of meaning. In a world of signifiers, a world in which everything seems weighted with sense, no ultimate signifier emerges, but only, if you will, a certain sense of sense. Meaning is what hovers just beyond knowing: "The correspondent, observing the others, knew that they were not afraid, but the full meaning of their glances was shrouded" (V, 89).

The men themselves become interpreters of meaning while they look at the shore:

> "What the devil is that thing?"
> "Why, it looks like a boat.
> "Why, certainly it's a boat."
> "No; it's on wheels."
> "Yes, so it is. Well, that must be the life-boat. They drag them along shore on a wagon."
> "That's the life-boat, sure."

> "No, by ——, it's – it's an omnibus. I can see it plain. See? One of these big hotel omnibuses."
>
> "By thunder, you're right. It's an omnibus, sure as fate. What do you suppose they are doing with an omnibus?" (V, 79)

In the first part of the story the men were viewed from a figurative balcony; here the perspective is reversed. But the result is much the same, for the new view, from sea to shore, also involves distance, and distance estranges. It estranges, in the balcony passage, by making the men seem merely picturesque; it alienates in the present scene by putting the interpreters so far from the sighted object that they cannot make it out. The gesturing man on shore cannot speak to those who would hear him because distance has in effect deprived him of language. Further, gesture, like the language of words, communicates only to the degree that its witnesses understand its conventions. But the men in the boat are interpreters without the necessary hermeneutic base on which to operate:

> "What's that idiot with the coat mean? What's he signaling, anyhow?"
>
> "It looks as if he were trying to tell us to go north. There must be a life-saving station up there."
>
> "No! He thinks we're fishing. Just giving us a merry hand. See? Ah, there, Willie."
>
> "Well, I wish I could make something out of those signals. What do you suppose he means?"
>
> "He don't mean anything. He's just playing." (V, 80)

The desire to confer meaning is a radically human desire. When the men in the boat relate to nature through language they are attempting, very fundamentally, to confer meaning. If they do not succeed, it is because language has become for them, as for all human beings, a second nature; and because this nature is different from that other one, which is mute because inanimate. When a man in an open boat talks to mute nature, we are more certain of his talking than of nature's listening. Recourse to speech has become a habit, a way of directing one's human feelings toward the inarticulate world: "The bird flew parallel to the boat and did not circle, but made short sidelong jumps in the air in chicken-fashion. His black eyes were wistfully fixed upon the captain's head. 'Ugly brute,' said the oiler to the bird. 'You look as if you were made with a jackknife.' The cook and the correspondent swore darkly at the creature" (V, 71).

The inarticulate world has nonetheless its own meanings, or at least its own way of sounding as if it does. Consider, for example, the noise of the shark: "Ahead or astern, on one side or the other, at intervals long or short, fled the long sparkling streak, and there was to be heard the whiroo of the dark fin" (V, 84). The onomatopeia of "whiroo" renders the shark palpably; and in a sense it speaks to the man – in this case, the correspondent – who hears it. But it speaks in a preverbal or, better, subverbal way. The noise is an energy, a force. It declares, without the use of words, *I am; fear me;* it establishes, to use Crane's own word, a presence: "The presence of this biding thing did not affect the man with the same horror that it would if he had been a picnicker. He simply looked at the sea dully and swore in an undertone" (V, 84). The correspondent uses language here in the same way as the other men, who either insulted the bird or cursed it. Language has become a way of striking out, a way of asserting my human condition against the nonhuman thing that confronts me.

From this one can slide easily into the notion that nature, in its own way, does the same. Such a possibility is approached ironically through the correspondent: "He tried to coerce his mind into thinking of [the full meaning in the other men's glances], but the mind was dominated at this time by the muscles, and the muscles said they did not care" (V, 89). The correspondent is, to be sure, in a special mood. His mind is on meaning, and he is trying harder than usual to interpret. But the idea that muscles can "say" merely localizes a pervasive phenomenon in the story:

> The billows that came at this time were more formidable. . . . There was a preparatory and long growl in the speech of them. (V, 77)

> A high cold star on a winter's night is the word [a man] feels that [nature] says to him. Thereafter he knows the pathos of his situation. (V, 85)

This attitude toward nature is not expressed *by* the correspondent so much as through him. That the other men share this attitude is established by the concluding sentence: "When it came night, the white waves paced to and fro in the moonlight, and the wind brought the sound of the great sea's voice to the men on the shore, and they felt that they could then be interpreters" (V, 92). Nietzsche goes so far as to assert that there is no such thing as facts, but only interpretations. Crane, it seems to me, does not go that far, though he heads in the same direction. His statement neither denies the existence of facts nor affirms the existence of truthful interpretation. Crane remains with his characters on "this" side of the problem, aware of the problem and therefore problematic in *his* interpretation of *their* interpretation.

We may be reminded again of Henry Fleming, who thought that he was more capable of construing meaning than he really was. In Henry's case we are often made to feel a kind of falseness. The youth cannot recognize his own desire, and this failure opens a gap between the truth of his being and his idea of it. For the men in the boat, however, the distance lies between human being and nature. The men are in accord with their desire; they really feel that they could then be interpreters. The problem is that this feeling does not create, as Crane says in a famous poem, a sense of obligation on the part of nature. The distance that separated Fleming from himself has become a distance separating this group of men (and perhaps, by implication, all human beings) from the nonhuman world. The inherent skepticism in this idea is reinforced by the overlapping qualifications of the sentence. First, we are not told that the men can become interpreters, only that they feel they are. Second, the prospect is put in the conditional tense, which diminishes the likelihood that the interpreting will come about. And third, we are told, not that the men will interpret, but that they will, as by an act of grace, "be" interpreters – a status to which the men may aspire but not necessarily attain. An alternative formulation, such as "they could then interpret," would have been less equivocal; but such a statement would have implied that the distance between man and nature is about to be spanned, whereas practically everything in the story says that it probably won't be. The final sentence, as it stands, does precisely the job it seems to do: It tells us how the men feel; and in the telling it confirms their desire but not their ability, to give meaning. Edwin H. Cady contrasts the view suggested here with the view ascribed to conventional naturalism:

> The true naturalist's truth must be that man is a part of nature and not other. Crane's sense of the indifference or hostility of nature to man was shared, for instance, by a Pilgrim Father (Brewster), a Massachusetts Bay Puritan (Winthrop), a rationalistic Calvinist (Edwards), a deist (Freneau, "The Hurricane"), by Melville (whatever he was), and by many varieties of non-naturalistic Darwinists. Like them, Crane did believe man was "other" – in Crane's case, man was human.[5]

Crane does indeed show the indifference of nature and he also shows indifference in the captain and the correspondent. But this is not the indifference felt by the Easterner in "The Blue Hotel." That quiet little man epitomized the failure of fraternity, a fact that Crane underlines by calling attention to his lack of compassion just as Johnnie lies collapsed in pain on the frozen earth. But the key point of the correspondent's experience of the poem is that he overcomes indifference, arriving at a state of sympathetic identification with the soldier of Algiers. The latter's suffering is an important juncture in what might be called the pattern of pathos, a pattern that connects this suffering with the hard labor of rowing, the constant physical discomfort in the boat, the lack of sleep, and the anguish of unknowing that besets the men whenever they try to discover the meaning of the things they see on the distant shore.

A recent study proposes that in the later years of the nineteenth century American literature gradually turned from an emphasis on ethos to an emphasis on pathos. In Henry James and Howells, as well as in the pragmatic philosophers and later Theodore Dreiser and Gertrude Stein, an "ethics of intensity" expresses the value newly placed upon the affective moments of experience – the crises of feeling, as it were – that are the personal register of whatever transpires interpersonally, and that an older tradition approached more explicitly in terms of character and social morality. As I read these writers, it is not that the ethical realm diminishes; it is rather that felt intensity comes to be relied on as a valid measure of shared reality. Reality itself, by William James's account, is of a piece with the intensity of one's experience:

> Speaking generally, the more a conceived object *excites* us, the more reality it has. The same object excites us differently at different times. Moral and religious truths come "home" to us far more on some occasions than on others. As Emerson says, "There is a difference between one and another hour of life in their authority and subsequent effect. Our faith comes in moments . . . yet there is a depth in those brief moments which constrains us to ascribe more reality to them than to all other experiences."[6]

The intensity of "The Open Boat," in contrast to the strident *Maggie,* is carefully controlled, not least by pungent locutions and laconic generalizations, such as "Shipwrecks are *apropos* of nothing": ". . . in their sentiment and point of view, such statements contrast keenly with the concerns and experience of the men in the boat. They do not contradict the men's experience, but they emphasize its seriousness and intensity."[7]

The latter qualities are evidenced by the much-discussed fate of the oiler, whose death seems particularly unjust. That it is also ironic is a point too well established to require further comment here. But it is only fair to note that his demise is not patly ironic and not a merely mechanical reversal of expectation. In "Flanagan" Crane explains that "The first mate was a fine officer, and so a wave crashed him into the deck-house and broke his arm. The cook was a good cook, and so the heave of the ship flung him heels over head with a pot of boiling water and caused him to lose interest in everything save his legs" (VII, 97).[8] Here Crane is not only clear about the causality behind the injuries but pointedly so, the idea being, apparently, to make the irony quite unmistakable, and to do this while remaining more or less aloof from the pathos. He is not aloof, however, from the question of justice. The two "and sos" leave the same taste of bitterness that occasionally creeps into Crane's reflections on the ways of the world. Knowing that protests do no good, he is nonetheless making one. But in "The Open Boat" causality is problematic and, instead of protesting, its author simply bears witness. Causality is problematic since Crane does not draw the type of connections he draws in the companion piece. While it is true that the oiler must be tired after the double shift and all the rowing, it is also true that he is "ahead in the race" (V, 90) after the men leave the boat and is "swimming strongly and rapidly" (V. 90). It may also be true that some current or undertow or other caprice of the sea undoes him. There is no way of knowing. We do know that, in another irony, the caprice of the sea has the opposite effect for the correspondent: "Then the correspondent performed his one little marvel of the voyage. A large wave caught him and flung him with ease and supreme speed completely over the boat and far beyond it. It struck him even then as an event in gymnastics, and a true miracle of the sea" (V, 91). When Crane later bears witness to the fate of the oiler, the tone is different: "In the shallows, face downward, lay the oiler. His forehead touched sand that was periodically, between each wave, clear of the sea" (V, 92).

The color of the sky, it seems in retrospect, is contingently unknown. In their particular situation, the gaze of the men is fixed at the level of the waves, the colors of which they do know, but if they were in a position to look up they would know the color of the sky as well. The particular refuses to let them, which is another way of expressing the ethics of their condition. For, where ethical issues are concerned, says Hannah Arendt, it is wrong to look for universals or valid generalizations; practical matters "always concern particulars; in this field, 'general' statements equally applicable everywhere, immediately degenerate into empty generalities. Action deals with particulars, and only particular statements can be valid in the field of ethics or politics."[9] Crane knows this, or his art does, which is why he goes on to mention "each particular part" of the correspondent's body (V, 92) as the latter falls to the sand. The condition of this man, of all the men, is the ensemble of particulars and details – the littles – that constitutes their situation. Nothing is too small for witnessing since the small is ultimately what even the great is made of.

Regarded in another way, ethics of intensity is intensity of ethics, which is to say that the condition in which the men find themselves from beginning to end is extraordinarily felt and felt to be extraordinary. Felt, but not said: "And after this devotion to the commander of the boat there was this comradeship that the correspondent, for instance, who had been taught to be cynical of men, knew even at the time was the best experience of his life. But no one said that it was so. No one mentioned it" (V, 73). What is finally problematic in the story, beyond the issues that have just been discussed, is the uncertainty about the role of the men as interpreters: Uncertainty as to their competence if they should eventually interpret, and uncertainty as to just what it is, after all, that is supposed to be interpreted. These limitations do not apply, however, to the correspondent's conviction about the best experience of his life. In that conviction there is nothing in the least problematic, there is no hedging, no vacillation, no doubt. Crane's desire to be unmistakable in meaning is here completely realized.

THE HOUSE OF CHANCE

"The Five White Mice" takes its title from the rhyme first recited by the New York Kid as he rolls for a winning ace, and again when he and his two companions, the 'Frisco Kid and Benson, enter upon a potentially violent confrontation with three Mexicans:

> "Oh, five white mice of chance,
> Shirts of wool and corduroy pants,
> Gold and wine, women and sin,
> All for you if you let me come in –
> Into the house of chance." (V, 42)

In itself the phrase "the house of chance" would indicate a place where chance operates; but if that is the criterion, the Kid already occupies the house, for chance is distinctly in operation as he makes his wager and rolls his dice. In context the house of chance in fact signifies a state of good fortune, a state so remote that the Kid can only pray for it. The extreme improbability of being admitted to the house is actually what makes his desire appropriate, that desire, and the condition in which he finds himself, being equally extreme. For two days his luck has been consistently bad, and only a kind of magical gesture can bring about a change. The bet that he can roll a fifth straight ace – the odds against which must be astronomical – is that gesture, and the fact that it works sets the pattern that will eventuate in the quality of experience that Crane calls "the unreal real."

In the opening episode two notions emerge. There is on the one hand luck, which is both a mysterious attraction between an individual and a sudden outcome in a game, or the absence of such an attraction; and there is on the other hand chance, which is intimately related to luck but must not be mistaken for it. Chance, a larger concept, is also a more rational one, in the broad sense of the term, a concept which the nineteenth century, with its accelerating sense of the changes wrought by the sciences and their technological extensions, could employ as a partial substitute for the older, poetically richer idea of Fortune. Chance in this sense names all that is random and beyond control, all that "just happens." But immediately one must distinguish Crane's attitude from that of Peirce, who found chance an ultimate constitutive agency that could be reconciled, he believed, with theories of evolution. Interesting as such a court may be, it is one in which Crane declines to testify, preferring to record the meaning of chance for immediate personal and social experience. Crane dramatizes the suddenness with which things happen, the pace of change that arises as one happening follows another. It is a rapid pace since wagering games move in brief episodes, each with its own climax, rising to a further climax which is final for all players in that each must at some point leave the game and must do so either as having won, lost or broken even.

"The Five White Mice," with its doubling of gambles, presents two durations, each with its own pace.[10] The first begins to accelerate as the drinkers in the Casa Verde bar throw dice repeatedly, giving themselves to a momentum determined by the very structure of the game, with its quick succession of climaxes leading to the grand climax of the final throw. The process revives the inertial dynamics of *Maggie* and *George's Mother,* where everyone seems to be led less by their desires than by a system of roles. The New York Kid submits to the game because "the cheerful hoots of the players supplemented now by a ring of guying non-combatants caused him to feel profoundly that it would be fine to beat the five queens" (V, 42). When the Kid appeals to the five white mice to admit him to the house of chance, his purpose is to win, whereas he had previously sought merely to gamble, which Crane sees as an activity governed less by the desire for victory (or for defeat) than by sheer interest in the playing. But the moment the New York Kid aspires to win, play becomes combat, and the Kid, assuming the role of the little man, brings on a double confrontation, first with the man he is trying to beat, then with the crowd.

Having mystified his spectators with his incantation, he defies the odds by wagering fifty American dollars that the remaining die, dramatically hidden under the cup, will be an ace. The calmness of his demeanor does not alter the fact that the wager is, in its own way, an outburst asserting that he has had all he can take. The result is further magic, a gesture of defiance that consolidates chance and the crowd into a single new opponent superseding his original opponent in the game. The Kid is not so much betting on the ace as he is betting on himself; by the same stroke he is betting against the crowd. He is saying that his magic stroke has turned his luck; he may also be saying that he has performed a mystification which will enable him to defeat the crowd, regardless of the outcome of his final throw. On this point Crane allows some ambiguity to remain. But there is no ambiguity about the fact that the Kid's magical gesture, the cold bluff of betting excessively against excessive odds, turns him into a loser who wins. He loses because the final throw produces a ten-spot and he wins because no one would wager that it would not be an ace. In his own way he has entered the house of chance, so long as this continues to be seen in its intersection with circumstance and character. While it is chance that determines the identity of the remaining die, the outcome of the challenge to the crowd is influenced by everything the Kid brings to the moment – the deliberateness of his movements, his incantation, his confidence, the size of his bet. Yet, despite this influence, the result of his defiance is not foreknown: Whether anyone accepts the bet remains within the province of chance. Without this possibility no wager is truly a wager, no bluff a bluff.

The Kid can influence the situation because of the aura that surrounds him and his counterpart the 'Frisco Kid. A companion piece entitled "The Wise Men" describes their mythic capacity to cavort day and night, only going to bed (in the opinion of one commentator) once in every two weeks. "The other folk frankly were transfixed at the splendor of the audacity and endurance of these Kids" (V, 26). Set apart in this way, the Kids possess something of the splendor of isolation surrounding the Swede, though they enjoy more good will, the term *kid* being an 1884 Americanism applied familiarly or intimately to any young person. In "The Wise Men" Crane describes the lengths to which they go in order to match a middle-aged bartender in a foot race against a younger man, their purpose being less to win a great deal of money (which they do) than to gull a drinking companion.

As in *George's Mother,* so in these stories about the Kids, money and work are derealized. "The Five White Mice" never accounts for the ability of the Kids, or anyone else, to pass their time in the pursuit of pleasure. Leisure is a given, a precondition of play, and is itself, to this extent, a form of play. With the exception of the bartenders and the waiters, no one works in either story, and the reason for the presence in the Casa Verde of "a gambler, a millionaire, a railway conductor and the agent of a vast American syndicate" remains as mysterious as the reason for the presence of the two Kids or Benson. The size of the Kid's bet implies a significant financial risk until we learn that his father is a financier and a millionaire. Money, then, is no serious thing. What is serious is the capacity to act, as an individual, in a crisis brought on, in particular circumstances, by chance.

PACE

We can already see, in the crisis belonging to the first phase of the story, a tension that reappears in the crisis of the second phase and helps account for its dynamics. This tension expresses itself as the difference between two kinds of pace. Now, pace is a source of appeal to an imagination as agonistic as Crane's, as is the related theme of pursuit.[11] Pace in Crane is typically a measure of competitive status, a way of telling who is winning or losing in a struggle such as a confrontation or a race, the former figuring in "The Five White Mice," the latter in a companion piece "The Wise Men: A Detail of American Life in Mexico." Like other patterns in Crane, the concern with pace appears early. Indeed, it is central to "Uncle Jake and the Bell-Handle," his first tale, which describes an old man's fear of being overtaken by municipal authorities for a minor contretemps. In *Maggie* Pete pursues the Johnson girl at a predatory pace, while Rufus Coleman in *Active Service* scurries after his beloved at various rates of speed, depending upon the means of transportation on which he must rely. *The Red Badge of Courage* is, among many other things, a study in the relativity of pace, pursuit, tempo, and an entire range of other phenomena providing both a temporal and a spatial gauge of position or progress.

The theme is central to "The Pace of Youth," in which Stimson, a father whose kinship to the little man is indicated by his character traits, learns that his daughter has eloped with one of Stimson's employes. Racing to hire a hack, Stimson discovers that the animal harnessed to it is old like himself whereas the horse pulling the couple is not:

> Ahead, that other carriage had been flying with speed, as from realization of the menace in the rear. It howled away rapidly, drawn by the eager spirit of a young and modern horse. . . . A sense of age made him choke again with wrath. That other vehicle, that was youth, with youth's pace, it was swift-flying with the hope of dreams. He began to comprehend those two children ahead of him, and he knew a sudden and strange awe, because he understood the power of their young blood, the power to fly strongly into the future and feel and hope again, even at that time when his bones must be laid in the earth. (V, 12)

In providing this glimpse at an overlooked pattern, I am suggesting that the two types of pace in "The Five White Mice," far from being a minor motif, are one of the story's key structuring and animating elements, and one of the key ways in which Crane builds up pressure to the breaking point. In the first phase of the story the tempo of begging, the shouting of the gamblers, and outpouring of emotional, racy words escalate toward the *peripeteia* of the Kid's cold bluff and toward the evocation of a mood for which there is no ready term. It is a mood created by the heightening of certain details – visual, aural, kinetic – and by bringing out the dark side of things, such as the "gnome-like cloaks" of the policemen (V, 40). The mood is enhanced by the manner in which interest becomes concentrated in the actions of the Kid and a strange new opponent: "The contest narrowed eventually to the New York Kid and an individual who swung about placidly in nefarious circles. He had a grin that resembled a bit of carving. He was obliged to lean down and blink rapidly to ascertain the facts of his venture but fate presented him with five queens. His smile did not change but he puffed gently like a man who has been running" (V, 41). Against this opponent and then, more climactically, against the crowd, the Kid brings to bear the defiance that has grown within him after his two days of bad luck and taunts. The very slowness of his movement contributes to a climax that the previous pace had led one to expect to be breathless. The *peripeteia* thus consists, on one level, of a reversal of pace. The Kid brings the reversal about because the pace is the one thing he can control; because he actually does control it he attains a momentary power. "Instantly he was presiding over a little drama in which every man was absorbed" (V, 42). On another level the *peripeteia* consists in a reversal of roles since the Kid loses again, yet wins by successfully carrying out his bluff.

The tension that creates what might be called the disjunctive dynamics of the second and last phase of the story also arises from a difference between two kinds of pace. One, a fast pace, advances the physical action of the story – the actual movements of the characters and the attitudes these movements express:

> A Mexican wheeled upon the instant. His hand flashed to his hip. . . . The New York Kid had almost instantly grasped Benson's arm and was about to jerk him away when the other Kid who up to this time had been an automaton suddenly projected himself forward. . . . But the Mexican's hand did not move at that time. Then the New York Kid took a sudden step forward. His hand was also at his hip. . . . His pace forward caused instant movement of the Mexicans. (V, 46–8)

The sequence recalls the episode in *Maggie* that proved to be intelligible without the characters' speech, while underlining the fact that "Five White Mice" is geared as much to physical circumstance as to character and chance. Crane draws a map of movements that delineates, first, a series of forward steps, then, after the Kid has drawn and aimed his revolver, a series of steps backward. The second, collateral pace is that of consciousness. The early phase of the story provides only a glance in the direction of consciousness when the taunting causes the Kid to feel that he would like to beat five queens. But, as in "The Open Boat," "Death and the Child," and "The Blue Hotel," consciousness comes increasingly toward the center as the narrative goes on; what is more, it is, as in those works, the consciousness of one who sees himself somehow apart from the situation even as he is caught in it. My use of the term *situation* derives from a perception attributed to that consciousness: "It was a new game; he had never been obliged to face a situation of this kind in the Beacon Club in New York" (V, 50). A situation is a nexus that raises a question of right action; brought on by chance, shaped by the circumstance in which it occurs, it depends upon a character for its resolution. In a small space of time (and often, as in "The Open Boat," in a small physical space as well) the character determines what he is by what he does; he resolves himself in attempting to resolve the situation, which is another way of approaching the phenomenon of condition.

In describing situation or condition Crane stretches in two directions at once, both toward the typical and toward the unique: "They had even gone to the trouble of separating the cigars and cigarettes from the dinner's bill and causing a distinct man to be responsible for them" (V, 40).

We feel a distance within this conception, not because the man is not actually "there," but because of the manner in which he is there. For his particularity – the basis for his being distinct – is oddly general. He is an anyone who is barely someone, a type sufficiently unique for us to distinguish him, but at the same time so general that we would never recognize him if we happened to run into him. He is stretched between being some unique man and being a man *tout court*.

We have been able to relate the dynamics of the action, up to this point in the story, to a difference between two paces (slow and fast) and a difference between two spheres of reference (general and particular on the one hand, unique and typical on the other). A third difference is a source of the dynamics of the concluding phase of the story. This is a difference between the pace of physical movement, illustrated by the last quotation, and the act of consciousness directed both toward the future and toward the past.

THE FUTURE AND THE PAST

As the Kid steps forward his consciousness goes forward too, but it also goes backward. Where thought directs itself and how long it stays there depends upon its interaction with everything else: the Kid's body and his uncertainty about the speed of his reflexes in relation to the weight and size of his revolver, the advance of the Mexicans, the drunken attitude of his American friends, and so on. Consciousness is seen to be a continuum extending from the present back into the past and forward into the future. Its first movement is toward the past:

> But the Mexican's hand did not move at that time. His face went still further forward and he whispered: "So?" The sober Kid saw this face as if he and it were alone in space – a yellow mask smiling in eager cruelty, in satisfaction, and above all it was lit with sinister decision. As for the features they were reminiscent of an unplaced, a forgotten type which really resembled with precision those of the man who had shaved him three times in Boston in 1888. But the expression burned his mind as sealing-wax burns the palm and fascinated, stupefied, he actually watched the progress of the man's thought toward the point where a knife would be wrenched from its sheath. (V, 47)[12]

Encountering his first corpse, Henry sees in the type and particularity of human mortality the prospect of his own death. Like that one, the face in the present passage is typical and anticipatory, but in a different way. The face that Henry sees predicts the future in a vague manner: There is a soldier who was alive and is now dead, and here, looking at him, is a soldier who is alive and will be dead. Thus the face signifies to Henry his own ostensible fate. But the face that the New York Kid sees is more specifically situated, its expression revealing a definite intention that is the necessary condition on which the Kid will form a definite intention of his own.

A further source of dynamic disjunction is the difference between the object of the Kid's retrospection as experienced immediately by the Kid himself and that object as it is experienced mediately by the author. The immediate object of the Kid's retrospection is a type of face that is vague because he has forgotten it, while the object that is mediately experienced, and that the author shows to us, is the face that this type "really" resembles. Thus Crane presents, not merely the consciousness of his character, but something beyond that consciousness. The reality suggested by "really" exists within a frame of reference widened to imply a more general, perhaps a universal significance in what is happening. In this way Crane furthers a perspective, introduced in the previous paragraph, recalling the perspective accompanying the Swede in his trek from the blue hotel to the Weary Gentleman Saloon: "There was no sound nor light in the world. The wall at the left happened to be of the common prison-like construction – no door, no window, no opening at all. Humanity was enclosed and asleep" (V, 47). The counterpart of this reality of the larger view is evoked by the "actually" that belongs to the Kid. Before, the Kid had not attained consciousness of that which has occurred; now the Kid does attain consciousness, but that of which he is conscious has *not* occurred. That which he experiences when he anticipates his enemy's move is in the future, as that which he did not experience (and which Crane provided for us) was in the past.

Reality comes to exist for the reader as something defined by the situations in which it emerges, but these situations, though different, are not mutually exclusive. The reader experiences both situated realities in a continuum created by the presentation in which the one unfolds so closely after the other that it is difficult to separate them. I believe we are not meant to separate them, because it is just that difficulty with which Crane is attempting to deal. I mean the difficulty of knowing where reality begins and ends and the difficulty of defining the role within reality of that something other, that presence of the *allotrios,* the strange, that makes us say at times that reality has become unreal. A fuller sense of what this means will emerge in a passage to be examined below.

As the New York Kid takes a further step toward his adversary – a step in space that is also a step in time, carrying him closer to the flashpoint of a fight – his consciousness veers in another direction: "Then the New York Kid took a sudden step forward. His hand was also at his hip. He was gripping there a revolver of robust size. He recalled that upon its black handle was stamped a hunting scene in which a sportsman in fine leggings and a peaked cap was taking aim at a stag less than one eighth of an inch away" (V, 47–8). The scale of this contrasts with the perspective that placed the characters against a background of all humanity and the world, yet has its own way of suggesting a type of enormity; for the revolver seems all the larger for containing a representation of a scene complete with a hunter and a stag. The concluding detail introduces the mock-epic flavor that Crane had attempted during the dice game when "Three kings turned their pink faces upward" (V, 40). This final shift shows that the pictured scene is very little after all, perhaps implying that the man who is thinking about it is somehow little too. Like figures on an urn, hunter and prey are held in time by their motionlessness in space, a tension creating a sense of anticipation checked by restraint – creating, in a word, suspense.

The situation recalls "Killing His Bear," but is more complex, both because it involves more variables and because of the care with which Crane traces the movement of consciousness in time:

> The Eastern lad suddenly decided that he was going to be killed. His mind leaped forward and studied the aftermath. The story would be a marvel of brevity when first it reached the far New York home, written in a careful hand on a bit of cheap paper topped and footed and backed by the printed fortifications of the cable company. But they are often as stones flung into mirrors, these bits of paper upon which are laconically written all the most terrible chronicles of the times. He witnessed the uprising of his mother and sister and the invincible calm of his hard-mouthed old father who would probably shut himself in his library and smoke alone. Then his father would come and they would bring him here and say: "This is the place." (V, 48)

The shift from conjectural future to remembered past still relates directly to his present situation; the same was true of his recollection of the scene on the revolver. What the Kid remembers and what he anticipates come together right now, in an intersection of times that Heidegger calls contemporaneity. The convergence of three times – past, future, and present – offers a clearing in which to realize one or another possibility. In this sense the times are together, and thus con-temporaneous. Chance, character, and circumstance express themselves through these times, each existing in some moment or duration, and all converging in this meeting of times. A crossroad situation develops, a time of suspense that can be broken only by some definite resolve. It is, if you like, a crisis, and St. John reminds us that crisis means judgment; it is a turning point at which one decides to go this way or that. The situation interrupts the narrative flow, so that the time seems to slow. Meanwhile, the physical action continues at a pace of its own which, if it could be followed separately, would look direct and swift. Because it cannot be, because the two paces play in and out of each other just as past, present, and future play in and out of each other, because of all this one might call the dynamics of the situation disjunctive.

To put it a little differently, the crossroads moment – the crisis – transpires in a time that stands out, a moment diverging from the temporality the previous phases of the narrative had led the reader to regard as normal. This divergence is the temporal mode Heidegger names "ecstasis" after the Greek *ecstasis,* meaning "standing outside," in the sense of being displaced or going beyond.[13] This newly situated time departs from previous narrative time as it departs from the previous time of the character. Narrative and character reach a crisis that is profoundly "temporal" in that past, present, and future converge in a situation calling into peril this character's very life. Until now, one thing had led to another in the "normal" way, which is to say that the leading seemed to take care of itself without becoming a focus of reflection. Now it does; now suddenly to this being who had not reflected upon time, time is revealed in all directions at once, all different, all co-present, all pulling him further into that crisis which is the temporal form of judgment.

THE UNREAL REAL

That is one, but only one, of the experiences Crane provides; for in his double vision he offers as well a transcendental vision that itself stands out from what has gone before:

> These views were perfectly stereopticon, flashing in and away from his thought with an inconceivable rapidity until after all they were simply one quick dismal impression. And now here is the unreal real: into this Kid's nostrils, at the expectant moment of slaughter, had come the scent of new-mown hay, a fragrance from a field of prostrate grass, a fragrance which contained the sunshine, the bees, the peace of meadows and the wonder of a distant crooning stream. It had no right to be supreme but it was supreme and he breathed it as he waited for pain and a sight of the unknown. (V, 49)

In "An Occurrence at Owl Creek Bridge" Bierce gives his hero a similar though fuller opportunity for imaginative flight, as Peyton Farquhar removes himself from his threatening situation into a scene of tranquility. Both authors then play the little dream off against the larger reality. The difference is that Bierce gives the dream a longer run before pulling it up short. Reality becomes a trick played upon illusion; one could say therefore that Bierce deals with the same spectrum as Crane – the spectrum of the real and the unreal – but traverses it by a different route. Bierce, if you will, goes a long way through the unreal and when he arrives at the real he just stops. Crane, for his part, goes round to the real through the unreal, and when he arrives he keeps on going, looking this way and that, not because he is lost but because he can't quite believe what he sees. Surely this strange business cannot be reality; yet it is; and all the while that this reality is revealing its intimacy with the unreal, there is another pair of eyes tracing the process on a map.

These eyes are what is missing from the conclusion of *The Red Badge of Courage,* where Henry Fleming traverses a similar spectrum, and what here provide that second standing-out, that ecstasis of perspective, which I anticipated in my remarks above. This is Crane's way of handling what amounts to a modern *topos.* Its beginnings remain obscure, though we find the term "unreal" in *Macbeth* (*OED,* 1605), and *Don Quijote* also takes it up. It is an attempt, in any case, to render the wonder of things as they are both in their familiarity and in the strangeness with which that familiarity is interpenetrated. Rudolf Bultmann says of modern literary realism:

> The analysis of the occasional moment unveils something totally new and elementary, the fullness of reality and the depth of life contained in every moment. In this moment a deeper reality, so to speak a more reality, appears. . . . It is difficult to describe this reality. It is not a metaphysical substance, but it is the ever-increasing result of the whole of our experiences and hopes, of all our aims in interpreting our life and our encounters, it forms itself apart from our purpose and consciousness, but it comes into consciousness in moments of reflection.[14]

The description, it seems to me, catches a good deal of the spirit that informs "The Five White Mice." The claim with which Crane might disagree is that the reality at issue for Bultmann is formed apart from human purpose and consciousness. Crane implies the opposite to be the case, hence everything depends upon what this particular young man thinks and how he acts. But Crane does try to convey the unexpected thrust of reality, its capacity for being "more real" by standing out from the horizon of the ordinary.

Crane's approach invites comparison with a pair of equally explicit statements on the sense of the real, the first by Longfellow (1839), the second by Whitman (1871):

> Life is real! Life is earnest!
> And the grave is not its goal;
> Dust thou art, to dust returnest,
> Was not spoken of the soul.
>
> *("A Psalm of Life," 11. 5–8)*

> This then is life,
> Here is what has come to the surface after so many throes
> and convulsions.
> How curious! how real!
> Underfoot the divine soil, overhead the sun.
>
> *("Starting from Paumanok," 11. 18–21)*

A sudden feeling for life's reality brings each speaker to the point of poetic outburst, or at least poetic exclamation – a point it becomes necessary to reach because both poets want to sharpen a sense they regard as having been dulled. Both speak by pointing in a straightforward manner – by some aesthetic standards, too straightforward. But in their main drift they diverge. Longfellow, who would enforce a moral truth in support of Christian doctrine and for the furtherance of Christian life, draws his adjectives from a barrel of synonyms, while Whitman yokes together qualities that strain in different directions. His sense of what is real is more mixed than Longfellow's, closer to Crane's. Without being less poetic than Longfellow – and indeed as a way of being more meaningfully poetic – Whitman is more the reporter. He seems to say the first thing that strikes him: "How curious!" Longfellow, more programmatically, states in two phrases what amounts to one bald intellectual thesis. Thus, while Longfellow's words stay on the same level, Whitman's mount, for the curious quality that interests him is not significant until the first exclamation becomes integrated with the second at the latter's higher level. For Whitman and Crane, differences not only exist within the same, they shape the same. That life is curious is essential to its reality, in Whitman's view, and in Crane's view reality itself includes an essential element of the unreal.

If anything, Crane yokes his contraries more forcibly than Whitman. "And now here is the unreal real," he declares, pointing to this wonder – a wonder consisting both in the peacefulness of the imagined scene and in its sheer incongruity – that unfolds for the reader in a dramatic but quiet way. The moral dimension that figures conspicuously in Longfellow and subtly in Whitman appears in the passage by Crane as well, transposed by irony into a minor key: "It had no right to be supreme but it was supreme."

The physical medium that precipitates the emergence of the unreal real is smell, the sense that provides immediate contact at once peculiarly palpable and peculiarly intimate. While shifting back and forth between the mediate and the immediate, Crane also shifts between the simultaneous and the successive: "But in the same instant, it may be, his thought flew to the 'Frisco Kid and it came upon him like a flicker of lightning that the 'Frisco Kid was not going to be there to perform, for instance, the extraordinary office of respectable mourner. . . . The New York Kid became convinced that his friend was lost. There was going to be a screaming murder" (V, 49). Perfect simultaneity is beyond the reach of discourse; Crane's description aims rather at a convergence of two lines of development in a single moment, a moment that discourse tends to make temporally extensive, when in fact nothing could be more – if you will – temporally *in*tensive. Everything is packed into this one long moment that ends with the drawing of the revolver. This is "the supreme moment" (IV, 50), the time when decision making passes over into action. The abstract possibility of drawing the gun becomes the concrete but strange reality of doing so. The moment of crisis is thus a moment of transformation; at the same time, it reveals itself as that process of reversal which Hegel regards as essential to consciousness and Aristotle as essential to drama:

> The cry and the backward steps revealed something of great importance to the New York Kid. He had never dreamed that he did not have a complete monopoly of all possible trepidations. The cry of the grandee was that of a man who suddenly sees a poisonous snake. Thus the Kid was able to understand swiftly that they were all human beings. They were unanimous in not wishing for too bloody combat. There was a sudden expression of the equality. . . . The whole thing had been an absurd imposition. He had been seduced into respectful alarm by the concave attitude of the grandee. And after all there had been an equality of emotion, an equality: he was furious. He wanted to take the serape of the grandee and swaddle him in it. (V, 51)

With the revelation the Kid realizes that he has won his second bluff; the final climax in the street seems merely to repeat the initial climax in the bar. But the confrontation effects a reversal that robs the bluffer's triumph of its meaning. To be sure, there was a problematic element even in the first bluff, which pulled victory from a losing toss. The final climax goes further, though; "something of great importance" is the fact that genuine victory is ultimately impossible.

In certain stories, such as "A Mystery of Heroism," Crane suggests, to the contrary, that some are braver than others. But if the present work suggests anything, it is the emptiness of such distinctions. The little man, striving to be bigger than the next, looks all the smaller when placed in a generic context, a life situation that is essentially the same for all human beings. Montaigne, as noted above, calls it by a broad name, the human condition; the key word for Crane – a word with a notably American resonance – is equality. It means, as Crane applies it: Where all are fundamentally equal none can ever be superior. Admittedly, one can think of nobler ways of stating the matter, but they would put an attractive front on a predicament that Crane keeps before us precisely as a predicament. It goes something like this. The fate of the New York Kid provides the central interest of the final confrontation. Everything depends upon what he decides to do and his competence a. doing it. But just as important is the decision his adversary makes and the latter's competence at following through. Thus, as Crane's emphasis on the grandee-like Mexican makes clear, the outcome of the confrontation gravitates around a competition between a pair of individuals.

Because of drink, the casual fraternal group to which the New York

Kid belongs, a group already less stable than the one in the open boat, possesses less solidarity than usual, which forces a solitary role upon the Kid. Thus the Kid acts within the group and, for practical purposes, independently of it, while his Mexican counterpart does the same. The result is a recognition of common humanity, or rather, that is part of the result, for the revelation of equality produces a reaction that Nietzsche would not hesitate to name as social resentment, *ressentiment*. "And after all there had been an equality of emotion, an equality: he was furious."

That central repetition is as evocative in its own way as Kafka's description of the initial predicament in "A Country Doctor": "I was in the courtyard all ready for the journey; but there was no horse to be had, no horse."[15] The difference is the degree to which the resentment can be externalized. In the case of the doctor the source of frustration is so pervasive, so intricately tied to his alienation from others and from himself, that there is no single thing to oppose. His frustration becomes indistinguishable from the mood or *Stimmung*, from the very "atmosphere" of the narrative. The Kid's resentment, on the other hand, lies nearer the surface. Being plaintive is not enough – he would complain outright if he only knew who was in charge. But the frustration he feels – and the frustration he represents – are, finally, as abortive as the doctor's, if in a different way.

The problem is not that he lacks an object to protest against, but that the object and his desire exist on different planes. For while the Kid's emotion is concrete, the thing that brings it out – the equality of emotion – remains as abstract as the conception standing behind it. This is the conception of a common humanity, a generic condition that is all-encompassing on the level of abstraction, but is narrowed drastically in the process of becoming concrete. For it is one thing to recognize that every person in the situation is theoretically the same, and another to differentiate the behavior of one of those persons to the point that everything gravitates around his thoughts, his ego, his emotions. The same becomes dissolved in difference, which is another way of saying that the abstract concept depicted by Crane never achieves corresponding concreteness. Up here on the level of abstraction and theory is the idea of common humanity, while down there on the level of particularity and practice is the reality of discrete entities, rattling against each other like shaken dice, each wanting to go its own way but balked by the presence of the others. It is as if one took the vision of "The Open Boat" – the vision of men acknowledging together their humanness – and passed it through the filter of an individualist ideology, so that it came out looking less like an image of community than like an illustration for the motto "Every man for himself." To draw the distinction another way: In "The Open Boat," community is, as we have seen, meaningfully particular;

while in "Five White Mice" it remains abstract. On the one hand there is a sense of common humanity and on the other a collection of individuals who never cohere socially; and even that sense remains fixed at the level of isolated initiative and isolated interpretation.

The final perspective is achieved by rendering the New York Kid's emotion with particularity while fixing the emotion of the others at the level of generality. On the Kid's side there is feeling, on theirs a concept of feeling. Thus the previous dualities in the story find their counterpart in a split between the abstract and concrete that is itself the reflection of an individualist orientation, an orientation that can never seize upon the possibility of solidarity simply because the latter never looks real enough to make the effort seem worthwhile. A world unto himself, the solitary person possesses a reality that is never quite that of anyone else – that certainly never matches perfectly the reality of that realm of otherness called the "world" – and that therefore makes the very idea of reality contingent and problematic, even at times unreal. The more isolated one is, the more unreal reality will appear, and the more one will resent a reality that reverses one's expectations at every step.

9

The Farther Shore: Poems

In an essay on Emerson, Kenneth Burke translates a famous line from the *Aeneid:* "And they stretched forth their hands, through love of the farther shore." Burke then expands in a direction that the author of the present study also tries to follow: "The machinery of language is so made that things are necessarily placed in terms of a range broader than the terms for those things themselves. And thereby, in even the toughest or tiniest of terminologies . . . we stretch forth our hands through love of a farther shore; that is to say, we consider things in terms of a broader scope than the terms for those particular things themselves."[1] Taking that remark as a cue, this chapter considers a scope broad enough to embrace Crane's major poems, with the goal, *inter alia,* of letting them talk to one another and to their totality; and with the further idea of letting that totality speak to whatever farther shore of meaning Crane's "lines" variously point toward. I believe this is part at least of what Burke means by "beyonding," and that such an approach accords with Crane's own view of his poetic corpus: "I suppose I ought to be thankful to 'The Red Badge,' but I am much fonder of my little book of poems, 'The Black Riders.' The reason, perhaps, is that it was a more ambitious effort. My aim was to comprehend in it the thoughts I have had about life in general, while 'The Red Badge' is a mere episode in life, an amplification" (*Letters,* p. 79).

Poetry about life in general is what other people tend to call philosophical, which is, in the main, the mode at which Crane's "lines" are inclined to aim. The philosophical poet is not much of a formalist, typically, but loves the interplay of ideas. By that criterion Crane is a philosophical poet. But no classification will ever corral him; for even if one grants that he offers reflections on life in general, he offers them, often, as stories, which means that, however idiosyncratically, he is also that *rara avis,* a narrative poet. His particular slant on narrative, one might add, takes him toward and sometimes into the "edifying" genres of fable, allegory, and riddle (to which I will return), which also makes him something of a traditionalist as well as a moralist.

None of this is meant to suggest that Crane does one thing in his poetry and another in his fiction. The fiction too is often reflective and poetic, as critics have observed, and is capable of turning philosophical, as it does in "The Blue Hotel" and "The Open Boat." In the words of James B. Colvert,

> The poetry and the fiction arise from an imagination profoundly affected by the historical breakdown of Protestant authority and the decline of romantic idealism. If in the times of Emerson and Hawthorne the assimilation of transcendental idealism to American Protestantism provided, Bernard Duffey has said, a coherent world view in which the "assumption of quest and celebration of openness were ready at hand as daylight ideals" and in which "emotions and grandly simple ideas were resolvable in intuitions of a spiritual order, consubstantial with nature," no such view was accessible to Crane. (X, *xxciii*)

What views Crane does adopt only the poems can tell; the plural is in order because to put the matter negatively, Crane's poetic testament does not tender "a coherent world view," if by that one means something highly self-consistent and systematic. To put the matter more positively, as well as more usefully, Crane stages a series of sorties into a variety of imaginary territories, ventures that are sometimes like Eliot's raid on the articulate; sometimes decadent, in a Beardsley vein; sometimes gnomic, like much of Pound, who admired Crane; and sometimes sublime in an American mode that Josephine Miles has helped us appreciate.[2] In the words of Werner Berthoff, Crane is "a visionary writer":

> Nothing quite like this naked magic-lantern works exists elsewhere in our literature. Even Poe's inventions carry a more consistent reference to common experience or to some stable conception of it. The nearest parallels to Crane's best manner are to be found, rather, in the work of certain graphic artists – in Daumier, perhaps, or above all in Goya, the rapt, strict master of the Tauromaquia and the Disasters of the War – work of a kind, moreover, that for all its transcendent purity of composition is like Crane's in being continuous with the documentary concerns of nineteenth-century journalism.[3]

The structure of this chapter generally accommodates itself to the structure of *The Black Riders* and *War Is Kind,* the verses of which act and react on one another like moments of a musing conversation in which ideas always ring loudly if not always clearly.

THE RIDE OF SIN

The title poem of *Black Riders and Other Lines* announces an advent that is also an emergence, a coming that is equally a coming-forth:

"Black riders came from the sea" (#1).[4] As in Emily Dickinson's "He preached upon 'breadth' until it argued him narrow," or Wallace Stevens's "I placed a jar in Tenessee," the event in question transpires within a relatively specific duration, in contrast with a more traditionally lyric duration evocative of a time suggestive of timelessness. The lines that follow develop auditory and kinetic aspects of the event:

> There was clang and clang of spear and shield
> And clash and clash of hoof and heel,
> Wild shouts and the wave of hair
> In the rush upon the wind:
> Thus the ride of sin.

If the riders are not charging to combat at least they are equipped for it. *Clang* and *clash* echo an episode in "The Black Dog" in which "A mug, a plate, a knife, a fork all crashed or clanged on the ground . . ." (VIII, 246) while anticipating "the wild clash of steel upon steel" in "In the Broadway Cable Cars" (VIII, 376). Metal hits earth, steel strikes steel: The passages attest to the mere oppugnacy of things. But while these little episodes show what follows, by a necessity of physics, from the conflict of objects, the sources of the action are at a remove. The clash of the utensils occurs apart from the protagonist in the first story while in the second the locus is outside the clashing. In contrast to these episodes the clang and clash of the riders is *of* and *with* the act, as merging aspects of a decisive kinetic moment.

The reader is constrained by the fact that Crane withholds the presence of the object at which the riders' act is aimed. Had such a presence been given, the reader would have been a disengaged third, witnessing a clash between two antagonists. As it stands, the poem, by interposing nothing between riders and readers, lets the former come, as it were, straight at you: The reader *feels* the onset of sin. If the copulative "There was" does nothing to sort out the impressions brought together in the lines, so much the better. Through this weakening of the verb, as it has been called,[5] impressions already exhibiting family resemblances are merged. The consequent feeling, for the reader, is a state like the one a sinner is presumed to experience. It is a passive state, for only the riders – the demonstrative presence in the poem – have the power to act; the implicit reader–sinner is at best the virtual object of their act.

The denouement turns out to be, for lack of a better term, the culminating phase of a "definition," to borrow from a word family of which Crane is rather fond. First comes the basic event, more or less simply announced, then its evocative amplification, then suddenly we are told what all this "means." Thus does Crane stall as long as he can, holding back the climactic statement – in which the climactic word is itself held back until the very last phrase. But now it is not merely late in the poem, it is – by the test of more usual allegorical treatments, in which the identity of sin would have been given – *too* late. What gives the experience meaning emerges only with the conclusion of the experience: Sin is with us before it is known to be sin.

Certainly apprehension of some sort occurs; whether some "deeper" understanding also occurs may be doubted. On the one hand the poem bypasses the leading expectation (as I have suggested) in order to meet an expectation that the reader did not know she or he had, an expectation subtly aroused by the turbulence, the wildness, and the sinister overtones of the central event. On the other hand, one cannot be entirely certain of the locus from which the ride is being defined. While "the ride of sin" sounds like the language of traditional morality, the main poetic energy is surely in the vivacity of the ride, which possesses an immediate experiential value before it receives a mediate moral one. The line that gathers the poem to a surprising final purpose also opens up a gap. Not only are we unable to identify the moral center of the poem, we are not even sure that it possesses one. Yet the nature of that word "sin," as it operates in the denouement, appears to invite such cognition. One must conclude, it seems, that the overview suggested by the final line can be situated only negatively, as existing apart from the kinetic event, much as the person in the cable car exists apart from the clash and clang, and hence as a trace left by the emergence of the final line as the ultimate signifier of what the lines preceding signify proleptically.

The poem enacts a complex process by presenting the emergence of the riders, then the emergence, as it were, of the ride itself. To put the matter a little differently, there is a coming-to-presence, which requires cognition, then a coming-to-consciousness, which requires *re*cognition. In bringing this process to a climax, the lines that attempt to define the ride represent an important shift. Whereas the preceding lines had seemed to deal with contingency (a particular "historical" moment when the riders came), we suddenly perceive that we have been, all along, in the realm of something rather more constant and general. One is left with the paradox that "sin" is called into question simultaneously with its appearance.

That Crane places his black riders at the head of the volume, which he also names for them, is sufficient warrant for looking to other poems for help in defining the extent to which the reader may justifiably fill in this or that indeterminacy. One notes, for example, the parallel between the movement of the riders and that of the mountains of poem 37, which suddenly march upon the first-person who has been watching them assemble, or that of the many red devils who run out of the poet's heart and onto the page. The first belongs to what I have called the pattern of advent, the second to the pattern of outburst. The coming of the riders is a bit of both: They are something "other," attacking from the outside, but also something that breaks out from within, the latter aspect being revealed only when we learn that the ride is the ride of sin.

Why are the riders black and what is the significance of the sea from which they come? Black, the principal color in the sixty-eight poems of the *Black Riders* volume, is associated not only with traditional themes such as nothingness and fear, but with change and sometimes with sheer physical movement as well, the value of what happens depending upon the situation. From the range of valuations, we may look for special relevance to the one expressed in the two poems (#32, #49), in which the color black is directly applied to persons in movement. Here it is not the derided object that is helpful, but the feeling of repugnance that "Black riders came from the sea" also, though not exclusively, conveys. For the feeling in the title poem is complex, containing elements of fear and repugnance and mystery (such as we also find in #10, #59, #67, and #68) compounded with a certain attractiveness as expressed in poem 23 by the lover's validating presence and in "Black riders" by that vivacity into which the main poetic energy of the poem is released. The compounding gives the riders a kind of dark glamour that makes them excitingly sinister without unduly restricting the reader's latitude of interpretation.

In opposition to Daniel G. Hoffman, who connects it with the unconscious, La France holds that the sea is typically "the emblem of external nature";[6] this polysemous word can also be related to life (a spawning ground of existence) or death (a place in which existence can end). The first notion does not help very much in reading this poem. If the sea meant the unconscious, the emergence of the riders would suggest the attainment of consciousness. Indeed, the entire poem would be on "this side" of the unconscious, an interpretation that paradoxically undervalues the significance of which a conscious–unconscious structure is at least potentially capable. It is not at the beginning that consciousness takes possession of the event depicted in the poem, but at the end: Only with the concluding line, as we have seen, does the meaning of the ride become a theme for a possible consciousness. The tension between consciousness and its counterstate inheres in the total development of the poem, and it is a tension that, far from being released at the outset, is maintained. This is one of the reasons why the poem has a surprise ending. The total effect of the lines is dissipated if one begins by identifying Crane's use of the sea with a single conventional symbol.

The sea, as that from which the action of sin emerges, is both outside and inside, like that movement of the riders which is both the advent of something far and "other," and the outburst of something from inside. The sin that rides out at the reader, though an affliction to be endured, is judged no more negatively than a natural event would be; neither is it judged affirmatively. This absence of a judgment makes objectionable that identification between reader and sinner to which I have referred.

With respect to technique, "Black Riders" exhibits patterns about which most commentators, including practicing poets like Hoffmann and Berryman, have relatively little to say. In this poem about riders rushing in the wind there are, for example, alliterations that require the breathy effort of the aspirate: *hoof, heel, hair.* The *wild* and *wave* in the same two lines, and the *wind* in the line that follows, aid the effect without being themselves aspirate. The effect of hurry is helped by *shield, clash, shouts,* and *rush,* which play up the spashing of the riders through the surf. By association, a word like wave weaves into the undulatory movement of the hair the idea of a mounted military group and of breakers, insofar as both come in waves. Eschewing pure rhyme, the poem links what Hoffman, glossing another poem, calls "identities":[7] *clang* and *clang, clash* and *clash;* there one also notes the polyptoton of *riders* and *ride* and the vowel rhymes of *shield* and *heel, wind* and *sin.*

Crane's juxtapositions avoid the orthodox precision of the rhymes in, say, Wilfred Owen's "Strange Meeting" (*hair, hour, here*), and are closer to the assonance in Stevens's "Bantams in Pine Woods" ("Chieftan Iffucan of Azcan in caftan of tan"). Each of the six line-ending words in Crane's poems contains a variation on a basic "i" sound; the first three are open "ee" sounds (*sea, shield, heel*), the fourth is *hair,* and the final two feature a closed "ih" sound; while in the second line *shield* and *spear* also share their vowel. Book 3 of *The Dunciad* offers an equally complex interplay between the same vowel when closed and open:

> H*e*re, *in* a dusky vale wh*e*re L*e*th*e* rolls,
> Old Bav*i*us s*i*ts, to d*i*p poet*i*c souls,
> And blunt the sense, and f*i*t *i*t for a skull
> Of sol*i*d proof, *i*mp*e*n*e*trably dull:
> *I*nstant, wh*e*n d*i*pt, away th*e*y w*i*ng th*ei*r fl*i*ght,
> Where Brown and Means unbar the gates of L*i*ght,
> D*e*mand n*e*w bod*ie*s, and *i*n Calf's array,
> Rush to the world, *i*mpatient for the day. (II, 24–30)

This gloss does not of course exhaust the aural resources either of Pope's verses or of Crane's. It does enable us to speak, with Poe, of an "intervolving" effect in both poems, but one that is structured differently in each. The vowel play in Pope develops within a sector delimited by a purpose (here, that of a quasinarrative, elsewhere, that of a mock encomium, and so forth), relating to the totality of other sectors in the book as part to whole, the book itself enjoying the same relation to the totality of books constituting *The Dunciad.* The range of play is further restricted by the behavior of the personages and by the relation between the larger delimited sector and the smaller ones monitored by the couplets. The result is an ensemble of components whose discreteness of identity is fairly represented by the symmetry of the rhymes; this is a further type of preciseness not to be sought in the poem by Crane.

The intervolving achieved by Crane tends toward a single unity of effect, to borrow again from Poe's terminology. While the components in Crane's verses never lose their identity, they come closer to doing so than do the verses of Pope. Their differences matter less, as it were, than their sameness. The problem is to *achieve* the same – to experience, by the end of the poem, what the ride of sin essentially is. That is why the poem concentrates on its own termination, which shows what all this had been leading to, but in a way that says that this is what has *always been*. Although one could make a similar claim for the darkness that concludes *The Dunciad,* the length and complexity of the latter work make it difficult for the darkness, as paradoxical revelation, to have the same immediacy of impact. Pope is more the fox seeing many things, Crane, at least in this poem, the hedgehog seeing one big thing.

Emily Dickinson's "The Robin's my criterion of tune" concludes with lines that anticipate the vowel play in Crane's poem:

> Without the snow's tableau
> Winter were lie to me –
> Because I see New Englandly.
> The Queen discerns like me
> Provincially.

Although the rest of the poem's eighteen lines end with words that are also artfully skewed, they present different focal points, such as the recurring *t* in *fits/it/taught,* or a metathesis with an elided consonant and elided modifier (*orchard-sprung/spurn*). In contrast with the structure of Crane's poem, which builds to a climax, Dickinson's poem fills out an opening premise: "The Robin's my criterion of tune." A comparison may also be made with Mallarmé's "Le Vierge, le vivace et le bel aujourd'hui," a sonnet consisting of exact rhymes on a traditional pattern (abba, abba, cdc, ede) plus variations on a basic vowel theme: *aujourd'hui, ivre, givre, fui; lui delivre, vivre, l'ennui; agonie, nie, pris; assigne, mépris, Cygne.* These recurring sounds create an aural atmosphere dominated by the Cygne, which, though mentioned earlier within a line, subsequently emerges in the upper case as the crucial presence, much as sin emerges in "Black Riders."

The difference is, first, that Mallarmé wagers heavily on the poem as linguistic ontology: With the emergence of *cygne* as *Cygne,* word is manifest as Word. But in Crane riders do not become Riders; they are revealed at a stroke as agents of that which by the same stroke emerges as sin. Thus, while Crane leans less than Pope toward difference, he leans more toward it than Mallarmé, which is why the rhyming vowels are more strained than the vowels in the lines by Mallarmé. Crane needs to keep them all within an aural nexus that, while it evolves gradually, must also surprise; conversely, though the sounds shift further than in Mallarmé, if they shift too far the denouement becomes *too* unexpected and the poem falls apart. Crane manages this precarious balance in the last two lines by placing wind before sin, eliding the final consonant in the first noun as Dickinson was fond of doing. Another vowel pattern, at which we have not looked, adds to the confluence in the poem's late stages. A guttural "uh" can be heard in each line of the poem, though the fact that this occurs thirteen times in all is less important than the fact that that sound is heard seven times in the last two lines: "In th*e* r*u*sh *u*pon th*e* wind: Th*us* th*e* ride *o*f Sin." The increased frequency indicates, in itself, a gathering momentum. At the same time it forms an important link between the "logic" of the concluding line, and the hastening toward it from the preceding line, by appearing first in the kinetic *rush* and then in the conjunctive *thus* that ushers in the final interpretation. Through these low, thoracic sounds the poem keeps in view the passional, pathic aspect of the experience that the final utterance never fully transcends.

THE CREATURE AND THE CREATION

In the desert
I saw a creature, naked, bestial,
Who, squatting upon the ground,
Held his heart in his hands,
And ate of it.
I said, "Is it good, friend?"
"It is bitter – bitter," he answered;
"But I like it
Because it is bitter,
And because it is my heart."

The explicit first-person who emerges here in poem 3 is not to be confused with the lyrical *I* of a poem such as "Little birds of the night," or with other types of presence also rendered in the grammatical first-person, such as the *I* in polemical poems attacking some god or the *I* in Crane's love lyrics (e.g., #40). These latter presences are immersed in their experiences, which are understood to be fully *their* experiences.

The first-person in the present work, by contrast, is of the type found in other poems, such as Poem 24:

I saw a man pursuing the horizon;
Round and round they sped.
I was disturbed at this;
I accosted the man.

"It is futile," I said,
"You can never – "
"You lie," he cried,
And ran on.

This first-person sees in the sense of bearing witness as well as in the sense of visually perceiving. Two experiences result: The experience of the creature who eats of his heart (or of the man who pursues the horizon), and the first-person's experience of that experience. The latter "metaexperience" is an encounter that is mediated but not explained. To this extent the first-person functions like Walter Benjamin's storyteller, who orally transmits a narrative that contains, openly or covertly, something useful:

> The usefulness may, in one case, consist in a moral; in another, in some practical advice; in a third, in a proverb or maxim. But if today "having counsel" is beginning to have an old-fashioned ring, this is because the communicability of experience is decreasing. In consequence we have no counsel either for ourselves or for others. After all, counsel is less an answer to a question than a proposal concerning the continuation of a story which is just unfolding. To seek this counsel one would first have to be able to tell the story. . . . Counsel woven into the fabric of real life is wisdom.[8]

The wisdom in the present poem depends upon our sense that somehow the encounter seems parabolic, though without being reducible to paraphrase.

Such a work thrives upon the tension created by the interposition of a presence that relates what happens but does not say what it means. The tension is a consequence of the need to have a presence lending authenticity and authority, and the conjoint need to prevent that presence from turning wisdom into mere information. A second tension arises from the fact that the reader of the poem has an experience of an experience of an experience. It might be said that we thus uncover two encounters, that of the first-person with the creature and that of the reader with this first encounter. At this point, however, we see the need for a further step, for the reader does not stop at the level of the first-person; the reader goes through that level to the creature, who is a more powerful presence in the poem not despite the transparency of the I but because of it. The one is there in order for the other to be there more: The first-person lets us see through him to the real opacity, the creature, who is the ultimate focus of the reader's experience.

That Crane employs the prounoun *who* does not in itself remove the creature from the realm of animality: At least as early as the Renaissance the term was used with reference to animals, either to imply something like personality, or as a substitute for *which* (*OED* sb. *who* II.11.b).

Dickens, for example, applies it to dogs. Although reference to the creature as a *he,* the possessive pronoun *his,* and the attribution of speech all unite to humanize this being, he is at the same time bestial, a term we tend to apply to human beings in order to suggest, for example, that in some way they are less than human. Conversely, we do not say that an animal is naked except perhaps to make, by incongruity, a comic point. As for the word *creature,* it means both a human being or any created being, and with about the same frequency. As Crane employs the word in *Maggie,* it indicates an extreme form of existence: Her boss is "a detestable creature" (*M,* pp. 66–7). The creature in the present poem is just as extreme, but in the other direction, for between the creature and the I there arises a spontaneous fraternity that is the poetic version of the good interpersonal relations in various tales and sketches. The first-person watches a creature whose conflict is with his own condition, which, evidently, is either brought on by himself, or if we follow the word *creature* back to some creator, has been brought upon by another. The origin of the situation remains unknown.

D. H. Lawrence advised his erstwhile friend Bertrand Russell to cease "being an ego and have the courage to be a creature."[9] Crane's heart-eater is both. The poem reveals a creature reduced to the essential, to the extremity of his own condition. But this creature is also an ego, an I who has made up his own mind about how to act and who speaks for himself. He is a being who, having decided to eat his heart out, validates the decision by becoming a connoisseur of the process. This is a type of magic, as understood both by Freud and by Sartre, in which a being attempts to derealize the disadvantage of his act by transforming it into an advantage. The creature does not merely accent the bitterness he cannot avoid; that is not sufficiently magical. He positively likes it. To state that he likes it because it is his own heart is to press the magic further. Such an utterance, as magic, as existential "logic," is perfect sense. How egotistical; how perverse: The creature acts for himself by acting against himself. No cultivation of *ennui* emerges, however, as in Baudelaire or Stendhal, no yielding to vertigo as in Baudelaire or Poe. We have, evidently, something closer to the sort of internalization, the *ressentiment,* that so exasperated Nietzsche. The creature turns inward a desire that might have been released into action in the world. Eating one's heart is the quintessential immanent act, apparently indistinguishable from the rituals of the Nietzschean slave. But the creature, again, goes a step further. His magic is based not upon the denial of the bitterness, but upon its recognition. The creature transcends the condition of the slave, who would make a virtue either of overlooking bitterness or of enduring it as the price of a future satisfaction. For Crane's creature, the

Biblical wisdom "To the hungry soul every bitter thing is sweet" (*Prov.* 27.7) is long on satisfaction but short on recognition.

The poem suggests that there is something admirable in the creature, a courage that is not the less remarkable for being at least partly self-destructive. It is a strange courage, a sacrifice of oneself for oneself. Even stranger: As something created, the creature is the produced; for his part he produces nothing, but consumes – himself. And though he has a body, which should be both producer and consumer, this body too is something produced, hence is acted upon as something to be consumed!

The posture the creature assumes is very different from the posture of the black riders. Whereas the latter are erect, the creature bends down in what would appear – on the basis of associations we have seen in the prose writings – to be an attitude of submissiveness. The stooping posture of Maggie's mother was an ironic variation on this pattern, however, and I believe that the creature's physical attitude is another. The creature is not humbled, but defiant. His squatting is a way of willfully hunkering down in his creatural condition, or proudly wallowing in his own bareness and beastliness. He is not unlike the desert anchorite who lives in vain visibility on a heap of dung. The difference consists in the greater value the creature reposes in himself, a value derived from a defiance as firm as the little man's defiance of the mesmeric mountain. Like the child who goes into the garden to eat worms, the creature aspires to reject his createdness. That he does so radically is an important part of what makes the first-person salute him as friend. It is not that the I "agrees" with him. The I seems rather to discern in this desert solitude a splendor of isolation that finds expression in a spontaneous sense of fraternity, the attitude drawing the reader toward a wonder at such self-completeness, one might almost say, such ultimacy.

A quarter of a century earlier T. H. Huxley had turned to Balzac's *La Peau de chagrin* for an illustration of his understanding of "the physical basis of life." Just as the magical wild ass's skin shrinks as the hero enjoys the benefits it makes possible, so, in the words of Huxley, "the matter of life is a veritable *peau de chagrin,* and for every vital act it is somewhat the smaller." Huxley goes on to describe the "catholicity of assimilation" by which he as a human being shares with the other animals, as all living things live off other living things, transforming the matter of others into their own.[10] Crane's creature, on the other hand, lives off himself, at the expense of himself. The waste by which the work of life (as Huxley calls it) is accomplished is here the waste of its very substance. The creature is his own fatal skin. His consuming is an attack on his having been produced, on his createdness: This human–animal condition is a fate, like his heart, which he has not made but which he can yet take into his own hands.

Another poem carries the reader back to the creation of the world itself:

> God fashioned the ship of the world carefully.
> With the infinite skill of an all-master
> Made He the hull and the sails,
> Held He the rudder
> Ready for adjustment.
> Erect stood He, scanning His work proudly.
> Then – at fateful time – a wrong called,
> And God turned, heeding.
> Lo, the ship, at this opportunity, slipped slyly,
> Making cunning noiseless travel down the ways.
> So that, forever rudderless, it went upon the seas
> Going ridiculous voyages,
> Making quaint progress,
> Turning as with serious purpose
> Before stupid winds.
> And there were many in the sky
> Who laughed at this thing. (X, 5)

The technique of the poem is more complex than may first appear. Crane employs *homoeoteleuton,* the concentration of same or similar endings – careful*ly*, proud*ly*, sly*ly* – supplemented with sound effects of the same type within lines – *noise*less, *rudder*less, *progr*ess – and by compounding of assonance: h*u*ll, r*u*dder, adj*u*stment. Although unstressed final syllables are to be found in the preceding poems, Crane does little with them. The most significant effect occurs in "Once there came a man," where *weeping, scuffle,* and *simplicity* appear as final words in the last three lines, laying the groundwork for a qualitative progression, as Kenneth Burke would call it, to the present poem, where the resources of such words are modified quantitatively *and* qualitatively: the former, in that the number is doubled, with three words of this type at the end of lines and three within lines; and the latter, in that the words are more closely attuned to one another. In the first set of three words, the second word is homologous to the first and the third makes a wry commentary on both. *Carefully* and *proudly* support the mastery of the maker, *slyly* undermines it. Homology goes further in the second set, with "quaint progress" echoing "ridiculous voyages," which are so because the ship that is "forever rudderless" has made "cunning noiseless travel." The last two word pairings that are similarly constructed ("serious purpose" and "stupid winds") etch in the impression, the first by denying the purposefulness of the ship's movement, the second by denying to the winds that create the movement the very possibility of carrying out the purpose.

The Miltonic inversions of lines 2–4 and line 6 are the rhetorical equivalent of the creator's erect and prideful posture. Although the lines that describe the actual movement of the ship are equally mimetic, the lines that follow are not:

> Mákiňg cúnnĭng noíselĕss tŕavĕl doẃn thĕ wáys.
> Sŏ thát, fŏrévĕr rúddĕrléss, ĭt wént ŭpón thĕ séas
> Going ridiculous voyages,
> Making quaint progress . . .

The first of these lines is trochaic, with a truncated concluding foot, while the second is iambic; but one glosses the next two lines at one's peril. First comes the "sly" phase, soothing and smoothly kinetic, then, as the ship attains the high seas, the metrical compass starts spinning. The reality of these voyages and this progress is exposed in prosaic, heavily judgmental language; by the norms of the preceding lines, these lines are themselves like ridiculous voyages whose progress is quaint.

The first part of the poem is predominantly pride, the last part fall; the first part pretension, the last part ridicule; the first part arrogance, the last part perspective. The poem calls creation into question by a temporizing of essence: By casting a view of the world – an idea about the way things are – into the form of a story. The action of the story as such (as distinguished from the verbal effects we have been examining) tends to undermine the importance of creation, first, by showing its contingency: It is by one of the nemeses of nineteenth-century faith, the phenomenon of chance, that the world came to be the way it is. Because the creation of the world, furthermore, is evidently a mere epiphenomenon there is no reason to doubt that the many who laugh in the sky, like the wrong that called, are in existence even while God is working on the ship, or that the chaos that the world comes to be is a mere extension of the lack of control already in the universe.

DISTANCE AND DESIRE

Poem 21 explores, among other things, the relation of distance and desire:

> There was, before me,
> Mile upon mile
> Of snow, ice, burning and sand.
> And yet I could look beyond all this,
> To a place of infinite beauty;
> And I could see the loveliness of her
> Who walked in the shade of the trees.
> When I gazed,
> All was lost
> But this place of beauty and her.
> When I gazed,

And in my gazing, desired
Then came again
Mile upon mile,
Of snow, ice, burning sand.

The first reversal, beginning with line four, turns attention away from the obstacles faced toward a more transcendent place, the description of the woman and of the first-person's gaze filling in some of the indeterminacy. The task of the second and final reversal belongs to the last five lines, which describe the onset of a desire that turns attention back to the obstacles. The place of infinite beauty is an essential place, promising a kind of otherworldly version of amorous union. Psychologically, the first-person, to borrow a phrase from *The Red Badge of Courage,* falls into a little trance. In existential language, the real world becomes transparent, only to turn once again, and suddenly, opaque. All at once the snow, ice, burning sand are "there" just as, but for his illusion, they have always been. Like the little man of "The Mesmeric Mountain," the first-person becomes lost in contemplation of something he wants to achieve; unlike the little man, he fails to achieve it.

Two parallels suggest themselves, one earlier in time and literary, the other contemporaneous and philosophical. The literary parallel is the moment at the opening of "The Fall of the House of Usher" when the narrator experiences a return to reality that he likens "to the after-dream of the reveller upon opium – the bitter lapse into every-day life – the hideous droppings of the veil."[11] The narrator, like the first-person of the poem, becomes newly aware of the otherness of the world, of the sheer resistance reality puts up against him. The other parallel is with the second of the three categories by which Peirce attempts to explain all phenomena. This second category he calls "the element of struggle," the category of fact, the world of experience. To experience is not merely to perceive, but to become acquainted with changes of perception. When one hears the whistle of a passing train go to a lower note, one has a sensation merely of that note but a *cognition* of the *change,* and that cognition is essential to genuine experience.

> It is the compulsion, the absolute constraint upon us to think otherwise than we have been thinking, that constitutes experience. Now constraint and compulsion cannot exist without resistance, and resistance is effort opposing change. Therefore there must be an element of effort in experience; and it is this which gives it its peculiar character.[12]

It is precisely the crucial element of experience, the oppositional element, of which the onset of desire makes the daydreamer newly aware. Desire presupposes effort, actual or potential, against whatever it is that resists.

It is precisely at the moment of desiring that the resistance of the world comes to the fore.

But, it may be objected, the poem makes no mention of desire in the first description of reality, where it must also be supposed to exist. The supposition is correct. What it overlooks is that the poem is a lived experience of the emergence of desire as a central mode of experience. With the return to the here and now the world is felt in the fullness of its resistance, which itself emerges as the polar sense (Peirce's term) of felt desire. If desire is not mentioned at first, this is because it is not yet earned through the action of the poem. The earning begins with that sense of the beyond which, when informed with desire, recalls the world to presence. Resistance is not added to the world; it is always, in virtue of the very effort one makes against it, present. Through the speaker, the poem reveals a distance between the ideal and the real that the emergence of desire holds open even as it returns us to the real. It is a distance of relation – an intimate distance, if you will – seen from the near side, then from the far side, then again from the near.

Compare poem 23:

> Places among the stars,
> Soft gardens near the sun,
> Keep your distant beauty;
> Shed no beams upon my weak heart.
> Since she is here
> In a place of blackness,
> Not your golden days
> Nor your silver nights
> Can call me to you.
> Since she is here
> In a place of blackness,
> Here I stay and wait.

Crane returns to the problem of distance and desire in poem 26:

> There was set before me a mighty hill,
> And long days I climbed
> Through regions of snow.
> When I had before me the summit-view,
> It seemed that my labor
> Had been to see gardens
> Lying at impossible distances.

Attention may now be focused on the relation between the last two poems and the present work. In an interplay of similarity and difference, the poem presents a vision of a desired object that is inaccessibly remote, as in poem 21; and there is, as in that poem, a sense of frustrated effort.

But in two important respects this poem differs from both of the others: first, in that the persona has no thought of another person; second, in the way it is structured. Poem 21 proceeds more or less circularly, through a negation of the here and now that leads to the place of infinite beauty, which, itself negated, gives way again to the here and now. Poem 23 is more of a mirror, the first rejection being followed by a second that reinforces the first. The present lines, by contrast, depict a kind of retroactive discovery, the turning point coming in the second sentence when the sighting of a new beyond, the distant gardens, suddenly defines the previously experienced realm, the regions of snow, as itself a beyond. With this recognition the poem reveals its likeness with poem 21 which, though differently structured, also describes a first-person separated from his object by a distance he thought he had overcome.

Compare that with poem 35:

> A man saw a ball of gold in the sky;
> He climbed for it,
> And eventually he achieved it –
> It was clay.
>
> Now this is the strange part:
> When the man went to the earth
> And looked again,
> Lo, there was the ball of gold.
> Now this is the strange part:
> It was a ball of gold.
> Aye, by the heavens, it was a ball of gold.

Unlike the one who climbs through regions of snow, this man has his goal constantly before him. That he achieves it sets him apart from other seekers until the discovery that the ball is clay undermines the distinction, whereupon it appears that he has not achieved his goal after all. This is the first reversal in the poem. The second reversal comes in the second part, and is doubled. Looking again, the man sees his object as once more a ball of gold, a retrospective discovery that invalidates the first discovery. There follows, seemingly, an "excess" of repetition, as the ball is said twice more to be a ball of gold. The final two statements differ, however, from the first statement ("Lo, there was the ball of gold"), which initiates the second reversal; for now the article is definite, confirming that the ball the man sees now is indeed the same ball that he saw before.

It is in this context that the next statement, and the next after that, returns to the wording "a ball of gold," with which the poem began, tying the ball now sighted to the ball originally seen. The point is no longer to underline the identity of the perceived object – this is established; the point is to confirm the *nature* of that object, to confirm that this selfsame ball is really made of gold. Equally significant is the manner in which the verb of being is employed in the three last statements about the ball. For, while the first states *where* it is, the penultimate and concluding clauses state *what* it is: "It was a ball of gold. / Aye, by the heavens, it was a ball of gold." The ostensible redundancy of the second part of the poem resolves the contradiction between the belief that the ball is of clay and the belief that the ball is of gold. Like the man who saw before him snow, ice, burning sand, and the man who climbed through regions of snow, the man who climbed for the ball of gold experiences a bitter version of the wonder that animates so much of Crane's writing. He is tardily surprised, taken unawares by a strange disjuncture: The desire he felt remains unfulfilled; the ball of gold was never achieved. What he has achieved is knowledge, but this he did not desire. He *could* not desire it, for he already had it: His ascent was based on the knowledge that the ball was a ball of gold. The irony of the poem is that this disjuncture comes about precisely through the resolution of the contradiction between the two beliefs. In the victory of the desired belief lies the defeat of desire.

This has its consequences for action. For the problem is not merely that we do not act as we should because we do not know what we need to know. The problem is that we could not act even if we did know. Truth is defined in terms of action; to achieve one's aim one must know its true nature. But it is precisely this knowledge that the effort to achieve dissolves. At the moment of optimal action the man is no different from the many who "do not know" – though more tragic than they, perhaps, since he has for a time a height of knowledge from which to fall. He is a victim of his own failings all the same.

In poem 29 we are asked to imagine how the world would look to a being who has actually achieved the farther shore:

> Behold, from the land of the farther suns
> I returned.
> And I was in a reptile-swarming place,
> Peopled, otherwise, with grimaces,
> Shrouded above in black impenetrableness.
> I shrank, loathing,
> Sick with it.
> And I said to him:
> "What is this?"
> He made answer slowly:
> "Spirit, this is a world;
> This was your home."

If "the land of the farther suns" suggests a Paradiso phase, the place to which the spirit returns smacks of the Inferno. This is what interests Crane, the fall into the world, or rather a fall back into it from a transcendent place whose attainment exacts a heavy price. Achieving a new home, the spirit loses his old one; the world of immanence, of earthly life and origin, has itself become inaccessible. The spirit's very ability to reach the beyond deprives him of the ability to come back. Authentic homecoming requires a home, which the spirit has truly lost. The consequence of this double achievement – arrival at the land of the farther suns and arrival at this place – is problematic. For the spirit, having left one place for another, leaves the latter place as well; his coming back is, as it were, full of going-away. We are less aware of his being here than of his not belonging here, a fact of which the unnamed respondent reminds us by his shift in tense: this *is* a world; this *was* your home.

The arresting technique this time is not the rhyming (*place, grimaces*) but those unwieldy words at the end of lines three and five. In the awkwardness of "a reptile-swarming place" and "black impenetrableness" and in their placement we recognize something that is specifically poetic, for the language of poetry, the Formalist Victor Shlovsky reminds us, "is a difficult, roughened, impeded language"; poetry is "*attenuated, tortuous* speech."[13] "A repitle-swarming place" is as cumbersome as the *herbstkräftig* which gives Mörike's famous "September-Morgen" its peculiar torque, and gets our attention in a similar way. It is in fact a typically German formation, the sort of thing skillful poets writing in English are supposed to avoid: Describe the swarming reptiles, don't turn them into a mere modifier, and above all don't force them into a hyphenated compound. Going against that advice, Crane hews a phrase that works because it conveys the repulsive quality in a foreign-sounding way, for it is precisely to an alien place, a realm to which he returns a foreigner, that the spirit finds himself. "Black impenetrableness" is similarly mimetic, a phrase that is almost too abstract and too stretched-out to get hold of. Introduced by the word "Shrouded," it is itself, in its own way, a shrouding word, impenetrable. This poem demonstrates, finally, the range of being covered by the first-person who appears throughout the collection. Variously a neutral observer, a sympathetic questioner, a man in quest of something, a self-important child, a polemical antagonist of orthodox religion, a sinner, and a lover, he becomes in these lines a spirit: a figure who has come to dwell, perhaps in a realm beyond earth and short of heaven, like the creatures in Poe's angelic dialogues, and one who is at any rate no longer human in the ordinary meaning of that term.

The neutral observer returns in poem 24:

> I saw a man pursuing the horizon;
> Round and round they sped.
> I was disturbed at this;
> I accosted the man.

"It is futile," I said,
"You can never – "
"You lie," he cried,
And ran on.

As in "I stood musing in a black world," illusion is associated with headlong movement: The runner is a one-man torrent of desire. Like the impetuous child of another poem, "I met a seer," he insults the man who would speak with him, the outburst revealing at once his self-preoccupation and the automatism of his behavior. A far horizon that is overtaken is in any case no longer a far horizon. In this sense the future of the man, the fact of his failure, is pregiven.

The action of poem 37 is another matter:

On the horizon the peaks assembled;
And as I looked,
The march of the mountains began.
As they marched, they sang:
"Aye! We come! We come!"

The action belongs to a time that Crane never specifically defines, but which resonates vaguely with Christian or Judeo-Christian overtones of revelation and apocalypse. If it is the time of "the triumphal march of justice" (#64), it is not yet, perhaps, the time of the marching blue battalions, who seem headed for genuine salvation. The present poem depicts a movement from the other pole, a movement of something bigger and older and probably threatening toward the witnessing man. Here is at once a moment of advent and a moment of challenge.

The distant mountains of poem 22 are the object of the little man's combative desire:

Once I saw mountains angry,
And ranged in battle-front.
Against them stood a little man;
Aye, he was no bigger than my finger.
I laughed, and spoke to one near me:
"Will he prevail?"
"Surely," replied this other;
"His grandfathers beat them many times."
Then did I see much virtue in grandfathers, –
At least, for the little man
Who stood against the mountains.

The size of the little man makes the nature of the being who poses the question suddenly problematic. If the little man is no bigger than his finger, the first-person would appear to be huge, possibly a giant or a god. His amused response to the little man's situation tends to support the latter possibility; this may well be the "laughter of the gods." Furthermore, only the little man is specifically identified as human; the speakers are simply "I" and "one," or "this other." Since the latter is at least a peer, and is superior, at least in knowledge, he would be on the same level as the interrogator.

But level can be defined differently. The smallness of the little man could be, for example, an effect of distance. Perhaps the two speakers are simply far away, in which case the prediction made by "this other" is an opinion, not a reliable prophecy. The poem on this reading exemplifies Crane's transcendental imagination, an imagination expressing an almost Nietzschean interplay between the human and the superhuman. Of these two interpretative approaches I suggest that the latter is the more useful; that the ontic status of the two speakers is left partly indeterminate; that the determinations that are made tend to locate them in a realm "beyond" the human, in the sense that it enjoys a historical overview, a temporal perspectivism, if you will, but is not ultimately "above" it; and that there is little need to press the search for their identities beyond that.

The little man desires, the first-person valuates. "This other" does too. The difference is that he offers a view much closer to the little man's own view than to that of the first-person. While "this other" articulates the immediate significance of the grandfathers' example for the little man's desire, the first-person judges as from a height, the moral distance between him and the little man being expressed by his neutrality regarding the value of the fight. He does not ask: Is it a good fight; should the little man be admired? His is the curiosity of a spectator, without a stake, who merely inquires about the odds. The little man does all the betting, and his wager is in terms of power. The first-person wants simply to know whether he has enough of it. When this other says that he probably does, the question is being addressed appropriately, in terms of power and probability.

The ethical dimension, reduced to the sphere of the little man, remains open for the spectatorial imagination in two directions. It is open both toward the future and toward the past: The first-person could assert that it is good that the little man will win, or could assert that it is good that his grandfathers made it possible for him to win. The alternatives are not symmetrical. To make the first assertion is to take a position regarding the contest; it is to choose the little man over the mountains. The other alternative involves the same commitment, though in a slightly more indirect way. When the first-person finally locates the good in the past, he avoids the dilemma by relativizing his judgment. There is virtue in grandfathers, not generally, but for this little man who had made this particular decision. The situation of the little man was framed, in effect, from the start. The question and its answer widen the frame to include a historical continuum from past to present to future, then the judgment of the first-person narrows it again. That it narrows, and the manner in which it narrows, makes manifest the relativity that results from the tension between desire and distance. Learning about the little man's grandfathers, the first-person responds immediately and affirmatively ("Then did I see much virtue in grandfathers") only to pull back: "At least, for the little man / Who stood against the mountains." The desire to distantiate is as firm now as it was when the first-person, noting the little man's situation and his small size, broke out in laughter.

The relation between a solitary, dauntless individual and his own peculiar tradition is one of the features that invites comparison between this poem and poem 27:

> A youth in apparel that glittered
> Went to walk in a grim forest.
> There he met an assassin
> Attired all in garb of old days;
> He, scowling through the thickets,
> And dagger poised quivering,
> Rushed upon the youth.
> "Sir," said this latter,
> "I am enchanted, believe me,
> To die, thus,
> In this medieval fashion,
> According to the best legends;
> Ah, what joy!"
> Then took he the wound, smiling,
> And died, content.

The age of the protagonist sets him apart from most of the other protagonists in the volume; this fact and the illusion he lives probably explain the parallel R. W. Stallman draws between the youth and Henry Fleming. But, as Hoffman observes, "there is surely a difference between the panic and courage of the novel and the satisfied nihilism of the poem."[14] The youth reminds us of the creature who eats his heart and likes it because it is bitter. The youth, too, finds a place within himself. The nature of what he finds, however, is transcendental in that it exists outside of himself. In this he resembles the little man who stands against the mountains. The little man has his grandfathers, the youth his legends, and there is virtue in both. The difference is that the youth lacks the family tradition enjoyed by the little man. Guided like Quijote by the fiction, he is, like him, enchanted. He also recalls that student of Cervantes, Tom Sawyer, but a Tom Sawyer crossed with the Swede of "The Blue Hotel," the radical loner whose play-acting is not, like Tom's, a thing of leisure. Nor is he reckless in the same way as the New York Kid in "Five White

Mice," who risks much on a throw of dice. The youth is a full-time play-actor who determines his own "values in a universe of chance," to use the Peircean phrase. Chance is overcome at the expense of his life. Let us consider more closely how this comes about.

The apparel of the youth cannot be armor, as is sometimes suggested. A small, hand-held blade is not going to kill a person encased in protective metal. The apparel may be metal-like in that, being of hard surface, it gives off light, but the point is the light and the manner in which it is given off. The most famous quotation in which the opening predicate occurs, "All that glitters is not gold," fairly catches the sense of something in which reality is subordinated to appearance. That the apparel is not metal, that it cannot ward off the blow, is a crucial aspect of the illusion and is the very material condition that makes it possible for the assassin to strike the victim dead. The effect comes through all the more clearly in contrast to a phrase he might have used, such as "raiment that shone." But that type of garment and light would have been altogether too numinous, too real, even too "religious." By contrast, the apparel of the youth is, so to speak, radiant in a shallow way.

Like the loner of poem 17, who goes into direful thickets, seeking a new road, the youth "went to walk in a grim forest" where he meets a man attired not in apparel but in garb. *Apparel,* interestingly, is a medieval word, while *garb* is a late seventeenth-century formation. Adding the phrase "of old days" enhances precisely that aspect of him which fascinates the youth: his appearance. It is idle to seek a determinate cause for the assassin's presence or his attitude. His presence and his attitude are a given which makes no more "sense" than the presence and attitude of the youth. They are equally, if you will, on the side of "anarchy." The "sense" is in what happens when they meet. What would happen if a youth like this met someone dressed in a manner he could interpret as belonging to an earlier, better age? That is the speculative premise of the action of the poem which, because it is a poem, needs no other justification.

The assassin appears to make the first move, like the mountains that march or range themselves in battlefront; and like the black riders from the sea he comes rushing. The phrase "scowling through the thickets" implies, on the other hand, that he was on the move when the youth ventured into the forest, and simply increased his speed. In principle the two are on the move together, the one in search of the other, much as in the riddle-poem that we will be looking at next. Victim and victimizer are partners in a kind of dance; and yet how differently they act, the one by pure mindless aggression, the other by a submission that is equally pure but full of mind. In this the youth again recalls the heart-eating creature, for it is through the belief that nourishes his life that his life is consumer. The quality of this belief is made clear through the plot and through a feature of technique that is easily overlooked. The poem employs a higher proportion of unstressed final syllables at the ends of lines than any poem since number 6, which relied on *homoeoteleuton.* That rhyme effect is not attempted here; the line-winding words fall, rather, into two counterpoised groups: those with grim or threatening overtones – *forest, assassin, thickets, quivering* – and those that are affirmative and bright – *glittered, fashion, legends, smiling.* The words in the first group convey a sense of the peril the youth faces, as it would appear to anyone but the youth, whose desire for a certain type of death is expressed by the "belief" words of the second group.

It is worth noting that the groups are first and second in order of appearance, and that their synchronic opposition is thus experienced by the reader diachronically. The neutral word *latter* – the word that does not fit into either of the two groups – comes appropriately in between. It is a referential word bridging the two parts of the poem by unobtrusively identifying the speaker of the second part with the silent protagonist of the first. The reasonable reader then hears from the lips of the youth all sorts of unreasonable things that the first part of the poem gives one no reason to expect. In the two concluding, codalike lines, the excess reaches the end of its run. The word on which the final stress falls, *content,* is the accentual reverse of the other line-ending words. By this, and by the very fact of its position, it calls attention to itself. The tradition in which the youth believes, holding him enchanted, brings contentment. The words "believe me," uttered so casually, are a fragment of the implied total statement that the youth makes to the assassin: Believe me even as I believe you. Like the little man who stood against the mountains, the youth can claim a tradition, but unlike him, he has no way of validating it interpersonally. The only other person who appears is co-opted without being consulted.

WISDOM

Poem 61, on a related theme, takes the reader into the general sphere of "wisdom" literature, which embraces such short forms as the riddle, the proverb, the parable, and longer forms of the fable, of which Crane composed four in prose:

> A man feared that he might find an assassin;
> Another that he might find a victim.
> One was more wise than the other.

Finding an assassin may mean that the first man becomes a victim – a sufficient cause for fear. The word *find* – instead of, say, *meet* – makes the feared encounter less pointed, but a normal individual would feel frightened at running across an assassin under any conditions. The break comes with the problematic second line. Assuming a symmetry with the preceding statement, the second man may fear that in finding a victim he will emerge as his complement, that is, an assassin. One argument against the man's fear in this case is Blakean. If you are an assassin there is no reason to fear finding a victim; do your tigerish business with a tiger's clean conscience. If we abandon this assumption and assume that the second man is just an ordinary fellow, we face the problem of a fear that is not ordinary. The poem does not say that the man would experience fear on finding an assassin, like anyone else; he feels it in advance. Perhaps he is neurotic. In any case, the fact that he fears in advance should draw our attention to another temporal aspect. The assassin has an ongoing capability that the victim lacks. You are only a victim of assassination once, but you can kill more than once, so that the assassin threatens more.

To find the solution to the riddle one does not have to settle on one or another of the possibilities surrounding the second man. One has instead to recognize that none of the theories pertaining to the second man provides as plausible an explanation for fear as the one pertaining to the first man. One can go a step further and abandon even the assumption that the first man may become a victim. The issue then becomes a simple choice between the assassin and the victim as sources of fear. That choice may be entirely too simple, which is why I have preferred to give greater attention to other considerations. At least it gets us back to the basic question of who is the wiser. Wisdom as understood here is closer to the *phronesis* or practical wisdom of Aristotle than to his higher wisdom. Being more wise than another means acting in a way that conduces to a good life, and in this light – for all the reasons stated – the first man is more wise than the other.

"The proverb illustrates a general principle by a special case. A riddle is an invitation to translate a metaphor and by doing so to perceive the similarity of apparently dissimilar things. Both are exercises in the search for simplicity."[15] Such riddles are nothing if not solvable. They still exist in the United States, though less abundantly than in Crane's day when they were a widely popular type of entertainment, often in the form of a little book of conundrums. Crane's lines, of course, may be either a riddle that happens to be in verse, or a riddle-poem. A riddle-poem aims higher, asks harder questions. If the present work is indeed such a poem, there is probably even more room for interplay than this brief analysis has been able to allow. But it may also be a simple riddle, a slight thing that one is in danger of overinterpreting. We cannot be sure, I think, which of these is the better choice. But we do know that the lines are about large matters similar to the ones raised in the poem about the youth and the assassin. Such an interpretation, without destroying the independence of the present work, allows it to comment on the other one, the gist of the comment being that someone who seeks out an assassin, instead of fearing him, is wise. This we already knew.

What is at issue, however, is more than knowledge in the narrow sense; for if the present work offers a cognitive perspective that enriches the other work, it is also an experience in its own right. The reader has to live through the enigma, has to wrestle with the difficulties until they are resolved, abandoned, or simply held indefinitely in suspense. The historical context for such an experience is the history of the genre itself. Riddles in various forms, Huizinga reminds us,[16] are secretly powerful, dangerous. An extreme form is the *Halsrätsel* or "capital riddle," which costs your head if you fail to solve it, the *aporia* which the Greeks employed as a parlor-game ("What is sweeter than honey?") being but a weakened form of this. Crane's three-line work is not a parlor-game, though nineteenth-century American versions of such may have exerted some influence on him. Neither is it, precisely, a capital riddle. Yet the fact that it concerns a life-and-death situation, an ultimate moment, brings it within the range of that neglected genre. This suggests why it may not be necessary to "clear up" the obscurity that it casts like a shadow. "The close connections between poetry and the riddle are never entirely lost. In the Icelandic *skalds* too much clarity is considered a technical fault. The Greeks also required the poet's word to be dark."[17] If Crane's word remains in this measure dark, the reader is left musing in a poetic black world not unrelated to the world of the lost seeker who was denounced in another poem for the blindness of his spirit. Riddling puts the reader, if only temporarily, in a situation that always fascinated Crane: the situation of someone who does not know.

Some of the poems following "I stood musing in a black world" swing back and forth between the polarity of this ignorance and a sure, if limited, wisdom or knowledge. Poem 51 makes a similar rejection in stronger terms, establishes the possibility of the latter, as a seeker flees from a tyrannical god:

> Then the man went to another god, –
> The god of his inner thoughts.
> And this one looked at him
> With soft eyes
> Lit with infinite comprehension,
> And said: "My poor child!"

The man becomes both knower and known: known because he is the object of the god's comprehension; knower because he is himself that knowing subject. This is not a withdrawal, like Henry Fleming's retreat, but a turning-inward viewed as an act of courage. Wisdom and the figure of the sage are inverted in folly and the figure of the fool, one of Crane's favorites, as in poem 13:

I

Blustering god,
Stamping across the sky
With loud swagger,
I fear you not.
. . . .

III

Withal, there is one whom I fear;
I fear to see grief upon that face.
Perchance, friend, he is not your god;
If so, spit upon him.
By it you will do no profanity.
But I –
Ah, sooner would I die
Than see tears in those eyes of my soul.

At first the poem seems headed in the same direction as Stevens's "Bantams in Pine Woods," but is not so antic or so consistently – and playfully – polemical. Like other works with polemical elements, this one gives one side of a contest as in the traditional *flyting,* in which opponents strive to deal word-death to the other. The attack on the foolish god simultaneously legitimizes the first-person's crucial claim: He has transcended fear. With the third section a reversal reinstates fear in the interest of a higher purpose. For if the first-person who does not fear the blustering god fears, instead, the god of his own soul, then the latter is the greater god.

This interiority in which the speaker finds safety and sympathy differs significantly from the interior castle of mystical tradition. Turning inward, the speaker experiences a numinous encounter: He finds his god. This interiority is not, however, an intimate space within a universal architecture of belief; it defines itself negatively, against an external legitimacy. The intimacy is in the dialectic, which keeps the opposition and the reconciliation warringly together, as evidenced in the final stanza by the two "liquid" expressions: the spit that the friend is rhetorically challenged to produce and the tears that the speaker's eyes will produce if he is not faithful to this, the greater god. The relation of the first-person to his god differs from the one so often found in the mystics, being affectionate rather than amatory. This is a kinship of sympathy grounded not in hierarchy but in equity, a kinship essentially fraternal.

This kinship – intimate, low-keyed, hidden from the world – is judged sufficient. Measured as it is by the experiencing subject himself, a similar notion of measure is implicit in poem 55:

A man toiled on a burning road
Never resting.
Once he saw a fat, stupid ass
Grinning at him from a green place.
The man cried out in rage:
"Ah! do not deride me, fool!
I know you –
All day stuffing your belly,
Burying your head
In grass and tender sprouts:
It will not suffice you."
But the ass only grinned at him from the green place.

If the poem attacks excessive pretension, it also dramatizes two kinds of experience, two kinds of desire. The man wants the ass to want more, forgetting that this is to measure the animal by an unwise standard; it is to hold that it should aspire to the kind of "greatness" Crane denounces elsewhere. What the ass does, does suffice. The epithet "fool" redounds to the man who fails to pluck the bough that the ass not only plucks but wears. Other poems have traced the distance between desire and its object; this one traces the distance between two desires. To the man the green place inhabited by the ass is inaccessible. He sees it, but the percept is foreign to his desire, which is so strong that he moves on, heedless of heat, indifferent to fatigue. It perhaps makes little difference whether one considers his essential place to be the burning road or the beyond to which it may lead: The one is so much the condition, the very premise of the other, that it is impossible to separate them.

While this man is not as explicitly helpless as the man who mused in a black world, he is heedless in a similarly frustrating way. The one toils on a burning road, the other leaps unhesitant, each in his way anticipating the headlong haste of the speeding spirit who appears in the final poem. The man on the road engages in the more negative of two general types of opposition in these poems. One is the opposition between an individual and some other who is genuinely opposed to him (e.g., the man who stands against the mountains). This is a "good" opposition, in that it summons one to manly duty, to courage; it is a chance to fight the good fight. The other type of opposition pits the individual against something that is merely other. The ass is not against the man. It is just an ass, sufficient to itself in its own and proper place. This one-sided antagonism might better be termed agonism, to designate a struggle without a true adversary. The man thinks he can be an interpreter of nature; his folly is that he reads it wrong.

GOD DEAD OR ALIVE
If God died – what then?

God lay dead in Heaven;
Angels sang the hymn of the end;
Purple winds went moaning,
Their wings drip-dripping
With blood
That fell upon the earth.
It, groaning thing,
Turned black and sank. . . .
But of all sadness this was sad, –
A woman's arms tried to shield
The head of a sleeping man
From the jaws of the final beast.

The poem complements "God fashioned the ship of the world carefully." There are, in the one setting, angels and purple winds, and in the other, winds and "many in the sky / Who laughed at this thing." The point is not that the winds are exactly the same winds or that the many are necessarily angels. The point is that neither in the beginning of the world nor in its end is God wholly of it. Neither coextensive nor coterminous with the world, God lives, or dies, apart. And yet, with the death of God the world does end after all – the earth turns black and sinks; only it takes a while, leaving time for a little picture of solidarity. The basic situation derives from the tradition of the sleeper, a figure who appears in Coleridge, Wordsworth, Byron, Shelley, and Poe.[18] Like Shelley's "magnetic lady," like Poe's Annie, the woman functions as guardian. But if in practical terms she fails – she can only *try* to shield – morally the effort is a triumph, the degree of which is suggested by the fact that she does not try to wake him. To allow the man to remain unconscious while interposing her own body between his head and the jaws of the beast, is great solicitude. Herein lies the moral force of the scene, small as it is, which carries the burden of the statement "but of all sadness this was sad." And it is the same force which, for tough-minded readers, saves the statement from excessive sentimentality and which, for the tender-minded, saves it from being sentimental at all.

The final poem in the volume reads:

A spirit sped
Through spaces of night;
And as he sped, he called:
"God! God!"
He went through valleys
Of black death-slime,
Ever calling:

"God! God!"
Their echoes
From crevice and cavern
Mocked him:
"God! God! God!"
Fleetly into the plains of space
He went, ever calling:
"God! God!"
Eventually, then, he screamed,
Mad in denial:
"Ah, there is no God!"
A swift hand,
A sword from the sky,
Smote him,
And he was dead.

The echoing voices, followed as they are by the swift violence from the sky, help to identify the spirit as a figure of failure. The first clue is in the verb *sped,* recalling poem 24: "I saw a man pursuing the horizon; / Round and round they sped," and a number of other works in which speed is associated with hastiness, rashness, or futility. It is not so much a question of time in the abstract but one of pace. If rate of movement is a correlative of a mode of being, the poems tend to suggest that the human mode of being attempts an accelerated pace at its own peril. Precipitate action, blind plunges, headlong pursuit bespeak the fool, or the failure, who are ultimately the same. All suffer from lack of perspective, expressed now in a temporal dimension. To be in haste is to be lacking in perspective. Consistently with this implicit view, Crane validates in poem after poem "slow" kinds of behavior: the figures of courage typically wait, firm in their resolve, whether alone, like the man who stood against the march of mountains, or together, like the men and women who abide by one another in the face of annihilation.

It is also consistent for God to triumph in poem 68 by swift action. God's sword stroke is not hasty or lacking in perspective; it is merely instantaneous, and as the instantaneous act of a divine being it expresses his special power of perspective. God has from the beginning an overview never available to the spirit, and is constrained as to pace or tempo. God can wait while the spirit hastens about and, when the fateful moment of denial occurs, can act in a flash. The speeding spirit (one almost wants to say "the little man") indulges in an outburst, a scream of denial that denotes his madness, and is punished. God in his own way is "guilty" of an outburst, too, but the fact is made irrelevant by the lack of any further framework in which to view what he does. God measures the spirit; no one measures God.

The position of poem 68 makes it in some sense an answer to poem 67, "God lay dead in heaven." The detail of the "black death-slime" is sufficiently reminiscent of other poems with Gothic gore to point up the difference between what happens in the two pieces. In the one, God turns black in death. In the other, despite the presence of black death-slime and his own ostensible absence, God is shown to be still alive. This is hardly a blow to orthodoxy, for it is impossible to remove the negative aspects of the central action from the affirmative ones. On the one hand, God still exists; and that is good. On the other hand, his existence is proven by an act of destruction; and if we cannot declare this bad, neither is there any assurance that it is good, except to those who will take belief at any price. The spirit who "sped" is "dead." The positioning of those two words, at the end of the first line and the end of the last, is, as I have suggested, a technical feature with meaning. It underlines the power of God, for it is not a mortal he destroys, but a spirit, a being whose superiority is shown by his ability to fly in space. It is not that whatever God does is right. The point is that whatever God does, is.

It is easy enough to say that Crane saves belief by means of this poem: It shows God in triumph after all. The poem does not stand alone, however, but relates to other works from which a variety of impressions arises, and whose totality cannot be left out of account. That totality gravitates to a considerable extent around the overall problem of God but also around the more particular problem of what we know and how we know it. It is what we mean when we speak of Crane's perspectivism – which, if it could be precisely defined to everyone's satisfaction, would no longer be perspectival. *Black Riders* is a restless book full of ideas, points of view, fresh starts, repetitions, and is to that extent inconclusive. The collection is more kaleidoscopic than cumulative. The last poem is not a finale, but the sixty-eighth poem in a series of sixty-eight poems, among which there is much interplay as well as interplay of many kinds. The collection does not build to a single crescendo. It is a series of collages, of discrete poetic entities and meaningful juxtapositions, whose "anarchy" and "ethical sense" meet in something like Hesiod's *eris,* the tension of beneficial strife.

MORALITY IN WAR

In the title poem of *War Is Kind* (#69), as elsewhere in the same volume, Crane offers a counter to his own aesthetics of war. War becomes a theme of moral judgment, the judgment being at once negative and severe.

> Do not weep, maiden, for war is kind.
> Because your lover threw wild hands toward the sky
> And the affrighted steed ran on alone,

Do not weep.
War is kind.

The "spondaic rhythm" to which one critic understandably refers can be heard in the opening line, with its six accents for just eight words.[19] But as in the opening passage of "The Open Boat," there occurs an interruption in the rhythm as the second line turns irregular and "prosey." This too is interrupted as line three returns to roughly the same accentual pattern as the opening line, after which the two-line, balladlike refrain rounds off the long apostrophe.

With the second apostrophe, focusing on the babe, the pattern recurs, the regularity of "Do not weep, babe, for war is kind," giving way to a long, bouncing line similar in structure to the second line in stanza one, after which, following the structure of the latter, a more regular rhythm returns both in the third line and in the refrain:

Raged at his breast, gulped and died,
Do not weep.
War is kind.

One notes not only the accentual emphasis of "heart hung humble" but the consonantal alliteration of that phrase together with the interweaving of pathic gutturals: *Mother, hung, humble, button,* setting the reader up for the "higher" vocality of the following line's *bright* and *splendid.* The case is a little different with "shroud of your son," which offers a closing guttural preceded by two contiguous diphthongs (*shroud, your*). The twisting and turning of the sounds are ululant in effect, all the more so because of the semantic pattern, which establishes the presence in every stanza, including the nonapostrophic "choruses" at which we have not yet looked, conditions calling for sorrow. Although that presence, in combination with the attitude of the voice addressing the maiden, the babe, and the mother, lays a foundation for lamentation, the lamentation does not come. It is effectively choked, forced back into the interiors of the words, so to speak, as if the keening, instead of being openly and loudly expressed, as by the mother herself, must somehow be contained. This produces a torsion in the reading, which keeps following the path of death and destruction only to discover that the path ends more or less where it begins, with the same ironic advice ("Do not weep") and the same unacceptable definition ("War is kind").

The complexity of the poem, both in structure and in irony, has been elucidated by Mordecai Marcus,[20] who contrasts the lamentations in the apostrophe-stanzas to the denunciations of the second group, consisting of stanzas two and four, which are interpolated between the three stanzas of the former group, tracing the modulations that occur within each group as well as between them. Adding to the complexity, the second and fourth stanzas each takes as a cue from the preceding stanza an element that fits into its own representation of war. After complementing this with apposite details of battle, it stirs the latter in with high-sounding effects familiar from military propaganda and jingoist jargon, then returns at the close to the attitude of rejection ironically expressed in the refrain with each apostrophic stanza's end.

Allow me to illustrate. The apposite element serving as a cue in the opening stanza is the action of the lover throwing his hands to the sky as he falls from his horse, which then runs on alone. The second stanza complements this with a series of warfield details spelled out, as in Expressionist poetic practice, in flashes that are similar in nature but not explicitly joined to one another: for example, "Hoarse, booming drums of the regiment / Little souls who thirst for fight." If the militaristic rhetoric has not already begun, it certainly becomes apparent in the lines that follow:

> These men were born to drill and die
> The unexplained glory flies above them
> Great is the battle-ground, great, and his kingdom –

Whereupon the note of rejection enters in the form of the bald statement, lacking even a predicate: "A field where a thousand corpses lie."

The pattern is repeated in the second stanza, with the dying father cueing the warfield details of flag and regiment, after which come the men born to drill and die, leading to the puncturing of illusion in three hard-hitting lines:

> Point for them the virtue of slaughter
> Make plain to them the excellence of killing
> And a field where a thousand corpses lie.

The mother in the concluding stanza evinces the humility appropriate for someone in a culture where men are born to drill and die and where the national flag flies in unexplained glory. In a conceit reminiscent of English Metaphysical poetry, her heart contrasts with the bright splendid shroud of her son even as it is fastened to that shroud, a relationship giving the greater weight to the shroud, the brightness and splendor of which suggests the kind of aura the militarist philosophy conspires to paint around the fallen.

Crane, as Stallman points out, is a man of moods.[21] Here the mood is plainly dark, the tone bitterly ironic, indicating a departure from the stance of an earlier poem (#113) about a mother-nurtured flower ultimately devoted to duty and nation. For the sacrifice a young soldier makes

> The nation rendered to him a flower
> A little thing – a flower

Aye, but yet not so little
For this flower grew in the nation's heart
A wet, soft blossom
From tears of her who loved her son

The trope that finally assimilates the flower anticipates the rhetoric of the later war writings:

A little thing – this flower?
No – it was the flower of duty
That inhales black smoke-clouds
And fastens its roots in bloody sod

This sounds like something the author of *The Red Badge of Courage* might have written as an afterthought to that novel, but it does not sound like that other afterthought – if such it was – that turns into "Do not weep, maiden, for war is kind." Indeed, if we did not know that the latter was written prior to Crane's first actual experience of battle, it could be taken as a testimonial to his disillusionment following Cuba and Greece. But the poet was disillusioned before the correspondent.

"There exists the eternal fact of conflict / And – next – a nere sense of locality," the opening lines of poem 127, provided a useful way in to *The Red Badge of Courage,* and could offer the same service in approaching many other works. As poet Crane always sees the here and now *sub specie aeternitatis.* The latter aspect is set forth in the first stanza in the form of conflict, which goes on indefinitely, but something else is ongoing, too, and that is the consequence following upon the mere sense of locality:

Afterward we derive sustenance from the winds.
Afterward we grip upon this sense of locality.
Afterward we become patriots.

Human identity grows into national identity, as if the American sense of place possessed the forming power of a fate, and nationalism becomes the means through which conflict is concretely carried out, leaving the we of the poem completely helpless: "The godly vice of patriotism makes us slaves."

In the second stanza the sense of locality is further historicized as the poet of 1899 pictures the Spanish–American war from the home front:

And the sacked sad city of New York is their record
Furious to face the Spaniard, these people, and crawling worms
before their task
They name serfs and send charity in bulk to better men
They place at being free, these people of New York
Who are too well-dressed to protest against infamy.

The city is sad because it is sacked and it is sacked in that its citizens have been dispatched to war along with the charity that is being shipped in bulk to dispossessed foreign civilians and refugees.

In a little-noticed companion poem (#128) written about the same time, the locus shifts to those civilians as they watch the American charity arrive:

> On the brown trail
> We hear the grind of your carts
> To our village,
> Laden with food

The villagers share with other inhabitants of Crane's imaginary world a sense that there is something important they know and something equally important that they do not know:

> We know you are come to our help
> But –
> Why do you impress upon us
> Your foreign happiness?
> We know it not.

DECADENCE

Poems 111 and 132 are the work that comes closest to the 1890s quality that is frequently called decadent. The poem is brief enough to be quoted in its entirety:

> There is a grey thing that lives in the tree-tops
> None know the horror of its sight
> Save those who meet death in the wilderness
> But one is enabled to see
> To see branches move at its passing
> To hear at times the wail of black laughter
> And to come often upon mystic places
> Places where the thing has just been.

The Expressionist technique of little or no punctuation makes each line come from nowhere, spontaneous and uncontrolled, and hence mysterious. *Black,* the main color word in the poems, makes the laughter awesome and also sinister, while *grey,* an in-between shade associated with fog, mist, and miasma, heightens a sense of mystery reminiscent of Poe (though not so much the Poe of the poetry, which is organized with metronome-like regularity, as the Poe of the tales, with their intangible atmospherics).

Applied to poem 132, the term "decadent" is descriptive rather than pejorative, indicating as it does that shock-effect aesthetic of the 1890s which highlighted eroticism, blended morbidity of mood with insouciance and irreverence, and indulged in theatricality of the Pierrot vein.

The roots of the decadent mode are largely French, however, and go deep into the work of Baudelaire, the poet to whom the following lines may be indebted:

> A naked woman and a dead dwarf:
> Wealth and indifference.
> Poor dwarf!
> Reigning with foolish kings
> And dying mid bells and wine
> Ending with a desperate comic palaver
> While before thee and after thee
> Endures the eternal clown –
> – The eternal clown –
> A naked woman.

The text in question is the seventh of the *Petits poèmes en prose*.[22] There, a colossal statue of Venus towers above a clown who lies prostrate at her feet. The loneliest of beings, the clown is made for one thing only, according to his own testimony, and that is "to understand and feel immortal Beauty." At the end of his entreaty Venus continues to stare off into space. Crane's poem offers similar characters and the status of each is similar as well in that Venus and the naked woman are superior to both the *fou* and the clown. But if Crane did know the French poem, he saw fit to rework it considerably. Crane's poem is retrospective. Whereas Baudelaire depicts a confrontation between Venus and a living clown, Crane's clown is already dead. All that remains is to draw some lesson from his relation to the woman, or at least to generalize about it in some meaningful way.

From the arrangement of words and lines, wealth and indifference appear to be apposite, respectively, to the naked woman and the dead dwarf. But on second thought it looks to be the other way around, as the dwarf is associated with kings, bells, and wine, and the woman, being above it all in her eternality, seems to embody indifference. This chiastic relation, being more unexpected and more contrastive than the other relation, should probably be given interpretative preference; then too, it helps along the irony by making the dwarf's *poor* a pun, for though he is so close to kings that he can reign with them, they are fools, and the end of reigning is only dying. The term *palaver* indicates wheedling, cajoling talk, the sort of discourse one improvises to gain advantage or retain position, but also, in an earlier sense deriving from Smollett, talk that is idle and pointless, and the likelihood is that Crane conflates them here to underline the finality and futility of the clown's speaking.

The poem presents two times and two clowns. One time is that of eternity, the other is the time of mortals. To the former belongs the woman clown, to the other the dwarf, and they are never, at least within the poem, synchronous: Although at first glance the juxtaposition in the opening line brings the two characters together, it actually posits their separateness, a state that the conjunction merely attests to. While the two characters have in common the fact that they are both clowns, the woman has the advantage of indifference, a condition like the coldness of God in "A man adrift on a slim spar" or the attitude of nature, as viewed by the correspondent, in "The Open Boat."

The nakedness of the woman may well have amatory implications, but precisely what they are is open to discussion. This is no *Liebestod.* The two characters are not lovers and do not die for and with one another. Nor is any other erotic prospect pursued in specific ways. It may be that for a male poet a woman thus undressed is simply assumed, in some vague way, to be "ready for love." Crane no more objects to being vague when necessary than he does to being unmistakable. But naked means more than undressed; it also means bare or exposed, possibly suggesting a certain vulnerability. The naked and the dead are beings in an elemental condition. Nor is this the only respect in which these examples of the elemental are similar. They are also similar in that each is an individual, a particular someone, who nonetheless functions as a type; but this individual-type, if that term may be used, is not identical with the paradigmatic figure of allegory who concretizes a concept. The naked woman and the dead dwarf are typifying individuals, discrete beings through whose mediation a representativeness emerges, such that eternality and clowning subtend any woman who is unclothed and exposed, and mortality and clowning any dwarf who is dead. The immanence of a larger representative in the individual-type is reinforced by the juxtaposition of definite and indefinite articles. *A* naked woman becomes *the* eternal clown, whereupon, by inverted restatement, *the* eternal clown becomes *a* naked woman.

APOCALYPSE

Apocalypse is frequently understood as a vision deriving from the revelation of the future experienced by St. John (*OED* 1), this revelation deriving from other Biblical prophecies, such as those of Daniel and Isaiah. The concept of an apocalypse is equivocal, as M. H. Abrams has observed, sometimes requiring the destruction of the present earth as the condition of achieving a new, transfigured earth, and sometimes signifying "a coming state of felicity on this earth after it shall have been renewed. . . ."[23]

In American literature apocalyptic fears and promises appear in authors as varied as Poe, who offers in *Eureka* a cosmogony in which the universe rushes back into itself, annihilating matter, and Emerson, who proposes an apocalypse of the mind. A problematic or apocryphal aspect is a frequent feature in the American canon, as in the familial destruction wrought in Charles Brockden Brown's *Wieland,* or in Melville's *The Confidence-Man,* where mention of the Apocrypha is taken for mention of the Apocalypse.[24]

For present purposes the apocalyptic mode is understood very broadly as entailing the possibility of an ultimate destruction that may or may not be followed by a redemptive or transcendental state.

Last things may be suggested on a small scale, as evidenced, for example, by the slouching beast in Yeats's "Second Coming." Poem 114, though lacking the framework of traditional reference employed by the Irish poet, depicts, near the end, a similar incident:

> A row of thick pillars
> Consciously bracing for the weight
> Of a vanished roof
> The bronze light of sunset strikes through them,
> And over a floor made for slow rites.
> There is no sound of singing
> But, aloft, a great and terrible bird
> Is watching a cur, beaten and cut,
> That crawls to the cool shadows of the pillars
> To die.

The conscious bracing of the pillars beneath the missing roof captures something of the dynamics of architecture, with its system of forces and counterforces striving intensely with and against one another, suggests the sense of loss represented by the destruction of the roof, and registers the incomprehension of the pillars, which do not know that they have nothing left to support. The fact that there are no slow rites on a floor that was made for them and no sound of singing implies that key religious customs or ceremonies have also vanished. Nothing human survives, only a cur and a bird. If the crawling of the former anticipates the slouching of Yeats's beast, it is not headed for rebirth and is not symbolic in any strong sense. Closer in nature to the beast is the great and terrible bird, a *mysterium tremendum* whose watchfulness seems at once indifferent, mysterious, and baleful. In contrast to the cur, no motion is attributed to this creature. It is not said to be hovering or circling, and neither is it perched. As befits a *mysterium,* it is essentially a presence, like a distillation of the very atmosphere.

Two major posthumous poems, 125 and 126, embody contrasting situations and two contrasting versions of the vision of last things. In the latter poem, "A man adrift on a slim spar," the immanence of the end turns, near the end of the poem, imminent. Extinction is suddenly here and now, in this scene, in this drowning. In the other poem, "When a people reach the top of a hill," or "Blue Battalions," the end, by contrast, is implicitly imminent throughout. For, in this more traditional apocalyptic treatment, the ultimate moment still lies at some farther shore in time.

> A man adrift on a slim spar
> A horizon smaller than the rim of a bottle
> Tented waves rearing lashy dark points
> The near whine of froth in circles.
> God is cold.
> The incessant raise and swing of the sea
> And growl after growl of crest
> The sinkings, green, seething, endless
> The upheaval half-completed.
> God is cold.

These and other lines in the poem are often said to be irregular in rhythm, and they are, but this does not mean that they are not rhythmical, or that they could easily be rearranged as acceptable prose. Most of the lines in each of the four-line stanzas have four stresses in the traditional English pattern favored in the Middle Ages and underlying blank verse: "A man adrift on a slim spar / A horizon smaller than the rim of a bottle," and so on. The most irregular stanza is the next to last, in which the poet turns from the long central stanza to the critical plight of the man, which is nearing a climax. In my scansion the lines carry, respectively, six, three, five, and five accents, a pattern that highlights the quickness of the second line, as accords with the kinesis of its "Inky, surging tumults." The structure of the poem also owes something to the rhythmic pattern of the stanzas, each of which begins with a line that is typically more regular than most of the other lines in the stanza, then ends with the precise regularity of the two-accent refrain, "God is cold":

> A man adrift on a slim spar . . .
> The incessant raise and swing of the sea . . .
> The seas are in the hollow of The Hand . . .
> A horizon smaller than a doomed assassin's cap . . .
> The puff of a coat imprisoning air . . .

The poem also owes a good deal to the alliterative use of *s,* which, while not strictly regularized, distributes the sounds with comparable frequency in each of the four-line stanzas. After the first four-line stanza sets the scene, with eight members of the *s* family (five unvoiced sibilants, two voiced, and one intermediate *sh*), the second stanza offers twelve (nine unvoiced and three voiced), the third, again twelve (nine unvoiced, two voiced, and one intermediate), and the fourth delivers eleven (nine unvoiced and two voiced), thus:

> The puff of a coat impri*s*oning air.
> A fa*c*e ki*ss*ing the water-death
> A weary *s*low *s*way of a lo*s*t hand

And the *s*ea, the moving *s*ea, the *s*ea.
God i*s* cold.

Ever experimental, Crane weaves a dense texture of sounds, producing unexpected effects and nuances that warrant a kind of microanalysis. Rather than undertake a traditional rhyme scheme, for example, Crane follows a pattern of what might be called frequency distribution, so that sounds with a family resemblance congregate in the same neighborhood. The first two stanzas offer a series of *r*-vowel pairings: *adrift, spar, horizon, smaller, rim, rearing, dark, near, froth, raise, growl, growl, green.* Emphasis occurs not only through rhythm but through sound, one notable technique being the sudden intervention in a prevailing pattern by a novel one. In stanza two the prevailing pattern derives from the recurrence of the *e* and *o* range, which dominates the first, third, and fourth lines and closes the second, but only after being interrupted by a pair of dissonant diphthongs:

The incessant raise and swing of the sea
And *growl* after *growl* of crest
The sinkings, green, seething, endless
The upheaval half-completed.

The device turns up the volume of the growling, which bursts forth from the background, into which it then sinks back. That emergence and the subsequent return to the prevailing pattern are subtly signaled, moreover, by transition words, *raise* and *crest,* that offer a combination of vowel sounds from the prevailing range and the *r* sounds that initiate the interruptive diphthongs.

A similar pattern occurs in the first stanza, where the crux, however, is an effect more nearly onomatopoeic. There *rearing* sets up an assonant rhyme in *near,* followed by two other *r* words in *froth* and *circles.* But the main effect is *near whine,* where the carryover off the diphthong of the first word to the second, with its aspirate shading into the long *i,* comes as near to replicating a near whine as the whiroo in "The Open Boat" replicates the sound of the shark sliding through the water.

Consonant distribution in the last four lines of the long central stanza works on the model of assonance to connect aurally words of distinctly different meanings. "Oceans may become grey ashes" is the most obvious instance, the two nouns signifying things that could hardly stand in greater contrast to one another. *Ashes* in turn anticipates *fishes* and *ships* – animate things versus technological artifacts. At the same time the similarity in sound complements a surprising similarity in the two types of beings, which are not usually thought of as sound-producing, but here make tumult on the one hand and utter cries on the other. These cries, finally, point toward *mice,* an assonant rhyme with *cries,* but Crane shrewdly puts a damper on the end of the stanza, as though to establish silence, by contrasting the unvoiced sibilant of the *s* sound in mi*c*e with the voiced sibilant of crie*s*. It is another way of saying what the line says implicitly, namely, that the mice do not make tumult or utter cries but are silently submissive.

In one instance Crane produces a distinctive effect by using an obsolete word for a current one. The word is *raise* in "the incessant raise," whereas the obvious choice here is *rise,* the substantive of the intransitive verb. *Raise* is a term, from 1538, for the act of raising (*OED* 1). By deploying it, Crane makes the sea seem the more active, as it raises not only the waves but, implicitly, the man and the spar and the ships as well. At the same time, not specifying that the sea also lowers these things creates an air of suspense to complement the general sense of menace.

The central stanza of the poem stands apart from the others, as do the choric stanzas in "Do not weep, maiden, for war is kind," and also works in counterpoint, but to a different effect. Whereas the latter provide the militaristic and political jargon for the apostrophic stanzas to debunk, the central stanza of poem 126 provides an overview, and an unsettling overview it is. That God may turn oceans into spray or grey ashes leaves no doubt about his omnipotence, but it does leave doubt about its employment, since the examples of God's might are not represented as actually happening. If *raise* furnishes an act with a specified object acted upon, this stanza furnishes objects acted upon without an act. Moreover, the motive for turning the oceans into a spray, a feeling of pity for a babe, is precisely the type of motive that could save the man adrift. The absence of the latter, and the merely conditional status of the former gesture, is another way of saying that God is cold. In another regard God is even colder; for the acts God can be envisaged as performing suggest no sense of measure, that criterion by which Crane so often implies attitude or judgment. To make a gesture of pity for a babe God wreaks destruction worthy of an apocalypse. If you are a mouse, the price of being beckoned by The Hand is the roaring, moaning death of oceans amid the tumult of fishes and the cries of ships. The implication, one may conclude, is that the cost of sparing mouse or man would be so out of line that the consequences of doing so would be worse than not sparing them.

Against this divine might everything else in the scene looms little. The spar is slim, the waves are no more than points, and the horizon that is first smaller than the rim of a bottle is subsequently "smaller than a doomed assassin's cap."

> This term "assassin," which Crane, like Emily Dickinson, was curiously given to using in nonpolitical contexts, combines in portmanteau fashion the word *sin* with the signification of murder or killing. So the drowning man may be an assassin after all, since natural depravity, as

> first inherited by Cain and by him passed on, led to the murder of a brother. "Assassin" further suggests the desperation of the victim (the term derives from *hashish,* smoked in the Orient by hired murderers to induce frenzy); and the cap of a doomed assassin is a powerful image of what the drowning man sees as the waves close over his head.[25]

This generally persuasive commentary by Hoffman might be modified in two ways. First, the poem does not indicate that the man is less worthy of sustenance than the mice. It indicates, rather, as I have implied above, that neither is shown to be saved; the poem at no point goes beyond saying what *may* happen. Second, how does one know that God would have salvation in mind if he decided to beckon the mice? Given God's immense potential for destruction, something less affirmative than sustenance could await the mice. Supporting Hoffman's reading, on the other hand, is the possibility that the second series of apocalyptic events, involving oceans, fishes, and ships, stands in the same relation to the beckoning as the first series stands in relation to the gesture of pity toward a babe, in which case the latter act would indeed invite the reader to see a beneficent intention in the gesture. The second consideration is the nature of the cap, which is less likely to be a fez or stocking-cap, neither of which makes obvious sense in the context, than the cap pulled down over the eyes in military executions,[26] which makes perfect sense. The plausibility of this alternative is obviously enhanced by the fact that Crane knew a great deal about military matters. Third, the cap is doubtless what the man sees as the horizon shrinks down to the size of his submerging head, and the sky, first reeling and drunken as the man is tossed about, and then no sky, is also what he would see, and is equally dramatic, almost terrifyingly so. But by the end of the stanza the locus becomes problematic. Though "A pale hand sliding from a polished spar" could be a picture taken in by the man, it is just as likely that Crane is letting the reader see what the man does not see, and probably more likely, given the fact that the line is calmer and more detached than the preceding lines in the stanza.

The concluding details no longer represent what the man sees or knows:

> The puff of a coat imprisoning air.
> A face kissing the water-death
> A weary slow sway of a lost hand
> And the sea, the moving sea, the sea.
> God is cold.

It is the reader and not the man who sees and knows that the coat is puffing with air, and only some locus other than the man's could see his coat and his face and his hand as *a* coat and *a* face and *a* hand. By the last line the man is gone and only the sea remains, moving but unmoved. An unmoved sea is a cold sea, in the sense of being unfeeling or indifferent, qualities signified in the reiteration "God is cold." The quality of physical coldness must of course be present too; in "The Open Boat" it is the first thing the correspondent notes: "The coldness of the water was sad; it was tragic. This fact was somehow so mixed and confused with his opinion of his own situation that it seemed almost a proper reason for tears. The water was cold" (V, 90). Crane could have said that God, like the sea, was cold, or something of the sort. In the absence of such an assertion, "God is cold" assimilates whatever associations the reader may have between the two types of coldness, any of which is likely to give the refrain extra force. The proposition is more safely construed, in any case, as a description rather than a definition, if by the latter term one means a making-definite that is binding in all circumstances.

Crane widens his lens in poem 82 to take in the apocalyptic fears and hopes of an entire populace.

> Toward God a mighty hymn
> A song of collisions and cries
> Rumbling wheels, hoof-beats, bells,
> Welcomes, farewells, love-calls, final moans,
> Voice of joy, idiocy, warning, despair,
> The unknown appeals of brutes,
> The chanting of flowers
> The screams of cut trees,
> The senseless babble of hens and wise men –
> A cluttered incoherency that says at the stars:
> "O, God, save us!"

The poem turns inside out the theme of Ambrosian world harmony that inspires Whitman's "Out of the Cradle Endlessly Rocking," while offering much the same sort of catalogue Whitman would repudiate on the grounds of its negativity. Nothing is the way it should be in the desperate world the poet describes. The wise men engage in henlike babble and trees, which are supposedly inanimate, cry out in pain. The hymn of voices calls to God while in fact it is addressing the stars; the form of address might as well be a hum as a hymn, being so incoherent that the poet has to speak for it, for the "says" points to what the incoherency means rather than what it literally expresses. From the first line of the second stanza – "Toward God a mighty hymn" – Crane implies that there is a God to address. If that is the case, then the problem may be bad aim: The babble doesn't know in which direction God lies, a shortcoming that may be an important aspect of their general incoherency.

Poem 83 in the *War Is Kind* collection tells another story:

> Once a man clambering to the house-tops
> Appealed to the heavens.

With strong voice he called to the deaf spheres;
A warrior's shout he raised to the suns.
Lo, at last, there was a dot on the clouds,
And – at last and at last –
God – the sky was filled with armies.

An appeal to such spheres may be a problem not of aim but of audience, which may be deaf either in the sense of incapable of hearing or in the sense of being unwilling to listen. It could also be that the man's aim is wrong after all, that God lies in another direction but answers the appeal by an act of grace. Like Hopkins in "The Wreck of the Deutschland," but more unmistakably, Crane reports a moment of epiphany.

In the equally apocalyptic poem 115, the farther shore looks to be coming closer as Crane's stance resembles more than usual that of Whitman:

Then sing I of the supple-souled men
And the strong, strong gods
That shall meet in times hereafter
And the amaze of the gods
At the strength of the men.

More typical of Crane is poem 130, the "Battle Hymn," another experimental piece that tries to do too much in too many ways, but serves as a crucible for creating the superior hymn of "When a people reach the top of a hill":

All-feeling God, hear in the war-night
The rolling voices of a nation
. . . .
Mark well, mark well, Father of the Never-Ending Circles
And if the path, the new path, leads
Awry then in the forest of the lost standards
Suffer us to grope and bleed apace
For the wisdom is Thine.

The new path will lead to the same beyond in which the supple-souled men and the strong gods meet, provided that it is the true path. The uncertainty shown on this score dissolves, in any case, as the temperature of the rhetoric rises and the collective persona reveals itself to be firm in resolve and energetically militant:

For we go, we go in a lunge of a long blue corps
And – to Thee we commit our lifeless sons,
The convulsed and furious dead.
(They shall be white amid the smoking cane)
For, the seas shall not bar us;
The capped mountains shall not hold us back
We shall sweep and swarm through jungle and pool,

Then let the savage one bend his high chin
To see on his breast, the sullen glow of the death medals
. . . .
His prize is death, deep doom.

Crane is trying, one senses, to keep it simple, because that is what the basic issue is, and to be more or less elevated and Longinian in style without being oratorical. But of course the poem is very oratorical ("Then – O, God – then bare the great bronze arm"). It is also dense and overcharged at points, as in the Blakean line "Swing high the blaze of the chained stars," which almost sounds like something from one of the English poet's prophecies. The main difficulty resides, however, in trying to yoke close-at-hand history to vast spiritual matters, the very problem that reduces the effectiveness of Blake's *The French Revolution*.[27] The war-night, which also smacks of Blake, turns immediately into a national business, so that when Crane refers to "a people," any reader is disposed to think this means the American people, an assumption reinforced by the color of the corps. Allusions to the smoking cane and to "jungle and pool" suggest Cuba during the Spanish–American War as the time of the poem's composition. But this unnecessary and nasty war, with its news-hungry correspondents and philandering filibusters, is far from being a sufficient occasion to what is partly but importantly an occasional poem. When the collective persona commits its lifeless sons to a God who accepts the superiority of U.S. over Spanish foreign policy, Crane comes uncomfortably close to the rhetorical smokescreen that the apostrophes of "Do not weep, maiden, for war is kind" so effectively puncture.

There are some nice touches, nonetheless, the Biblical sounding "amid the smoking cane" being one example. Crane's other crack at a workable refrain falls short. Hoffman complains that "The chanting disintegrate and the two-faced eagle" represents "grammatical confusion," one of a series of objections he himself counters by implicitly praising "the suggestive, incantatory movement of incremental parallelism and functional refrain."[28] On the second score Hoffman is entirely right, and if one does not so readily agree with the first, one can still see why the point is raised. It is more precise to state, it seems to me, that the line is somewhat ambiguous; but this is a situation easily solved if we recognize that the poem is still in the mode of invocation that begins with "See" and then goes to "Bend and see." "Disintegrate" is in the same tense, which means that Crane is asking God to disintegrate the chanting and the two-faced eagle too. The chanting comes from "him of the many lungs," later "the savage one," who is responsible for the war to which the poem objects and would replace with the higher battle, aided by God, against such war.

It is on the path to victory over the savage, and not in the theatre of the present war, that the collective first-person commits the lifeless sons. As for the eagle, it is two-faced for carrying on that war – an additional consequence of which is the virtual civil war for which the poem calls – while purporting to symbolize the peace and harmony of *e pluribus unum*.

If "Blue Battalions" is equally militant it is less military.[29]

> When a people reach the top of a hill
> Then does God lean toward them
> Shortens tongues, lengthens arms.
> A vision of their dead comes to the weak.
> The moon shall not be too old
> Before the new battalions rise
> – Blue battalions –
> The moon shall not be too old
> When the children of change shall fall
> Before the new battalions
> – The blue battalions –

People is one of Crane's favorite words. He is already using it in his early news reports: "We, as a new people, are likely to conclude that our mechanical perfection, our structural precision, is certain to destroy all quality of sentiment in our devices, and so we prefer to grope in the past when people are not supposed to have had any structural precision" (VIII, 665; cf. VIII, 653). The association of people and nation (*OED* 1, 1292) continues in *The Red Badge of Courage* as news of a great war inspires Henry to enlist: "This voice of the people, rejoicing in the night, had made him shiver in a prolonged ecstasy of excitement" (II, 6). When Crane speaks of "the people of this stricken district" in "Nebraska's Bitter Fight for Life," he refers to those "belonging to a place or constituting a particular concourse, congregation, company or class" (*OED* 2, 1300). Allusion to an American Indian tribe as a people (X, 185) reminds us that the first sense entails races and tribes as well as nations. In Nebraska Crane also calls attention to "the profound and dogged courage of the American people who have come into the West" (VIII, 411), pointing to the composite ethnic nature of the American population.

People in "Blue Battalions" may also be a conflation, this time of senses one and two: sense one because they may be seen to constitute a broad community such as a tribe, race, or nation, sense two because they may constitute a smaller one as well; if the latter is the case, they resemble the "we" who in "Battle Hymn" set themselves against those fellow countrymen who would prolong an unjust war. Crane's noun is highly resonant, in any case, setting the stage as it does for an action not only of national but of cosmic magnitude. The hill the people climb is an important part of that action. Hills, mountains, and peaks abound in Crane's writings.

Hills are one of the first things seen in his war novel; Maggie imagines faraway places where, according to God, little hills sing, while in poem 26 "a mighty hill" looms before a seeker who, having once climbed through its regions of snow, discovers "gardens / Lying at impossible distances." Hills are connected with vision and the visionary. Sighted, they can serve as an orientation or a limit, a horizon, an obstacle, a form of communication, or, as in the case of the mighty hill just mentioned, a goal. Although this is its role in "Blue Battalions" as well, in the latter there is no disappointing discovery of distances. Distance in Crane's second battle hymn is temporal and bridgeable, being a space of future time in which the rise of the new God-led battalions is imminent. The poem promises that distance will eventually be overcome through desire, thanks to the intercession of God.

"When a people reach the top of a hill" is not only a hymn in prose, as already observed, but a much better one than "Battle Hymn." Whereas the latter does not clearly delimit the nature and function of its parts, "Blue Battalions" does. In each of the three stanzas a four-line sequence establishes a basic situation, first in the present tense, then in the future, then again in the present, while the inset choral lines counterpoint with "Blue battalions" as the refrain. The chorus also has a temporal function: When the opening lines of the first stanza finish their work in the present tense, the chorus pick up in the future: "The moon shall not be too old / Before the new battalions rise."

The opening lines of the second stanza follow the lead of the preceding chorus by continuing in the future tense:

> Mistakes and virtues will be trampled deep
> A church and a thief shall fall together
> A sword will come at the bidding of the eyeless,
> The God-led, turning only to beckon.

At this point the ensuing chorus reverses the direction of the opening lines by returning to the present tense, but not to the same space of time established in stanza one:

> Swinging a creed like a censer
> At the head of the new battalions
>   – Blue battalions –
> March the tools of nature's impulse
> Men born of wrong, men born of right
> Men of the new battalions
>   – Blue battalions –

The present tense serves a preparatory function in the first stanza, explaining how God meets the climbing people halfway, bending toward them in order – by lengthening arms and shortening tongues – to let their actions speak louder than their words. By contrast, the present tense in the second chorus describes a later time when the conditions set forth early in the stanza, such as the falling together of church and thief, are envisaged as having already come about. The blue battalions are not a phenomenon to be anticipated but one to be witnessed here and now.

The final stanza's opening lines continue the focus on the present, which, as the poet turns to prayer, is seen in the chorus to be continuous with the future:

> Then swift as they charge through a shadow,
> The men of the new battalions
> – Blue battalions –
> God lead them high. God lead them far
> Lead them far, lead them high
> These new battalions,
> – The blue battalions

These last, strongly rhythmic repetitions need to be taken more or less musically. Music plays a more prominent role in Crane's canon than is commonly realized, from the "heroic song" (VII, 42) that Henry whistles in "The Monster" to the "cruel and monotonous music" chanted by Whilomville children, signifying in both cases Chaucer's "Sounds in melodic or harmonic combination" (*OED* 2, 1381). Specific songs are legion, as in "Pull for the Shore, Sailor, Pull for the Shore," and the ever-popular "Boom-de-ay," and often Crane provides the text as well (VIII, 120).

Crane is very fond of *hymn,* which he usually employs in the prose, in a figurative sense, as in "a hymn of twilight" (II, 49) and "the hymn of the end." *Chorus* functions in a similar way in "the chanted chorus of the trees" (II, 49) and "A chorus of colors" (X, 60), in contrast to the literal "Grand chorus" (VIII, 46) at the end of a parodic musical "happening" roughly corresponding to what were once called musical "varieties." A report on a musical review featuring "Rule Britannia" comes to a climax with a minstrel-show song entitled "Hev' you seen a colored coon called Pete!", recalling Crane's early "Grand Concert" (VIII, 611). Comments on numerous other musical performances, singers, and instrumentalists appear in a variety of reports and sketches; nor should we forget the play with music for which Crane wrote the script while at Brede Place, and that Crane himself was the leading tenor in a church choir.[30] Notable too are evocative uses of musicality, as in "a firing-line . . . is nothing less than an emotional chord, a chord of a harp that sings because a puff of air arrives or when a bit of down touches it" (VI, 129). A passage from "The Pace of Youth," in which band music is heard from a pavilion, has something almost visionary about it: "They walked home by the lakeside way and out upon the water those gay paper lanterns sang to them, sang a chorus of red and violet and green and gold, a song of mystic lands of the future" (V, 10).

Crane's interest in rhythm is everywhere apparent, not least in the use of the term, as when "they took their trot about the deck in perfect rhythm to the music of the band" (IX, 112), signifying "Movement marked by the regulated succession of strong and weak elements, or of opposite or different conditions"(*OED*,7.*gen.*, 1855). It is not surprising, given Crane's penchant for archaisms, that he prefers the older *rhythmical* over *rhythmic,* which sprang up in Britain during the American Civil War; in Crane's novel about the war, interestingly, one finds "rhythmical noises" (II, 46) and its adverbial counterpart as well (II, 22).

As in musical structure, word position and sequence, while satisfying an innate desire for pattern and recurrence, also work incrementally, in the manner of a *crescendo,* to increase volume and intensity. Once "blue battalions" is positioned after "new battalions," the ensuing sequences in which the same words occur add little or nothing of distinct semantic novelty. Rather, they first hypostatize, then confirm a presence, a four-beat rhythmic vowel and consonant series with a halo effect on other word positions and sequences, such as occurs when one hears a *leitmotiv*. With each return of the word series the new–blue battalions become more present, more here and now, more real, and at the same time they are mnemonically intensified, such that this musical phrase, without being a phrase in actual music, echoes like one, lingering, fading, then returning in full force like the onomastic presences that sound forth at the climax of certain tales by the highly musical Poe: At the end of "Ligeia," "Morella," and "Eleanora" the narrator rings out each heroine's euphonic name. Musicalized repetition taps some reservoir of affectivity that other arts seem to tap less directly and spontaneously. Energized by this source, the repeated terms lift themselves to a higher emotional power, meaning "more" than the words say *sensu strictu* – the point that Poe keeps trying to make in his aesthetic writings as well as his poems. The onomatopoeic *Ulalume* comes to express the very ululation of grief much as blue battalions come to express the very essence of new spiritual militancy on the march.

The *crescendo* effect at the end of poem 125 is enhanced by the increase in tempo that begins in the line "Then swift as they charge through a shadow." Normally an adjective, *swift* is here an adverb, a medieval application now sanctioned lexically only for poetic purposes. The sense may be "great speed or velocity," in a short period of time, or "after a very short, or no, interval of time" (*OED adv*. 1, 2, 3), and is likely a conflation of all three, the idea being that the battalions are charging with speed *and* without delay. The *crescendo* effect is further enhanced by the strong beats in the imperative of the invocation. The lines can be scanned, to be sure, on the pattern of *la-dee-da* metrics: "Gŏd leád thĕm hígh. Gŏd léad thĕm fár / Léad thĕm fár, léad thĕm hígh." But Crane, as we have amply seen, is as spondaic as possible under a given circumstance, and the circumstance here is all energy and assertiveness and intensity and speed, hence: "Gód leád thém hígh. Gód leád thém fár / Léad thém fár, leád thém hígh." This poem is no thing of piping ditties but a thing of blaring trumpets and rolling drums.

Attention now turns to three cruxes, the first of which is the relation of "the children of change" to the battalions in the first stanza. " 'The children of change are the fallible mortals who in their unwisdom rule the earth, and "change" is the false god they praise.' "[31] Given Crane's concern for duty and fidelity, change may imply, somewhat more specifically, a pattern of inconstancy on the part of the people, a lack of conviction with respect to their god, of the sort that Biblical prophets were wont to denounce. Doesn't the adjective in "new battalions" itself signify change, however? It goes, but the change is of a different order entirely. At issue is a genuine and permanent transformation, an apocalyptic conversion: After this change there shall be no other.

Hoffman wisely approaches the second crux, "the eyeless" of the second stanza, by quoting a letter from Crane:

> "Tolstoy's aim is, I suppose – I believe – to make himself good. It is an incomparably quixotic task for any man to undertake. He will not succeed; but he will even succeed more than he can ever himself know, and so at his nearest point to success, he will be proportionately blind. This is the pay of this kind of greatness." If this has any bearing on the poem, we may interpolate, "A sword will come at the bidding of the wholly good."[32]

The quotation does indeed have bearing on the poem, though the assumption underlying Crane's words – that the eyeless are the wholly good – is not quite unpacked by the words themselves. The assumption is supplied by Arendt, who remarks that "the moment a good work becomes known and public, it loses its specific character of goodness, of being done for nothing but goodness' sake. When goodness appears openly, it is no longer goodness. . . . Goodness can exist only when it is not perceived, not even by its author. . . ."[33] Thus the following, from poem 18:

> Presently God said:
> "And what did you do"
> The little blade answered: "Oh, my lord,
> "Memory is bitter to me
> "For if I did good deeds
> "I know not of them."
> Then God in all His splendor

Arose from His throne.
"Oh, best little blade of grass," He said.

Crux three, "the tools of nature's impulse," echoes the views of Crane's minister father, who regards as blameless even the impulse that opposes right behavior.[34] In *The Red Badge of Courage* nature appears in the colors and changes of the opening scene, the sky with its wafer, the squirrel taken for a symbol, the "golden processes" that go on during battle, and the ray of sun at the conclusion, to name but a few examples. Nature in Crane's pastoral scenes is something "with a deep simple heart" (III, 328), which women seem able to peer into, but is also the source of the storm that swirls around the blue hotel and throws Nebraskans into physical and economic misery. Nature is the color of the sky, which the men in a boat do not know, and is equally the colors of the sea, which they do know. It is human beings in themselves and in their relations to the landscape, especially the sky, the sea, and the earth, and the traditional elements, of which the two most prominent in Crane are air and fire; and nature is animals, of which there are examples too numerous to cite, but the chief of which are horses, birds, bears, panthers, and snakes:

> Suddenly from some unknown and yet near place in advance there came a dry shrill whistling rattle that smote motion instantly from the limbs of the man and the dog. Like the fingers of a sudden death, this sound seemed to touch the man at the nape of the neck, at the top of the spine, and change him, as swift as thought, to a statue of listening horror, surprise, rage. (VIII, 65)

Santayana might have had this passage before him when he observed: "Though hardly in itself poetry, an animal cry, when still audible in human language, renders it also the unanswerable, the ultimate voice of nature." Here is the very cry of nature's impulse, of which animal being is, in Crane's sense, the tool, even as are his marching men – a view more than a little reminiscent of Blake's vision of creatural existence. "There is no utterance so thrilling as that of absolute impulse," Santayana continues, "if absolute impulse has learned to speak at all." When all human interests are fused together – animal, social, and moral alike – when all then fasten intently on one idea, the resulting power of expression is a thing unmatched, as exemplified by the contributions of the Hebrew prophets to the leading source of borrowings in Crane, the Bible; and the philosopher finds in them certain qualities also evident in Crane at his best. "The age of these prophets possessed . . . a fresh and homely vocabulary; and the result was an eloquence so elemental and combative, so imaginative and so bitterly practical, that the world has never heard its like. Such singlemindedness, with such heroic simplicity in words and images, is hardly possible in a late civilisation. Cultivated poets are not unconsciously sublime."[35] By the philosopher's standards, Crane cannot be unconsciously sublime, which is another way of saying he is a sentimental poet in Schiller's sense: "In the state of civilisation . . . when this harmonious competition of the whole of human nature is no longer anything but an idea, the part of the poet is necessarily to raise reality to the ideal, or what amounts to the same thing, *to represent the ideal.*"[36] A modern poet like Crane will discover that war is not distinctly Homeric but that distinctly Biblical modes of expression are still viable if properly fitted into a given context and modified where necessary. Thus "a tree-shaded land, where everything was peace" (I, 129) echoes Job 1.21, and "it will rain for forty days and forty nights" (VIII, 253) echoes Gen. 7.4, to cite but two of many instances. That Crane is not oblivious to this practice is demonstrated in a Whilomville tale by "the rains came and the winds blew in the most biblical way when a certain fact came to light" (VII, 137).[37]

The invocation to the seven mad gods of the sea in "The Open Boat" is in the nature of an oath, a common mode of expression in Crane, in comparison with prayer, which is infrequent. An exception is the ironic invocation to Popocatepetl in the fable "The Voice of the Mountains," and the chant of the five white mice borders on this mode. But "Blue Battalions" exhibits several features characteristic of Biblical nonpsalmic prose prayer, which, according to Moshe Greenberg[38] offers, *inter alia,* petition ("God lead them high. God lead them far") and narrative (the story line in the three stanzas). The poem approximates a third feature, prophetic oracle, by predicting the apocalyptic appearance of the blue battalions. All three features add considerably to the already considerable resonance of the poem.

To deploy such features in a new context is, in a sense, to make them over, and the same applies to direct quotation.

> Whenever a word appears in a radically new context it has a radically new sense: the expression in which it so figures is a poetic figment, a fresh literary creation. Such invention is sometimes perverse, sometimes humorous, sometimes sublime; that is, it may either buffet old associations without enlarging them, or give them a plausible but impossible twist, or enlarge them to cover, with unexpected propriety, a much wider or more momentous experience.[39]

This is a fair representation not only of Crane's practices but of the techniques of Melville, Whitman, or Hawthorne, or, for that matter, John Berryman, who wrote the first major study of Crane. The emphasis at the present juncture falls, however, on the third characterization, "sublime," which is precisely the quality in "Blue Battalions" that I have been trying to get at:

> The force of experience in any moment – if we abstract from represented values – is emotional so that for sublime poetry what is required is to tap some reservoir of feeling. If a phrase opens the flood-gates of emotion, it has made itself most deeply significant. Its discursive range and clearness may not be remarkable; its emotional power will quite suffice.[40]

In feeling, structure, tone, mood, and diction, "When a people reach the top of a hill" meets the criteria for sublime poetry, which Josephine Miles sees as central in American literature: "This 'tenth muse lately sprung up in America' was more Hebraic than the other nine muses; and sought sometimes the high style of ceremony, not always the low style of colloquy, because she held strongly to Biblical and Pindaric tradition."[41] The qualification of "sometimes" applies equally to Crane, who employs all three levels of style, the so-called low, middle, and high, as well as satire, grotesquerie, and word-death. But in "Blue Battalions," and less successfully in "Battle Hymn," Crane gives poetic form to impulses that elsewhere lead to the military sublime, an uplifted and uplifting form that transfigures secular militarism into militant spirituality. It may also be taken to represent the emotional power of Crane's art in general. The power comes, at least in part, from the ability to express the large in the little, the presence of eternity in a grain of sand, as Blake would have it, or of the godhead in a wasp, as Edward Taylor would have it.[42] The power comes from energy of impulse fused into image and event, another impulse from nature in Crane's sense: "Every animal when goaded becomes intense; and it is perhaps merely the apathy in which mortals are wont to live that keeps them from being habitually sublime in their sentiments."[43]

Crane keeps that intensity so alive at times that it broaches the unreal real and the limits of expression: "and as each new impulse bubbles to the surface he feels himself on the verge of some inexpressible heaven or hell. He needs but to abandon himself to that seething chaos which perpetually underlies conventional sanity . . . to find himself at once in a magic world, irrecoverable, largely unmeaning, terribly intricate, but, as he will conceive, deep, inward, and absolutely real." The scene of such experience is the soul, by which is meant, not a doctrinal entity or essence, but "an animating current widely diffused throughout the cosmos, a breath uncreated and immortal as a whole, but at each point entering some particular body and quitting it, in order to mingle with the air, the light, the nether darkness, or the life of the god from which it came."[44] A scene thus expanded is a fitting one for Crane, who keeps one eye on the blade of grass and the other on the color of the sky, who stands squarely in the here and now while peering intensely at the farther shore, who travels the realm of primordial experience and lives to write of it. This writing is made possible not only by his personal gifts but the inherent discursive potential in such experience:

> In this muddy torrent words also may be carried down; and if these words are by chance strung together into a cadence, and are afterwards written down, they may remain for a memento of that moment. Such words will have some quality – some rhyme or rhythm – that makes it memorable. . . . For the man himself . . . they may consequently have a considerable power of suggestion, and they may even have it for others, whenever the rhythm and incantation avail to plunge them also into a similar trance.[45]

Which is to say, not that Crane is possessed, but that his art possesses.

The readers it affects the most, where the sublime is concerned, are probably those who are looking for something besides discursive range and clearness. Now Crane himself has such range and clearness, as attested by the variety of his techniques, themes, perspectives, and ideas, a variety so broad as to defy any summative characterization. No category has ever corralled him or ever will, as indicated by, among the other things, attempts to tag him as a naturalist, an impressionist, an expressionist, a realist, and an existentialist, and to discern in his ideas signs of skepticism, atheism, agnosticism, and piety, depending on whether the labeler believes that Crane continues in the religious tradition of his Methodist forbears, makes nominal use of it *faute de mieux* or out of habit, uses it without being certain of what he thinks or wants the reader to think of it, rebels against it on occasion, or rejects it altogether. Crane has discursive range and clearness enough, but he offers rhythm and incantation too, and grotesquerie and comedy, and a passion for earthly fraternity, and something even beyond that. The challenge to comprehend him in this regard comes not only from his inimitable way of seeing and saying, but from the company he keeps; for surely he belongs with those who stretch forth their hands, through love of the farther shore.

Notes

1. Introduction

1 Joseph Conrad, *Last Essays* (New York: Doubleday, Page & Company, 1926), p. 103.

2 Conrad, p. 103.

3 Tony Tanner, *The Reign of Wonder: Naivety and Reality in American Literature* (1965; rpt. New York: Harper & Row, 1967), p. 10.

4 R. W. Stallman, *Stephen Crane: An Omnibus* (New York: Knopf, 1952), p. *xxxix,* is apparently the first critic to have insisted on Crane's plurality of styles. Crane's extensive use of parody, and what comes to replace it, is examined by Eric Solomon, *Stephen Crane: From Parody to Realism* (Cambridge, Mass.: Harvard Univ. Press, 1966). The relation of stylistic questions to questions about knowledge – which will become a focus later in this chapter – is addressed by Frank Bergon in "Voices of Perception: Crane's Prose Style," the first chapter of Bergon's *Stephen Crane's Artistry* (New York: Columbia Univ. Press, 1975), pp. 1–29.

5 Larzer Ziff, *The American 1890s: Life and Times of a Lost Generation* (New York: Viking, 1966), pp. 185–6.

6 Kenneth Burke, *Language as Symbolic Action: Essays on Life, Literature, and Method* (Berkeley: Univ. of California Press, 1968), pp. 37*ff.*

7 Quoted in Eric Solomon, *Stephen Crane in England* (Columbus: Ohio State Univ. Press, 1964), p. 67.

8 Henry David Thoreau, *Walden* (Harmondsworth: Penguin, 1983), p. 373.

9 Kenneth Burke, *The Philosophy of Literary Form: Studies in Symbolic Action,* 3rd ed. (1941; rpt. Berkeley: Univ. of California Press, 1973), p. 144.

10 Stallman, *Stephen Crane: An Omnibus,* p. *xx.*

11 Preface to *Stephen Crane,* rev. ed. (New York: Twayne, 1980). The most recent review of the critical tradition, as of this date, is by Chester L. Wolford, *The Anger of Stephen Crane: Fiction and the Epic Tradition* (Lincoln: Univ. of Nebraska Press, 1983), pp. 6–15.

12 The translation, by E. J. Trechmann, is furnished by Erich Auerbach in *Mimesis: The Representation of Reality in Western Literature* (Princeton: Princeton Univ. Press, 1953), pp. 286, 287. On the contradictions in Crane's personality see Thomas Gullason, *The Complete Novels of Stephen Crane* (New York: Doubleday,

1967), p. 19. On the contradictions in his reputation see Stallman, *Stephen Crane: An Omnibus,* p. *xxi.*

13 Alexis de Tocqueville, *Democracy in America* (New York: Random House–Vintage, 1954), I, 443.

14 Arnold, *A Study of History* (Oxford: Oxford Univ. Press, 1961), XII, 278.

15 *America: A Dutch Historian's Vision from Afar and Near,* trans. Herbert H. Rowen (New York: Harper & Row, 1972), pp. 32–3.

16 Alan Simpson, *Puritanism in Old and New England* (Chicago: Univ. of Chicago Press, 1955), p. 23.

17 Wilson Carey McWilliams, *The Idea of Fraternity in America* (Berkeley: Univ. of California Press, 1973), p. 475. Other key aspects of the late nineteenth-century American cultural milieu are discussed by Eric J. Sundquist in "The Country of the Blue," the introduction to his *American Realism: New Essays* (Baltimore: Johns Hopkins Univ. Press, 1982), pp. 3–24.

18 Quoted in David Levin, *History as Romantic Art: Bancroft, Prescott, Motley, and Parkman* (Stanford: Stanford Univ. Press, 1959), p. 62. The examples I employ are drawn from Levin.

19 *The Complete Tales of Henry James,* ed. Leon Edel (New York: Lippincott, 1961), I, 50–1.

20 *The Collected Works of Ambrose Bierce* (New York and Washington: Neale, 1909–1912), I, 374–6.

21 *The Collected Works of Ambrose Bierce,* I, 376–7.

22 Citations for Crane are to *The Works of Stephen Crane,* ed. Fredson Bowers, 10 vols. (Charlottesville: Univ. of Virginia Press, 1969–1975); further references appear parenthetically by volume and page number. Citations from the correspondence are to *Stephen Crane: Letters,* ed. R. W. Stallman and Lillian Gilkes (New York: New York Univ. Press, 1960), hereafter cited parenthetically as *Letters,* followed by the page number.

23 *The Yellow Book: Quintessence of the Nineties,* ed. Stanley Weintraub (New York: Doubleday, 1964), p. 351.

24 Sergio Perosa, "Naturalism and Impressionism in Stephen Crane's Fiction" in *Stephen Crane: A Collection of Critical Essays,* ed. Maurice Bassan (Englewood Cliffs, N.J.: Prentice Hall, 1967), p. 88. On Crane's "epistemological existentialism" see Donna Gerstenberger, " 'The Open Boat': Additional Perspectives," *Modern Fiction Studies* 17 (1971–1972): 577–61.

25 See Yosal Rogat, "The Judge as Spectator," *University of Chicago Law Review* 31 (1964): 213–56.

26 *Linguistics and Literary History: Essays in Stylistics* (Princeton: Princeton Univ. Press, 1948), p. 73.

27 *Eras and Modes in English Poetry,* 2nd ed. (Berkeley: Univ. of California Press, 1964), p. 238.

2. The Little

1 Lewis Mumford, *Technics and Civilization* (1934; rpt. with new introduction, New York: Harcourt Brace Jovanovich, 1963), p. 126.

2 *The Human Condition* (Chicago: Univ. of Chicago, 1958), p. 52.

3 Marcel Proust, *Remembrance of Things Past,* trans. C. K. Scott Moncrieff (New York: Random House, 1934), I, 158–9.

4 Walter Pater, *The Renaissance: Studies in Art and Poetry,* ed. Donald L. Hill (Berkeley: Univ. of California, 1980), pp. 110–11.

5 Hamlin Garland, *Main-Travelled Roads* (New York: New American Library, 1962). Page references in parentheses are to this edition. Crane may also have been influenced by the "little captain" in Whitman's "Song of Myself."

6 Ambrose Bierce, *In the Midst of Life and Other Tales* (New York: New American Library, 1961), p. 33.

7 *In the Midst of Life,* p. 33.

8 *Emerson's Essays* (New York: Crowell, 1936), p. 389.

9 Henry David Thoreau, *Walden* (Harmondsworth: Penguin, 1983), p. 336.

10 "The Genteel Tradition in American Philosophy" in George Santayana, *Winds of Doctrine* (New York: Harper, 1957), p. 199.

11 *Adventures of Huckleberry Finn,* eds. Sculley Bradley, Richmond Croom Beatty, and E. Hudson Long (New York: Norton, 1961), p. 230.

12 Joseph Katz, quoted by R. W. Stallman in the introduction to his edition of *Sullivan County Tales and Sketches* (Ames: Iowa State Univ. Press, 1968), p. 17.

13 *Cf.* Frank Bergon, *Stephen Crane's Artistry* (New York: Columbia Univ. Press, 1975), p. 18.

14 See "A reinterpretation of 'The Fall of the House of Usher' " in Leo Spitzer, *Essays on English and American Literature,* ed. Anna Hatcher (Princeton: Princeton Univ. Press, 1962), pp. 51–66.

15 Daniel Defoe, *Robinson Crusoe* (New York: Random House, 1948), pp. 58–9.

16 *Stephen Crane: From Parody to Realism* (Cambridge, Mass.: Harvard Univ. Press, 1966).

17 The significance of this for an overall understanding of Crane is demonstrated by James B. Colvert, "Stephen Crane's Magic Mountain," in *Stephen Crane: A Collection of Critical Essays,* ed. Maurice Bassan (Englewood Cliffs, N.J.: Prentice-Hall, 1967), pp. 96–105.

18 "The Structural Study of Myth" in Claude Lévi-Strauss, *Structural Anthropology,* trans. Claire Jacobson and Brooke Grundfest Schoepf (New York: Basic Books, 1963), pp. 206–31.

19 Mircea Eliade, *The Sacred and the Profane: The Nature of Religion,* trans. Williard R. Trask (1959; rpt. New York: Harper & Row, 1961), p. 26.

20 On the basis of common techniques of narrative handling, diction, tone, and point of view, Crane's fables would include "The Voice of the Mountain" (May 1895), "How the Donkey Lifted the Hills" (June 1895), "The Victory of the Moon" (July 1895), and "The Judgment of the Sage" (January 1896), in VIII, 88–98. William L. Andrews, "A New Stephen Crane Fable," *American Literature* 47 (1975), 113–14, would add to the canon "How the Ocean Was Formed," written in early 1894.

21 Leo Spitzer, "Classical and Christian Ideas of World Harmony (Prolegomena to the Interpretation of the Word 'Stimmung')," *Traditio* 2 (1944), 409–64, and 3 (1945), 307–64.

22 *The Principles of Psychology* (1890; rpt. New York: Dover, 1950), II, 593.

23 Rudolf Otto, *The Idea of the Holy: An Inquiry into the Non-Rational Factor in the Idea of the Divine and Its Relation to the Rational,* ed. John W. Harvey (1923; rpt. New York: Oxford Univ. Press, 1958), p. 26.

24 Kenneth Burke, *Language as Symbolic Action* (Berkeley and Los Angeles: Univ. of California, 1968), p. 386.

3. Conflict as Condition

1 Donald Pizer, "Stephen Crane's *Maggie* and American Naturalism," *Criticism* 7 (Spring 1965): 168–75, brings out the chivalric aspects of Jimmie's defense of social honor and finds the key to Bowery morality in this and other instances of theatricality. On this topic see Elizabeth Burns, *Theatricality: A Study of Convention in the Theatre and in Social Life* (New York: Harper & Row, 1972), and Erving Goffman, *The Presentation of Self in Everyday Life* (New York: Doubleday, 1959).

2 David M. Fine, "Abraham Cahan, Stephen Crane and the Romantic Tenement Tales of the Nineties," *American Studies* 14 (1973): 95–107; *cf.* Thomas A. Gullason, "The Prophetic City in Stephen Crane's 1893 *Maggie,*" *Modern Fiction Studies* 24, 1 (1978): 129–38.

3 *The Collected Papers of Charles Sanders Peirce,* ed. Charles Hartshorne and Paul Weiss, Vols. 1–6, and Arthur W. Burks, Vols. 7 and 8 (Cambridge, Mass.: Harvard Univ. Press, 1931–1935/1958), 8.346. Hereafter I follow the established practice of citing volume and page number parenthetically.

4 Charles Dickens, Preface to *The Old Curiosity Shop* (Garden City: Doubleday, 1961), p. 6.

5 "Die Briefe des Zurückgekehrten" in Hugo von Hofmannsthal, *Ausgewählte Werke in zwei Bänden,* ed. Rudolph Hirsch (Frankfurt: Fischer, 1971), II, 484.

6 *Science and the Modern World* (1925; rpt. New York: Free Press, 1967), p. 64.

7 On the parodic aspect of the portrait see Solomon, *Stephen Crane: From Parody to Realism,* p. 39.

8 Jan Mukařovský, "Standard Language and Poetic Language," in *A Prague School Reader on Esthetics, Literary Structure, and Style,* trans. Paul L. Garvin (Washington, D.C.: Georgetown Univ. Press, 1964), pp. 17–30.

9 *Mimesis: The Representation of Reality in Western Literature,* trans. Willard R. Trask (Princeton: Princeton Univ. Press, 1953), p. 189.

10 *Attitudes toward History* (1937; rev. 2nd ed. Boston: Beacon, 1961), pp. 308–14.

11 See the bibliographical essay in *Readings in Existential Phenomenology,* ed. Nathaniel Lawrence and Daniel O'Connor (Englewood Cliffs, N.J.: Prentice-Hall, 1967), pp. 404–5; Ludwig Binswanger, *Henrik Ibsen und das Problem der Selbstrealisation in der Kunst* (Heidelberg: Lambert Schneider, 1949), and David Halliburton, *Edgar Allan Poe: A Phenomenological View* (Princeton: Princeton Univ. Press, 1973), pp. 263*ff.*

12 *From Max Weber: Essays in Sociology,* trans. and ed. H. H. Berth and C. Wright Mills (New York: Oxford Univ. Press, 1946), pp. 192–3.

13 *The Ethics of Aristotle,* ed. J. A. K. Thomson (1953; rpt. London: Penguin Classics, 1970), p. 66.

14 *Mimesis,* pp. 468 *ff.*

15 *Principles of Psychology,* I, 439–40.

16 *Rumor and Reflection* (New York: Simon and Schuster, 1952), p. 181.

17 *Deceit, Desire, and the Novel: Self and Other in Literary Structure,* trans. Yvonne Freccero (Baltimore: Johns Hopkins Univ. Press, 1965). Girard considerably modifies and greatly expands his methodology in *Le Violence et le sacré* (Paris: Grasset, 1972); but his earlier interpretation of desire in the novel remains useful, as in the present case.

18 Frank W. Noxon, "The Real Stephen Crane," *Chicago Step-Ladder* 14 (January 1938): 4–9, first called attention to Crane's knowledge of Goethe's theory of color. See also Robert L. Hough, "Crane and Goethe: A Forgotten Relationship," *Nineteenth-Century Fiction* 18 (September 1962): 135–48; Stallman, "Stephen Crane: A Revaluation" in *Critiques and Essays on Modern Fiction: 1920–1951: Representing the Achievement of Modern American and British Critics,* ed. John W. Aldridge (New York: Ronald, 1952), pp. 244–69 (see esp. pp. 252–4); Stallman, *Stephen Crane: An Omnibus* (New York: Knopf, 1952), pp. 185–7; Robert C. Basye, "Color Imagery in Stephen Crane's Poetry," *American Literary Realism, 1870–1910* 13 (1980): 122–31; and Katharine G. Simoneaux, "Color Imagery in Crane's *Maggie: A Girl of the Streets,*" *College Language Association Journal* [Morgan State Univ., West Virginia] 18 (1974): 91–100, which offers a precise tabulation of the colors in *Maggie* and explores their significance.

19 Crane's expressionist tendencies have been noted by Bergon, *Stephen Crane's Artistry,* p. 72; Bill Christopherson, "Stephen Crane's 'The Upturned Face': An Expressionist Fiction," *Arizona Quarterly* 38 (2) (Summer 1982): 147–61; Charles Walcutt, *American Literary Naturalism: A Divided Stream* (Minneapolis: Univ. of Minnesota Press, 1956), p. 86; David Werner, *The City as Metaphor* (New York: Random House, 1966), pp. 55*ff.;* Jean Cazemajou, "*The Red Badge of Courage:* The 'Religion of Peace' and the War Archetype," in *Stephen Crane in Transition; Centenary Essays,* ed. Joseph Katz (Dekalb: Northern Illinois Univ. Press, 1972), pp. 59, 63; and Thomas A. Gullason, "Tragedy and Melodrama in Stephen Crane's *Maggie,*" in *Maggie: A Girl of the Streets (A Story of New York),* ed. Thomas A. Gullason (New York: Norton, 1979), p. 249. Milne Holton, *Cylinder of Vision: The Fiction and Journalistic Writing of Stephen Crane* (Baton Rouge: Louisiana State Univ. Press, 1972) considers the possibility that Crane produces expressionism, but decides that "*dramatic impressionism*" (p. 2) is more fitting. He nonetheless finds that in Chapter 17 of *Maggie* Crane comes closer "to real expressionism" than at any time before "The Blue Hotel" and on the same page notes the "impressionistic rendering of scene" in the chapter. He also finds in an early scene a correlate of qualities in the painting of Edvard Munch, who is often regarded as a major forerunner of the Expressionist movement.

20 Goethe citations are from Hough (see n. 18).

21 *The Complete Works of Edgar Allen Poe,* the "Virginia Edition," ed. James A. Harrison (New York: University Society, 1902), XIV, 128.

22 *Cf.* Thomas A. Gullason, in "The Permanence of Stephen Crane," *Studies* *in the Novel* 10 (1978): 89, and Ada Farrag Graff, "Metaphor and Metonymy: The Two Worlds of Crane's *Maggie*," *English Studies in Canada* 8, 4 (1982): 432–3.

23 On Talmage and Brace see R. W. Stallman, *Stephen Crane: A Biography* (New York: Braziller, 1968), p. 73; on Fawcett see Solomon, *Stephen Crane: From Parody to Realism,* pp. 25–6. *Cf.* Thomas A. Gullason, "The Prophetic City in Stephen Crane's *Maggie*," *Modern Fiction Studies* 24 (1978): 129–37.

24 See Marcus Cunliffe, "Stephen Crane and the American Background of *Maggie*," *American Quarterly* 7 (Spring 1955): 37.

25 Solomon, *Stephen Crane: From Parody to Realism,* pp. 33–4.

26 Jean-Paul Sartre, *Search for a Method,* trans. Hazel E. Barnes (New York: Knopf, 1963), pp. 163–4.

27 *Stephen Crane: Letters,* ed. R. W. Stallman and Lillian Gilkes (New York: New York Univ. Press, 1960), p. 133.

4. Doing Without

1 James B. Colvert, "Introduction" to *George's Mother,* I, 103*ff.*

2 *Letters,* p. 158.

3 Albert Camus, *L'Etranger* (Paris: Gallimard, 1944), p. 9.

4 "The Color of This Soul," the final chapter of Berryman's literary biography, argues at length for the application to Crane of a theory espoused by Freud, and is far and away the most controversial aspect of this seminal book.

5 *Creative Fidelity,* trans. Robert Rosthal (New York: Farrar, Straus and Giroux, 1964), pp. 154–6.

6 *The Human Condition* (Chicago: Univ. of Chicago Press, 1958), pp. 8–9.

7 See *From Max Weber: Essays in Sociology,* trans. and ed. H. H. Gerth and G. Wright Mills (1946; rpt. New York: Oxford Univ. Press, 1958), p. 193.

8 Wilson Carey McWilliams, *The Idea of Fraternity in America* (Berkeley: Univ. of California Press, 1973), pp. 379–80. *Cf.* Johann Huizinga, *America: A Dutch Historian's Vision, from Afar and Near,* trans. Herbert H. Rowen (Harper & Row, 1972), pp. 32*ff.*

9 Jean-Paul Sartre, *Critique of Dialectical Reason,* trans. Alan Sheridan-Smith, ed. Jonathan Ree (London: New Left Books, 1976), p. 430.

10 Max Scheler, *The Nature of Sympathy,* trans. Peter Heath (London: Routledge & Kegan Paul, 1954), p. 152.

12 Thorstein Veblen, *The Theory of the Leisure Class* (1899, 1912; rpt. New York: New American Library, 1953), p. 210. If Crane does not demonstrate explicit knowledge of this trend, it is hard to imagine that he was unaware of it, given the religious environment in which he was raised, his reporting on religious activities, the sensitivity to trends that marks his coverage of events, and above all given the public pronouncements by clergymen and the fact that a reliable contemporary like Veblen could report the "belief" as "current."

13 Henry James, *The Princess Casamassima* (1886; rpt. New York: Harper & Row, 1962), p. 410.

14 Richard Hofstadter, *The Age of Reform* (New York: Knopf, 1955), p. 82. For works on the city see John Z. Guzlowski and Yvonne Shikany Eddy, "Studies of the Modern Novel and the City: A Selected Checklist," *Modern Fiction Studies* 24 (1978): 145, 147–53).

15 "And just as the driver of a newly-come car with a blue light began to blow his whistle and pound his dash board and the green conductor began to ring his bell like a demon which drove the green driver mad and made him rise up and blow and pound as no man ever blew or pounded before, which made the red conductor lose the last vestige of control of himself and caused him to bounce up and down on his bell strap as he grasped it with both hands in a wild, maniacal dance, which of course served to drive uncertain Reason from her tottering throne in the red driver, who dropped his whistle and his hook and began to yell, and ki-yi and whoop harder than the worst personal devil encountered by the sternest of Scotch Presbyterians ever yelled and ki-yied and whooped on the darkest night after the good man had drunk the most hot Scotch whiskey; just then the left-hand forward wheel on the rear van fell off and the axle went down" (VIII, 275–6).

16 Leo Spitzer, *Essays on English and American Literature* (Princeton: Princeton Univ. Press, 1962), pp. 14–36.

17 "Experiments in Another Country: Stephen Crane's City Sketches," in *American Realism: New Essays* (see Chapter 1, n. 17), p. 153. Trachtenberg is especially sensitive to the ways in which Crane's perspectivism works experimentally to render lived experience.

5. Eternal Fact and Mere Locality

1 See Jean-Pierre Vernant, "Ambiguity and Reversal: On the Enigmatic Structure of *Oedipus Rex*," in Vernant and Pierre Vidal-Naquet, *Tragedy and Myth in Ancient Greece* (Atlantic Highlands, N.J.: Humanities Press, 1981), pp. 96–7.

2 Leo Spitzer, "Linguistic Perspectivism in the Don Quijote," in his *Linguistics and Literary History: Essays in Stylistics* (Princeton: Princeton Univ. Press, 1948), p. 57.

3 George Sherburn, "Fielding's Social Outlook" in *Eighteenth-Century English Literature,* ed. James L. Clifford (New York: Oxford Univ. Press, 1959), pp. 257*ff.*

4 Solomon, *Stephen Crane: From Parody to Realism,* p. 87; *cf.* R. W. Stallman, *Stephen Crane: An Omnibus* (New York: Knopf, 1952), p. 198; Frederick Newberry, "*The Red Badge of Courage* and *The Scarlet Letter,*" *Arizona Quarterly* 38 (1982): 101–15; and Robert Dusenberry, "The Homeric Mood in *The Red Badge of Courage,*" *Pacific Coast Philology* 23 (1968): 31–7.

5 Kenneth Burke, *A Grammar of Motives* (1945; rpt. Cleveland and New York: World, 1962), p. 506.

6 Eric Solomon, "The Structure of *The Red Badge of Courage,*" *Modern Fiction Studies* V (Autumn 1959): 230–1.

7 *The Portrait of a Lady,* ed. Robert D. Bamberg (New York: Norton, 1975), p. 117.

8 Robert Shulman, "*The Red Badge of Courage* and Social Violence: Crane's Myth of His America," *Canadian Review of American Studies* 12 (1981): 15–17.

9 *Stephen Crane: Letters,* ed. R. W. Stallman and Lillian Gilkes (New York: New York Univ. Press, 1960), p. 158.

10 Jean-Pierre Vernant, *The Origins of Greek Thought* (Ithaca: Cornell Univ. Press, 1982), pp. 62–3.

11 Georg Lukács, *The Theory of the Novel: A Historico-Philosophical Essay on the Forms of Great Epic Literature,* trans. Anna Bostock (Cambridge, Mass.: M.I.T. Press, 1971), p. 66.

12 Chester L. Wolford, *The Anger of Stephen Crane: Fiction and the Epic Tradition* (Lincoln: Univ. of Nebraska, 1983), pp. 62–3. Wolford, who enlarges our understanding of Crane's response to Greek antiquity in general and his relation to the epic in particular, is commenting on a Crane passage quoted in part at the beginning of the next section. See also Warren D. Anderson, "Homer and Stephen Crane," *Nineteenth-Century Fiction,* 19 (June 1964): 77–86.

13 I am indebted to W. R. Johnson, *Darkness Visible: A Study of Vergil's "Aeneid"* (Berkeley: Univ. of California Press, 1976), p. 78, for the translations and for the overall tenor of this commentary.

14 Solomon, *Stephen Crane: From Parody to Realism,* p. 73.

15 Helpful discussions include Claudia C. Wogan, "Crane's Use of Color in *The Red Badge of Courage,*" *Modern Fiction Studies,* 6 (1960): 168–72; and Reid Maynard, "Red as Leitmotiv in *The Red Badge of Courage,*" *American Quarterly* 30 (1974): 135–41.

16 *The Works of Francis Bacon,* ed. James Spedding, Robert Leslie Ellis, and Douglas Denon Heath (London: Longmans, 1870), VI, 588.

17 Stendhal, *Love,* trans. Gilbert and Suzanne Sale (Hammondsworth: Penguin, 1975), p. 60; *cf.* p. 59.

18 *The Poetical Works of John Greenleaf Whittier* (Boston: Houghton-Mifflin, 1892), II, 100.

19 Ralph Waldo Emerson, *Nature* (Boston: James Monroe, 1836), p. 14.

20 Henry David Thoreau, *Walden* (Harmondsworth: Penguin, 1983), p. 90.

21 Paul F. Reichardt, "Gawain and the Image of the Wounds," *PMLA* 99 (1984): 154–61.

22 *Opposition: A Linguistic and Psychological Analysis* (Bloomington: Indiana Univ. Press, 1967), p. 34.

23 *Opposition: A Linguistic and Psychological Analysis,* pp. 96–7.

24 Scott C. Osborn, "Stephen Crane's Imagery: 'Pasted like a Wafer,' " *American Literature* 23 (November 1951): 362; James B. Colvert, "The Origins of Stephen Crane's Literary Creed," in *Stephen Crane's Career: Perspectives and Evaluations,* ed. Thomas A. Gullason (New York: New York Univ. Press, 1972), p. 179, n. 18; Jean G. Marlowe, "Crane's Wafer Image: Reference to an Artillery Primer?" *American Literature* 43 (1972): 645–7; Jean Cazemajou, "The 'Religion of Peace' and the War Archetype," in *Stephen Crane in Transition,* ed. Katz, 62.

25 Stallman, "The Scholar's Net: Literary Sources," *College English* 17 (October 1955): 20–7; La France, *A Reading of Stephen Crane,* p. 100.

26 Thomas Kearney, *General Philip Kearney: Battle Soldier of Five Wars* (New York, 1938), p. 267.

27 On structure see Norman Lavers, "Order in *The Red Badge of Courage,*" *University Review* (Kansas City), 32 (1966): 287–95, and Clinton S. Burhans, Jr., "Twin Lights on Henry Fleming: Structural Parallels in *The Red Badge of Courage,*" *Arizona Quarterly* 30 (1974): 149–59.

28 In addition to McWilliams, *The Idea of Fraternity in America,* and Huizinga, *America,* previously discussed, see George W. Johnson, "Stephen Crane's Metaphor of Decorum," *PMLA* 78 (1963): 250–6.

29 Vernant, *The Origins of Greek Thought,* p. 47.

30 Solomon, *Stephen Crane: From Parody to Realism,* p. 96.

31 Stephen Crane, *The Red Badge of Courage: An Episode of the American Civil War,* ed. Henry Binder (New York: Norton, 1979).

6. The Mysteries of Heroism and the Aesthetics of War

1 Garland, "The Return of a Private," p. 140.

2 It is this in part that invites the reader to see in Collins a more socially aware and ethically sensitive character than his youthful counterpart in *The Red Badge of Courage;* see Colvert, VI, 25–6.

3 Gibson, *The Fiction of Stephen Crane,* observes that in the present case, as in "The Veteran," "The heroic act is meaningful whether or not it achieves its ends" (p. 92).

4 *A Reading of Stephen Crane,* p. 194. *Cf.* Stallman, *Stephen Crane,* p. 335: "His vainglorious triumph is symbolized by the indifference of two jesting lieutenants who jostle the bucket until the water spills and the bucket 'lay on the ground empty.' The empty bucket suggests the emptiness of his heroism."

5 Immanuel Kant, "Analytic of the Sublime" in *The Critique of Judgement,* trans. James Creed Meredith (Oxford: Oxford Univ. Press, 1952), pp. 112–13. Without reference to Kant, Berthoff, *The Ferment of Realism,* p. 229, speaks of the "frontline terrors and sublimities" of Crane's war novel. On the sublime in American painting and Dickinson's poetry see Albert J. Gelpi, *Emily Dickinson: The Mind of the Poet* (Cambridge, Mass.: Harvard Univ. Press, 1965), pp. 124*ff.*

6 Kant, p. 110.

7 Berryman, p. 265, contends that "War Memories" is "just behind some of this work," referring to the roster of canonical writings. Stallman, *Stephen Crane,* p. 490, calls "War Memories" the best piece in *Wounds in the Rain.* To La France it is one of Crane's three best sketches. See *The Chief Glory of Every People: Essays on Classic American Writers,* ed. Matthew J. Bruccoli (Carbondale: Southern Illinois Univ. Press, 1973), p. 42. La France later commends Will C. Jumper, author of a 1958 Stanford dissertation, as "the first to perceive the structural grounds for judging 'War Memories' a major work. . . ." See *American Literary Realism, 1870–1910* 7 (1974): 129.

Proposing that Crane uses images "in a new way" in "War Memories," Holton, *Cylinder of Vision,* p. 250, remarks that images in the piece "often gratuitously occur, set apart from their background and represented almost as if they are the real concertization of recollection." Nagel, in *Stephen Crane and Literary Impressionism,* p. 138, takes note of the self-consciousness with which Crane deploys his images in this work: "Yes, they were the birds, but I doubt if they would sympathize with my metaphors" (VI, 232–3).

8 Colvert, VI, *xxxii–xxxiii,* points out that the passage "obviously elaborates a pattern of imagery" from "Four Men in a Cave."

7. Community and Crisis

1 Thomas Gullason, "The Symbolic Unity of 'The Monster,' " *Modern Language Notes* 75 (1960): 663–7.

2 See the discussion in Edward W. Said, *Beginnings: Intention and Method* (New York: Basic Books, 1975), pp. 83–4, *et passim.*

3 *Illuminations,* trans. Harry Zohn, ed. Hannah Arendt (1968; rpt. New York: Schocken, 1969), pp. 86–8.

4 Said, *Beginnings,* p. 125.

5 Berryman, *Stephen Crane,* p. 192.

6 Solomon, *Stephen Crane: From Parody to Realism,* p. 222.

7 Wiebe, *Search for Order,* pp. 113*ff.*

8 Quoted in LaFrance, *A Reading of Stephen Crane,* p. 206.

9 Wiebe, *Search for Order,* p. 56.

10 Wiebe, *Search for Order,* p. 58.

11 Tanner, *The Reign of Wonder,* p. 34.

12 Solomon, *Stephen Crane: From Parody to Realism,* p. 203.

13 *Stephen Crane: An Omnibus,* ed. Robert Wooster Stallman (New York: Knopf, 1952), p. 535.

14 The foundations of this order, which is that of so-called bourgeois society, are analyzed in C. B. Macpherson, *The Political Theory of Possessive Individualism: Hobbes to Locke* (Oxford: Clarendon, 1962).

15 On the literary function of scene see *A Grammar of Motives and a Rhetoric of Motives* (1945, 1950; rpt. Cleveland: World, 1962), pp. 3*ff.*

16 Both quotations are from *On Phenomenology and Social Relations,* ed. Helmut R. Wagner (Chicago: Univ. of Chicago, 1970), pp. 92, 93.

17 Quoted in Eric Bentley, *The Life of the Drama* (New York: Atheneum, 1964), p. 60.

18 Georg Lukács, *The Theory of the Novel,* trans. Anna Bostock (Cambridge, Mass.: MIT Press, 1971), p. 51.

19 A helpful source on this and related aspects of vernacular American architecture is John A. Kouwenhoven, *Made in America: Industrial Arts in Modern Civilization* (New York: Doubleday, 1948).

20 The problematic ending of the story has occasioned much interesting commentary. See, for example, Bergon, *Stephen Crane's Artistry,* pp. 124–31; James Trammell Cox, "Stephen Crane as Symbolic Naturalist: An Analysis of 'The Blue Hotel,' " and the Gentle Reader, *Studies in Short Fiction* 1 (1964): 224–6; Bruce L. Grenberg, "Metaphysics of Despair: Stephen Crane's 'The Blue Hotel,' " *Modern Fiction Studies* 14 (1968): 203–13; Marvin Klotz, "Stephen Crane: Tragedian or Comedian, 'The Blue Hotel,' " *University of Kansas City Review* 27 (1961): 170–4; and Alan H. Wycherly, "Crane's 'The Blue Hotel': How Many

Collaborators?" *American Notes & Queries* 4 (1966): 88, and Robert F. Gleckner, "Stephen Crane and the Wonder of Man's Conceit," *Modern Fiction Studies* 5 (1979): 280.

21 La France, *A Reading of Stephen Crane,* p. 213.

22 For a general approach to this phenomenon see Elizabeth Burns, *Theatricality: A Study of Convention in the Theatre and in Social Life* (New York: Harper & Row, 1972).

23 "Stephen Crane's Metaphor of Decorum," *PMLA* 78 (1963): 254.

8. The Ethics of Their Condition and the Unreal Real

1 Among the valuable discussions of the language of the story is Harold C. Martin, "The Development of Style in Nineteenth Century American Fiction," *English Institute Essays* (New York, 198), especially pp. 126–33. The shift in perspective is discussed by James B. Colvert, "Structure and Theme in Stephen Crane's Fiction," *Modern Fiction Studies* 4 (1959): 199–208. Shifts in attitudes are described in Milne Holton, *Cylinder of Vision: The Fiction and Journalistic Writing of Stephen Crane* (Baton Rouge: Louisiana State Univ. Press, 1972), pp. 161*ff.* Crane's are related to larger issues by Solomon, pp. 157–76, and LaFrance, pp. 195–205. *Cf.* R. W. Stallman, "Stephen Crane: A Revaluation," in *Critiques and Essays on Modern Fiction, 1920–1951: Representing the Achievement of Modern American and British Critics,* ed. R. W. Stallman (New York: Ronald, 1952), p. 259.

2 *On the Nature of Things,* trans. Martin Ferguson Smith (London: Sphere Books, 1969), p. 141.

3 *Martin Chuzzlewit* (New York: New American Library, 1965), p. 407.

4 William Bysshe Stein, "Stephen Crane's *Homo Absurdus,*" *Bucknell Review* 7 (1959): 168–88, brings the story into the mainstream of modern treatments of the existentially absurd. In " 'The Open Boat': Additional Perspective," *Modern Fiction Studies* 17 (1971–1972): 557–61, Donna Gerstenberger enlarges upon her existential reading of Crane's epistemology. The first to explore this basic viewpoint is Peter Buitenhuis, "The Essentials of Life: 'The Open Boat' as Existentialist Fiction," *Modern Fiction Studies* 5 (1959): 243–50.

5 *Stephen Crane,* revised ed. (New York: Twayne, 1980), p. 132. By contrast, Richard P. Adams, "Naturalistic Fiction: 'The Open Boat,' " *Tulane Studies in English* 5 (1954): 137–46, portrays Crane as a true naturalist. For Charles C. Walcutt, Crane is the quintessential naturalist; see "Stephen Crane: Naturalist and Impressionist" in his *American Literary Naturalism: A Divided Stream* (Minneapolis: Univ. of Minnesota Press, 1956), pp. 66–86. A more pluralistic view is offered by Mordecai Marcus, "The Threefold View of Nature in 'The Open Boat,' " *Philological Quarterly* 61 (1962): 511–15.

6 Quoted in Anthony Channell Hilfer, *The Ethics of Intensity in American Fiction* (Austin: Univ. of Texas Press, 1981), p. 7.

7 Bergon, *Stephen Crane's Artistry,* p. 88.

8 For more on the subject see William Randel, "The Cook in 'The Open Boat,' " *American Literature* 34 (1962): 405–11.

9 *The Life of the Mind* (New York: Harcourt Brace & Jovanovich, 1971), I, 200.

10 Berryman, who is intrigued by the story, complains, *Stephen Crane,* p. 109, that its two halves fall apart. Noting the same structural arrangement, Gibson, *The Fiction of Stephen Crane,* p. 121, rightly characterizes the second section as being superior.

11 Pursuit and flight constitute one of the structuring patterns in *The Red Badge of Courage; George's Mother* features a fight on the run as Corcoran is pursued by a nameless opponent. Finally, amorous pursuit of a woman by a man is the central theme of *The Third Violet* as well as *Active Service.*

12 The concern with faces and with damaging process – here the burning sealing-wax – converage in a nexus that Michael Fried explores in detail in *Realism, Writing, Disfiguration: Thomas Eakins and Stephen Crane* (Chicago: Univ. of Chicago Press, 1986). Fried's texts include *The Red Badge of Courage,* "The Upturned Face," "The Monster," and "Death and the Child."

13 *Being and Time,* trans. John Macquarrie and Edward Robinson (New York and Evanston: Harper & Row, 1962), p. 277, n. 2.

14 *History and Eschatology: The Presence of Eternity* (New York: Harper and Row, 1957), p. 108.

15 Franz Kafka, *The Complete Stories,* ed. Nahum N. Glazer (New York: Schocken, 1979), p. 220.

9. The Farther Shore

1 *Language as Symbolic Action: Essays on Life, Literature, and Method* (Berkeley: Univ. of California Press, 1968), p. 200.

2 *Eras and Modes in English Poetry,* 2nd ed. (Berkeley: Univ. of California Press, 1964), pp. 224–50.

3 *The Ferment of Realism: American Literature, 1884–1969* (New York: Free Press, 1965), p. 232.

4 Numbers in parentheses are the numbers assigned to the poems in Vol. 10 of the Virginia edition of *The Works of Stephen Crane.* When the number of a poem is not given, I identify the text by volume and page number.

5 Orm Overland, "The Impressionism of Stephen Crane: A Study in Style and Technique," in *American Norvegica: Norwegian Contributions to American Studies,* ed. Sigmund Skard and Henry H. Wasser (Philadelphia: Univ. of Pennsylvania Press, 1966), p. 279.

6 *A Reading of Stephen Crane,* p. 160.

7 *The Poetry of Stephen Crane,* p. 41.

8 Walter Benjamin, *Illuminations,* ed. Hannah Arendt, trans. Harry Zohn (New York, 1968; rpt. New York: Schocken, 1969), pp. 86–7.

9 Quoted in *A D. H. Lawrence Miscellany,* ed. Harry T. Moore (Carbondale: Illinois Univ. Press, 1959), p. 170.

10 *Prose of the Victorian Period,* ed. William E. Buckler (Cambridge, Mass.: Harvard Univ. Press, 1958), pp. 520–1.

11 *The Complete Works of Edgar Allan Poe,* ed. James A. Harrison (New York: The University Society, 1902), the "Virginia edition," II, 273.

12 Peirce, 1.336.

13 *Russian Formalist Criticism: Four Essays,* trans. Lee T. Lemon and Marion J. Reis (Lincoln: Univ. of Nebraska Press, 1965), pp. 22–3.

14 *The Poetry of Stephen Crane,* p. 253.

15 Anatol Rapoport, "The Search for Simplicity," in *The Relevance of General Systems Theory: Papers Presented to Ludwig von Bertalanffy on His Seventieth Birthday,* ed. Ervin Laszlo (New York: Braziller, 1972), p. 16.

16 Huizinga, *Homo Ludens,* p. 108. See also "The Self-Enclosure of the Riddle" in Albert Cook, *Myth and Language* (Bloomington: Indiana Univ. Press, 1980), pp. 225–33.

17 *Homo Ludens,* p. 135.

18 Halliburton, *Edgar Allan Poe: A Phenomenological View,* p. 45.

19 Cazemajou, *Stephen Crane (1871–1900),* p. 452.

20 "Structure and Irony in Stephen Crane's 'War Is Kind,' " *College Language Association Journal* 9 (1966): 274–8.

21 "Stephen Crane: A Revaluation," in Aldridge, *Critiques and Essays on Modern Fiction,* p. 571.

22 On the Baudelaire connection see Richard E. Peck, "Stephen Crane and Baudelaire: A Direct Link," *American Literature* 37 (1965): 202–4; Cazemajou, *Stephen Crane (1871–1900),* p. 481 *et passim;* Hoffman, *The Poetry of Stephen Crane,* p. 118 *et passim.*

23 *Natural Supernaturalism: Tradition and Revolution in Romantic Literature* (New York: Norton, 1971), pp. 41–2.

24 Douglas Robinson, *American Apocalypses: The Image of the End of the World in American Literature* (Baltimore: Johns Hopkins Univ. Press, 1985), rightly arguing for the centrality of the literature of "last things" in the American canon, offers intertextual readings of Emerson's early *Nature, Poe's The Narrative of Arthur Gordon Pym,* William Faulkner's *Absalom, Absalom!,* and John Barth's *Giles Goat-Boy.*

25 Hoffman, *The Poetry of Stephen Crane,* pp. 98–9.

26 George Monteiro, "Crane's 'A Man Adrift on a Slim Spar,' 20," *Explicator* 32 (1973): Item 4.

27 David Halliburton, "Blake's *French Revolution:* The *Figura* and Yesterday's News," *Studies in Romanticism* 5 (1966): 158–68.

28 *The Poetry of Stephen Crane,* p. 162.

29 In contrast to Hoffman, Harland S. Nelson, "Stephen Crane's Achievement as a Poet," *Texas Studies in Literature and Language* 4 (1963): 564–82, downgrades "Blue Battalions" and other late poems in favor of early works, which are more epigrammatic and parabolic, and are frequently anthologized. Ruth Miller, "Regions of Snow: The Poetic Style of Stephen Crane," *Bulletin of the New York Public Library* 72 (1968), 328–49, disagrees with Hoffman's view of Crane's lyricism, arguing that his craft is essentially dramatic. Joseph Katz, " 'The Blue Battalions' and the Uses of Experience," *Studia Neophilologica* 38 (1966): 107–16, connects "Blue Battalions" to Crane's first experience of battle at Velestino, noting that he identified with the Greek army, which wore blue uniforms, in contrast to the Turks, who wore black.

30 Stallman, *Stephen Crane,* p. 20. For further evidence of Crane's musicality see pp. 30, 35, 47, 51, 52, 54, 60, 65, 70.

31 *The Poetry of Stephen Crane,* p. 137.

32 *The Poetry of Stephen Crane,* p. 171.

33 *The Human Condition* (Chicago: Univ. of Chicago Press, 1958), p. 74.

34 *The Poetry of Stephen Crane,* p. 171. As the place to start when considering the question of Crane and religiosity, Cade, *Stephen Crane,* p. 114, properly identifies "The War in Heaven" chapter in Daniel G. Hoffman, *The Poetry of Stephen Crane* (New York: Columbia Univ. Press, 1956). In the first two chapters of his dissertation, "*A Methodist Clergyman – of the Old Ambling-Nag, Saddle-bag, Exhorting Kind*": *Stephen Crane And His Methodist Heritage,* Clarence Oliver Johnson analyzes the secondary literature on Crane's debt to his religious forbears.

35 George Santayana, *Reason in Art* (1905; rpt. New York: Dover, 1982), p. 87.

36 Friedrich von Schiller, *On Simple and Sentimental Poetry,* in *Criticism: The Major Texts,* ed. Walter Jackson Bate (New York: Harcourt, Brace & World, 1952), p. 411.

37 Johnson, "*A Methodist Clergyman,*" pp. 257–60, lists numerous Biblical allusions in Crane's writings. In "Son of Thunder: Stephen Crane and the Fourth Evangelist," *Nineteenth-Century Fiction* 24 (1969): 253–92, Daniel Knapp makes a provocative case for Crane's reliance on the Gospel of St. John.

38 *Biblical Prose Prayer as a Window to the Popular Religion of Ancient Israel* (Berkeley: Univ. of California Press, 1983), p. 7.

39 *Reason in Art,* p. 97.

40 *Reason in Art,* pp. 97–8.

41 Josephine Miles, *Eras and Modes in English Poetry,* 2nd ed. (Berkeley: Univ. of California Press, 1963), p. 228.

42 Albert J. Gelpi, *The Tenth Muse: The Psyche of the American Poet* (Cambridge, Mass.: Harvard Univ. Press, 1975), p. 51. Types of experience similar to those described by Santayana in the quotations that follow are examined by Gelpi from a psychological point of view.

43 *Reason in Art,* p. 89.

44 Santayana, *Realms of Being* (1940; rpt. New York: Cooper Square, 1972), p. 329.

45 *Reason in Art,* p. 90.

Index